Handbook of Social Cognition
Volume 3

HANDBOOK OF
SOCIAL COGNITION

Volume 3

Edited by
ROBERT S. WYER, JR.
THOMAS K. SRULL
University of Illinois

LAWRENCE ERLBAUM ASSOCIATES, PUBLISHERS
1984   Hillsdale, New Jersey   London

Lawrence Erlbaum Associates, Inc., Publishers
365 Broadway
Hillsdale, New Jersey 07642

Library of Congress Cataloging in Publication Data

Main entry under title:

Handbook of social cognition.

Includes bibliographical references and indexes.
1. Social perception—Addresses, essays, lectures.
2. Cognition. I. Wyer, Robert S. II. Srull, Thomas K.
[DNLM: 1. Cognition—Handbooks. 2. Social perception—
Handbooks. BF 311 H2367]
HM132.H333   1984   302'.12   84-6021
ISBN 0-89859-338-7 (v. 1)
ISBN 0-89859-339-5 (v. 2)
ISBN 0-89859-340-9 (v. 3)
ISBN 0-89859-337-9 (set)

Printed in the United States of America
10 9 8 7 6 5 4 3 2

Contents

Preface

Social cognition is currently the most active and dynamic area in psychology. New and important theoretical developments are occurring on a regular basis. Moreover, the flurry of research activity in this area has reached proportions one could never have anticipated as little as 10 years ago. It was a rare event in the mid-1970s to meet someone who was specifically interested in social cognition. In contrast, it is now difficult to meet anyone at all who does not profess to be working on some problem related to this general domain of inquiry.

The emergence of social cognition as a major area of psychology reflects, at its core, a convergence of two hitherto distinct disciplines in pursuit of a common set of problems. This convergence was not instigated by any single individual, nor was it stimulated by any specific set of empirical findings. Rather, it occurred spontaneously as a result of the independent recognition by researchers in each discipline that continued advancement in their own area required at least a partial understanding of phenomena being investigated in the other. For example, social psychologists had long been concerned with the effects of situational and individual difference variables on judgments and behavioral decisions. However, they began to realize that their past efforts had largely been restricted to a description of simple input-output relations. That is, experimental investigations were examining the relations among certain classes of stimulus variables and certain classes of overt responses. Evidence bearing on these relations often provided very little insight into the fundamental psychological processes that underlie their existence. Thus, many social psychologists began turning to cognitive theory and methodology for guidance in conceptualizing the underlying processes that mediate such judgments and decisions.

Simultaneously, researchers in cognitive psychology began to realize that continued advancement in their work would require a far more serious consideration of the role of real-world knowledge in the interpretation and cognitive organization of new information. Accordingly, they literally began to move from the "word" to the "sentence," and then to the type of complex stimulus materials that are very similar to those of traditional interest to social psychologists. At the conceptual level, researchers interested in the processing of prose material began talking about things like empathy, the role of attributions in comprehension, and the subjective identification of the reader (an inherently social being) with one or more characters in a story. Moreover, a concern with the role of prior knowledge in interpreting and organizing new information led mainstream cognitive psychologists to consider the effects of self-referential knowledge, and of transitory cognitive and emotional states, on the processing of information. Consequently, questions related to the role of the "self-concept" in responses to information, and the influence of emotional and affective states on information processing, which had long been of interest to social psychologists, suddenly became the focus of attention of many cognitive psychologists as well.

Even these brief historical descriptions convey the fact that investigators with quite different perspectives and backgrounds appeared to spontaneously converge on a common set of problems to which both sets of knowledge and skills were necessary. Consequently, the institutional boundaries that have historically existed between many areas of cognitive and social psychology have become more and more artificial, and the "cognitive" and "social" labels attached to researchers in these areas are often more a reflection of their past history than of their current theoretical and empirical interests.

The present set of volumes reflects this convergence. In combination, the volumes provide a comprehensive treatment by both cognitive and social psychologists, often in collaboration, of issues that are central to social information processing. The volumes are intended to be a resource for researchers trained in both traditional disciplines, permitting them to review the most important conceptual and empirical advances in each area. In doing so, the volumes are intended to increase further the cross-disciplinary communication and cross-fertilization of ideas that we believe is required for continued progress, and that anticipates what we believe will ultimately be an even more formal integration of these two historically distinct disciplines.

The handbook is divided into three volumes. Volume 1 provides an overview of central issues in the field. Two chapters (Ostrom; Holyoak & Gordon) focus on how traditional concerns in social and cognitive psychology have blended into the new discipline of social cognition. Other chapters provide a review and analysis of three basic phenomena that cut across theory and research in the area: social categorization (Lingle, Altom, & Medin), the nature and functions of schemata (Brewer & Nakamura; Rumelhart[1]), and cognitive heuristics (Sherman & Corty).

The focus of Volume 2 is on various aspects of memory, including methodological issues associated with the study of social memory (Srull), theoretical and empirical issues surrounding the cognitive representation of social information (Wyer & Gordon), and reviews of recent theory and research in the areas of social memory (Hastie, Park, & Weber), semantic and episodic memory (Shoben), and visual memory (Klatzky).

Volume 3 addresses a variety of topics of interest to both cognitive and social psychologists concerned with various aspects of social information processing, including the role of automatic and controlled processing of social information (Bargh), implications of theory and research on story comprehension for the interpretation of social events (Black, Galambos, & Read), the dynamics of social communication (Kraut & Higgins), the role of the self in information processing (Greenwald & Pratkanis), and output processes in social judgment (Upshaw).

A project such as this simply could not be completed without the help of many people. Most important, we want to thank the large number of investigators who, as a result of their day-to-day research activities, have made this one of the most enjoyable and exciting areas in which to work. We also owe a large debt to each of the authors. Their enthusiasm and commitment to the project is reflected in the universally outstanding chapters of the handbook. We have found our interactions with them during the course of the project to be professionally stimulating and personally rewarding.

The contributions of others are less obvious. We owe a special note of thanks to Professor Jon Hartwick of McGill University. He has been an important source of intellectual stimulation to us for many years, and our early discussions with him were instrumental in the decision to embark on the project.

Finally, we want to express our gratitude to Larry Erlbaum for his confidence and encouragement throughout the project, as well as for giving us an absolutely free hand in trying to accomplish our objectives. Without his advice, encouragement, and gentle prodding, the project would not have been nearly as successful or rewarding.

Robert S. Wyer
Thomas K. Srull

[1]The chapter by Rumelhart, unlike the others in this handbook, is an adaptation of an earlier theoretical analysis of cognitive schemata. It is included in the present handbook because the conceptualization is extremely important and the earlier version was targeted to a very small audience. The original version appeared in *Theoretical issues in reading comprehension: Perspectives from cognitive psychology, linguistics, artificial intelligence, and education*, a volume edited by R. J. Spiro, B. C. Bruce, and W. F. Brewer (Lawrence Erlbaum Associates, 1980).

Contents

1 Automatic and Conscious Processing of Social Information

John A. Bargh
New York University

Contents

Interest in automatic processes is a natural accompaniment to our enduring fascination with the nature of consciousness. The recent surge of interest in automatic phenomena owes much to the current Zeitgeist of social cognition: the turn, in the middle of the last decade, away from the model of rational, scientific man and towards a model of man as cognitively limited and subject to all sorts of distortions as a result. Although opening shots had already been fired in this insurrection (e.g., Jones & Nisbett, 1971; Kanouse, 1971; Taylor & Fiske, 1975; Tversky & Kahneman, 1973, 1974), the breakthrough came with the Carnegie

1

Symposium of 1975 (Carroll & Payne, 1976). The basic assumption that people are rational, capable, and systematic processors of all information relevant to their judgments and decisions was undermined by the evidence that they heavily favor the use of concrete over abstract information (Abelson, 1976; Nisbett, Borgida, Crandall, & Reed, 1976), are severely limited in the ability to combine different sources of information (Dawes, 1976), and are biased simply by the natural and necessary use of simplifying categorization procedures (Hamilton, 1976). These and later findings of people's failure to consider all or even most of the available relevant information when making social judgments (e.g., Major, 1980; Nisbett & Ross, 1980; Snyder & Swann, 1978) have fostered the currently widely-held belief that people have only a limited conscious involvement with their social environment.

At about the same time, cognitive psychologists were developing the distinction between that mode of processing that was under the control of the person and that which was not (LaBerge & Samuels, 1974; Posner & Snyder, 1975; Schneider & Shiffrin, 1977; Shiffrin & Schneider, 1977). Conscious or *control processes* were described as flexible and easily adapted to the particular features of the current situation, but severely restricted in scope at any given time by a limited processing capacity. *Automatic processes,* on the other hand, were said to be effortless and not restrained by capacity limitations. They are relatively static sequences of processing that developed out of frequent experience within a particular stimulus domain, and which are triggered by those stimuli without the necessity of conscious intent or control. Even though this phenomenon has been discussed by psychologists for more than a century (see James, 1890), it has only recently been empirically demonstrated with sufficient rigor to be widely and confidently accepted.

In the first part of this chapter, the historical development of the two-process model is traced, and the contemporary theoretical and empirical work of cognitive researchers such as Posner, Shiffrin and Schneider, and Logan is discussed in detail. Based on a critical examination of these more recent conceptualizations of automaticity, and the somewhat fuzzy line of demarcation that emerges between automatic and conscious processes, a clarification is proposed. This includes a consideration of just how much influence automatic processes should be expected to have on thought and behavior. The second part of the chapter consists of a review of the several areas of social cognition research that have applied (and misapplied) the automatic/conscious processing model, in order to evaluate what is and what is not automatic in social information processing.

As social cognition had ample evidence for half of this two-process model—namely, the limited conscious abilities of people to deal with social information—it is not surprising that the concept of automatic processing was quickly embraced as well. In the last 5 years it has been invoked as an explanation for (1) the disproportionate influence of salient information in social judgment (e.g., Taylor & Fiske, 1978), (2) causal attributions (e.g., Smith & Miller, 1979), (3) attitude-behavior consistency and discrepancy (e.g., Langer, 1978; Wicklund, 1982), (4) attitude change (Fiske & Dyer, 1982; Petty & Cacioppo, 1979), (5) objective self-awareness (Hull & Levy, 1979), (6) depression (Kuiper, Olinger, & MacDonald, in press), (7) social interaction (Langer, 1978, 1982), (8) the focal role of the self in phenomenal experience (Kuiper & Derry, 1981; Markus & Smith, 1981), and (9) category accessibility effects (Higgins & King, 1981). The widespread use of the concept illustrates the centrality of the automatic/controlled process distinction to social cognition. But there is a very real danger that the "automatic" label has been so widely applied that the distinction may cease to have any real meaning.

What Automaticity is Not

Automaticity as Irrationality.   One way in which the term "automatic" can be misused is by equating it with "irrationality" itself. In this application, characteristic of the research on "mindlessness" (e.g., Langer, 1978), a failure to consider all available relevant information signifies the absence of conscious processing, which means, by default, the person must have been operating "on automatic." That is, a failure to properly use the relevant information is taken to be evidence that it was never consciously noticed in the first place. Since it has been pretty well established that people tend not to make the best use of information even when they *are* consciously dealing with it (e.g., Dawes, 1976; Nisbett & Ross, 1980), such reasoning not only obfuscates the real meaning of "automatic," but also, by implication, equates consciousness with rationality.

Automaticity as the Null Hypothesis.   A second problem has been the seductiveness of using automaticity as a *deus ex machina* to be called in when no evidence of a mediating controlled process can be found for a given effect. For example, if no reliable correlation is obtained between, say, recall of behavioral information and attributions, it is concluded that the latter did not depend on any subsequent processing that should have been reflected in better memory for the information involved, and so must have been made automatically at the time the information was presented. While this explanation certainly is not ruled out by the lack of correlation, it equally certainly is not demonstrated, for the same reason that one cannot prove the null hypothesis.

Automaticity as Lack of Awareness.   Cognitive theorists (e.g., Posner & Snyder, 1975; Shiffrin & Schneider, 1977) have labeled as "automatic" those cognitive processes that proceed outside of awareness, whether they are stimulus-driven or consciously instigated. There seems to me to be a major difficulty with equating automaticity with lack of awareness, however. A person lacks awareness of nearly all his or her cognitive processes, even those consciously triggered. Thus, if every process to which a person did not have conscious access was considered automatic, the vast majority of cognitive processes would be, and the automatic/conscious distinction would lose all meaning.

Take, as an example of the problem of defining automaticity of a cognitive process as a lack of awareness of that process, the study by Higgins, Rholes, and Jones (1977). Subjects in this study were not aware of the influence that a given mental category of social information (e.g., "reckless"), activated in a previous, apparently unrelated context, had on their later impressions of a target person. Based on the equation of automaticity with a lack of awareness in the cognitive literature, Higgins and King (1981) considered these findings, along with similar results by Srull and Wyer (1979, 1980), to be evidence of automatic category effects. Yet the subjects in these experiments were demonstrating the same lack of introspective access to their thought processes as did subjects in the experiments reported by Nisbett and his colleagues (Nisbett & Bellows, 1977; Nisbett & Wilson, 1977a, 1977b). In these latter studies, subjects also were presented with influential stimuli, and were even consciously using these stimuli to make judgments, but were *still* unable to distinguish influential from noninfluential stimuli any better than nonparticipating observers. Thus, lack of awareness of the influence of a stimulus is not sufficient evidence of an automatic process, for people apparently lack awareness even of processes that they are actively controlling. In fact, given the limited capacity of consciousness, it would be maladaptive to be conscious of much of *how* we know something, for this would mean less consciousness for *what* we need to know (Bateson, 1972). I propose, therefore, that lack of awareness of a process should not be a sufficient criterion of automaticity. There has to be something more to the concept of automaticity for it to be of real service.

Cause and Effect in Thought

If we ask what was the cause of the differential impressions formed by subjects in the Higgins et al. (1977) and Srull and Wyer (1979, 1980) studies, we can answer at two levels. In one sense the cause was the different categories that were temporarily active for subjects in the various conditions. Going back one step, we could say the cause was the different priming stimuli (trait terms or behavioral exemplars) to which subjects were exposed and which resulted in the activation of the different categories. Of course, both were causes of the effect, but the active category was the proximal or immediate cause, and the priming stimulus materials were the distal or remote cause:

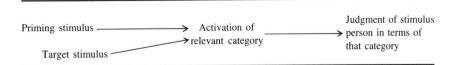

Now we must ask if the subject's conscious intent or control played any role in this causal chain. We can see that it does, for the subject paid conscious attention to the priming stimuli during the first of the two experimental sessions. The causal chain is actually thus:

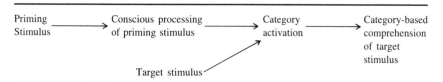

Thus the intervention of the subject's conscious control was necessary for the effect to occur. Subjects may not have been aware of the way in which the activated category influenced the later processing of the description of the stimulus person, but they *were* aware of the stimuli that activated the category in the first place. The important point is that the immediate cause of the effect was the conscious activation of the category, *not* the priming stimuli themselves. If a process requires conscious intent of any kind to be completed, we should not consider it automatic. Thus the effect of the priming stimuli on impressions of the stimulus person in these studies was not automatic, although the effect of the activated category could be argued to be so, as subjects were not aware or in control of its influence on their inferences. As discussed above, however, it is not very meaningful to label as automatic *internally* instigated processes (such as category activation resulting from conscious attention) that subsequently operate outside of consciousness. To do so would be analogous to arguing that a kicked football moves of its own accord once it loses contact with the foot. Therefore, we will here define automatic processes as *those which are under the immediate control of the environment.* All that an automatic process requires is the presence of a triggering stimulus configuration; no conscious intervention of any kind is necessary.

Distinguishing between immediate and ultimate causes in this way also helps to escape the "problem of volition" (Kimble & Perlmuter, 1970). It has been argued that models of information processing that include an "executive" or set of "control processes" are merely inserting a homunculus or "little man in the head" into the system, which is of course no explanation at all (see Neisser, 1967, pp. 292–295). Such mechanistic devices fill the same gap in our knowledge of cognition as did the *will,* and earlier, the *soul.* To locate ultimate causation of any kind in consciousness or the will is therefore unscientific, according to this reasoning, and so it is contended that *all* thought is under the control of the environment either directly or through its effect on associative mechanisms of the brain (e.g., Anderson & Bower, 1973; Skinner, 1971, p. 195). According to this perspective, then, every thought is automatic, and man is like Spinoza's conscious stone, believing it flies freely through the air only because it is not aware of the source of its movement. I hope to preserve the utility of the automatic/conscious dichotomy by distinguishing between those cognitive processes *directly* instigated by external stimulation and those the immediate cause of which is some conscious and intentional process.

MODELS OF AUTOMATIC AND CONSCIOUS PROCESSING

Habit Formation

The division between mental processes that are under conscious control and those that are not is nothing new; in fact, as the principle of "habit formation" it is one of the oldest concepts in psychology. In his *Principles of Psychology* (1890), William James reviewed the arguments of several writers who had advocated such a model. James cites the physiologist Carpenter, writing over a hundred years ago:

> The psychical principles of *association,* indeed, and the physiological principles of *nutrition,* simply express—the former in terms of mind, the latter in terms of brain—the universally admitted fact that any sequence of mental action which has been frequently repeated tends to repeat itself; so that we find ourselves automatically prompted to *think, feel,* or *do* what we have been before accustomed to think, feel, or do, under like circumstances, without any consciously formed *purpose,* or anticipation of results. (in James, 1890, vol. 1, pp. 111–112)

James concluded that frequent use of a mental sequence results in its removal from conscious control, as well as from conscious awareness, and that this was absolutely necessary in order to free limited consciousness from the numerous mundane requirements of life (1890, vol. 1, pp. 113–114). He differentiated between *voluntary* and *involuntary* attention; the former characterized by its effortfulness, being directed by intentions and purposes, the latter by its ease and reflexiveness (1890, vol. 1, pp. 416–420). A further distinction was made between *immediate* and *derived* sources of involuntary attention. By "immediate" was meant those stimuli that naturally or instinctively draw our attention: either by their "mere force," i.e., those that are intense, looming, or suddenly changing; or are by their nature directly exciting to us as a species—in James's classic list, "strange things, moving things, wild animals, bright things, pretty things, metallic things, words, blows, blood, etc., etc., etc." (1890, vol. 1, p. 417). *Derived* involuntary attention is directed towards those areas of the environment in which one has considerable experience and familiarity. The function of voluntary attention was argued to be to preserve the focus of thought through inhibition of the processing of competing stimuli:

Effort is felt only when there is a conflict of interest in the mind. . . . Dynamically, . . . that may mean . . . that the associative processes which make Z triumph are really the stronger, and in A's absence would make us give a passive and unimpeded attention to Z; but, so long as A is present, some of their force is used to inhibit the processes concerned with A. Such inhibition is a partial neutralization of the brain-energy which would otherwise be available for fluent thought. (vol. 1, p. 451)

To summarize James's processing model: due to the necessity of freeing limited consciousness, those stimulus events that are frequently experienced eventually come to be processed without the necessity of conscious involvement. Habitual mental sequences deal with the invariances in the environment, allowing conscious capacity to be flexibly allocated to variable situational and personal requirements. We shall see that the contemporary reawakening of interest in consciousness has resulted in a model that is not appreciably different from that outlined by James.

Initial Automatic Analysis of the Environment

It is widely recognized that an individual's conscious processing capacity is limited at any given time[1] (e.g., Boring, 1933, p. 194; Broadbent, 1958; Kahneman, 1973; Mischel, 1979; Norman & Bobrow, 1976; Posner & Snyder, 1975; Schneider & Shiffrin, 1977). On logical grounds alone it is clear that considerable amounts of cognitive work must go on outside of conscious awareness:

Suppose that on the screen of consciousness there are reports from many parts of the total mind, and consider the addition to consciousness of those reports necessary to cover what is, at a given state of evolution, not already covered. . . The next step will be to cover the process and events occurring in the circuit structure which we have just added. And so on. Clearly the problem is insoluble, and every next step in the approach to total consciousness will involve a great increase in the circuitry required. It follows that all organisms must be content with rather little consciousness. . . (Bateson, 1972, pp. 142–143)

Up to a certain point, then, we are not aware of the analysis of environmental stimuli. How *much* analysis goes on prior to conscious awareness has been a

---

[1]The notable exception is Neisser (1976; Hirst, Spelke, Reaves, Caharack, & Neisser, 1980; Spelke, Hirst, & Neisser, 1976), who contends that the human ability to acquire complex skills demonstrates that capacity does not have fixed limits. Shiffrin and Dumais (1981) have called this position unreasonable in light of the consistent performance asymptote in their target detection paradigm, even with extensive practice. Still, the real difference here may be semantic, as most view skill acquisition as a process of reducing capacity demands through practice so that more and more can be accomplished within the fixed limits.

matter of some debate. Broadbent's (1958) original filter theory of attention, which reintroduced consciousness as a topic for research in experimental psychology, held that inputs were screened for entry into consciousness on their physical characteristics. But dichotic listening experiments by Moray (1959) and Treisman (1960) demonstrated that *meaningful* unattended inputs were also noticed by subjects. This led Deutsch and Deutsch (1963) to propose that all inputs were fully analyzed for meaning unconsciously, with entry into consciousness determined by this analysis.

The Moray (1959) and Treisman (1960) experiments had not shown *all* stimuli to break through the attentional barrier, however. In the Moray (1959) study, the only unattended stimulus to be noticed was the subject's own name (and then only a third of the time); in the Treisman (1960) study, only words with a high conditional probability of occurring were able to draw attention. More recently, experiments by Lewis (1970) and Corteen and Wood (1972) have been cited as evidence that all stimuli are fully analyzed for meaning prior to reaching consciousness, but their procedures do not permit such a conclusion to be drawn.[2] An experiment by Treisman and Geffen (1967) undermined the complete-analysis position, by showing that subjects are not able to detect targets in an unattended message as well as they can in an attended message. It appears, therefore, that stimuli reaching the sensory apparatus are automatically processed to a certain degree, perhaps up to the extraction of physical features, and that some, but not all, stimuli receive more extensive initial analysis.

What determines the level to which an environmental stimulus will be automatically processed? Bruner's (1957) discussion of categorization procedures posited a preconscious stage of "primitive categorization," in which a rather gross analysis of the environment into distinct objects or events takes place. This is followed by a process of cue search, which depending on the stimulus event can either be a continuation of the original automatic perceptual sequence, or a consciously-directed examination of the feature space. The amount of consistent

---

[2]Lewis (1970) presented stimuli to the unattended ear in a dichotic listening task, and found that unattended words that were semantically related to simultaneously-presented attended words interfered with their shadowing. Lewis concluded that words on the unattended channel receive full semantic analysis. Treisman, Squire, and Green (1974) replicated the Lewis (1970) experiment, however, and found the interference to occur only for words presented very early in the list, and *not* for all semantically-related word pairs. This suggested that it may take time for efficient focusing of attention to develop in the shadowing task. Before that occurs, some attention is given to the to-be-ignored channel, producing interference, which cannot therefore be attributed to any routine automatic analysis of all inputs.

Corteen and Wood (1972) obtained greater galvanic skin responses to the presentation of unattended words that had previously been associated with an electric shock. In a replication of this study, Dawson and Schell (1979) found the effect only for conditioned stimuli that had been given substantial amounts of *conscious* processing; i.e., those that were temporarily still active. Neither the Lewis (1970) nor the Corteen and Wood (1972) studies can be considered as evidence of full analysis of all sensory inputs.

experience one has had with the stimulus is said to determine how far it will be processed automatically:

> In highly practiced cases or in cases of high cue-category probability linkage, a second process of more precise placement based on additional cues may be equally silent or 'unconscious'. . . In such instances there is usually a good fit between the specifications of the category and the nature of the cues impinging on the organism. . . Where the fit to accessible categories is not precise, or when the linkage between cue and category is low in probability in the past experience of the organism, the conscious experience of cue searching occurs. (Bruner, 1957, p. 130)

Neisser (1967) also endorsed a model in which automatic analyses of the environment served as the grist for the mill of conscious processes. What he denoted as *preattentive processes* segregated the stimulus field into figural units, to which focal attention then gives further analysis. Like James, Neisser considered some preattentive processes to develop out of sufficient experience with the stimulus event, while others are innate (1967, p. 101). Like Bruner, he considered the perceiver to be an active explorer of the environment; perception involved a *construction* of the environment based on the output of the preattentive processes (pp. 193–198).

The Interaction of Conscious and Automatic Processes

Based on research in the Stroop and semantic priming paradigms, Posner and Snyder (1975) and Logan (1980) proposed models in which a stimulus automatically activates those mental structures that have been chronically associated with it. Conscious processing, however, is said to be able to inhibit competing automatic processes from entering consciousness. In the Stroop paradigm, subjects are instructed to report one dimension of a stimulus, such as the color in which a word is printed. Unreported dimensions of the stimulus, such as the word's meaning, interfere with the task if they are incompatible with the reported dimension (see Kahneman, 1973; Logan, 1980). The semantic priming paradigm requires subjects to make a judgment about a stimulus, such as whether or not it is a meaningful word. When a priming stimulus that is associatively related to the target word (e.g., FRUIT as a prime for APPLE) is presented just prior to the target, response time is facilitated (e.g., Schvaneveldt & Meyer, 1973). In both paradigms, subjects are to attend to only one stimulus dimension, but irrelevant dimensions influence subjects' responses despite their efforts to ignore the irrelevancies.

Posner and Snyder (1975) concluded from these studies that a stimulus will automatically activate a specific neural pathway, and that this activation will facilitate the processing of other stimuli that use the same pathway without interfering with other ongoing processing. Conscious activation of a pathway, on the other hand, was also said to facilitate that pathway, but at a "widespread cost or inhibition in the ability of *any* other signals to rise to active attention" (p. 66). Posner and Snyder (1975, p. 55) proposed three operational criteria for an automatic process: it may occur (1) without intention, (2) without giving rise to conscious awareness, and (3) without producing interference with other ongoing mental activity. Conscious processing, on the other hand, requires attention, gives rise to awareness, and does interfere with other processing.

The most important contribution of the Posner-Snyder model is the specification of how the automatic and attentional processes interact. Automatic processing of stimulus inputs was characterized as proceeding in parallel and outside of conscious awareness, but inhibited from achieving consciousness by the conscious-attention mechanism. Neely (1977) provided a test of this hypothesized interaction. He presented subjects with words that either primed their own semantic category (e.g., BODY—heart), or, through a conscious expectancy induced by instructions from the experimenter, primed a different category (e.g., BODY—sparrow). In this latter condition, therefore, subjects had a conscious expectancy for a name of a type of bird when they saw the BODY prime, while BODY should also automatically prime its own category of body part names. It was found that BODY facilitated the decision of whether or not body part names were words at short intervals between prime and target (about 250 milliseconds). The BODY prime interfered with such decisions at longer intervals, however, when the conscious expectancy for bird names had had time to develop and to inhibit other processing, such as the automatic activation of body part names. In support of the Posner and Snyder (1975) theory, conscious attention worked to inhibit the results of automatic processing, reversing the usually facilitative semantic priming effect.

Logan and Zbrodoff (1979) reversed the usal Stroop effect in the same way. Subjects were to report the word that was presented either above or below a fixation point. Responses became faster to the word BELOW when it was above the fixation point, and to the word ABOVE when it was below the fixation point, when due to their greater frequency such trials came to be expected by subjects.

Logan (1980) has developed a model similar to that of Posner and Snyder to explain the Stroop and semantic priming phenomena. Automatic effects are assumed to be relatively permanent in sign (facilitative or inhibitory) and size over variations in situational context and the individual's purposes. The relatively flexible attentional effects are said to vary in sign and magnitude as current purposes demand. The model further assumes that the automatic and attentional effects associated with each stimulus dimension are combined additively in making a response decision. For example, in the Stroop test, the word RED printed in red ink has a facilitative or positive automatic weight associated with the irrelevant dimension of the word meaning, and so the magnitude of the attentional weight required to report the ink color is decreased. On the other hand, the word GREEN printed in red ink has an inhibitory or negative automatic weight associated with it, and so the attentional weight needed to achieve the response criterion and report the ink color as "red" is greater. *When automatic and attentional processes are dealing with the same environmental features, less conscious attention is needed; when they are concerned with different environmental features, more conscious attention is necessary to maintain its focus.*

As did the Bruner (1957) and Neisser (1967) models before them, those of Posner and Snyder (1975) and Logan (1980) consider automatic processes to be those set in motion by the presence of a stimulus, and not requiring the involvement of consciousness. They are contrasted with processes under the individual's control that are limited in focus at any given time. The Posner-Snyder and Logan models extend the earlier work by also treating how the conscious and automatic modes interact in the processing of stimulus events.

The Development of Automaticity

Based on a thoroughgoing series of experiments in the target detection paradigm, Shiffrin and Schneider (1977; Schneider & Shiffrin, 1977; Shiffrin & Dumais, 1981) developed the most comprehensive of the two-process theories. Before each experimental trial, subjects were presented with several items (either consonants or digits), called the *memory set*. Their task was to report the occurrence of any memory set members in the rapidly-presented series of 20 *frames* (each containing four elements—either digits, consonants, or random dot patterns). The dependent variables were the memory set size (the number of items in the memory set; either 1 or 4), the frame size (the number of characters presented in each frame), and the frame time (how many milliseconds each frame in a given trial was presented). Memory set size and frame size multiplicatively combined to determine the *memory load*.

Subjects were given extensive training in the detection paradigm, but the nature of this training procedure varied. In the *consistent-mapping* condition, the memory set targets were always digits and the distractors (items in the frames that were not in the memory set) were always consonants, across all trials. In addition, items in the memory set never appeared as distractors, and vice versa. In the *varied-mapping* condition, memory set items and distractors were randomly interchanged across trials, and were all from the same category (i.e., either all consonants or all digits).

Results of these experiments (Schneider & Shiffrin, 1977) showed that target detection performance in the varied-mapping conditions markedly deteriorated with increases in memory load, while the performance of subjects after thousands of trials in the consistent-mapping conditions was not affected by load. In other words, when the targets to be detected were frequent and consistent, they came to be noticed no matter how much processing capacity was being used to hold the target set in memory. When the nature of the targets was completely inconsistent, detection ability was dependent on the amount of available capacity. Schneider and Shiffrin (1977) concluded that subjects in the consistent-mapping conditions learned *automatic-attention responses* for the memory set items, so that conscious attention was automatically drawn to them upon their presentation.

A further set of studies (Shiffrin & Schneider, 1977) found that when a consistently-mapped target subsequently appeared as a distractor, it still drew attention and so interfered with controlled processing. This occurred even when the consistently-mapped target was presented in a frame location that subjects were instructed to ignore as irrelevant.

Shiffrin and Schneider (1977) presented a general theory of information processing, focusing on the complementary roles played by automatic and controlled modes. Automatic processes are those that are well-learned and stored as a sequence of nodes in long-term memory, are not demanding of attention unless containing an automatic-attention component, are difficult to alter or suppress, are not affected by current demands on capacity, and which become active in response to particular internal or external inputs without the necessity of active control by the individual. Controlled processes are flexible and easily established and modified, are highly demanding of processing capacity, and so are very dependent upon the amount of capacity available for their successful operation. The two modes can and do operate simultaneously, although automatic processes perform the initial analysis of sensory inputs, and furnish the results to controlled processing.

A major contribution of the Shiffrin and Schneider research is the empirical demonstration of the development of automaticity. Considerable and consistent experience with a stimulus was found to be necessary. A further series of studies by Schneider and Fisk (1982a) has investigated the *degree* of consistency required. These experiments varied the percentage of trials that an item appeared as a target versus a distractor. It was found that as long as an item was equally or more likely to be a target than a distractor, automatic detection developed, but the more consistently an item was a target, the stronger the automatic processing component. Thus, it appears that automatic processes can develop where there is less than perfect consistency of experience with a stimulus, although the more consistent one's experience with the stimulus, the stronger the automatic process that develops.

Comparison of the Models

The Shiffrin-Schneider, Posner-Snyder, and Logan models are virtually identical. All view automatic and controlled processes as separate modes, and emphasize the role of intention in distinguishing between the two. Automatic processes can operate in parallel, are not affected by how much of the limited capacity is currently available, and are not under the person's control. Conscious or controlled processes, conversely, are serial in nature, are capacity-limited, and are intentional on the part of the individual. Automatic processes develop out of considerable and relatively consistent experience with an environmental object or event, and so are comparatively fixed and inflexible, while control processes are adaptable to novel and unusual situations.

The Shiffrin-Schneider model differs from the others in its inclusion of automatic-attention responses. This violates two of Posner and Snyder's (1975) criteria for an automatic process, since automatic-attention responses theoretically give rise to conscious awareness and interfere with ongoing mental activity. Shiffrin and Dumais (1981) therefore proposed two "rules" of automaticity, and defined a process as automatic if it satisfied either of the rules. Rule 1 was that "any process that does not use general nonspecific processing resources and does not decrease the general nonspecific capacity available for other processes is automatic" (p. 116). On this criterion all three models would agree. Rule 2, however, proposed that "any process that always utilizes general resources and decreases general processing capacity whenever a given set of external initiating stimuli are presented, regardless of a subject's attempt to ignore or bypass the distraction, is automatic" (p. 117). The existence of such automatic attention responses, however, is not conclusively demonstrated by the Shiffrin-Schneider experiments. In their paradigm, the subject's very task was to search the frames for the presence of targets, and so they were devoting conscious attention to the stimuli. Even when an item was presented to a to-be-ignored frame location it was likely to receive at least some attention, especially when the subject's total concentration was directed to the visual information in front of him or her. In terms of Logan's (1980) model, it could well have been the presence of conscious attention *combined* with the automatic effect of the consistently mapped target that allowed it to enter consciousness. Thus, there is no real evidence against the Posner-Snyder and Logan position that control processes can override automatic processes when the two are in conflict. What is needed is data on the conscious awareness of automatically processed information when attention is demonstrably focused elsewhere.

Suggestive but not conclusive on this point are the dichotic listening studies of Moray (1959) and Nielsen and Sarason (1981) that found the subject's own name and sexual words, respectively, to *occasionally* break through the attentional barrier and be noticed. No other type of word was noticed, not simple words repeated 35 times in the Moray study, nor other emotionally salient words in the Nielsen and Sarason study. More importantly, these words did not *always* attract attention (for example, subjects in the Moray study noticed their name in the unattended channel only about one-third of the time on the average), which would be expected if the reaction to consciously attend was *automatic*. Furthermore, it is unclear from the very nature of the shadowing task employed in both studies whether the effect was not just due to a switching of *conscious* processing to the to-be-ignored channel. In the Nielsen and Sarason study, for instance, subjects who were presented the sexual words were much more likely than other subjects to make errors in shadowing the attended channel, which indicates a possible focusing of conscious attention on the sexual word content and away from the target channel. A demonstration of automatic attention responses showing that the configuration of stimuli always draws attention when presented, and which rules out the involvement of conscious processing, has thus far not been made. The evidence therefore favors the Posner-Snyder-Logan position that automatic processing does not require attention, and that conscious processes dominate and inhibit automatic processes when the two are in conflict.

A second difference is that Shiffrin and Schneider include internally-instigated automatic processes as well as those that are set in motion by external stimulation alone. Logan (1979) restricts the scope of automaticity to those processes set in motion by an environmental event without the need of any conscious intervention:

> Attention refers to a central process that coordinates and controls performance in some task environment. Performance is considered automatic to the extent that it is coordinated without attentional control, and the development of automaticity with practice refers to a transfer of control from attention to reliable characteristics of the task environment. (p. 189)

The same conclusion has been reached by investigators of human problem-solving abilities (see, e.g., Kaplan & Kaplan, 1982, pp. 167–168). For example, deGroot's (1965) classic study of chess masters found that the only difference between masters and novices was in their initial perception of the problem, not in how they subsequently manipulated this information. In other words, the higher level of analysis and abstraction reached by the masters' automatic processing of the stimulus configuration, on which their control processing then operated, was the difference between them and the novices. I noted in the introduction the problems inherent in defining as automatic mental processes that are started by intention but then proceed without awareness. It is not that the automaticity of such processes is questioned so much as that the utility of the automatic/conscious distinction is essentially lost in this definition, given one's *general* lack of awareness of one's cognitive processes. For these reasons the "stimulus-driven" definition is strongly advocated here.

The Extent of Automatic Influence

Since automatic processes are under the immediate control of environmental stimuli, either due to innate predispositions or to frequent and consistent experience with those stimuli, it is apparent that their influence will be almost exclusively at the perceptual end of the information processing spectrum. The more abstract a mental representation—that is, the more removed it is from sensory experience—the later it will develop, and the less frequently it will become active (Hebb, 1949; Kaplan, 1976; Newell & Rosenbloom, 1981). Therefore, the less likely it will be to become activated automatically. This would seem to be a very functional arrangement; it would be counterproductive for a species that uniquely possesses the flexibility of the conscious processing system to place very many behavioral responses under the control of the environment (see Campbell, 1974, pp. 332–337).

Perception, by most accounts, involves an interaction between the environmental stimuli that are currently present and the individual's readiness to perceive some over others. We have been concerned up to this point with structural readinesses, relatively fixed and permanent and developed out of long-term experience with a particular stimulus event. But such "top-down" influences can also be due to transitory mental states—temporary activation of certain representations due to current plans, goals, and needs that increase their power over perception and thought (Bruner, 1957; Erdelyi, 1974; Higgins & King, 1981; Neisser, 1967, 1976; Wyer & Srull, 1981). Automatic processes can exert their "bottom-up" influence and give prominence to some stimuli over others, but, as pointed out in the last section, active perceptual sets driven by motives and intentions can override these "suggestions" and grant emphasis to other stimuli that better suit present purposes. One can conceptualize motives as higher-order schemata that direct the controlled search of the environment (Cohen, 1981; Neisser, 1967, 1976), or as resulting in the temporary activation of certain representations that are then more sensitive to the presence of relevant stimuli (Erdelyi, 1974; Higgins & King, 1981). In either case, the subsequent recall of social information has been found to be markedly dependent on such transitory states (Cohen, 1981; Higgins, McCann, & Fondacaro, 1982; Jeffrey & Mischel, 1979). In his critique of the man-as-computer analogy, Dreyfus (1972) notes that a major difference between human and mechanical intelligence is that humans continually organize available information in terms of current needs. In other words, there is no objective factual knowledge to be had, because what is learned from a situation is dependent on one's situational goals. People are active explorers of their environment, not passive recipients of stimulation (Bruner, 1957; Neisser, 1976; Taylor, 1981), and this limits the potency of automatic effects.

Unless attention is directed to an automatically activated location in long-term memory, the activation will persist for only a second or two (Glucksberg & Cowen, 1970; Norman, 1969; Peterson & Kroener, 1964), and the result of such processing will not be stored in memory (Moray, 1959; Neisser, 1964; Schneider & Fisk, 1982b). In other words, a stimulus event must receive conscious attention if it is to be stored in long-term memory (Broadbent, 1958; Erdelyi, 1974; James, 1890; Neisser, 1967; Shiffrin & Schneider, 1977).[3] Moray (1959), for

---

[3]In studies that have been taken by some to be exceptions to this general rule, Hasher and Zacks (1979) contended that spatial location, time, frequency of occurrence, and word meaning are "en-

example, found no recognition memory for words that had just been presented up to 35 times in the unattended channel. Erdelyi (1974) has pointed out the adaptiveness of such a processing system, which preserves the clarity of one's long-term cognitive map of the environment by not cluttering it with additional instances of what one already knows well.

AUTOMATIC AND CONSCIOUS PROCESSING OF SOCIAL INFORMATION

What are the implications of automatic processing for social psychology? It seems to be most clearly relevant for social perception, for a considerable amount of interpretive work could automatically occur for certain stimuli, with these elaborations being treated by the perceiver as being as unquestionably veridical as any other "raw sensory experience" (cf. James, 1890, vol. 2, p. 301). The power of self-relevant stimuli in social judgments (e.g., Markus & Smith, 1981) may be due to their favored status in the initial automatic analysis of sensory data. As another example, there may be automatic pathways associated with chronically accessible categories, so that stimuli consistent with them automatically activate the category itself (Bargh & Pietromonaco, 1982; Higgins, King, & Mavin, 1982). Some have argued that the negative mind-set that characterizes the depressive may be the result of just such automatic inferences (MacDonald & Kuiper, 1982). In addition, an automatic spread of activation from the internal representation of an environmental object to the attitude associated with it has been hypothesized recently to be necessary for attitude-behavior consistency (e.g., Fazio, Powell, & Herr, 1983).

These are effects driven solely by automatic processes. As we have seen, however, perception is also influenced by conscious control processes. Salience effects, as I will argue below, can be attributed to the greater degree of conscious attention given to unexpected stimuli, due to the absence of automatic assistance in their processing. A major focus of recent attitude change research has been on the role of involvement, which appears to modulate the role such active processes play (Chaiken, 1980; Petty & Cacioppo, 1979). With low message-recipient involvement, the automatic effects may be stronger than the attentional

---

coded automatically into memory" (p. 358), but they emphasized that "the person must be *attending* to the input in question" (p. 358–359) for this to occur. Kellogg (1980) had subjects look at faces while performing an auditory multiplication task, and found that subjects later reliably recognized these faces that, he claimed, they had not consciously attended. Subjects had been looking at the faces, and so it is hard to believe that they had not been consciously aware of them, at least momentarily. The only measure of awareness taken was a self-report based on subjects' memory of how much conscious attention they had given to the faces. A lack of memory does not mean a lack of momentary awareness (e.g., White, 1980), and the validity of the self-report measure of attention is questionable.

effects, whereas the reverse may be true under conditions of high involvement. Thus, which sources of information are more influential—those emphasized by automatic processing, or those augmented by conscious attention—will depend on the amount of conscious attention deployed. This line of research is doubly important because it concerns the conditions under which people are and are not in control of their perceptual experience.

This brings us to the question of the degree of control that is typically exerted, which is the focus of the research on "mindlessness." We have seen that there are good reasons to doubt that the stimulus environment directly and automatically controls much in the way of actual behavior, so Langer's (1978) rather strong claims about "automatic" social interaction should not be taken too literally. While the "mindlessness," salience, and attitude change evidence does not satisfy the criteria for automatic effects because of intervening conscious processing, it does show that automatic input into the controlled processing that *then* makes the response decision is the more powerful determinant under conditions of low conscious involvement. That is, to the extent that conscious processes do not play a role in perception, the information they operate on to make inferences and behavioral choices depends on automatic analyses of the environment. In terms of Logan's (1980) additive model, in such situations the permanently strong automatic effect outweighs the relatively weak attentional effect in the competition for conscious attention.

It has been noted that with all of the recent attention given to the structure and content of schematic representations of the social environment, there is a relative lack of knowledge of the processes that operate on these representations (Fiske & Linville, 1980; Wyer, 1980). Especially needed is an understanding of how the various representations become active to exert their influence on processing (Nisbett & Ross, 1980, p. 36). The automatic/controlled process model shows great promise in helping to fill this need, and has already found a home within social cognition. We will now review these relevant areas of social cognition research.

Innately Interesting Stimulus Properties

The more intense a stimulus event, the greater the resultant activation of the internal representations associated with it, and the more likely it is to be consciously noticed (Neisser, 1967). Intense stimuli contribute a greater automatic input into the perceptual process, requiring less attentional effort to be noticed, as is demonstrated by the decrease in reaction time to a stimulus with increases in its intensity (Teichner & Krebs, 1972). People also seem to be "prewired" to notice changing features of the environment, such as motion and contours, and this appears to be explainable in terms of its adaptive value (Neisser, 1967).

Another innate bias is the human preference for visual information over that from other sensory modalities. As a species we are highly dependent on visual data (Campbell, 1974, p. 334; Kaplan, 1976), and we give it greater weight in social judgments. Vivid, concrete verbal information that is easily visually imaged has been argued to have a disproportionate impact on people's judgments relative to less easily imageable abstract statistical information (Nisbett et al., 1976; Nisbett & Ross, 1980; but see Taylor & Thompson, 1982). The person or other aspect of the environment on which visual attention is focused is usually judged to be the causal agent in the social situation (Fiske, Kenny, & Taylor, 1982; Jones & Nisbett, 1971; McArthur & Post, 1977; Storms, 1973; Taylor & Fiske, 1975), even when the perceiver is highly distracted from the verbal content of the situation (Taylor, Crocker, Fiske, Sprinzen, & Winkler, 1979). The conclusion that the effect of visual information on social judgments constitutes an automatic response to stimulus qualities (Taylor et al., 1979; also by McArthur, 1980, 1981) is not justified, however, because subjects were intentionally attending visually to the stimulus persons. Furthermore, the study by Fiske et al. (1982) showed that recall of visual information considered relevant by the subjects to judgments of causality was a significant mediator of such judgments. Since memory requires conscious attention, it appears that the influence of visual information on causal judgments is not automatic, but rather reflects the greater automatic perceptual emphasis given to visual data, thus affording it more weight in the subsequent conscious judgment. This was the conclusion reached by Fiske et al. (1982, p. 123).

Salience Effects

Other stimuli are given figural emphasis not because of their own properties per se, but because of the contrast between them and the current context or the perceiver's temporary or long-term expectancies.[4] This emphasis is due to differential *conscious* attention to unexpected stimuli, and has been argued to be a very adaptive use of limited attention (Fiske, 1980; Hastie, 1981; Shiffrin & Schneider, 1977). In terms of the present discussion, unexpected or novel information is given little if any automatic processing in the initial perceptual analysis, and therefore requires relatively greater amounts of conscious attention in order to be processed once it is

---

[4]In defining salience as stimulus features that, by virtue of their situational or general unexpectedness, attract greater amounts of conscious attention, I depart from the somewhat broader definition recently proposed by Fiske and Taylor (1984). They defined salience as features of stimuli in context that usually, but not necessarily, attract attention. Included in their set of salient stimuli, however, are those that would attract attention for reasons other than their unexpectedness, such as goal-relevant stimuli and those that dominate the field. I believe that limiting the concept of salience to apply only to those stimuli that attract attention due to their inconsistency with temporary or long-term perceptual hypotheses is useful, because attention allocation attributable to salience defined in this way can be more easily differentiated from that driven by needs and motivation or by properties of the stimulus itself such as size or intensity.

consciously noticed. For example, Fiske (1980) presented subjects with slides depicting either extremely or moderately positive or negative behaviors. Extreme and negative behaviors were given more attention (measured in terms of looking time) and subsequently had more impact on impression ratings. Fiske (1980) argued that social perceivers have a chronic expectancy for people to behave in a mildly positive manner in public, so that negative or extremely positive behavior is unexpected and draws more attention. Friedman (1979) found the same result in the processing of common scenes, such as kitchens, farms, and living rooms. She measured first eye fixations to these pictures, and showed that first fixations to unexpected items, such as a hippopotamus in the farm pond, were approximately twice as long as those to expected items.

It therefore appears that stimuli consistent with expectancies are more likely to be noticed but are then given minimal conscious attention, while unexpected events are less likely to be noticed, but, if they are, draw considerable attention. If the expectancy is a chronic, long-term feature of the perceptual system, the advantage of consistent stimuli is due to automatic processing; if the expectancy is temporary it is attributable to an active conscious set (Bargh, 1982; Higgins & King, 1981). A demonstration of the processing effects of an active expectancy was made by Hastie and Kumar (1979). They presented subjects with a series of behaviors that were either consistent, inconsistent, or irrelevant with regard to an initial description of the stimulus person. For example, the stimulus person was described as "honest and sincere," and then subjects read behavioral descriptions of that person, some of which were of dishonest, some of honest, and others of neutral acts. The proportion of consistent to inconsistent behaviors was varied in different experimental conditions. It was found that subjects best recalled inconsistent behaviors, followed by consistent and then neutral behaviors. Furthermore, the advantage of inconsistent items in recall was greater the fewer inconsistent behaviors that were presented. Hastie and Kumar (1979) concluded that the items that were inconsistent with the initial expectancy were more informative as to the subject's character, and so received more attention and were consequently easier to recall. It also appeared that the active expectancy changed over the course of the experiment in response to the actual mix of consistent and inconsistent behaviors presented, for the recall advantage of inconsistent behaviors diminished as the mix approached equality. This is testimony to the flexibility and adaptiveness of conscious perceptual sets.

Hastie (1981) argued that such effects should only occur when the perceiver has sufficient time to devote differential attention to the inconsistent items. In support of this, Srull (1981, Experiment 4) found that in a replication of the Hastie and Kumar study, loading conscious attention with a simultaneously-performed secondary task eliminated the recall advantage of incongruent behaviors. Therefore, when information is available only briefly, and is being presented at a fast rate, automatic processes should play a greater role. Bargh, Thein, and Friedman (1983) conducted a replication of the Hastie and Kumar (1979) study,[5] but controlled the presentation rate of the behavioral information so that subjects could not allocate different amounts of attention to the various items. Each behavioral description was presented for just enough time for subjects to read through the behavior once before the next one was presented.

Two groups of subjects participated: those who did ("Chronics") and those who did not ("Nonchronics") possess a chronically accessible mental category for stimuli related to honesty. Following the selection criteria of Higgins et al. (1982), subjects were considered to have a chronic sensitivity to stimuli consistent with those personality trait categories that first came to mind when they were asked to describe various types of people. It was assumed that the subjects used this category so frequently in social perception and judgment that they were capable of automatically processing information consistent with it.

Subjects were instructed to form an impression of the stimulus person while reading the behavioral descriptions. Half of the subjects read about a person who performed mainly honest behaviors, while the remaining subjects read mainly dishonest behavioral descriptions. It was predicted that Nonchronics would not be able to discriminate in their impressions between the stimulus person who was mainly dishonest and the one who was mainly honest. This was because they were assumed to lack the ability to automatically process honest or dishonest behavioral information, and because they were not given the time necessary to allocate different amounts of conscious processing to the two types of behavior. Chronics, on the other hand, were hypothesized to be sensitive to the difference between the honest and the dishonest stimulus persons. Being able to automatically process the honest behavioral stimuli would free the load on memory caused by the rapid presentation rate, and so Chronics would be able to devote some attention to the dishonest behaviors. Consequently, their impressions of the honest and dishonest stimulus persons should differ. This was what was found (see Table 1.1).

It thus appears that salient information in the environment is that which must be given relatively greater (conscious) attentional processing, either because it does not receive much in the way of automatic processing, or because its internal representation is not part of a currently active conscious set. This follows directly from Logan's (1980) additive model of attentional effects: the amount of attention needed to consciously process a stimulus is lessened by the amount of automatic processing and the amount of conscious activation it is already receiving.

Some have contended that causal attributions are made automatically, based on salient stimuli, as part of the act of perception (McArthur, 1980; Smith & Miller, 1979; Taylor et al., 1979; Taylor & Fiske, 1978), but given that the

---

[5]We are grateful to Reid Hastie for providing the stimulus behaviors used in the Hastie and Kumar experiment.

TABLE 1.1
Mean Overall Impression Rating of the Stimulus Person by the
Chronicity of the Subject and the Behavior Proportion Presented
(Bargh, Thein, & Friedman, 1983)

	Proportion of Behaviors Presented	
	12 Honest/ 6 Dishonest	12 Dishonest/ 6 Honest
Honest Chronics	5.50[a]	3.73[b]
	(19)	(23)
Nonchronics	5.29[a]	4.68[a]
	(22)	(22)

Ratings ranged from 0 to 10; 10 is highly positive. N's per cell in parentheses. Means with different superscripts in the same row are reliably different at $p < .01$; means with different superscripts in the same column are reliably different at $p < .04$. Means with the same superscript are not reliably different at $p > .25$.

possibility of conscious involvement was not ruled out by the design of these studies, and the differences found between attributions and impressions made under versus not under time pressure (Strack, Erber, & Wicklund, 1982), this conclusion does not seem warranted at this time. Rather, the available evidence supports the view that the disproportionate impact of salient information is due to the greater conscious attention it receives, resulting in its greater likelihood to be used in subsequent conscious inferential procedures.

Self-Relevance and Chronically Accessible Categories

Another kind of information that has a disproportionate influence on later judgments and memory is that which has been frequently experienced. Such stimuli come to have automatic pathways associated with them that ensure that they will be noticed upon their detection by the sensory apparatus, unless this will conflict with ongoing conscious purposes. The results of the Bargh et al. (1983) experiment implied that behavioral stimuli consistent with an individual's chronically accessible categories are automatically processed.

There are alternative interpretations of such automatic effects. One view, already mentioned, is that certain categories of social stimuli are so frequently experienced that they are eventually able to activate their internal abstract representation automatically (Bargh & Pietromonaco, 1982; Higgins & King, 1981). Another hypothesis is that the self-representation, or self-schema, automatically screens stimuli for further processing (Hull & Levy, 1979; Kuiper & Derry, 1981; Markus & Smith, 1981). A third possibility considers the emotional salience of the inputs to be the determining factor (Nielsen & Sarason, 1981). Each of these alternatives will be considered in turn.

Automatic Processing of Self-relevant Information.   If frequency of processing is the key to the development of automatic processing of a given stimulus, then those stimuli that are self-relevant should be given extensive automatic analysis. People are constantly experiencing events with themselves as the central focus (e.g., Greenwald, 1980), and so those dimensions of environmental information that comprise one's internal representation of oneself should correspond to extremely accessible mental categories. Indeed, self-relevant information has been found to be more efficiently processed and more easily accessed in memory (Markus, 1977; Ross & Sicoly, 1979). Self-relevant stimuli easily attract one's attention as well (Brenner, 1973; Geller & Shaver, 1976; Hull & Levy, 1979).

Geller and Shaver (1976) made some subjects self-aware by placing a mirror and a videocamera in front of them while they performed a variant of the Stroop task. Other subjects performed without the mirror and camera present. Some of the words used in the Stroop test were "self-relevant" for people in general, as determined by pretest ratings; these were such words as "disliked," "proud," and "popular." Geller and Shaver found that these self-relevant words resulted in markedly greater interference in naming the ink color of the word, but only for the self-aware subjects. Based on this result, and especially the fact that the temporarily self-aware subjects did *not* show any greater interference on the self-irrelevant control words than did the non-self-aware subjects, Hull and Levy (1979) proposed that self-awareness does not correspond to greater *conscious* attention to self-relevant information (as theorized by Duval & Wicklund, 1972), but to an automatic emphasis in perception. That is, if self-awareness constituted a conscious attentional focus on self-relevant stimuli, this would mean less attentional capacity would be available for the Stroop task, and so it should have resulted in an *overall* decrement in color-naming speed for Geller and Shaver's (1976) self-aware subjects. Since there was no decrement shown for the control words, Hull and Levy (1979) argued that interference was due to an automatic and not a conscious process.

Hull and Levy (1979) attempted to show that dispositionally self-aware people showed the same sensitivity to self-relevant information as did the situationally self-aware subjects in the Geller and Shaver (1976) study. High and low self-conscious subjects judged each of 30 words on its length, meaningfulness, or self-descriptiveness. High self-conscious subjects recalled more words judged as self-relevant than did low self-conscious subjects.

The results of the Geller and Shaver (1976) and Hull and Levy (1979) experiments do not provide evidence of automatic processing of self-relevant information, as claimed by Hull and Levy. For one thing, the manipulations of self-awareness used have been shown to focus *conscious* attention on the self (Wicklund & Hormuth, 1981), and so the obtained results depend on the self-represen-tation being already activated in memory and not solely on the presence of the self-relevant information. Secondly, Hull and Levy's (1979) results concern the *recall* of self-relevant information, and do not demonstrate any attentional dif-ference—the obtained advantage for dispositionally self-aware subjects could instead be due to a more accessible structure operating during retrieval.

To provide a strict test of automatic processing of self-relevant stimuli, Bargh (1982) conducted a variation of the dichotic listening paradigm. Subjects were selected for the experiment based on whether or not they considered the trait of independence to be an important part of their self-concept, following the pro-cedure of Markus (1977). Their task was to repeat out loud (shadow) the words played to one ear, while ignoring the words played to the other ear. This was a difficult task, as the words followed each other at a very fast rate (less than a second each).

One channel contained common nouns, the other contained trait adjectives. At the same time a noun was played to one ear, an adjective was played to the other. Some subjects shadowed the noun channel, while others shadowed the adjective channel. One section of the adjective list was comprised of trait words related to independence, such as "leader" and "assertive," while the preceding and succeeding sections were of adjectives unrelated to independence.

Several measures of subjects' degree of awareness of the contents of the unattended channel were taken. A recognition memory test on unattended stimuli was administered to all subjects at the conclusion of the shadowing task. The number of shadowing errors made during the task were tabulated. Finally, in a momentary-awareness control condition, a separate group of subjects engaged in the shadowing task but were stopped halfway through the word list and ques-tioned on their awareness of the unattended stimuli. None of these measures revealed that subjects had any awareness of the unattended channel contents.

At several times during the shadowing task, subjects responded as quickly as they could to a light that went on at unpredictable intervals. Reaction time to this probe stimulus constituted the measure of how much attentional capacity was taken at that moment by the shadowing task (Kantowitz, 1974; Posner & Boies, 1971). Assuming a limited conscious processing capacity, the more attention being allocated to the primary shadowing task, the less would be available for reacting to the probe stimulus, and the longer the reaction times should be. Capacity usage was assessed before, during, and after presentation of the inde-pendent trait adjectives.

If the independent trait words are automatically processed by those subjects for whom they are self-relevant, whether because of the words' self-relevance per se or because they correspond to very frequently-activated mental categories (see next section), two predictions can be made from Logan's (1980) additive model. First, the automatic effect associated with the independent-related words should necessitate *less* conscious attention for the shadowing task when the independent adjectives are presented to the attended channel. This is because the focus of the attentional and automatic processes is the same. Second, automatic processing of the independent adjectives presented to the unattended channel should require relatively *greater* amounts of conscious attention to be allocated to the shadowing task in order to keep the independent words from consciousness. Both of these predictions were upheld. Subjects for whom the independent words were self-relevant took less time to respond to the probe light when they shadowed the independent adjectives, but took more time to react when the independent adjectives were in the unattended channel, relative to subjects for whom the independent stimuli were not self-relevant. There were no reaction time differences between the two groups of subjects on the probes taken when the independent words were not being presented. These results provide strong support for the existence of automatic processing of social stimuli: subjects were not aware of such processing, it occurred despite their intention not to process the contents of the unattended channel, and it did not interfere with their performance on the shadowing task.

Automatic Category Activation.   Are these automatic processes attributable to the self-relevance of the independent-related words, as argued by those who postulate that the self-representation acts as an automatic filter for incoming stimuli (Hull & Levy, 1979; Kuiper & Derry, 1981; Markus & Smith, 1981)? Or do automatic effects occur for any frequently-encountered category of social information, of which those that are self-relevant are a subset? Higgins et al. (1982) argued that an individual possesses a certain limited set of chronically accessible categories that develop out of extensive experience with certain kinds of social information, and that are more readily employed in the processing of any social stimulus event, self-relevant or otherwise.

Higgins et al. (1982) had each subject read a behavioral description of a target person, containing information relevant both to that subject's accessible and inaccessible trait categories. The accessibilities of subjects' trait categories were determined by their responses to a free-response measure taken weeks earlier, on which they provided trait descriptions of various types of people. In two experiments, more inaccessible than accessible trait-relevant behavioral information was deleted from subjects' reproductions of the stimulus material and from their impressions of the target person.

Earlier studies (Higgins et al., 1977; Srull & Wyer, 1979, 1980) had found recently-active categories to exert a greater influence on the interpretation of ambiguous social information, but the Higgins et al. (1982) findings are attributable instead to long-term structural differences in category accessibility among subjects. The *locus* of this effect cannot be determined from the results of the study, however, for the differential retention could be due to the advantage of the more accessible structure in retrieval, or to an automatic perceptual emphasis on stimuli consistent with the chronic categories, or both. An experiment by

Bargh and Pietromonaco (1982) furnished results that address both this issue of the locus of chronic category accessibility effects, and that of the necessity of self-relevance in automatic processing effects for social information.

The content of self-representations has been found to be heavily biased toward positive information (Bradley, 1978; Greenwald, 1980; Markus, 1980). Thus, information consistent with chronically accessible but *negatively*-valued trait categories should *not* be automatically processed if the determinant of such effects is self-relevance, but *should* be automatically processed if the criterion is chronic accessibility. It was assumed (somewhat pessimistically, perhaps) that stimuli related to the trait concept of hostility would have been frequently processed by people in general, and so would correspond to a chronically accessible category for the average person. Because of its negative quality, however, we assumed that hostility would not be part of the average person's self-representation.[6]

Category-consistent stimuli were presented to subjects below the threshold of conscious awareness, to see whether this resulted in the activation of the hostile trait category. Subjects first performed a vigilance task in which they detected very brief flashes of light on a monitor screen. The flashes were actually words, although subjects were not informed of this. The subject's task was to press a button as quickly as possible every time a flash occurred. The location and time of appearance of each flash was made unpredictable, and combined with their brief presentation ensured that subjects had no conscious awareness of the word contents. Several manipulation checks confirmed this.

Depending on the condition to which the subject had been assigned, either 0, 20, or 80 of the 100 trials consisted of hostile-related words, with the remainder neutral control words. Immediately after completing the vigilance task, subjects read a brief behavior description of a stimulus person that was ambiguous with respect to the trait of hostility. Their subsequent ratings of the stimulus person, on trait dimensions related and unrelated to hostility, revealed that the greater the proportion of hostile words to which a subject was exposed outside of awareness, the more hostile and negative was his impression. Thus it appears that the hostile-related stimuli were automatically processed, resulting in differing levels of activation of the hostile-trait category (or some more general category such as ''unpleasant''; see below) depending on the proportion of hostile-related stimuli presented.

These results suggest that chronically accessible categories for social information are automatically activated by the presence of category-consistent information in the environment. They also argue against the position that it is self-relevance alone that is critical in the screening of the stimulus field, as people are

---

[6]A later survey of 560 students at New York University confirmed this assumption: less than one percent could be considered as having hostility as a dimension of their self-representation, using the Markus (1977) criteria.

also vigilant for the presence of frequently-processed but not self-relevant stimuli as well. Furthermore, both the Bargh (1982) and the Bargh and Pietromonaco (1982) findings support the Posner and Snyder (1975) and Logan (1980) position that conscious processing dominates automatic processing and inhibits it from reaching awareness. Such results run counter to the hypothesized existence of automatic attention responses (Shiffrin & Schneider, 1977), because even such frequently-processed stimuli as those that are self-relevant can be inhibited from attaining consciousness when controlled processing is fully deployed on other stimuli.

Automatic Processing of Emotionally Salient Stimuli. It is not clear from either the Bargh et al. (1983) or the Bargh and Pietromonaco (1982) results *which* social category was automatically activated. In both studies, the same pattern of ratings was obtained for traits related and unrelated to the stimulus trait dimension. Thus one cannot tell from these experiments whether the stimulus automatically activated the specific relevant category (i.e., that for honesty or hostility) with this activation then spreading to associated trait categories, or that some more global concept, such as "pleasant" or "evil," was directly activated. Higgins et al. (1977) found that only trait adjectives that were relevant to the description of the stimulus person had an influence on subsequent impressions, however; positive and negative adjectives that were not related to the description had no effect. Therefore, it appears that consciously-attended trait stimuli directly activate their specific relevant categories, and not some more global affective representation (although the activation of the specific category can then spread to evaluatively similar trait categories that are associated with it in memory; see Srull & Wyer, 1979, 1980), but whether or not this is also true of automatically processed trait stimuli remains to be seen.

It is also possible that *no* specific category activation took place in the Bargh (1982) and Bargh and Pietromonaco (1982) experiments, and that subjects were automatically processing the emotional content of the stimuli. Both self-relevant and hostile stimuli are emotionally salient; the former type because information implicating the self is highly affect-laden (cf. Zajonc, 1980a). Zajonc (1980b) and Nielsen and Sarason (1981) have recently argued, in keeping with the classic New Look position (cf. Erdelyi, 1974), that the affective quality of a stimulus can be processed outside of conscious awareness. Although frequency of processing has been strongly supported in the experimental literature as the cause of automatic effects, in studies in which single characters (Shiffrin & Schneider, 1977) or nonsocial category members (Neely, 1977) have been used as stimuli, this does not mean that it is necessarily a sufficient cause of such effects where more complex social information is concerned.

Bargh and Bond (1983) pitted the frequency and emotional salience hypotheses against each other by replicating the Bargh and Pietromonaco (1982) study for both an emotionally salient and an emotionally neutral trait (as determined by pretesting), with people who either had or did not have a chronically accessible category for such trait information as subjects. If the subconscious priming effect found by Bargh and Pietromonaco occurred only for subjects exposed to the emotionally salient trait primes, regardless of the accessibility of the subjects' cognitive categories for that trait, the emotional salience of the stimuli would be found to be the critical factor in producing the effect. If, on the other hand, only those subjects in possession of a chronically accessible category corresponding to the trait stimuli showed the effect, regardless of the emotionality of the trait dimension, then category accessibility and not stimulus emotionality would be supported as the causal factor.

The analysis of the impression ratings (see Table 1.2) revealed reliable main effects for priming ($F (1,77) = 4.78, p = .03$) and trait emotionality ($F (1,77) = 6.83, p = .01$) for Chronics, but no interaction between the two factors ($p > .25$). No reliable effects were found for Nonchronics. Thus, category accessibility was required for automatic processing of the primes, but among those subjects possessing an accessible category, trait emotionality independently elevated impression ratings. In other words, it is not the emotional salience of the stimulus that causes it to be processed outside of awareness, but a sensitivity to the presence of that stimulus by the relevant category born of frequency of use. If that activated category contains an affective response, however, then the emotionality of the trait dimension comes into play and exerts an independent influence on impressions. This effect of emotional salience also occurs if the category is activated consciously by the behavioral description itself, as evidenced by the main effect of emotionality in Chronics' ratings and the absence of an interaction of trait emotionality with priming. The clear implication is that affective responses depend on category activation, supporting the traditional category-based model of affect (e.g., Bartlett, 1932) over stimulus- or feature-based models. Moreover, the apparently additive nature of the effects of chronicity, emotionality, and priming, verified by a subsequent hierarchical multiple regression

TABLE 1.2
Mean Impression Ratings by Trait Emotionality, Category
Accessibility, and Priming (Bargh & Bond, 1983)

		Emotionally Salient Trait (Kindness)	Emotionally Neutral Trait (Shyness)
Chronics			
	Priming	7.39	6.52
	No Priming	6.63	6.22
Nonchronics			
	Priming	6.24	6.39
	No Priming	6.18	6.17

Ratings ranged from 0 to 10; a rating of 10 indicated extremely kind or shy.

analysis, suggests an additive model of category accessibility. Frequency of use (chronicity), recency of use (priming), and affect associated with the category seem to independently increase the accessibility and thus the influence of that category in information processing.

Summary.   The evidence supports a close correspondence between the concepts of automatic processing and chronic category accessibility. Both are assumed to develop from frequent processing of a certain set of stimuli, and both have been found to exert their influence without the need of conscious direction. The individual differences in chronic accessibility found by Bargh (1982), Higgins et al. (1982), Bargh and Bond (1983), and Bargh et al. (1983) underscore the fact that the extent and content of the automatic analysis of the social environment varies among people. The automatic inferences made by people involved in the same social situation may be very different, yet feel just as unshakably real to each individual involved, because the inferences are not the outcome of any process the person is aware of or has control over. That a person one has just met is "friendly," or "sinister," or "manipulative" may seem just as self-evident as that he has a beard or that she talks very fast.

APPLICATIONS TO SPECIFIC RESEARCH DOMAINS

Up to this point the emphasis has been on the theoretical mechanisms underlying automatic and conscious processing. The final section focuses on more specific areas of social psychological research that have been reinterpreted recently in terms of the automatic/conscious processing distinction.

Depression

It may be that automatic inferences play a role in the development and maintenance of depression. Beck (1967) has argued that the depressive's negative affect is a response to an automatic negative categorization of his or her behavior and the reactions of other people to it. The depressed person is not aware of this inferential procedure, just of the bad feelings that result from the conclusion. Higgins et al. (1982) and Kuiper and Derry (1981) have recently suggested that the depressive possesses relatively accessible negative categories and relatively inaccessible positive ones, so that negative information is more likely to survive the initial automatic screening of the environment and be consciously noticed. To elaborate a bit on this idea, it could be that the negative automatic input into conscious processes leads to a greater likelihood of negative responses by the depressive to the situation in turn, resulting in a greater probability of negative feedback, and so on. It is easy to see how a temporary negative mood state could lead to chronic depression if the negative mental categories become very frequently used due to the operation of this vicious cycle. Furthermore, one reason for the syndrome's resistance to change may be that the depressive is not aware of his or her automatic negative bias, and so cannot correct for it with conscious processes. When information comes into consciousness with a strong subjective feeling of truth to it, it must be very difficult to unequivocally accept another's (or your own) word that things aren't really so bad.

Currently, the only account of an experimental test for automaticity in depressives' information processing is an experiment by MacDonald and Kuiper (1982; see also Kuiper, Olinger, & MacDonald, in press). Three groups of subjects participated: clinically depressed, normals, and nondepressed psychiatric controls. All rated 30 depressed and 30 nondepressed content adjectives on their self-descriptiveness. While performing the self-rating task, half of the subjects also engaged in a memory task, in which their attentional capacity was loaded by having to remember six digits during each adjective rating trial. According to Logan (1979), loading memory in this way will interfere with a task to the extent that it requires attention in order to be performed. The effect of the memory load should be larger in treatment conditions that demand more attention and smaller in those that require less attention. In the MacDonald and Kuiper (1982) experiment, the conditions requiring less attention should be those in which subjects rate adjectives consistent with their hypothesized accessible categories (i.e., depressives rating depressed-content adjectives and normals rating non-depressed-content adjectives) and the conditions demanding more attention should be those in which subjects rate adjectives which are not consistent with their chronic perceptual set (i.e., depressives rating nondepressed-content adjectives and normals rating depressed-content adjectives). Therefore, a null interaction between the memory load and the other factors in the analysis of adjective rating time variance would indicate an automatic component in the self-ratings for both depressed and normal subjects, while an interaction would indicate an attentional process.

MacDonald and Kuiper (1982) reported that memory load did not interact with the other factors, and so concluded that automaticity was involved in the self-referent processing of all subjects. As noted above, however, a null interaction indicates automaticity only when there is a task dimension that creates different levels of attentional demand. Examination of the average rating times showed that *both* depressed and normal subjects took longer to say "yes" to depressed than to nondepressed-content adjectives, so the category-consistency dimension apparently did *not* produce different levels of attention demand as hoped by the investigators. Also, the subjects' conscious intent and awareness were engaged in processing the adjectives, which clouds the interpretation of the effect as an automatic process. Another difficulty is that the authors do not report the p-value of the null interaction; since they are in effect trying to prove the null hypothesis, a very lenient criterion value for nonsignificance should have been employed (such as $p > .25$) to protect against a Type II error. Thus it appears that the MacDonald and Kuiper data cannot be taken as evidence of automaticity in depressive self-reference.

More convincing on this issue would be demonstration of an *absence* of a main effect for memory load in depressives' processing of negative content, accompanied by the existence of an effect in their processing of positive content. The reverse pattern would be expected for normals. Such a "zero-slope" memory load test is considered by Logan (1979) to be a stronger demonstration of the presence of automatic processing (see also Shiffrin & Schneider, 1977). The question of whether such automatic effects occur only in the processing of self-relevant information (a position advocated by Kuiper & Derry, 1981) or reflect the operation of chronically accessible categories that influence the processing of information about others as well (Higgins et al., 1982) could be addressed by having subjects make both self- and other-ratings on the positive and negative dimensions. Another possibility would be to have depressed and normal subjects perform a lexical decision task (i.e., "Is this a meaningful word?"; Schvaneveldt & Meyer, 1973) on positive, neutral, and negative adjectives and nonwords presented below the threshold of conscious awareness. Automatic processing would be indicated by a greater-than-chance performance on the task for a certain type of content, along with faster decision times.

Attitude-Behavior Consistency

Several researchers have now argued that, for one reason or another, the low degree of consistency between measured attitudes and overt behavior is due to a weak association between the mental representations of the object and the attitude toward it. Langer (1978) noted that the inconsistency may be due to the fact that people typically don't think about their attitudes toward the stimulus when they act towards it. Abelson (1976) has pointed out the importance of direct experience with an attitude object in increasing consistency. Wicklund (1982) also emphasized that the responses involved in answering attitude items and those involved in the behavior toward the attitude object may be completely separate and distinct in memory. The common theme is that attitude-behavior consistency is poor because the representation of the object and the representation of the attitude are only weakly connected in long-term memory. Thus, the solution to the problem is to strengthen this associative bond, either by having the person consciously think about his or her attitude before behaving (Langer, 1978; Wicklund, 1982), or by giving the person direct experience with the attitude object (Abelson, 1976).

Fazio and his colleagues have recently shown that strengthening the association in memory between an object representation and its evaluation does indeed improve consistency. In one study (Fazio, Chen, McDonel, & Sherman, 1982), the accessibility of some subjects' attitudes towards various puzzles was increased by having them copy their responses to the attitude questions onto blank forms. These subjects then showed greater consistency between their stated attitudes towards the puzzles and their subsequent choice of puzzles to work on during a 'free-play' period, than did subjects who only marked down their evaluations of the puzzles one time. Fazio, Powell, and Herr (1983) gave subjects either direct or indirect experience with various puzzles, before assessing their evaluations. Again, some subjects made extra copies of their evaluations, and the remaining subjects did not. In a second, purportedly unrelated experiment on "color perception," subjects were exposed to either their most or least preferred puzzle in order to unobtrusively activate subjects' mental representation of the puzzle. Finally, in a third study, their attitudes toward puzzles in general were assessed by having them judge whether another person's willingness to work on a series of problems for the experimenter was due to extrinsic reasons or an intrinsic liking for solving puzzles. These final ratings were in the direction of the puzzle-attitude that had been recently activated, but only when the object-attitude link was strong (i.e., only in the direct experience and repeated expression conditions).

Fazio et al. (1983) propose a model in which one's perception of an attitude object is mainly responsible for one's behavior towards it. Thus, if the attitude is so strongly associated with the object representation that when the latter is automatically activated in perception, activation automatically continues to spread to the attitude representation, the attitude will have an influence on behavior toward that object. Such a model is clearly in line with the criteria for an automatic effect, but since the subjects in the Fazio et al. (1982) and Fazio et al. (1983) studies differed only in the *temporary* activation state of their mental apparatus, these studies do not conclusively demonstrate automatic attitude activation. This is because conscious attention was necessary to activate the attitude and produce the effect. It remains to be shown that the same process occurs *without* the need of consciously-produced activation manipulations; that is, for long-term attitudes formed on the basis of considerable direct experience. The results of the studies by Fazio and his colleagues make such a finding seem quite likely.

Attitude Change

For information to be stored in long-term memory, conscious processing is required. Generally, the more extensive the conscious processing, the more accessible the memory. This is why direct experience with an attitude object and conscious consideration of the attitude were hypothesized to increase attitude-behavior consistency. In the same vein, persuasion researchers have recently suggested that attitude changes resulting from deliberate conscious attention to the contents of the persuasive message are more permanent and predictive of behavior towards the attitude object than are changes that are due to message-irrelevant cues such as the source's attractiveness or expertise (Chaiken, 1980;

Cialdini, Petty, & Cacioppo, 1981; Petty & Cacioppo, 1979, 1981; Petty, Cacioppo, & Goldman, 1981). Attitude shifts due to careful conscious evaluation of the message have been labelled the "central route," and those attributable to non-content stimuli have been called the "peripheral route" to persuasion (Petty & Cacioppo, 1981). Chaiken (1980) referred to the two forms as "systematic" and "heuristic" message processing.

One major factor in determining which type of processing the recipient will give the message has been found to be his or her *involvement* with the attitude issue. For example, Chaiken (1980) manipulated the subjects' involvement with the message topic by having some of them believe that they would be discussing the topic again in the near future. Petty and Cacioppo (1979) presented subjects with a message advocating decreased dormitory visitation privileges; some subjects were told the plan was to go into effect at their school (high involvement), and others were informed the proposal concerned another university (low involvement). In both studies, the final attitudes of the involved subjects were more dependent on the quality of the arguments in the persuasive message, while those of the noninvolved subjects were determined more by superficial features of the situation, such as the sheer number of supporting arguments regardless of their quality (Chaiken, 1980), or the expertise of the source (Petty & Cacioppo, 1979; Petty et al., 1981).

Petty and Cacioppo (1979), Chaiken (1980), and Fiske and Dyer (1982) have proposed that personal involvement with the attitude issue results in more cognitive effort devoted to the message contents; low involvement leads to less effort made. Petty and Cacioppo (1979) and Fiske and Dyer (1982) contend that low involvement is characterized by the use of automatic processing strategies in the situation, while high involvement leads to the use of controlled processing. Chaiken (1980) argued that degree of involvement determines whether a heuristic (reliance on more accessible information) or a systematic (careful evaluation of arguments) processing strategy will be employed. Chaiken's conceptualization of the roles of consciousness and automaticity in attitude change is probably closer to the mark, as there is no evidence that the attitude change *itself* is the result of an automatic process, just that with low conscious involvement there is less conscious control exerted over the perceptual process, and thus automatically furnished data play a greater role. High involvement results in a greater conscious role in the selection of stimuli for further processing, inhibiting the automatic inputs from having much of a say in the subsequent conscious evaluation of the message. The attitude change itself is therefore not automatic but the result of a conscious process. The informational input into that process, however, is determined largely by the automatic, effortless perceptual analysis of the situation under conditions of low involvement, and by a consciously-directed perceptual search when there is high involvement.

A very valuable feature of this research is its concern with the interaction of automatic and controlled processes dealing with social information. The personal relevance of an attitude issue appears to influence the relative power of automatically-produced versus consciously-produced data in the message evaluation process. Involvement produces greater attentional effort, which increases the size of the attentional effects on perception relative to the automatic effects; under conditions of low involvement/effort, the latter may be the stronger of the two. An important question for future research is *how* the personal relevance of an issue occasions greater attention to the message arguments. One possibility is given by Fiske and Dyer (1982), who suggest that those personally involved in an issue possess more efficient knowledge structures for issue-relevant information, so that more processing capacity remains for consideration of the arguments. This does not explain why making the *same* issue more or less personally relevant (e.g., visitation rule changes at the subject's or a different university; Petty & Cacioppo, 1979) has the same effect. Perhaps self-relevance of an issue results in the frequently-used categories relevant to the self-concept being used to process the information, requiring less conscious attention to do so, again with relatively greater capacity left over. In either case, it is clear that without *some* help in relieving the strain on capacity, there may not be enough to simultaneously weigh the quality of several arguments in a persuasive message, as evidenced by people's typically poor ability to integrate multiple pieces of information (Dawes, 1976; Posner, 1973).

Scripts and "Mindlessness"

Langer and her colleagues (Langer, 1975, 1978, 1982; Langer, Blank, & Chanowitz, 1978; Langer & Imber, 1979) have argued that the degree of conscious control exerted in social information processing is usually very low. They have characterized this phenomenon as "mindlessness"—not consciously making use of all of the relevant information in a given situation. Langer has contended that mindlessness can result from overlearning situational cues so that behavior in these routine situations is "performed automatically" (1978, p. 36):

> We typically have assumed that virtually all behavior other than overlearned motor acts are performed with conscious awareness. Perhaps a more efficacious strategy is one that assumes that by the time a person reaches adulthood, (s)he has achieved a state of 'ignorance' whereby virtually all behavior may be performed without awareness . . . unless forced to engage in conscious thought. (1978, p. 40)

The concept of mindlessness is based on script theory (Abelson, 1976, 1981; Schank & Abelson, 1977). A *script* is a mental representation of a type of situation, abstracted from many encounters with it, that preserves its recurring features and the temporal order in which they occur. Like any other knowledge structure, scripts provide expectations for what is likely to occur next. Langer (1978, p. 39) argued that these well-learned scripts take control of behavior away from conscious consideration of relevant situational cues.

The evidence offered in support of this claim comes from studies of compliance to routine requests, in which compliance rate differed as a function of how the request was phrased. In the Langer et al. (1978) study, for example, people using a copying machine were interrupted and asked in various ways to let another person use the machine. The person asked to be allowed to make either a small (5) or large (20) number of copies. When the request followed the form assumed to be the routine one by the experimenters, with the statement of the favor followed by a reason for the request (e.g., "Excuse me, I have five pages. May I use the xerox machine, because . . . ?"), compliance in the small request condition was the same regardless of the legitimacy of the reason given ("because I have to make copies" versus "because I'm in a rush"). Compliance was lower if no reason was given at all. In the large request condition, the quality of the request did make a difference in the rate of compliance. Langer et al. (1978) argued that as long as the effort involved in acceding to the request was low (as in the five-copy condition) and the request followed the expected structure (i.e., polite and with a reason given), the request was processed mindlessly and compliance behavior was automatic. The necessity of high effort expenditure (20 copies to be made) or the failure of the request to follow the expected format resulted in the involvement of conscious attention, with the quality of the reason given making a difference in the rate of compliance.

The major difficulty with interpreting this study or the others like it as demonstrating automatic social behavior is that there seems to be no reason to rule out conscious involvement in the compliance decision, in any of the experimental conditions. First, attention must be paid to the size of the request to determine how effortful compliance would be. Next, a conscious judgment of the worthiness of the request could be made based on the quality (or lack) of the reason given (see Abelson, 1981, p. 721). With a small request, the quality of the request needed for compliance is not great, so that saying "because I have to make copies" is sufficient.[7] With a large request, the hurdle is set higher: now the reason had better be a good one. This was Abelson's (1981, p. 721) analysis of the Langer et al. (1978) experiment, and he emphasized the role of consciousness in script enactment:

> The present concept of scripts does not necessarily imply total automaticity of performance and is not equivalent to Langer's concept of 'mindless' behavior. One obvious way in which 'mindful' behavior enters scripts is that acts of thinking can appear explicitly in the specified event sequence. (Abelson, 1981, p. 723)

Although this is only one of several studies Langer and her associates have conducted in order to demonstrate that social behavior can be performed without ongoing active conscious information processing, in none of these studies is

---

[7]The phrasing of what was intended by Langer et al. to be a "placebic" reason is unfortunate, because "I *have* to make copies" strongly implies the presence of a good reason. A more convincing placebo would have been "because I *want* to make copies."

there sufficient evidence to rule out conscious direction of behavior. In fact, what they *do* indicate is that well-learned scripts function as do any other mental representation or schema, and direct the search of the environment for needed information. That is, the features of the situation automatically activate the relevant script, which then directs the *conscious* process of searching for further cues to verify the script as an adequate model of the situation (Bruner, 1957; Neisser, 1976). The result is that certain pieces of information are selected by the script over others that may actually be more relevant and useful in the current situation, but which are not part of the script. Such a model can account for the results of other "mindlessness" studies as well. In the "illusion of control" experiments (Langer, 1975), the activation of a skill script rather than a chance script biases the interpretation of the chance situation that follows. Similarly, the loss of access to details of task performance by those who have overlearned the task (Langer & Imber, 1979) can be attributed to the development of a more abstract script for the task that deals with higher-level units of information. Thus, experiments that Langer has considered to be evidence of "automatic" social behavior can be seen instead as good support for a processing model in which an automatic analysis of the social environment is followed by a consciously directed exploration and response production.

It should be emphasized that if the definition of "mindlessness" is restricted to refer just to the phenomenon that certain relevant information is overlooked or not used as rationally as it should have been, there is certainly plenty of evidence in support of it. Chronic and temporary perceptual sets, visual information, and intense stimuli all result in biases in both the selection and the evidential weight of environmental information. Our limited processing capacity means that we will miss a lot of what is going on around us, and will have a hard time thinking very straight about it even if we do notice it. But Langer equates mindlessness with a state of "reduced cognitive activity" in which "conscious attention is not being expended" (1982), arguing that individuals can conduct complex interactions automatically (1978), and such a position is certainly not justified by the data. Unfortunately, this latter sense of the concept is what researchers and the lay public alike tend to come away with from these experiments. A better summary of the mindlessness studies would be that, as with the salience and persuasion research, when people exert little conscious effort in examining their environment they are at the mercy of automatically-produced interpretations.

The degree of attention typically exerted in social interaction, the effect that different levels of conscious engagement have, and the determinants of such involvement are important topics for further study. It appears that conscious involvement is in part a function of the routineness of the situation. What percentage of the social situations an individual participates in are routine, necessitating only minimal conscious attention? How much attention is actually given to these routine situations? For example, how complete and accurate are people's memories of what just occurred (e.g., the contents of a seemingly routine but

illegitimate request)? Given that consistency of experience is an important determinant of the development of automatic processing, the greater consistency of
social behavior within situations than within people (cf. Mischel, 1968; Nisbett
& Ross, 1980) would mean that automatically-activated situational representations (i.e., scripts) are likely to exert a major influence on all aspects of social
cognition.

CONCLUSIONS

The most useful conceptualization of automatic processing of social stimuli is
one that considers as automatic those cognitive processes that are directly under
the control of the environment, and that do not require conscious processing of
any kind. Automaticity characterizes the initial analysis of all sensory data, but
the extent of this analysis is greater for some stimuli than others. Those with
which one has had more frequent and consistent experience, such as those that
are self-relevant and consistent with chronically accessible categories, receive
more elaborate initial processing. Also, with direct experience or enough conscious consideration of one's attitude toward an environmental object or event,
that attitude comes to be automatically activated when the object or event is
perceived, increasing attitude-behavior consistency. Thus, automatic processes
in perception emphasize information that is consistent with one's expectations.
This leaves the limited conscious attention to be reserved for unexpected, salient
stimuli that are of greater potential danger or informativeness. Conscious perceptual sets are able to override these automatic suggestions, however, and direct
attention to those stimuli that best fit current purposes or observational goals.

Because the more abstract mental representations are activated less frequently, they are less likely to become active automatically. Automatic effects
are therefore typically limited to the perceptual stage of processing, with conscious processing then operating on the automatically-furnished data. There is no
evidence supporting the belief that social behavior is often, or even sometimes,
automatically determined. Under what is probably the more common condition
of low conscious participation in the perceptual process, however, automatically-
accentuated stimuli are more likely to be used in subsequent conscious decisions
and to be stored in memory. Thus, when one is not involved in an attitude issue,
different features of a persuasion situation may be consciously processed than
when one is highly involved, and this has consequences for the outcome of the
persuasion attempt.

Automatic processing is a natural and necessary part of how people divide up
their cognitive workload. It results occasionally in biases and misinterpretations
and ignorance of relevant information, but that does not mean that our minds are
stuck in low gear. Far from characterizing a state of diminished cognitive ac-

tivity, or ''mindlessness,'' which needs to be rectified by an increased conscious awareness of the environment, automatic processing delivers to the quite limited conscious processing vastly more information than it could ever provide for itself. The system seems to be quite functional as it stands.

ACKNOWLEDGMENTS

Preparation of this chapter was supported in part by a Research Challenge Fund grant from New York University. I am indebted to Bob Wyer, Tory Higgins, Susan Fiske, and Thom Srull for their constructive criticisms of an earlier draft. Portions of the research discussed in this chapter were presented at the 1982 American Psychological Association convention in Washington, D. C., and at the 1982 meetings of the Society for Experimental Social Psychology in Nashville, Indiana.

REFERENCES

Abelson, R. P. Script processing in attitude formation and decision-making. In J. S. Carroll & J. W. Payne (Eds.), *Cognition and social behavior*. Hillsdale, N.J.: Lawrence Erlbaum Associates, 1976.

Abelson, R. P. Psychological status of the script concept. *American Psychologist*, 1981, *36*, 715–729.

Anderson, J. R., & Bower, G. H. *Human associative memory*. Washington, D.C.: Winston, 1973.

Bargh, J. A. Attention and automaticity in the processing of self-relevant information. *Journal of Personality and Social Psychology*, 1982, *43*, 425–436.

Bargh, J. A., & Bond, R. N. *Cognitive involvement in the subconscious processing of affect: The necessity of categorization for automatic influences on impressions.* Unpublished manuscript, New York University, 1983.

Bargh, J. A., & Pietromonaco, P. Automatic information processing and social perception: The influence of trait information presented outside of conscious awareness on impression formation. *Journal of Personality and Social Psychology*, 1982, *43*, 437–449.

Bargh, J. A., Thein, D., & Friedman, D. *Category accessibility and perceptual hypotheses: Consequences for the attentional selection, recall, and use of category-consistent and inconsistent person information.* Unpublished manuscript, New York University, 1983.

Bartlett, F. C. *Remembering*. New York: Cambridge University Press, 1932.

Bateson, G. *Steps to an ecology of mind*. San Francisco: Chandler, 1972.

Beck, A. T. *Depression: Clinical, experimental, and theoretical aspects*. New York: Harper & Row, 1967.

Beck, A. T. *Cognitive therapy and the emotional disorders*. New York: International Universities Press, 1976.

Boring, E. G. *The physical dimensions of consciousness*. New York: Century, 1933.

Bower, G. H., Black, J. B., & Turner, T. J. Scripts in memory for text. *Cognitive Psychology*, 1979, *11*, 177–220.

Bradley, G. W. Self-serving biases in the attribution process: A reexamination of the fact or fiction question. *Journal of Personality and Social Psychology*, 1978, *36*, 56–71.

Brenner, M. The next-in-line effect. *Journal of Verbal Learning and Verbal Behavior*, 1973, *12*, 320–323.

Broadbent, D. E. *Perception and communication*. London: Pergamon Press, 1958.

Bruner, J. S. On perceptual readiness. *Psychological Review*, 1957, *64*, 123–152.

Campbell, B. G. *Human evolution*. Chicago: Aldine, 1974.

Carroll, J. S., & Payne, J. W. (Eds.). *Cognition and social behavior*. Hillsdale, N.J.: Lawrence Erlbaum Associates, 1976.

Chaiken, S. Heuristic versus systematic information processing and the use of source versus message cues in persuasion. *Journal of Personality and Social Psychology*, 1980, *39*, 752–766.

Cialdini, R. B., Petty, R. E., & Cacioppo, J. T. Attitude and attitude change. In M. Rosenzweig & L. Porter (Eds.), *Annual review of psychology*, vol. 32. Palo Alto, Calif.: Annual Reviews, 1981.

Cohen, C. E. Goals and schemata in person perception: Making sense from the stream of behavior. In N. Cantor & J. F. Kihlstrom (Eds.), *Personality, cognition, and social interaction*. Hillsdale, N.J.: Lawrence Erlbaum Associates, 1981.

Corteen, R. S., & Wood, B. Autonomic responses to shock-associated words in an unattended channel. *Journal of Experimental Psychology*, 1972, *94*, 308–313.

Dawes, R. M. Shallow psychology. In J. S. Carroll & J. W. Payne (Eds.), *Cognition and social behavior*. Hillsdale, N.J.: Lawrence Erlbaum Associates, 1976.

Dawson, M. E., & Schell, A. M. *Electrodermal responses to attended and nonattended significant stimuli*. Paper presented at the meeting of the Society for Psychological Research, Cincinnati, 1979.

deGroot, A. D. *Thought and choice in chess*. The Hague: Mouton, 1965.

Deutsch, J. A., & Deutsch, D. Attention: Some theoretical considerations. *Psychological Review*, 1963, *70*, 80–90.

Dreyfus, H. L. *What computers can't do*. New York: Harper & Row, 1972.

Duval, S., & Wicklund, R. A. *A theory of objective self-awareness*. New York: Academic Press, 1972.

Erdelyi, M. H. A new look at the New Look: Perceptual defense and vigilance. *Psychological Review*, 1974, *81*, 1–25.

Fazio, R. H., Chen, J., McDonel, E. C., & Sherman, S. J. Attitude accessibility, attitude-behavior consistency, and the strength of the object-evaluation association. *Journal of Experimental Social Psychology*, 1982, *18*, 339–357.

Fazio, R. H., Powell, M. C., & Herr, P. M. Toward a process model of the attitude-behavior relation: Accessing one's attitude upon mere observation of the attitude object. *Journal of Personality and Social Psychology*, 1983, *44*, 723–735.

Fiske, S. T. Attention and weight in person perception: The impact of negative and extreme behavior. *Journal of Personality and Social Psychology*, 1980, *38*, 889–906.

Fiske, S. T., & Dyer, L. *Cognitive analysis of involvement in persuasion*. Paper presented at the meetings of the American Psychological Association, Washington, D.C., 1982.

Fiske, S. T., Kenny, D. A., & Taylor, S. E. Structural models for the mediation of salience effects on attribution. *Journal of Experimental Social Psychology*, 1982, *18*, 105–127.

Fiske, S. T., & Linville, P. W. What does the schema concept buy us? *Personality and Social Psychology Bulletin*, 1980, *6*, 543–557.

Fiske, S. T., & Taylor, S. E. *Social cognition*. Reading, Mass.: Addison-Wesley, 1984.

Friedman, A. Framing pictures: The role of knowledge in automatized encoding and memory for gist. *Journal of Experimental Psychology: General*, 1979, *108*, 316–355.

Geller, V., & Shaver, P. Cognitive consequences of self-awareness. *Journal of Experimental Social Psychology*, 1976, *12*, 99–108.

Glucksberg, S., & Cowen, G. N. Memory for nonattended auditory material. *Cognitive Psychology*, 1970, *1*, 149–156.

Greenwald, A. G. The totalitarian ego: Fabrication and revision of personal history. *American Psychologist*, 1980, *35*, 603–618.

Hamilton, D. L. Cognitive biases in the perception of social groups. In J. S. Carroll & J. W. Payne (Eds.), *Cognition and social behavior.* Hillsdale, N.J.: Lawrence Erlbaum Associates, 1976.

Hasher, L., & Zacks, R. T. Automatic and effortful processes in memory. *Journal of Experimental Psychology: General,* 1979, *108,* 356–388.

Hastie, R. Schematic principles in human memory. In E. T. Higgins, C. P. Herman, & M. P. Zanna (Eds.), *Social cognition: The Ontario symposium,* vol. 1. Hillsdale, N.J.: Lawrence Erlbaum Associates, 1981.

Hastie, R., & Kumar, P. A. Person memory: Personality traits as organizing principles in memory for behaviors. *Journal of Personality and Social Psychology,* 1979, *37,* 25–38.

Hebb, D. O. *Organization of behavior.* New York: Wiley, 1949.

Higgins, E. T., & King, G. Accessibility of social constructs: Information-processing consequences of individual and contextual variability. In N. Cantor & J. F. Kihlstrom (Eds.), *Personality, cognition, and social interaction.* Hillsdale, N.J.: Lawrence Erlbaum Associates, 1981.

Higgins, E. T., King, G. A., & Mavin, G. H. Individual construct accessibility and subjective impressions and recall. *Journal of Personality and Social Psychology,* 1982, *43,* 35–47.

Higgins, E. T., McCann, C. D., & Fondacaro, R. The "communication game": Goal-directed encoding and cognitive consequences. *Social Cognition,* 1982, *1,* 21–37.

Higgins, E. T., Rholes, W. S., & Jones, C. R. Category accessibility and impression formation. *Journal of Experimental Social Psychology,* 1977, *13,* 141–154.

Hirst, W., Spelke, E., Reaves, C. C., Caharack, G., & Neisser, U. Dividing attention without alternation or automaticity. *Journal of Experimental Psychology: General,* 1980, *109,* 98–117.

Hull, J. G., & Levy, A. S. The organizational functions of the self: An alternative to the Duval and Wicklund model of self-awareness. *Journal of Personality and Social Psychology,* 1979, *37,* 756–768.

James, W. *The principles of psychology.* New York: Holt, 1890.

Jeffrey, K. M., & Mischel, W. Effects of purpose on the organization and recall of information in person perception. *Journal of Personality,* 1979, *47,* 397–419.

Jones, E. E., & Nisbett, R. E. The actor and the observer: Divergent perceptions of the causes of behavior. In E. E. Jones et al. (Eds.), *Attribution: Perceiving the causes of behavior.* Morristown, N.J.: General Learning Press, 1971.

Kahneman, D. *Attention and effort.* Englewood Cliffs, N.J.: Prentice-Hall, 1973.

Kanouse, D. E. Language, labeling, and attribution. In E. E. Jones et al. (Eds.), *Attribution: Perceiving the causes of behavior.* Morristown, N.J.: General Learning Press, 1971.

Kantowitz, B. H. Double stimulation. In B. H. Kantowitz (Ed.), *Human information processing: Tutorials in performance and cognition.* Hillsdale, N.J.: Lawrence Erlbaum Associates, 1974.

Kaplan, S. Adaptation, structure, and knowledge. In G. T. Moore & R. G. Golledge (Eds.), *Environmental knowing.* Stroudsberg, Pa.: Dowden, Hutchinson and Ross, 1976.

Kaplan, S., & Kaplan, R. *Cognition and environment.* New York: Praeger, 1982.

Kellogg, R. T. Is conscious attention necessary for long-term storage? *Journal of Experimental Psychology: Human Learning and Memory,* 1980, *6,* 379–390.

Kimble, G. A., & Perlmuter, L. C. The problem of volition. *Psychological Review,* 1970, *77,* 361–384.

Kuiper, N. A., & Derry, P. A. The self as a cognitive prototype: An application to person perception and depression. In N. Cantor & J. F. Kihlstrom (Eds.), *Personality, cognition, and social interaction.* Hillsdale, N.J.: Lawrence Erlbaum Associates, 1981.

Kuiper, N. A., Olinger, L. J., & MacDonald, M. R. Depressive schemata and the processing of personal and social information. In L. B. Alloy (Ed.), *Cognitive processes in depression.* New York: Guilford Press, in press.

LaBerge, D., & Samuels, S. J. Toward a theory of automatic information processing in reading. *Cognitive Psychology,* 1974, *6,* 293–323.

Langer, E. J. The illusion of control. *Journal of Personality and Social Psychology,* 1975, *32,* 311–328.

Langer, E. J. Rethinking the role of thought in social interaction. In J. H. Harvey, W. J. Ickes, & R. F. Kidd (Eds.), *New directions in attribution research,* vol. 2. Hillsdale, N.J.: Lawrence Erlbaum Associates, 1978.

Langer, E. J. *Minding matters: The mindlessness/mindfulness theory of cognitive activity.* Paper presented at the meetings of the Society for Experimental Social Psychology, Nashville, Indiana, 1982.

Langer, E. J., Blank, A., & Chanowitz, B. The mindlessness of ostensibly thoughtful action: The role of "placebic" information in interpersonal interaction. *Journal of Personality and Social Psychology,* 1978, *36,* 635–642.

Langer, E. J., & Imber, L. G. When practice makes imperfect: Debilitating effects of overlearning. *Journal of Personality and Social Psychology,* 1979, *37,* 2014–2024.

Lewis, J. Semantic processing of unattended messages using dichotic listening. *Journal of Experimental Psychology,* 1970, *85,* 225–228.

Logan, G. D. On the use of a concurrent memory load to measure attention and automaticity. *Journal of Experimental Psychology: Human Perception and Performance,* 1979, *5,* 189–207.

Logan, G. D. Attention and automaticity in Stroop and priming tasks: Theory and data. *Cognitive Psychology,* 1980, *12,* 523–553.

Logan, G. D., & Zbrodoff, N. J. When it helps to be misled: Facilitative effects of increasing the frequency of conflicting stimuli in a Stroop-like task. *Memory & Cognition,* 1979, *7,* 166–174.

MacDonald, M. R., & Kuiper, N. A. *Automaticity of information processing in clinical depressives.* Paper presented at the meeting of the Society for Experimental Social Psychology, Nashville, Indiana, 1982.

Major, B. Information acquisition and attribution processes. *Journal of Personality and Social Psychology,* 1980, *39,* 1010–1023.

Markus, H. Self-schemata and processing information about the self. *Journal of Personality and Social Psychology,* 1977, *35,* 63–78.

Markus, H. The self in thought and memory. In D. M. Wegner & R. R. Vallacher (Eds.), *The self in social psychology.* New York: Oxford University Press, 1980.

Markus, H., & Smith, J. M. The influence of self-schemas on the perception of others. In N. Cantor & J. F. Kihlstrom (Eds.), *Personality, cognition, and social interaction.* Hillsdale, N.J.: Lawrence Erlbaum Associates, 1981.

McArthur, L. Z. Illusory causation and illusory correlation: Two epistemological accounts. *Personality and Social Psychology Bulletin,* 1980, *6,* 507–519.

McArthur, L. Z. What grabs you? The role of attention in impression formation and causal attribution. In E. T. Higgins, C. P. Herman, & M. P. Zanna (Eds.), *Social cognition: The Ontario symposium,* vol. 1. Hillsdale, N.J.: Lawrence Erlbaum Associates, 1981.

McArthur, L. Z., & Post, D. D. Figural emphasis and person perception. *Journal of Experimental Social Psychology,* 1977, *13,* 520–535.

Mischel, W. Personality and assessment. New York: Wiley, 1968.

Mischel, W. On the interface of cognition and personality: Beyond the person-situation debate. *American Psychologist,* 1979, *34,* 740–754.

Moray, N. Attention in dichotic listening: Affective cues and the influence of instructions. *Quarterly Journal of Experimental Psychology,* 1959, *11,* 56–60.

Neely, J. H. Semantic priming and retrieval from lexical memory: Roles of inhibitionless spreading activation and limited-capacity attention. *Journal of Experimental Psychology: General,* 1977, *106,* 226–254.

Neisser, U. Visual search. *Scientific American,* 1964, *210,* 94–102.

Neisser, U. *Cognitive psychology.* New York: Appleton-Century-Crofts, 1967.

Neisser, U. *Cognition and reality.* San Francisco: Freeman, 1976.

Newell, A., & Rosenbloom, P. S. Mechanisms of skill acquisition and the law of practice. In J. R. Anderson (Ed.), *Cognitive skills and their acquisition.* Hillsdale, N.J.: Lawrence Erlbaum Associates, 1981.

Nielsen, S. L., & Sarason, I. G. Emotion, personality, and selective attention. *Journal of Personality and Social Psychology*, 1981, *41*, 945–960.

Nisbett, R. E., & Bellows, N. Verbal reports about causal influences on social judgments: Private access versus public theories. *Journal of Personality and Social Psychology*, 1977, *35*, 613–624.

Nisbett, R. E., Borgida, E., Crandall, R., & Reed, H. Popular induction: Information is not necessarily informative. In J. S. Carroll & J. W. Payne (Eds.), *Cognition and social behavior*. Hillsdale, N.J.: Lawrence Erlbaum Associates, 1976.

Nisbett, R., & Ross, L. *Human inference: Strategies and shortcomings of social judgment*. Englewood Cliffs, N.J.: Prentice-Hall, 1980.

Nisbett, R. E., & Wilson, T. D. Telling more than we can know: Verbal reports on mental processes. *Psychological Review*, 1977, *84*, 231–259. (a)

Nisbett, R. E., & Wilson, T. D. The halo effect: Evidence for unconscious alteration of judgments. *Journal of Personality and Social Psychology*, 1977, *35*, 250–256. (b)

Norman, D. A. Memory while shadowing. *Quarterly Journal of Experimental Psychology*, 1969, *21*, 85–93.

Norman, D. A., & Bobrow, D. G. On the role of active memory processes in perception and cognition. In C. N. Cofer (Ed.), *The structure of human memory*. San Francisco: Freeman, 1976.

Peterson, L. R., & Kroener, S. Dichotic stimulation and retention. *Journal of Experimental Psychology*, 1964, *68*, 125–130.

Petty, R. E., & Cacioppo, J. T. Issue-involvement can increase or decrease persuasion by enhancing message-relevant cognitive responses. *Journal of Personality and Social Psychology*, 1979, *37*, 1915–1926.

Petty, R. E., & Cacioppo, J. T. *Attitudes and persuasion: Classic and contemporary approaches*. Dubuque, Iowa: Wm. C. Brown, 1981.

Petty, R. E., Cacioppo, J. T., & Goldman, R. Personal involvement as a determinant of argument-based persuasion. *Journal of Personality and Social Psychology*, 1981, *41*, 847–855.

Posner, M. I. *Cognition: An introduction*. Glenview, Ill.: Scott, Foresman, 1973.

Posner, M. I. *Chronometric explorations of mind*. Hillsdale, N.J.: Lawrence Erlbaum Associates, 1978.

Posner, M. I., & Boies, S. J. Components of attention. *Psychological Review*, 1971, *78*, 391–408.

Posner, M. I., & Snyder, C. R. R. Attention and cognitive control. In R. L. Solso (Ed.), *Information processing and cognition: The Loyola symposium*. Hillsdale, N.J.: Lawrence Erlbaum Associates, 1975.

Ross, M., & Sicoly, F. Egocentric biases in availability and attribution. *Journal of Personality and Social Psychology*, 1979, *37*, 322–336.

Schank, R. C., & Abelson, R. P. *Scripts, plans, goals, and understanding*. Hillsdale, N.J.: Lawrence Erlbaum Associates, 1977.

Schneider, W., & Fisk, A. D. Degree of consistent training: Improvements in search performance and automatic process development. *Perception & Psychophysics*, 1982, *31*, 160–168. (a)

Schneider, W., & Fisk, A. D. *Processing with and without long-term memory modification: Attention, level of processing, and word frequency*. Technical Report HARL-ONR-8203. Champaign: University of Illinois, Human Attention Research Laboratory, 1982. (b)

Schneider, W., & Shiffrin, R. M. Controlled and automatic human information processing: I. Detection, search, and attention. *Psychological Review*, 1977, *84*, 1–66.

Schvaneveldt, R. W., & Meyer, D. E. Retrieval and comparison processes in semantic memory. In S. Kornblum (Ed.), *Attention and performance IV*. New York: Academic Press, 1973.

Shiffrin, R. M., & Dumais, S. T. The development of automatism. In J. R. Anderson (Ed.), *Cognitive skills and their acquisition*. Hillsdale, N.J.: Lawrence Erlbaum Associates, 1981.

Shiffrin, R. M., & Schneider, W. Controlled and automatic human information processing: II. Perceptual learning, automatic attending, and a general theory. *Psychological Review*, 1977, *84*, 127–190.

Skinner, B. F. *Beyond freedom and dignity*. New York: Knopf, 1971.

Smith, E. R., & Miller, F. D. Salience and the cognitive mediation of attribution. *Journal of Personality and Social Psychology*, 1979, *37*, 2240–2252.

Snyder, M., & Swann, W. B., Jr. Hypothesis-testing processes in social interaction. *Journal of Personality and Social Psychology*, 1978, *36*, 1202–1212.

Spelke, E., Hirst, W., & Neisser, U. Skills of divided attention. *Cognition*, 1976, *4*, 215–230.

Srull, T. K. Person memory: Some tests of associative storage and retrieval models. *Journal of Experimental Psychology: Human Learning and Memory*, 1981, *7*, 440–463.

Srull, T. K., & Wyer, R. S., Jr. The role of category accessibility in the interpretation of information about persons: Some determinants and implications. *Journal of Personality and Social Psychology*, 1979, *37*, 1660–1672.

Srull, T. K., & Wyer, R. S., Jr. Category accessibility and social perception: Some implications for the study of person memory and interpersonal judgments. *Journal of Personality and Social Psychology*, 1980, *38*, 841–856.

Storms, M. D. Videotape and the attribution process: Reversing the actors' and observers' point of view. *Journal of Personality and Social Psychology*, 1973, *27*, 165–175.

Strack, F., Erber, R., & Wicklund, R. A. Effects of salience and time pressure on ratings of social causality. *Journal of Experimental Social Psychology*, 1982, *18*, 581–594.

Taylor, S. E. The interface of cognitive and social psychology. In J. H. Harvey (Ed.), *Cognition, social behavior, and the environment*. Hillsdale, N.J.: Lawrence Erlbaum Associates, 1981.

Taylor, S. E., Crocker, J., Fiske, S. T., Sprinzen, M., & Winkler, J. D. The generalizability of salience effects. *Journal of Personality and Social Psychology*, 1979, *37*, 357–368.

Taylor, S. E., & Fiske, S. T. Point of view and perceptions of causality. *Journal of Personality and Social Psychology*, 1975, *32*, 439–445.

Taylor, S. E., & Fiske, S. T. Salience, attention, and attribution: Top of the head phenomena. In L. Berkowitz (Ed.), *Advances in experimental social psychology*, vol. 11. New York: Academic Press, 1978.

Taylor, S. E., & Thompson, S. C. Stalking the elusive 'vividness' effect. *Psychological Review*, 1982, *89*, 155–181.

Teichner, W. H., & Krebs, M. J. Laws of the simple reaction time. *Psychological Review*, 1972, *79*, 344–358.

Treisman, A. M. Contextual cues in selective listening. *Quarterly Journal of Experimental Psychology*, 1960, *12*, 242–248.

Treisman, A. M., & Geffen, G. Selective attention: Perception or response? *Quarterly Journal of Experimental Psychology*, 1967, *19*, 1–17.

Treisman, A. M., Squire, R., & Green, J. Semantic processing in dichotic listening? A replication. *Memory & Cognition*, 1974, *2*, 641–646.

Tversky, A., & Kahneman, D. Availability: A heuristic for judging frequency and probability. *Cognitive Psychology*, 1973, *5*, 207–232.

Tversky, A., & Kahneman, D. Judgment under uncertainty: Heuristics and biases. *Science*, 1974, *184*, 1124–1131.

White, P. Limitations on verbal reports of internal events: A refutation of Nisbett and Wilson and of Bem. *Psychological Review*, 1980, *87*, 105–112.

Wicklund, R. A. Self-focused attention and the validity of self-reports. In M. P. Zanna, E. T. Higgins, & C. P. Herman (Eds.), *Consistency in social behavior: The Ontario symposium*, vol. 2. Hillsdale, N.J.: Lawrence Erlbaum Associates, 1982.

Wicklund, R. A., & Hormuth, S. E. On the functions of the self: A reply to Hull and Levy. *Journal of Personality and Social Psychology*, 1981, *40*, 1029–1037.

Wyer, R. S., Jr. The acquisition and use of social knowledge: Basic postulates and representative research. *Personality and Social Psychology Bulletin*, 1980, *6*, 558–573.

Wyer, R. S., Jr., & Srull, T. K. Category accessibility: Some theoretical and empirical issues concerning the processing of social stimulus information. In E. T. Higgins, C. P. Herman, & M.

P. Zanna (Eds.), *Social cognition: The Ontario symposium,* vol. 1. Hillsdale, N.J.: Lawrence Erlbaum Associates, 1981.

Zajonc, R. B. Cognition and social cognition: A historical perspective. In L. Festinger (Ed.), *Retrospections on social psychology.* New York: Oxford University Press, 1980. (a)

Zajonc, R. B. Feeling and thinking: Preferences need no inferences. *American Psychologist,* 1980, *35,* 151–175. (b)

2 Comprehending Stories and Social Situations

John B. Black
Yale University

James A. Galambos
Yale University

Stephen J. Read
Northwestern University

Contents

Social behavior is fascinating to the common person as well as to the psychologist. This fascination is apparent in the frequency with which we discuss, evaluate and attempt to understand the behavior of our peers, our family members, our leaders, and even that of total strangers. The fascination is manifest in the stories we tell to others. A story is interesting because it affords us the opportunity to view characters with novel personalities perceiving and dealing with social situations and problems. We understand such stories using the knowledge and cognitive mechanisms with which we understand the behavior of people we know.

     Both social situations and stories about them conform to a *social logic* (or must be made to conform to such a logic if they are to be made comprehensible to us). Application of this social logic involves representing a particular behavior of a person, with a particular personality, in a particular situation. We find the behavior of a person in a situation to be **reasonable,** if we can fit together an explanation of it based on what we know about the person and the situation. Social logic guides our attempts to comprehend social behavior by integrating our perceptions with our knowledge of similar situations or similar people. The integration is accomplished using inferences of various kinds.

There is great flexibility in the inferences we can make, and thus in the range of possible ways in which we comprehend social behavior. We can understand a behavior by focusing on one of the components. For example, suppose we were trying to explain the behavior of one of our friends, Ralph. Ralph always gives handouts to beggars who ask for them. One natural way to explain this is by inferring that Ralph is a good samaritan. Thus, we make this behavior understandable using our knowledge of a particular personality trait. Our social logic also specifies rules of combination of information from multiple knowledge sources. For example, we might explain (but not condone) why Ralph would ignore his childhood friend, Sam, when Ralph is dining at a fancy restaurant with Mr. and Mrs. Upper-Crust. Our explanation might involve our knowledge of Ralph's desire for upward social mobility, as well as our understanding of how acknowledging the friendship in that particular situation might detract from the image Ralph is trying to present. Even in a fairly simple case as this, we must integrate our knowledge of Ralph, Sam, Mr. and Mrs. Upper-Crust, friendship, image-making, restaurants, and so forth. Our social logic even specifies ways in which to resolve the apparently contradictory behavior of Ralph in the two examples; perhaps Sam is in competition with Ralph for the benefits of higher social station, or Sam recently had an affair with Ralph's wife. Alternatively, it may be that Ralph is not really a good samaritan, but that giving small handouts to beggars makes him feel more important. This explanation also accords with the social logic.

The social logic which we employ to unify our understanding is quite complex and difficult to study. Our approach is to examine some of its characteristics by isolating the types of inferences that are made in comprehension and some of the types of knowledge structures that support the inferences and consequently come to be integrated in the understanding of behavior. Some of these inferences relate our knowledge to features of the context in which the behavior occurs. Other inferences link different actions in the situation with one another. After we discuss some of the different type of inferences that have been examined in the research on story comprehension, we present a model of the integration of knowledge that occurs during comprehension.

We take the perspective that the study of social situations in stories **is** the study of social situations. There are, of course, differences that involve the participant-observer distinction and the mode in which the information is presented (i.e., verbal versus nonverbal). Nonetheless, the higher level cognitive processes that are involved in **comprehending** why someone did something to/with someone else, reflect the same social logic whether the object of comprehension is presented in personal experience or in a story. The influence of the understanding on subsequent behavior of the understander may differ, but the comprehension process is the same. In both cases, the understander takes individual items of information and puts them together to form a cohesive and comprehensible whole. When we observe people behaving, the relationships between the actions are not given. Rather, we must infer how one action is related to another, or how an action is related to the personality of the actor or to the situation in which the action occurs. This is exactly what is studied in research on story comprehension. Thus, it is important that psychologists interested in social cognition be aware of the story comprehension research (just as story researchers should look to findings in social cognition to guide their theories).

In the last few years, there has been a large amount of research done concerning how people understand and remember stories. We cannot cover all of this research here (see Graesser, 1981 and Stein & Trabasso, in press for more extensive surveys), so we focus on the research we consider to be most relevant to social cognition. In particular, we concentrate on research concerning the kinds of inferences readers make in order to understand a story and the kinds of knowledge needed to make these inferences. Other kinds of approaches to story understanding that we do not cover (although we cite results from these approaches that are relevant to our perspective) are the approaches that focus on the **concept** of a story such as the story grammar (Mandler & Johnson, 1977; Rumelhart, 1975; Stein & Glenn, 1979; and Thorndyke, 1977), narrative structure (Brewer & Lichtenstein, 1981) and fuzzy concept (Stein, in press) approaches.

The chapter is divided into three sections. In the first section, we describe a number of the inferences that must be made in order to comprehend a social event (whether in a story or not). The source of these inferences is the various knowledge structures that are brought to bear on the problem of comprehending the input. Thus, we describe not only the type of inference, but also the kinds of knowledge structures that give rise to them. In the second section of the chapter we present a model of how these various kinds of knowledge are integrated during comprehension. In the final section, we attempt to reframe the results of some social cognition studies in terms of our comprehension model.

INFERENCES MADE DURING STORY UNDERSTANDING

Our understanding of any social situation is considerably richer than would be given by any mere transcript of the proceedings. A story writer exploits our propensity (indeed, our compulsion) to read between the lines; to draw inferences based on our knowledge. Observers of real social situations similarly augment the data presented to their senses using their prior knowledge. It is only through inference that the sense data become unified into a representation which will permit us to respond appropriately. In this section we describe some of the varieties of inference that are involved in comprehension. It is useful to separate these inferences into two general classes—*coherence inferences* and *memory-unit inferences*. The distinction between the types is related to the type of knowledge that is involved in supporting the inference. The coherence inferences provide "local" linkages between pairs of statements in a story or actions in some social situation. The sort of knowledge that supports coherence inference is that which represents relations among actions as causal or conventional sequences which are done in the service of a particular goal, or in the accomplishment of a specific familiar activity. On the other hand, the memory-unit inferences are "global" linkages that tie together packages of story statements into memory units at a higher level. The knowledge that supports these inferences is more abstract and involves the representation of general patterns of relationships among goals and activities which is independent of the situational content. This distinction will become clearer as we discuss examples of the two general types.

Each of these two classes of inference is further sub-divided into three different types of inference and we give examples of each type. The three major types of coherence inferences are *causal, goal-related,* and *point of view* inferences. In the next few pages we will describe each of these using a number of examples. The higher-level memory unit inferences also fall into three categories. Two categories are determined by the kind of memory structure involved in the inference—i.e., *goal-based episodes* and *plot units;* while the third category are the inferences linking *deviations* from these memory units to the standard or expected parts of the unit. Our classification is neither complete nor exhaustive. Nonetheless, the inference types we describe are of crucial importance to the comprehension of stories and of the social behaviors they depict. We hope that this work lays the foundation for continued investigation of social logic inferences.

Coherence in Stories

In this section, we present the evidence for three kinds of coherence relations in the representation of stories in the memories of readers. Two of these are strong forms of coherence, while the third is weaker. One of the strong forms occurs when one statement describes an action that directly causes the action in another statement. The other strong form, which is more motivationally oriented, relates the sources of goals with the goals themselves and the plans for attaining them. The third, weaker form of coherence is consistency in the point of view from which the story is told. The point of view is also important because it affects the inferences that establish causal and goal-related coherence.

Causal Inferences.   Kintsch (1974) and Kintsch and van Dijk (1978) proposed that a minimal criterion for coherence in a text is that the statements in the text refer to common objects, people and/or concepts. However, for stories this criterion is not enough to produce coherence. For example,

> John took a psychology course at Yale.
> Susan registered for a history course at Yale.
> Rita dropped a psychology course at Yale.

is rather incoherent even though the concepts of *course* and *Yale* are common to all the statements and *psychology* to two of them. In fact, explicit repetition of such concepts is not necessary for coherence. For example,

> The boulder rolled down the mountain.
> The hut in the valley was crushed.
> Many people were severely injured.

is quite coherent, but there is no explicit repetition of concepts at all. What makes this sequence of statements coherent? The sequence is coherent because the reader can link the statements by making causal inferences. Thus the boulder not only rolled down the mountain, but presumably crushed the hut thereby injuring many people. Making such inferences links the statements with implicitly common concepts (boulder is implicit in all the statements), but more importantly there are implicit causal relations between the statements. Thus an important criterion for coherence in stories is establishing causal links between the sentences.

Schank (1975) proposed that story episodes are stored in the memories of readers as networks of story "conceptualizations" linked by causal relations. The examples in the previous paragraph support this idea and there is also a substantial set of empirical results that support it. In particular, Mandler and Johnson (1977) found that causally-related episodes in children's stories were remembered better than ones not causally-related. Similarly, Black and Bern (1981) experimentally manipulated whether a causal inference could be made linking pairs of statements or whether such inferences were blocked. For example, one causally-related pair of statements was:

> He walked over to the refrigerator bumping a bowl he had left on the table.
> Suddenly it fell off the edge and broke.

The causal inference here is that bumping the bowl caused it to fall and break. The non-causal form of this pair merely replaced "bumping" with "seeing." These statements were recalled together much more in both cued and free recall when they were causally-related than when they were not. Further memory evidence for the causal-network memory representation for stories is provided by Trabasso, Seco, and van den Broek (in press) and Black and Bower (1980) finding that story statements on the main causal path through the story network are remembered better than those on side paths. Trabasso et al. also showed that memory effects that were earlier attributed to differences in story grammar category (e.g., setting, attempt to attain goal, etc.), were more likely due to the number of causal connections between the story statements.

If the linking causal inferences become an intimate part of the representation of a story in memory, then the readers would frequently be unaware after a delay that they did not explicitly read the implicit causal statements. This is what Bower, Black, and Turner (1979) found in the special case of script-based stories. Scripts were proposed by Schank and Abelson (1977) as a major source of causal inferences. A script is a knowledge structure of causally-related conceptualizations that represent what we know about the standard actions, objects, and actors in common conventional situations. Thus, for example, if we read

John sat down in a restaurant.
He ordered roast beef for dinner.

we know that when he sat down a waitress (or waiter) came over to his table and that he gave the order to the waitress after choosing what he wanted from the menu. It is our knowledge about restaurants embodied in the restaurant script that allows us to make these causal inferences. Bower, Black, and Turner found that after a short delay (30 minutes) subjects who had read such script-based stories would be fairly certain that they had read about a waitress coming to the table: that is, the subjects false alarmed on a recognition test to standard script actions that were omitted from the story.

If understanding a story involves establishing causal links between the statements, then the harder it is to establish such links the longer it should take to read the statements. Studies by Haberlandt and Bingham (1978), Bower et al. (1979) and Abbott, Black, and Smith (1982) have shown this implication of the causal-network memory representation to be true. In particular, Haberlandt and Bingham found that subjects took longer to read triples of sentences when there were no causal relations between them than when there were. Apparently the readers paused and searched in vain for causal relations in the non-causal case, only to finally give up and move on. Bower et al. (1979) and Abbott et al. (1982) examined less severe cases. In particular, they varied the "gap size" between statements in script-based stories as measured by the number of standard script actions that were skipped between the two statements in the story text. Here the "gap size" is the measure of how difficult it is to form a causal link between the statements and, in general, the results showed that the reading time increased with gap size.

Goal-Related Inferences.   Another kind of relation between story statements that makes stories coherent is goal-related linkage. Such links connect the source of goals (e.g., if it is raining or a story character is a policeman then we expect certain goals), the goals themselves, and the plans for attaining the goals. As with causal relations, we can construct a sequence of statements without any explicit repetition of concepts but which is quite coherent because there are implicit goal-related links between the statements. For example,

> Suddenly it started raining.
> Everyone headed for the store.
> The entire stock of umbrellas was depleted.

This sequence is coherent because goal-related inferences tell us that everyone was headed for the store in order to buy umbrellas (plan) to protect themselves (goal) from the rain (the source of the goal).

Abbott and Black (1982) provided memory evidence for goal-based links similar to the evidence we described for causal links. In particular, they compared subjects' free recall of triples of statements in a story that were either linked by repetition of several common concepts or were linked by goal-related inferences. The results showed that if one statement was recalled from a goal-related triple then the other statements in the triple were likely to be recalled, whereas the statement recall in the concept-repeitition triples was basically independent. The strength of the goal-related links was also shown in a recognition priming task. Here the time to recognize a statement as having been in the story was faster when it was preceded by another story statement from a goal-related triple, but no speedup was observed when it was preceded by a statement from a concept-repetition triple. Lichtenstein and Brewer (1980) have shown similar effects in the recall of actions that were presented to subjects on video-tape. When a behavior is shown with the goal that it serves, it is better recalled than when the goal is not shown. This supports our contention that observed behavior is comprehended in the same fashion as behaviors presented in stories.

As with causal links, the harder it is for the reader to establish the goal-related links in a story, the longer it takes to read the story. Seifert, Robertson, and Black (1982) found that when they left a goal or plan statement to be inferred, the next statement in the story took longer to read than when the goal or plan statement was explicitly stated. For example, the last statement in

> He wanted to be king.
> He was tired of waiting.
> He thought arsenic would work well.

took longer to read in this version, than when the plan ("He decided to poison the king.") was explicitly stated (here it would be inserted as the next to last statement). Smith and Collins (1981) manipulated the goal-related "gap size" between two statements in a text and found that the reading time increased with the gap size: that is, the more goal-related inferences needed to be made to connect two story statements, the longer the statements took to read.

Point of View.   A weaker form of coherence in stories is provided by maintaining a consistent point of view. The point of view is determined by who is the main character and by the perspective in the fictional story-world from which the story is told. Thus,

> John worked in the front yard.
> Then he went inside.

maintains a consistent point of view because John is the actor in both sentences and the actions are described from a location in the front yard. If the second sentence had said "came" instead of "went" then the point of view would change as one went from the first sentence to the second and the sequence would be less coherent. Black, Turner, and Bower (1979) found that such changes in point of view caused sentences to take longer to read, to be rated as less comprehensible, to be misremembered as having a consistent point of view and to be rewritten to be consistent when subjects were asked to edit the story. These results seem to indicate that the memory representation for a story maintains a consistent point of view.

The point of view from which a story is told also affects the causal and goal-related inferences that the reader makes when reading the story. In particular, Black (1982) and Bower (1978) found that people exhibited the same actor-observer attribution bias when reading a story that they exhibit in social situations. In social situations, this bias is to attribute the causes of behavior to the actor when one is an observer and to the situation when one is the actor (Jones & Nisbett, 1971). In Black's study, all the subjects read a several page story about three characters going water skiing. However, half the subjects read a one page introduction to the story designed to identify the boat driver as the main character, while the other half read an introduction that identified the skier as the main character. Later, all the subjects took a recognition test which included various items corresponding to potential causal and goal-related inferences. Which inferences the readers made (as measured by false recognition) depended on their point of view (i.e., who they saw as the main character). Readers in the skier condition false alarmed to items identifying the causes of unfavorable actions by the skier as being the situation (e.g., The tall waves caused the skier to fall down) or the other character (e.g., The driver turned the boat too sharply so the skier fell down). On the other hand, readers in the driver condition false alarmed to items identifying the skier as the cause of his troubles (e.g., The skier was clumsy and fell down). This data indicates that the reader tends to take the role of the main character and imagine the events in the story as though they were this character. With data from a recall experiment, Abelson (1975) also showed that the point of view affects memories for general features versus details about the situation. If readers are viewing a story scene from a hotel balcony, then they remember *general* aspects of the scene better; but if they are viewing from a character walking on the street below, then they remember *details* of the scene. Thus, the point of view from which a story is told seems to affect how the story is understood and remembered in several ways.

Higher-Level Memory Units in Stories

In the previous section, we described the three major kinds of coherence relations that connect statements in the memory representation of a story. However, although these interconnected story statements manifest local consistency, they do not form a uniform network representation of the story as a whole. Instead, groups of statements that are linked by coherence inferences can be considered as memory units, and these units can be themselves linked by inferences which apply at a higher level of abstraction. The higher-level memory unit that has been most fully researched is the goal-based episode, but recently higher-level units corresponding to standard goal-outcome patterns (plot units) have also begun to be investigated. In this section, we describe the research supporting these higher-level units, then describe how deviations from the standard parts of such units are represented in memory.

Goal-based Episodes.   The most important contribution of the "story grammar" approach to story understanding may well be the proposal that the goal-based episode is the major constituent of stories (Mandler & Johnson, 1980; Rumelhart, 1977). A goal-based episode is a particular goal (or subgoal if it is subordinate to other goals), the plan of actions to attain it, and the outcome of trying that plan. If these episodes are truly separate memory units, then we would expect them to exhibit some independence in memory.

Black and Bower (1979) found that these episodes showed independence in free recall. In particular, they manipulated the length of episodes and found that the length of an episode affected the recall of the actions in that episode but not the recall of actions in other episodes. For example, one story they used had an overall goal of trying to find a book on a university campus. The story consisted of two episodes: one episode described trying to find the book in the library (which failed), while the other described trying to find the book in the bookstore (which succeeded). Black and Bower created a "short" version of each episode by including the goal (finding book in library), three actions in service of the goal (entering library, looking in card catalog, and finding location), and the outcome (the book was not there). They also created a "long" version of each episode by including five other actions (e.g., asking the librarian) that probably occurred in the episode. Adding the five actions in a given episode increased the recall of the original goal, outcome, and three actions for that episode, but had no effect on the recall of statements in the other episode. Thus the goal-based episodes showed independence in free recall and adding more statements filling in the gaps between episode components increased their recall.

Other evidence that episodes act like separate chunks in memory is provided by Mandler (1978) and Glenn (1978). In particular, Mandler found that when she interleaved the actions from two episodes in a story, her subjects (especially children) tended to separate the actions into episode clusters during free recall: that is, the actions of a given episode were recalled together even though they were separated in the original text. Glenn (1978) found that her subjects tended to elaborate short elliptical stories in free recall. These elaborations were linking statements that tended to make the stories more coherent. However, the length of the episodes was the critical determinant of whether elaboration would occur, not the total length of the story.

Haberlandt (1980) also found evidence that episodes function as independent units. In particular, when he measured the reading time for each statement in a story, he found that readers spent a relatively long time reading the beginnings and ends of episodes. This finding seems to indicate that each time readers encounter a new episode, they spend time in the beginning activating the knowledge needed to understand the rest of the episode (e.g., the relevant plan or script) and at the end they pause to integrate and store the entire episode package as a unit in memory. Thus Haberlandt's reading time results complement the memory results in validating the hypothesis that goal-based episodes are processing and memory units in story understanding.

The effects of goal hierarchy on recall provide another kind of evidence that goal-based episodes are basic building blocks in the memory representation for a story. Sometimes stories form a hierarchy of goals in which attempts to attain a goal evokes other goals which have to be attained first. In such cases the episodes for the subordinate goals are embedded in the episode for the overall goal. For example, if we revised the "book" story described earlier so that the student in the bookstore needed to go to the bank to get money to buy the book, then the bank episode would be embedded in and subordinate to the bookstore episode. Numerous investigators (e.g., Black & Bower, 1980; Graesser, 1981; Thorndyke, 1977) have found that the more subordinate such episodes are (i.e., the lower in the goal hierarchy), the worse they are recalled. This finding is consistent with a memory retrieval process that starts at the top of the goal hierarchy and works its way down. Thus the lower in the hierarchy an item is, the more likely that at least one link has been forgotten, so the more likely the item is to be unretrievable. Since goal-based episodes are the basic units of analysis in these hierarchies, these results also validate their usefulness.

Plot Units.   Another important higher-level memory unit in stories that has only recently begun to be investigated is what Lehnert (1981) termed "plot units." Plot units are particular patterns of goals and outcomes that form standard thematic units. Plot units are composed of causally linked mental states (states of desire or goals), positive outcomes of a plan, and negative outcomes of a plan. For example, the "competition" plot unit consists of mental states between two characters with mutually exclusive goals where the same event results in the failure of one character's goals (i.e., a negative event for that character), and the success of the other character's goals (a positive event for that character). Thus, two people trying to go to a dance with the same other person or two people bidding at an auction for the same antique are instances of the competition plot unit.

So far, two kinds of evidence suggest that people utilize plot units when understanding stories. First, Lehnert (1981) and Lehnert, Black, and Reiser (1981) showed that plot unit networks predicted what readers would include in short summaries of stories. Second, Reiser, Black, and Lehnert (1982) found that subjects use plot unit configurations when categorizing and writing stories. Empirical research on summarization has been stymied in the past because good short summaries include statements not in the original story. For example, a concise summary of

> Bill and Tom both applied for a job at Cognitive Engineering, Inc. They both submitted impressive resumes and interviewed well, but Tom was hired in the end.

would be "Bill and Tom competed for a job but Tom got it," but the essential idea of competition here was not explicitly stated in the story. With memory studies, one can always score for the gist of the statements in the text, but for summarization one expects to get statements not in the text. Plot units provide a solution for this research problem, because the plot units tell us under what conditions to look for particular kinds of generalizations in the summaries.

The summarization research with plot units has found that the more pivotal the plot unit in a story (i.e., the more causal connections it has with other plot units in the story), the more likely it is to be included in a summary and that the more of the plot units in a story that are included in a summary of the story the better the summary will be rated by independent evaluators. The story categorization research has shown that subjects categorize stories according to their plot unit configurations. Thus, for example, subjects group stories involving competition, denied request, retaliation, and fleeting success (a four plot unit configuration) into the same story category regardless of specific content, but group stories involving competition, a denied request, change of mind, and success born of adversity (another four plot unit configurations) into a different category. Similarly, when asked to write a story like a story they are shown, subjects write stories with basically the same plot unit configuration as the original. These plot unit networks probably also predict memory (e.g., statements related to the pivotal plot unit are probably also the most likely to be recalled), but such predictions have not been tested yet.

Deviations From Standard Units.   Our discussion of higher-level units so far has only dealt with cases in which the story statements fit the standard expectations for the units, but now we discuss what happens when story statements deviate from the standard. What happens is that the deviation becomes a salient part of the memory representation because it is stored as a correction to the standard unit within the current context. For example, if one walks into McDonald's expecting to be seated and have a waitress come over, then one's expectations fail and the deviations are stored as corrections to the standard restaurant script in the context of fast-food restaurant (in actuality, it is probably the reverse—one learns about McDonald's before standard restaurants). This general notion of schema + correction is actually an old one (e.g., Bartlett, 1932; Woodworth & Schlosberg, 1954), but more specific versions have recently been proposed by Graesser (1981) and Schank (1982).

The basic idea of a schema-plus-correction theory of memory is that what a person remembers of an experience is the general schema that applies plus the deviations from that schema. Thus, for example, if a person read a story episode about going to a restaurant, then later the person will be confused about which of the standard restaurant actions were stated in the story but would remember the deviations better. Graesser (Graesser, Gordon, & Sawyer, 1979; Graesser, Woll, Kowalski, & Smith, 1980) confirmed this prediction by showing that even irrelevant actions like "John took a pen out of his pocket" in a restaurant were remembered better than the standard actions in the restaurant script after the memory results have been corrected for guessing.

While confirming the schema-plus-correction predictions, the irrelevant deviations from a schema is a weak case in which the reader can do little more than tag the irrelevancy as deviating from the schema. Bower et al. (1979) used stronger kinds of corrections in which the deviations could be causally related to the schema. In particular, they used deviations from scripts that were obstacles that blocked the standard script actions from occurring (e.g., the waitress does not come over to the table), errors in the standard actions (e.g., ordering a hamburger but getting a hotdog), and distractions which interrupted the standard flow of the script (e.g., stopping to talk to a friend about a football game in a restaurant). The results showed that these causally related deviations were remembered much better than either irrelevancies like Graesser used or the standard script actions.

Thus a strong kind of correction that one can make to a schema is to relate the deviation causally to the schema. Mio and Black (1979) also found if there is more than one deviation to a schema in a story, then readers try to make a causal inference linking the deviations: that is, when looking for a cause for one deviation, the readers tried to find a causal link to the other deviation. For example, if the story is a standard restaurant story with two deviations then the reader would try to link the deviations causally. Thus if there is an important political figure visiting the restaurant (one deviation) and the food is better prepared than usual (the other deviation), then the readers would see the important visitor being the reason for the better food. In cases like this, Mio and Black found that subjects would later falsely recognize statements corresponding to these causal linking inferences. This corresponds to what Taylor and Fiske (1978) called "top of the head phenomenon." In particular, when looking for the cause of a behavior, the initial tendency is to attribute the cause to a currently salient part of the situation. When reading a story that mostly fits a standard schema, salient parts of the story are the deviations from the norm, so these deviations are prime initial candidates for causes.

In the next section we develop a model for the processing that occurs during comprehension. The model is based on research in story understanding but it is potentially applicable to the understanding of observed experiences as well. Specifically, the comprehension of social behavior in common situations might be explained using this model, if we relax some of the assumptions about how knowledge is activated during the comprehension process (i.e., while we describe how "words" activate knowledge structures, it seems quite likely that the same structures could be activated by non-verbal stimuli). We describe much of this model in a fairly general way and then work out some of the specifics by re-examining some of the empirical results discussed in this section.

A FILTER ACTIVATION MODEL OF COMPREHENSION

One of the major assumptions behind much of the research described in this chapter is that knowledge structures of various different types are activated early in the processing of prose and that they guide the interpretation and perception of subsequent material. We have discussed the utilization of memory units such as scripts, and plot-units. In serious attempts to simulate the comprehension of narrative it has been necessary to develop and implement a wide variety of differing sorts of knowledge structures. In this section we summarize some of the work done in the Yale Artificial Intelligence Project on understanding narrative. We do this within the framework of the development of a model for prose comprehension. Clearly we are able to only skim the surface and the reader is encouraged to see Dyer (1982) for a brief history of the work in the Yale AI Project and a detailed discussion of different types of knowledge structures and the interactions among them, and Schank (1982) for a general blueprint of the directions that the Project will be following in the future.

To understand prose (or the world) one must have knowledge about the events, situations, people, and things that one is likely to encounter. A story about a policeman who, while eating lunch in a restaurant, recognizes a criminal sitting in a nearby booth would be incomprehensible without knowledge of what policemen are, what they do, what restaurants are like, what kinds of relationships exist between policemen and criminals, and so forth. Thus not only does a comprehender need to know the meanings of the words but also must have knowledge about the conceptual relations between them. Thus a restaurant is a place to purchase food to eat on the premises. It also is a situation in which a variety of things typically happen in a particular order; including getting a menu, ordering the meal, being served by someone, leaving a tip, and so forth. Knowledge structures like scripts have been postulated as the way in which this sort of knowledge is represented in memory. Similarly in social psychology, person prototypes and stereotypes can be considered as structures that represent concepts such as policeman and criminal, but features that extend beyond the definitions of these words. As was pointed out in earlier sections, it is necessary for the comprehender to have this sort of information available to make a passage coherent by supporting linking inferences.

Activating Knowledge Structures

The first question that needs to be addressed in any process model of prose comprehension is how the relevant knowledge structures come to be available to the comprehender. How are they accessed so that they can be used to support coherence and memory unit inferences? Shank and Abelson (1977) discussed the activation of the script during prose comprehension. Clearly the easiest way to activate the script is to refer to it by name, or by the main concept of the knowledge structure. Thus, the occurrence of the word "restaurant" in the midst of some story will lead to the activation of the knowledge structure representing information about restaurants and what sorts of things happen there. The occurrence of this script name can be in the title of the story or in the setting section. Studies by Bransford and Johnson (1972) and Thorndyke (1977) indicate the importance of the presence of information which permits the activation of a relevant knowledge structure. In general, the availability of knowledge structures is a major component of what provides the *context* of a story (or of propositions therein).

Interaction of Filters and Story Information.   We view the comprehension of a story by analogy with a chemical filtration system. In such a system, chemical filters (knowledge structures and associated concepts) in a solution (the internal representation) interact, or bind, with other substances introduced into the system (input from the sentences in the story). Concepts from the story enter the comprehension system where they interact with filters. This interaction has processing consequences including the activation of other structures. When a concept is encountered, the knowledge structure becomes available to the comprehension process. These structures, however, are not static, passive representations; when activated, they have a strong impact on subsequent processing. One major impact is on what sorts of filters are established to interact with subsequent input. So filters activate knowledge structures which, in turn, activate (and de-activate) other filters. Subsequent information is contextualized (i.e., understood in the context provided by the knowledge structure) because it is processed by filters that were established by that knowledge structure. An internal representation is built up via instantiation (by input from the story) of the active knowledge structures.

The notion of a filter is akin to that of a *production system* used in Artificial Intelligence simulations. Production systems (Anderson, 1976; Newell, 1973) are constructs that have two major components: *tests* and *actions*. The filter's test component examines the input (or other activated structures) to determine whether its test conditions are met. If a pattern to which the filter is sensitive is encountered, then the filter carries out its actions. The particular test conditions and actions performed can be arbitrarily complex. Thus, there can be a filter for a single lexical item which, when encountered, is merely added to some list. There can also be filters that are sensitive to complex configurations in the internal representation and which function by performing a long list of actions which may effect wholesale modification of that representation.

Distinctiveness and Centrality. The organization and content of these knowledge structures, prior to their instantiation in stories, has a great effect on the comprehension process. In a series of studies, Galambos and colleagues (Galambos, 1981, 1982a, 1982b; Galambos & Black, 1982; Galambos & Rips, 1982) have examined the components and characteristics of 30 common activities that appear to have script-like qualities (e.g., Changing a Flat Tire, Shopping for Groceries, Cashing a Check). In most of these studies, a reaction time technique was used which was adapted from the verification paradigms in semantic memory experiments. These techniques were used to map out relations among the component parts of an activity. These components are the specific *actions* which are performed in order to accomplish the activity. The technique has also been used to investigate the relations between the component actions and the activity concept. A number of these relations are discussed in Galambos (1982a).

In Galambos (1981) and Galambos and Rips (1982) the concept of the *centrality* of actions in their activities was investigated. Actions that were more important to the performance of the activity were more easily retrieved from the knowledge representation than those that were less important. A second important factor is called the *distinctiveness* of an action. An action is said to be distinctive to an activity if it occurs in few if any other activities. The typical experiment (e.g., Galambos, 1981) to demonstrate the importance of an action's distinctiveness involves presenting subjects with a phrase describing an action followed (after a delay of 1 second) by the name of an activity. The task was to decide whether or not the action is a component of the activity. Subjects were significantly faster in making this decision if the action they saw was distinctive to the activity than if it was not distinctive.

It is important to note that distinctiveness and centrality may vary independently. For example, in the restaurant activity, the action *see the head waiter* is highly distinctive (it occurs in few if any other activities), but is low in centrality (it is not a critically important action in the activity). On the other hand, the action *eat the meal* is very important (and thus highly central), but is not particularly distinctive as it can occur in a wide variety of other situations (e.g., one can eat on a plane, at home, while on a picnic in the park, and so forth).

In Galambos and Black (1982), we examined the effects of the distinctiveness and centrality of script actions on the way in which the script knowledge becomes available to the comprehension system. Specifically, we were interested in how the script is initially accessed and how the component parts of the script are then made available to the system. Subjects saw pairs of script actions, and their task was to report whether or not both actions were from the same activity. On some trials, the first action in the stimulus was highly distinctive to its script, while in other trials, the first action was not particularly distinctive. Furthermore, the centrality of the second action was varied. (We also controlled for the match between the order of presentation of the stimulus, and the sequential order of the two actions in standard restaurant experiences. In each condition in the experiment the order of presentation of the actions matched their normal temporal sequence on exactly half of the trials.) Thus, two of the stimuli for the restaurant activity were:

1. *See Head Waiter—Eat the Meal*
2. *Eat the Meal—See Head Waiter*

The prediction was that responses to stimulus 1 would be faster than those to stimulus 2. The only difference between these two stimuli is the order in which the items are presented. The first item in each pair was presented one and a half seconds before the second item appeared. One of the most interesting findings of this experiment was that subjects were significantly faster to decide that the actions in the first stimulus (See Head Waiter—Eat the Meal) were both from the same activity than they were to make the same judgment when the order of presentation of these same actions was reversed (as in 2).

The explanation of this result is that the distinctiveness of the first action (in stimulus 1) permits the activation of the restaurant knowledge structure and the centrality of the second action permits the easy recognition that this action is part of that activity. In stimulus 2, the first action is not distinctive, and the second action is not very central, to the restaurant script. According to our hypotheses, stimulus 2 has two strikes against it, even though it contains the same two actions as in stimulus 1. From a processing point of view, the order of presentation in stimulus 2 is exactly wrong. For all the twelve stimulus conditions in this experiment, there was a marked advantage for stimuli in which the first action was high in distinctiveness compared to those in which the first action was not distinctive. Furthermore, for those trials where the first action *was* distinctive, the centrality of the second action also had a significant effect on the subjects' decision.

The relevance of this for prose comprehension is quite straightforward (and the experiments to demonstrate it are in progress). When one encounters a sentence about an action which is distinctive to a knowledge structure, that knowledge structure becomes activated. Less distinctive actions may not provide sufficient information to activate a particular structure. Thus, a sentence about seeing a head waiter will activate the restaurant script, whereas a sentence about eating a meal (in the same place in a story) is less likely to activate that script. The activation of a knowledge structure leads to the establishment of expectations (in the form of new filters for the subsequent input). The particular expectations that become available are likely to be expectations for actions that are more central to the knowledge structure. The less central components of the activity are less likely to be explicitly established as expectation filters, at least on the initial activation of the knowledge structure. So, when the restaurant script is activated (for instance, by an explicit reference to a restaurant in some preceding sentence), there may be a specific expectation (in the form of a filter or set of filters becoming present in the internal representation) that a meal is to be eaten. Since the action of seeing a head waiter is not very central, the system is less likely to establish an expectation for the information about this action. (Of course, since this action is part of the restaurant script, there may be little or no decrement in comprehension performance, since when such information occurs, it may be easily incorporated into the internal representation using script-supported inferences.)

The Functionality of Knowledge Structures. The actions in an activity (as well as other features of the activity) are represented in a knowledge structure as filters. The filters must be associated with these knowledge structures in order for relevant information to activate the correct structures. It is parsimonious to consider the knowledge structure itself as a complex of filters. On this view, it is merely an expository convenience to describe filters as being ''associated'' to a knowledge structure. The knowledge structure **is** a set of filters. It is in this sense that we view the knowledge structure as an active processing structure. While it is true that the knowledge structure is a repository of declarative information about an activity or a personality type, it is, more fundamentally, a *functional* organization of that information. The function, which the structures serve, is to process or comprehend relevant perceptions. Knowledge structures are organized in ways that facilitate the performance of these functions.

For example, in our study of distinctiveness and centrality, we demonstrated the functionality of these two characteristics of script structures. A knowledge structure which represents the distinctiveness of its components can be rapidly and unambiguously activated when one of the distinctive components is encountered. A knowledge structure which represents the centrality of its components can prepare for subsequent input in a more efficient fashion.

Clearly the script structure is not the only type of knowledge structure that functions in this manner. For instance, consider a knowledge structure representing information about policemen, (their role in society, what sorts of things they do, and perhaps their relationships to other members of society). When a word is encountered that is relevant to this sort of knowledge, one of the filters associated to the policeman structure interacts with this information. This interaction results in the activation of the associated knowledge structure and the binding of the information to that structure. If we encounter a situation where someone is reciting the Miranda rights to someone else, it is reasonable to infer that the person doing the speaking is a policeman, since that is one of the things present in our knowledge structure about policemen. This action of reciting the Miranda rights is distinctive to the policeman knowledge structure. The activation of this knowledge structure allows us to comprehend the situation and the behavior of the people involved.

The knowledge structure is thus selectively attentive to information which it represents. Upon encountering such information, the structure becomes active and processes the information. The specific processes that are initiated (and the nature of the inferences that are made) will depend on a variety of things. Some of these are the prior state of the knowledge structure (e.g., whether or not it had been activated previously); the state of the internal representation of the narrative (or encounter) up to that point, and the significance of the particular bit of information involved. Nonetheless, the general function of the processing is to augment, or change the internal representation in order to fit in the new information.

Knowledge structures differ in their organization and content (and thus have different processing ramifications). Moreover,not all information in a story will be mere instantiations of pre-existing knowledge structure defaults. Comprehension processes must relate the novel characteristics of a situation with the mundane aspects. In the next section, we discuss how our model incorporates different sorts of novel information.

The Continuum of Comprehension Complexity

In any comprehension situation there is a subtle mix of the familiar and the novel. Knowledge structures in memory represent the familiar. Perception gives us information to help select the appropriate knowledge to bring to bear in understanding the novel aspects of the situation. Novel information can be encountered in a number of forms. It can be as mundane as that a particular character's name is Bill. Another kind of novelty is the deviation from standard structures, that we discussed above. In this case, the novelty is a function of the clash with the context provided by the knowledge structures actively guiding the comprehension of a story. Another sort of novelty might be an unfamiliar juxtaposition of different knowledge structures. It is possible that someone has not experienced the policeman/criminal relationship in the context of a restaurant. In all these cases, comprehension will be a matter of organizing the representation of the input by combining the novel aspects with the familiar. The processes involved in these combinations will differ depending on what sorts of combina-

2. COMPREHENDING STORIES AND SOCIAL SITUATIONS 63

tions are required. We examine a number of different types of knowledge structures and some processing strategies for tying them together with information presented in a narrative.

In order to approach the question of how the processing done by the knowledge structures can affect the developing internal representation of a story, it is necessary to consider several different types of input, ranging from predicted information to completely novel material. A particular item of input from the prose passage can stand in a number of different relationships to the existing internal representation. The status of any particular item of information is a function of the nature of the internal representation of the text at the point that the information is encountered. Many studies of text processing show that one small change in some relatively early part of the story can strongly influence the understanding of other sentences. The general explanation for this type of effect is that context is important to processing. The filter model provides the outline of a more specific mechanism for how this influence is manifest.

To make this point, let us consider some of the different types of input that can be processed by the comprehension system. We can think of these different types of input as falling at various point on a continuum of "comprehension complexity." This continuum represents the extent of processing that needs to be done for a given input (relative to some context or state of the internal representation of the story). As we noted above, one type of input is that which is *predicted* from the prior story information. This sort of information is probably the most directly integrated. At the other extreme is information that is *novel* from the perspective of the comprehension system. When a novel bit of information is presented, it is likely to require complex processing (perhaps including working out the interactions between multiple knowledge structures) to determine how it fits with what has gone before—if indeed it can be fit in. Predicted information interacts strongly with a filter that has been set up for just that purpose. Novel information may not react strongly with any active filters and may require further processing. In between is information which needs differing amounts (and varieties) of processing.

At any point, the system will contain a large number of activated filters. These filters are established by different knowledge structures used in the internal representation. The filters are associated with the knowledge structures that activate them, thus providing the mechanism whereby the information (in interacting with some filter) comes to be integrated into the internal representation in the correct fashion. For any given state of the system, some filters are strongly activated while others are at a background level of activation. For example, consider a story where the reader encounters a sentence about seeing a head waiter, and where nothing else relevant to the restaurant activity has been mentioned previously. In this situation, the filter, that interacts with this input, was at a background level of activation prior to occurrence of the sentence. This sentence contains novel information, relative to the state of the comprehension system. Compare this with the state of the system after the restaurant knowledge structure has been activated. The activation of this knowledge structure results in the establishment of some of its filters; including the filter for information about eating a meal. This filter is strongly activated in the comprehension system. When a sentence about eating is encountered, the filter provides the means of incorporating that information with the restaurant structure (i.e., the filter binds with the input information and, since the filter was initially activated by the restaurant knowledge structure, the input is comprehended by that structure). The activation levels of the filters can vary over a wide range. We suppose that filters can even be inhibited (i.e., have their activation levels suppressed below their background activation) in order to avoid potential ambiguity. When a weakly activated filter interacts with some input item it may require additional processing (activating other knowledge structures and their filters) to integrate the item with the internal representation. Thus, differences in the activation levels of filters is the basis for the differences in comprehension complexity.

In addition, it is important to note that information that is not caught by some subset of those filters will be caught by others and not discarded. This sort of filtration, therefore, involves parallel processing—all active filters are combing the input simultaneously. Input will interact with the type of filter that can process it most effectively (that with which it most strongly interacts). Novel information may not be caught by an active filter that is associated with the internal representation. It thus may need a good deal of additional processing to be integrated into that representation.

We discuss some of the different types of relations that incoming information can have to the comprehension system. The first of these is how information can be *predicted* by the characteristics of the internal representation. We will distinguish predicted from *expected* information. A third type is information that needs to be *explained* by a comprehension system. Finally, we examine some ways in which *novel* information is understood.

Predicted Information.   We will start with the simplest case: that of explicitly predicted information. Although it seems unlikely that we *always* (or even usually) generate specific conscious predictions of subsequent input, we sometimes do. This will occur when previous information in the prose (together with the knowledge structures used in its representation) so highly constrains the context that we can confidently generate an explicit prediction concerning some aspect of the subsequent input. Predictions, in this sense, are clearly attempts to economize in comprehension since, if readers can "get the point" of some part of the text, they need not listen as carefully as they might if they needed to obtain more information before they could understand. When a predicted bit of information is presented it will interact immediately with the knowledge structures that are being used to comprehend the input (i.e., those which have been previously activated). In these cases, the comprehension system was highly prepared for the particular information and its role in the underlying representation of the text has been worked out ahead of time. Thus, there will be little difficulty in the comprehension of explicitly predicted information because not only is the identity of the information "known" in advance, but its relationship to the other story information is also previously determined. It is in cases of explicit prediction that the filter metaphor is perhaps most apt. The predicted information is immediately incorporated into the knowledge structure since the filter with which it interacted is strongly associated to the internal representation which activated it initially.

Expected Information.   Clearly most information in prose will not be explicitly or consciously predicted and will require somewhat more complex processing to recognize and represent it. We will now consider information that requires somewhat more processing than that required for explicitly predicted information. This is information which is *expected* given the prior information and internal representation set up in comprehending it. Expectation is weaker than prediction in that there is a much wider range of information that is consistent with the prior context without being explicitly predicted. We have already discussed some script-based expectations. These are not nearly as strong as the explicit predictions discussed above. Rather, expectations are preparations to perceive information that will easily fit with the prior context. An expectation is an activated area in a knowledge structure (serving as a filter since it is still uninstantiated by input from the story). Expectations are important in that, even if they are not explicitly instantiated (and they typically have a high likelihood of being instantiated), they may nonetheless be used in drawing inferences to provide coherence for items that otherwise might remain unrelated (and thus not fully comprehended).

For example, consider the case of reading a story about a policeman. In such a story we might encounter the information that he is carrying a gun. This can easily be fit into the representation of the story because the knowledge structure about policemen contains the information that they may have guns. It need not be a *prediction,* in that the story may well have proceeded with no reference to any gun. Nevertheless, the occurrence of information about the gun can be said to be expected insofar as it is part of a knowledge structure that has previously been accessed. Information about guns, badges, nightsticks, criminals, sirens, speed traps can be expected to occur in the story with higher certainty than can information about insects, mathematics, furniture, and volcanos in that the knowledge structure about policemen contains reference to items in the former list. Furthermore even if the lexical item *gun* does not actually occur in the story, the filter for it is active and may interact with other configurations of information in the internal representation. For instance, if we find out that a criminal was shot in efforts to subdue him, we can infer that the shot came from the policeman's gun. Because the expectation is active, it can be used to filter the input as well as to provide necessary bridging inferences. Thus, a filter that was set up for expectation purposes actually is used in the process of *explaining* the connection between the knowledge structure and an otherwise potentially anomalous occurrence. Expectation and explanation are two very general and important uses of knowledge structures.

Since expectations play such an important role it is important to try to be as explicit as possible as to their function in processing stories. Clearly there is a wide range of things that can be expected, in the sense we are developing. In the treatment of some example of these, it is useful to describe some of the specific processing models of the comprehension system that have been developed in the domain of artificial intelligence. In order to design a functioning comprehension system (i.e., in the form of a computer program that actually processes text), a number of important problems (as well as some detailed theoretical solutions) have been examined.

Simulations of Story Comprehension.   The principle of using expectations associated with knowledge structures to guide processing was first used in a Yale Artificial Intelligence model by Riesbeck (1975), in an English language parser called ELI (English Language Interpreter). ELI was designed to be general in that it did not depend on any specific topic domain (as opposed to Winograd's SHRDLU, 1972, which dealt with a highly constrained microcosm called the "blocks-world" consisting only of movements of variously shaped and colored blocks on a table). ELI parsed sentences into a semantic representation based on the theory of Conceptual Dependency (Schank, 1973). In this theory, the semantic contents of words are represented as primitive ACTs, such as INGEST (introducing some substance into the body, e.g., eating, drinking, and breathing), or ATRANS (abstractly transferring possession of something, e.g., taking, giving, stealing, and buying). These ACTs are related by the Conceptual Dependencies (CD). The English word "eat" is conceptually related to an actor (who does the eating) and an object (which is eaten). In ELI, lexical items would access CD structures (ACT plus relations) where the uninstantiated relations could be used as expectations for subsequent input. Encountering the word "eat" leads to the expectation that an edible object may be mentioned. When the object is encountered, the INGEST conceptualization becomes fully instantiated and is then incorporated into the representation of the story. In terms of the filtration model, the knowledge structure for the concept of eating is activated when the word "eat" is encountered. Some of the processes that are initiated are the connection of the eating concept with the actor in the internal representation of the narrative and the setting up of an expectation that some edible object may be encountered.

Aside from easing the comprehension processing load, having active expectations allows for word sense disambiguation by "presetting" the system to understand a word or phrase in the relevant way. Dyer (1982) uses the example,

Bill ate a hot dog.

where the object is easily understood as a frankfurter rather than a canine with elevated temperature because of the expectation arising from the prior occurrence of the instance of INGEST. Once again this can be understood as an instance where the appropriate filter binds with the input element and, in so doing, incorporates it into the internal representation in the correct fashion.

Explainable Information.   *Explanation* of information requires a little more comprehension effort than merely filling an expectation. Our previous example of comprehending information about the shot from the policeman's gun was a simple case of explanation. Another was the earlier example of the causal explanation of John's ordering roast beef in a restaurant. Recall that in this latter example, the restaurant script provided the source for causal inferences. Subjects in Bower et al.'s. (1979) experiments falsely reported they had actually read sentences explicitly stating these inferences in the story (whereas the inferences were only implicit).

Scripts provide the context from which more complex expectations can arise than those available from ACTs. Furthermore, this kind of knowledge structure also serves as source for justifying explanatory inferences. Thus, a particular bit of information from the text can be explained by incorporating it into the script. There are probably a wide range of different sorts of explanations, and the distinction between an explanation and an expectation is not clear cut. In the restaurant example, the inferences that the main character looked at a menu, chose a meal, and told the waitress what he wanted, and that the waitress brought it to him, are all based on the SCRIPT. Some of this information is probably activated in the form of an expectation filter which (when we find out the food is being eaten by the main character) is subsequently incorporated as an explanation (of the presence of the food). The presence of the script makes this explanation quite simple (so simple, in fact, that such inferences may never need to be explicitly drawn unless the issue of ordering the meal figures in later portions of the story or in questions asked at some later time). Cullingford (1978) developed this notion of scripts in a program called SAM (Script Applier Mechanism) which understood simple stories by providing this type of knowledge structure to support explanatory inferences.

Of course many of the explanations that are needed to understand a narrative will not be so simple. Insofar as the information does not fit into a simple stereotypical sequence of events it will not be explained by reference to a SCRIPT. Specifically, a mental state of some character which causes him to act in some non-stereotypical way will be hard to represent since the SCRIPT will not contain all possible ways in which specific instances can deviate from the norm. More generally, motivations and intentions of human actors are not systematically represented in SCRIPTs. In order to explain information in the narrative relating to these issues, Wilensky (1978) used general planning and goal knowledge structures. His program, PAM (Plan Applier Mechanism) explained the actions of characters by using the character's goals to infer a plan which the character used to achieve them.

The standard example here is a story including the following:

> Jack was hungry.
> He looked for his Michelin Guide.

In order to comprehend how these two propositions are related, it is necessary not only to know that a Michelin Guide is a listing of restaurants and their locations. This sort of information might be stored with the Michelin guide concept. However it is also important to know that one plan for satisfying the goal associated with being hungry is to eat, and that restaurants are places where one can eat. All this information allows one to understand Bill's plan (find location of restaurant in guide, go to restaurant, and eat—thus satisfying his goal). A generalized goal knowledge structure allowed PAM to infer relationships among the actions of a character. In this system non-stereotypical sequences of actions could be understood as being related insofar as they fit into a plan to accomplish some goal. In doing this, PAM needed knowledge structures that represent human intentions and motivations. Explanations that depend on this kind of knowledge are typically more difficult because there is a much greater amount of variability in the ways in which goals can be achieved. The empirical studies by Abbott and Black (1982) and Seifert et al. (1982) underscore this point.

Goal knowledge structures represent patterns or configurations of relations among items of information. Knowledge structures such as these need not be contentful in the way that scripts are (i.e., scripts explicitly encode particular objects and actions involved in some particular situation). Goals, plans, Memory Organization Packets (or MOPs, Schank, 1982), Thematic Abstraction Units (TAUs, Dyer, 1982) are all knowledge structures that are sensitive to configurations of information rather than to specific physical objects and actions. While we do not have the space to discuss each of these in detail, it will be illustrative to consider an example of the processing done by the filter model when one of these structures is involved in the comprehension of a story. For simplicity, let us imagine that the comprehension system encounters a word that indicates a goal (words like want, hope, plan, need or expressions of states with standard goals like X was hungry, thirsty, and so forth). (As we mentioned in the case of initially activating a script, a knowledge structure need not be activated by the explicit presentation of the name of the structure.)

When information in the input interacts with one of the filters in a goal knowledge structure, that structure is activated. This structure abstractly represents information about goals and how they are realized. This includes the information that plans are usually involved in attaining a goal, and that the object of the goal is relevant to the type of plan to be employed. The structure then provides a general representational substrate that can serve as a source of inferences or expectations for subsequent text material. This means that the goal structure may serve as the backbone of the internal representation of the subsequent part of the story. Goal structures may activate filters for differing plans that may be involved in achieving the particular goal. There may also be filters for information relevant to the object of the goal, the felt immediacy of the goal, an for the particular type of plan. The sort of plan will be a function of the way the goal is articulated in the story.

For instance, if the goal filter originally encountered the phrase:

Bill is hungry.

a general goal structure would be activated. This, in turn, would lead to the activation of a filter for the plan to achieve the goal. Since hunger (i.e., the desire to satisfy the hunger) is the particular type of goal, only those plans that would lead to the achievement of this type of goal are made active. Thus, those plan filters that are sensitive to information about restaurants, or eating in general, or food in general are established. Subsequent information will interact with one of these filters. This will have two sorts of effects. First, this new information will be bound to the plan to accomplish the goal. Second, some of the other plans may become inactive. Continuing our example, if the sentence:

Bill went into a restaurant.

were encountered, the system is prepared to understand this as an instantiation of the plan to accomplish the goal of satisfying hunger.

Notice that in this case a script (restaurant) is serving as a filter activated by a plan structure. These relationships among the filters and the knowledge structures that activated them, will allow the correct interpretation of the subsequent information about eating. Thus, the information in the sentence:

Bill ate a meal.

will be contextualized as an action in a script which was entered in the course of a plan to fulfill a particular goal of the main character of the story. Thus the internal representation of even this simple part of a story provides a rich source of inferences as well as a highly cohesive understanding.

As we mentioned above, when a particular plan filter is instantiated, other competing plan filters decay, since the goal structure no longer needs to keep them active. Thus, a filter for grocery shopping (that might have been initially activated as a possible plan to achieve Bill's goal) will probably decay, or even be deactivated, when the information about the restaurant is encountered. Thus the filtering is dynamically made more sensitive and more specific as more information is acquired. The initially uninstantiated, abstract goal structure can be elaborated and changed to incorporate the specific details from the text passage.

To return to the use of the filter system in explaining input, we can discuss how the information about the Michelin guide is "explained" when it is encountered in the story. First of all, note that this phrase is indeed likely to need explaining, since it is not typically part of the general goal structure or even of the general plans associated with the hunger goal. The method of explanation involves two basic aspects: (1) accessing the word (or in this case, phrasal) knowledge structure for Michelin Guide and (2) representing the relevance of this concept to the goal structure associated with hunger. Dyer's (1982) BORIS (Better Organized Reading and Inference System) makes these two phases explicit.

The first aspect can be called the "bottom-up" aspect. A word or phrase will be represented in terms of the general knowledge necessary for the interpretation of the item. This information is then used to guide search of the existing higher level knowledge structures in order to find the relevant place to fit the new input. Thus Dyer's assumption that input items must "explain themselves" involves processing driven by the information in the representation of the item. In this case a filter may be activated by the low-level structure that encodes the word or phrase. This filter will be sensitive to and interact with other information already present in the internal representation. The second (or "top-down") aspect involves the application of processing associated with the more general knowledge structure that is found by the bottom-up processes. This might include representing new relations in the goal or plan structure and result in establishing new filters (or "spawning" new "demons" as Dyer calls them).

Note that the explanation done by the comprehension system involves a great deal of interaction between differing structures. In the example of the Michelin guide, a top down process under the control of one set of active knowledge structures (ncluding a goal structure) is integrated with a bottom-up process which involves another set of structures. Dyer's simulation employs many kinds of knowledge structures beyond the ones we have space to consider here. In order to control the ways in which those structures interact in the development of a coherent representation of a story, there are a number of special processing demons (filters) which have the specific job of recognizing when different developing structures can be fit together. When particular configurations of information are recognized, this special sort of filter functions to connect the otherwise unlinked structures. Filters such as these may subordinate one knowledge structure so that it is under the processing control of another. They may break down one structure and incorporate the information represented therein in another structure.

Some of these filters are specifically defined in terms of two particular structures that are to be integrated. For instance, there are knowledge structures for *affective states*. If a story contains the following sentences:

Sam insulted Bob.
Bob was angry.

then after reading the first sentence, the internal representation may reflect (among a number of other things) that one of Bob's high level goals (that of maintaining his self-esteem) has been threatened. When the second sentence is encountered, a filter associated with the affective state representing **anger** interacts with the new input. When an affective state is activated a filter is activated that will interact with some configuration of information that might have caused the affect. In this case, the configuration which represents the threatened goal and the action that activated this structure is present in the internal representation. This configuration will interact with the affect filter and the filter connects the thwarted health goal with affect structure. The filter allows the representation of the causal connection between the insult and the anger. This is only a very simple example of the sort of knowledge structure integration that typically plays an important part in the comprehension process. Much of this integration is done by filters which are not, strictly speaking, sensitive to the raw input, but which look for and operate on knowledge structures that were previously activated by input occurring at different points in the story.

Novel Information. Integrations of knowledge structures are often necessary in adequately representing information that is novel. Furthermore, integration of novel information may well require the most processing and perhaps the most extensive reorganization of the internal representation. It is this increased processing which may account for the advantage that novel information (of certain sorts) enjoys in tasks of memory for the story at later points. This is related to the studies by Craik and Tulving (1975), which demonstrated that the increased processing of a to-be-remembered item, increases its retention.

We discuss two sorts of novel information; deviations from expected information, and information which is merely unrelated to the present state of the internal representation. Recall that in our discussion of deviations from scripts, there were two sorts of deviations; *obstacles* which blocked causally related script actions from occurring (studied by Bower et al., 1979), and *irrelevancies* which were unrelated to the script (studied by Graesser, 1981). Both types were recalled remarkably well in later memory tests.

Deviations, such as obstacles, present the comprehension system with a contradiction of an active expectation. When an expectation (manifested as an active filter associated to some knowledge structure) is not only unfilled but is explicitly denied, a number of modifications must be made in the internal representation. The nature of these modifications will depend on the severity of the obstacle. If a restaurant no longer has the dish that was ordered, it may be necessary to merely iterate the menu examination-meal ordering actions in the script. Thus, the filters for those actions may be reactivated. If, however, the obstacle is that the chef has suddenly left the restaurant and there is no one to prepare any food, it may be necessary to record the failure of a higher level plan to achieve the goal of satisfying one's hunger. This may lead to the (re)activation of other plans (or at least, to the activation of a plan to search for another restaurant). Here, as when a filter was set up by an affect knowledge structure to find a goal structure, there may be special purpose filters that are sensitive to this sort of deviation. These filters function to reactivate other structures, and to tag those parts of the internal representation that are affected by the deviation. An interesting empirical question is how well the information leading up to the deviation (like the initial action of ordering the meal that was not available) is remembered. Our hypothesis is that it would also benefit from the additional processing that these deviation-detecting filters would perform on it.

The second type of novelty is information which is irrelevant to the existing representation of the story such as the unrelated information in some of Graesser's studies. Irrelevance is operationally defined in the filter model in terms of information that does not interact with any active filter or knowledge structure. It is clearly the case that truly irrelevant information is rare in stories. Some information merely conveys details that are not directly part of the main causal chain in the story. Nonetheless, a necessary assumption of the comprehension system, is that all information is potentially important for understanding the story. This is an implementation of the Gricean (Grice, 1967) principle that participants in any communicative situation make their contributions relevant to the topic at hand. Thus the system will probably try quite hard to make seemingly irrelevant information fit with the existing representation of the story.

Novel information may cause a number of errors in representation. For example, the information may be wrongly integrated with the existing structure since, even though it may only interact weakly with some filter, that weak interaction may be the best the system can do. This can result in the information being associated to the representation in an inappropriate manner. Second, the novel information may really be the start of a new part of the story. In this case, the information appears irrelevant to what has gone before, but the relations may become clear at some later point. The comprehension system will be unable to determine the difference between a truly irrelevant detail and an item that starts a new portion of the story. This is another reason for the assumption of relevance, and consequently for the necessity to attempt to apply whatever processing available to the novel information. The upshot of this is that novel information may receive a greater amount of processing than information that can be more straightforwardly integrated into the representation. This additional processing is an increased load on the system. This may account for the difficulty of understanding disconnected stories where there are a series of sentences which contain information which is novel with respect to that in the prior sentences. Furthermore, the additional processing of novel information also may account for its increased retention as measured in subsequent memory tests.

This concludes our discussion of the different levels on the continuum of comprehension complexity. We have shown how the filter model can account for a wide variety of types of information. The issues we've discussed are at the center of a theory of comprehension since, whatever the ultimate form of such a theory, it must explain how input information is integrated with our prior knowledge and how knowledge of various types interact in comprehension. The filter model provides a convenient framework for understanding a number of these issues. The design of the model was guided by the results of studies by researchers in Artificial Intelligence and the psychology of text understanding. After discussing a few remaining points of the model, we attempt to provide a few examples of how it might provide a useful framework for some of the findings in the psychology of social cognition. We believe that it is the right time to attempt this synthesis of the different disciplines studying cognition.

Additional Issues Concerning the Filter Model

De-activation of Structures. In the description of the model, we have had occasion to introduce a large number of different filters and structures in order to adequately represent a story. One concern is that there are just too many processing structures, or too many filters, in the comprehension system at any given point. In the context of artificial intelligence models this is a major problem, given the constraints of the memory size and processing speed of a computer. Similarly, in human comprehenders, short term memory capacity and processing limitations impose constraints on the model we have been developing.

One way of dealing with the problem is to have a reasoned way of de-activating previously activated filters. In passing we have alluded to one way in which this can be done. Those knowledge structures that caused the activation of a filter in the first place, can **de-activate** it. This would typically happen when the purpose it was to have served (finding a specific sort of information) has been achieved. For instance, a number of general plan filters may be activated by a goal structure associated with "hunger" (going to the grocery store, cooking, going to a restaurant, asking one's mother for a snack, etc.). When one of these filters is instantiated, the goal structure can de-activate the others. A second approach is to allow the activation of the filters to decay if they are not instantiated. Activated structures could be forced out of the "active" queue (the length of which may be related to some limited capacity memory store). Alternatively, the activation level of a structure may decrease through time if the structure is neither re-activated by a controlling process nor instantiated by input.

Yet another way of influencing the number of active filters is by not activating as many of them in the first place. Galambos and Black (1982) found evidence suggesting a limitation in the number of filters initially activated by a knowledge structure; specifically only filters for the more central components of a script may be activated.

Finally there is some interesting recent research by Sharkey and Mitchell (1981) which addresses the inhibition of knowledge structures. In this experiment subjects were presented with sentences that described script events. These sentences were followed by a lexical decision task. This is a task where subjects are asked to decide whether a string of letters is a word. The speed with which this decision is made is a measure of the activation level of the words. Thus, after reading a story about a common situation (like a children's birthday party), subjects can decide more rapidly that the letter string, CANDLE, is a word, than if they had read a story that had no relation to candles. (Of course, the string, CANDLE, does not actually appear in either story.) Sharkey and Mitchell found this to be the case with a number of stories about common activities. However, perhaps the most interesting finding was lexical decision to the word CANDLE after a story about a party that also includes sentences about leaving the party and beginning another activity (e.g., "Ron left the party and went to the laundromat. He put his laundry in the washer.") The lexical decision time to the word CANDLE is now no faster than for unrelated words. Apparently, the birthday party knowledge structure has been de-activated in the space of a few short sentences.

There is insufficient space to treat these solutions in greater detail. The point is that there appear to be a number of reasonable ways to handle the problem of too many activated structures. Which ones of these are the easiest to implement, or the most empirically motivated, remains an issue to be resolved by further research.

"Errors" Made by a Filter Model of Comprehension.   As we noted in our prior discussion of distinctiveness in script memory, we believe that the distinctiveness of concepts will influence both the ease with which the internal representation is constructed and the certainty that the comprehender feels about his understanding of the story. In general, the way in which the internal representation is set up (in terms of which knowledge structures are activated) will be subject to a number of factors in addition to distinctiveness. One of these may be the concreteness of the information filtered. Thus it may be easier to activate knowledge structures when concepts encountered in the input are specific (perhaps imageable) instances than if they are abstract characterizations. This may have been part of the reason that subjects in the studies by Nisbett, Borgida, Crandall, and Reed (1976) were better able to deal with, and showed a marked tendency to favor, logically weaker but more concrete evidence. Our claim is that the concreteness is like distinctiveness in that it facilitates the use of pre-existing knowledge structures, even when the use of these structures may be inappropriate.

This is only one sort of error made in a filter model of comprehension. Another was the inappropriate integration of novel information. These types of errors are not a failing of the model, but rather are a virtue. That is, we may be able to explain seemingly irrational or erroneous behavior of subjects in psychology experiments using constructs of our model. For instance there is a tendency (discussed by Spiro, 1980) for subjects to reconstruct stories in such a way as to make a number of ambiguous details fit a particular schema. This included adding spurious explanations and inferences that were not present in the input but which made that input more consistent with the schema. This sort of result is due to the integration of inferences into the internal representation which were uninstantiated active expectations or to the misinterpretation of details in such a way as to force them into the representation. This is a version of what Taylor and Crocker (1980) call the *illusory data base* problem and it arises from using a reasonably appropriate schema "too enthusiastically." There are wide variety of errors which might fall in this category including the type of overgeneralization that leads to prejudice against a stereotyped person.

Another source of mistake is the establishment of a particular knowledge structure as the most general structure controlling the processing (by influencing which filters are activated). It may be that a different but perhaps related structure is more appropriate to the task of representing the particular story. For instance, it is quite possible that a number of scripts can be simultaneously activated by concepts filtered from the input. It may turn out that a situation will be somewhat misrepresented if there is no way to choose between the alternative structures for representing it, and one of these is merely chosen randomly, or perhaps, because it was the first to be activated. In this case, subsequent information may be misinterpreted. The filters set up by the choice of one of them to be the main controlling structure may not interact with some important details or may fail to capture their importance. This version of error may be more obvious in the case of activations of different person prototypes. Thus a single characteristic about the protagonist of a story (particularly if it is distinctive to some prototype structure), may cause one prototype to be activated, when some other is more appropriate. Subsequent behaviors of this protagonist may be misinterpreted since the incorrect prototype was chosen as the main processing structure in building the representation.

As we said above, these features of the model can provide a framework for explaining social behavior of individuals. This thesis rests on the reasonable assumption that the same knowledge structures that are used to comprehend text plays a role in understanding the behavior of others as well as in the explanations one gives of one's own behavior.

APPLICATIONS TO SOCIAL COGNITION

Research on story understanding, particularly the work on knowledge structures is applicable to a wide range of problems in social psychology. In the following we outline what we see as its general relevance to social psychology, and then spend some time trying to apply it in more detail to two specific areas. First, the work on story understanding and knowledge structures is applicable to the general problem of how people encode and remember the social behavior they observe. The other example we discuss is application to how people's political beliefs and attitudes affect the ways in which they encode and remember political events in the media. Other areas of application have been discussed elsewhere by others, so we will not discuss them here. In particular, Abelson (1981) discussed the relevance of scripts to how people behave in social situations including an interesting treatment of the Latane and Darley (1970) studies in terms of the activation of a "helping script." Another important area of overlap between the model expressed here and issues from social cognition is the work by Cantor and Mischel (1979) on person prototypes. It seems to us that a person prototype might be considered a type of knowledge structure, with traits as component filters. If so, then this work is quite straightforwardly integrated into the model of comprehension we offer as a framework for understanding social information. Finally, the work by Wyer and Srull (1980) in relating scripts to attribution and person memory is another approach that is congenial to our own.

Observing Social Behavior

First, we will deal with the general problem of how this work is applicable to understanding the ways in which people perceive and encode the social behavior which they observe. While there are some obvious and important differences between comprehending text, and perceiving and encoding live behavior there are also some important similarities. In both domains, the critical question is how people take individual items of information and put them together into a cohesive and comprehensible whole. As we said at the outset, when we observe people behaving, the relationships between their actions is not given; it is not obvious on the surface of things. Typically, we must infer how one action is related to another. In order to do this we must use our knowledge of behavior to make sense of people's actions. This is precisely the problem that faces the individual reading a narrative.

It seems obvious that much of the knowledge we need to understand actual behavior is that which we use in understanding text. Thus, in order to understand live behavior we need knowledge of such things as scripts, we need knowledge of the kinds of goals people have and the various plans that they can use to achieve them, and we need many of the other kinds of knowledge which are so crucial for the understanding of narratives.

Very little work in social psychology has been done on the ways in which people perceive and encode live behavior. Perhaps one reason for this has been the lack of theoretical work on the types of knowledge structures that are needed. It may be that the work on text comprehension has provided a first step towards a theory of the necessary knowledge structures.

What work has been done in social psychology points to the need for such knowledge structures as we have discussed. For instance, Zadny and Gerard (1974) demonstrated that people's memories for an observed interaction were a function of their experiences about the intentions of the actors. For instance, in one study, subjects observed a videotape of several people talking and walking around an apartment. Some subjects were told that the actors in the videotape were just waiting for a friend to get back, others were told that the people were looking for something to steal, while others were told that the actors were looking for drugs. Subjects recalled best those objects and those items of dialogue which were consistent with their beliefs about the actors' intentions. These results are consistent with the work in story understanding we described earlier which demonstrates that knowledge of an actor's goals plays a central role in the processing of stories.

In terms of the filter model of comprehension, the explanation of the Zadny and Gerard results can be made on the basis of the knowledge structures that are actively involved in the establishment of filters. First, the goal structures active in the comprehension of the actor's intentions have activated filters for the subsequent input. These filters interact with objects and items of conversation and in so doing organize them into a coherent causal chain. The general form of this chain is given by the type of goal structure that was involved in the activation of the filters in the first place. The difference between the different conditions in the experiment is a difference in the type of goal knowledge structure that is activated initially. Furthermore, the items that were most easily incorporated by the goal structure (and the plan and script structures activated under the processing control of the goal structure) into the internal representation are those which will be better remembered. Finally there is the use of these structures in the reconstruction of the story at the later point of testing. Thus subjects may make post hoc inferences based on these structures to reconstruct some of what might have happened and what some of the objects might have been. These possibilities are quite amenable to empirical test. As described earlier, Black and Bern (1981) showed that statements in stories are better remembered when they are causally connected and numerous studies we described showed that people reconstruct causal linking inferences using various kinds of knowledge.

There is additional research in social psychology which can be tied into our present concerns. Newtson and his colleagues (Newtson, 1976; Newtson, Engquist, & Bois, 1977) have extensively examined the ways in which people break behaviors down into their component actions. What they have done is to have people observe short segments of behavior and indicate, by pressing a button, when one action ends and another begins. They have shown that people can do this with reasonable reliability. There are several interesting aspects to their results. First, it appears that people can vary their level of analysis and the size of their units. Thus, depending on instructions people will use small or large units in breaking down the behavior. Further, the larger units will contain within them the smaller units. That is, the smaller units do not go across the boundaries specified by the larger units. On the basis of this and other results, Newtson argues that people are analyzing the behavior in terms of the goal-subgoal relationships, and that they can choose which level in the hierarchy to use as the unit of analysis. This analysis in terms of goal-subgoal relationships has some interesting parallels in the work on story understanding related to goal hierarchies. For example, Lichtenstein and Brewer (1980) examined both stories and videotapes in terms of goal-subgoal relationships.

This work also has some parallels with the possible organization of scripts. Abbott and Black (1980) and Galambos (1982a) have provided evidence that scripts are organized hierarchically, in terms of the goal-subgoal relationships involved in the performance of the script activities. The analyses performed by the subjects in Newtson's studies may have been guided by these script-like structures.

Newtson also looked at how unitization of behavior was affected by its predictability. He had subjects observe a videotaped sequence of behavior that started out being fairly ordinary and predictable. However, several minutes into the tape the actor started to behave in very unpredictable ways. Newtson found that when the behavior became unpredictable (or increasingly further towards the novelty end of the comprehension complexity continuum), the subjects started to break it down into smaller units. It appears that as long as the actions are predictable (or at least expectable), the active filters will adequately incorporate them into the fairly high level units which activated those filters. However, when the behavior becomes unpredictable there are no filters from the higher level structures available to interact with the novel input. As we suggested before, it appears that one way of dealing with novelty is to use smaller knowledge structures (perhaps at the level of word meanings) to activate other larger knowledge structures. Thus, breaking the behavior into smaller units may aid the comprehension process by permitting the activation of knowledge structures other than the ones currently active. Further, breaking the behavior down into smaller units may aid subjects in finding a way to explain the novel information in terms of changing specific aspects of the existing internal representation. In general this strategy may involve interaction with filters that are several times more specific or detailed than those used to incorporate predictable information. Thus, a move to chunk the behavior in smaller units is the external manifestation of the attempt to integrate it using more specific filters.

Something similar might happen when people are trying to understand a narrative. As long as things are going according to expectation people may simply monitor the high level actions and check that events are consistent with that. However, when something unpredictable happens people might much more carefully track lower level actions. Doing so might be particularly effective in trying to identify a new structure which can be applied to understanding the unpredictable actions. It may also be the most effective way to try to develop an explanation for this unpredictable event. This suggests that when people encounter an unexpected event in a story or in real life, they may remember the unexpected event much better. Bower, Black, and Turner (1979) found precisely this in a study of the role of scripts in memory for stories. They discovered that people recalled interruptions to the normal flow of the script much better than they recalled the script actions.

This result overlaps with observations of how we remember people. Both Hastie (Hastie & Kumar, 1979; Hastie, 1980) and Srull (1981) have found that when subjects are given an expectation about the kind of person someone is, and are then presented with a list of behaviors this person performed, subjects reliably recall behaviors that are inconsistent with the expectation better than they recall behaviors that are consistent with it. However, other researchers have found that people remember consistent information better than inconsistent information (e.g., Berman, Read, & Kenny, 1982; Picek, Sherman, & Shiffrin, 1975). There are a number of possible reasons for this discrepancy. It may be that differences in experimental procedure account for the different observations. Thus it might be that the degree of inconsistency in the Hastie and Srull studies is greater than in those that find better memory for consistent information. Another possible reason lies in the differences between the studies in the relationship between subject's expectancies and the information they receive. For instance, in the Hastie and Srull studies, subjects receive an expectancy based on a trait descriptor of an individual and then are given examples of different behaviors the individual performed. In the Berman, Read, and Kenney study, the expectancy subjects receive is based on a trait descriptor and then subjects are given further trait information. A possible source for reconciling these results may be to consider the processing characteristics involved in the two types of study. In both, the activated knowledge structure is a particular trait representation. The filters associated with this structure will be realizations of expectancies that comprise characteristics of this trait. The particular items in the experiment will, of course, influence the type of processing. However the filter model allows for advantages for both consistent and inconsistent information. Consistent information is easily recalled because it is easily reconstructed from the knowledge structures that were involved in initially representing it. Inconsistent information also gains in recall since it was more difficult to incorporate during comprehension and therefore has the benefit of increased processing. It is necessary to design studies which isolate the effects due to comprehension and those due to recall in order to resolve the apparent discrepancy.

Interestingly, Hastie (1980) has provided some evidence that people in his studies are more likely to remember the inconsistent behavior when they spend time trying to explain the inconsistency. This fits with our model and with Bower, Black, and Turner's (1979) suggestion that inconsistent actions will be better remembered because they will receive a greater amount of processing.

Attitudes and Political Beliefs

The work on story understanding may prove quite useful in another area. Social psychologists have long been interested in how people's attitudes and political beliefs might affect their memory for political information. There is a tradition of research in this area which goes back at least 40 years. While the basic finding seems to be that people remember better information which is consistent with their attitudes (e.g., Jones & Aneshansel, 1956; Jones & Kohler, 1958; Levine & Murphy, 1943; Malpass, 1969; Tyler & Voss, 1982; Weldon & Malpass, 1981), the findings are somewhat inconsistent with several failures to replicate, thus complicating the literature (e.g., Greenwald & Sakamura, 1967; Waly & Cook, 1966). Unfortunately, it's not clear why the findings are so variable. However, it might be possible to bring considerable light to this area by carefully considering how people's political beliefs and attitudes might affect their encoding of and memory for political information. (Our comments in this section might well be applied to attitude-memory issues in general.)

A central point of our argument has been that people engage in extensive inferencing when they read a text. Since many of the connections in a text are left implicit, such inferencing is essential for connecting together the elements in a text. In order to make these inferences people must bring to bear their knowledge and beliefs about the world. This suggests that people's attitudes and beliefs may affect their responses to political information by influencing the inferences they make when processing it.

This effect may take a number of forms. For instance, people with certain beliefs may lack the knowledge needed to arrive at a cohesive representation for a text. This failure may have several effects. First, people may simply fail to understand the text. Second, because they have failed to link togehter the items in the text, the internal representation of it does not itself cohere and they may later find it much more difficult to remember. Part of this problem may be the absence of sufficiently activated knowledge structures which can be used to aid recall through reconstruction. Several writers have suggested that the links among items in a text can be used to retrieve other items. Thus, a well connected text is likely to be better remembered than is a poorly connected one. Some research indicates that this is the case. For instance, events that are connected together in a causal chain are better remembered.

The influence of people's beliefs on inference making may have effects on people's responses to political information. It is possible that people with different beliefs may draw different inferences from the same material. Since these inferences may become part of the representation, people with different beliefs may end up with different information in the representation. Thus, they might remember different things or they may draw different conclusions from the same material. Another possibility is that the different inferences people draw may serve to connect the text in very different ways.

It should be possible to relate the inferences people make to specific aspects of their belief systems. Belief systems can be thought of as very high level knowledge structures at least in their processing implications. Like knowledge structures, they have associated filters which interact with many different types of configurations of information. Once activated these knowledge structures set up other filters which can influence perception of the world or of stories about it.

For instance, Carbonnell (1979) has suggested that one major component of people's political beliefs is a complex of knowledge about their own goals and the goals of their opponents. To the extent that an individual's beliefs about an opponent's goals differs from someone else's beliefs about the opponent's goals (and furthermore, these beliefs may differ from the opponent's beliefs about his own goals), we might expect that the individuals will make very different inferences and attributions concerning the opponent's behavior. As a result, each of these people may have quite different representations of the opponent's behavior. This has several implications. One possibility is that people with different beliefs will remember the event in the same way, but will simply ascribe different meanings to it. A second possibility is that the event will be remembered differently. For, as we suggested above, the way in which elements are connected together may affect the ways in which they are remembered.

People may also have different beliefs about the nature of physical causation. An extremely religious person may believe that God intervenes in man's affairs and thus may believe that a specific outcome shows God's hand. A less religious person may attribute an outcome to more mundane factors. As a result, they may make very different inferences when reading about an event and they will probably represent the event in very different ways.

There are other ways in which people's political beliefs and attitudes may affect their memory for events. Much of the research we covered earlier suggests that our memory for events is reconstructive (e.g., Graesser, 1981; Bower et al., 1979): that is, when people learn about an event they typically learn a general schema and only some of the details, so that when they remember they use their knowledge of the world to fill in gaps and produce a coherent memory. Thus it seems quite possible that people may reconstruct their memory for political events in line with the way the events are reconstructed using their pre-existing belief structures.

There is some evidence for this. Read and Rosson (in press) measured people's attitudes toward nuclear power and then had them read a news story about a fire at a nuclear power plant. In a later recognition test, people falsely recognized items which were consistent with their own position on nuclear power. This was true both for totally new recognition items and for items which were distortions of originally presented items. Further, this effect increased with delay. This suggests that people reconstruct events in line with their beliefs and attitudes.

We would like to deal with one other way in which people's beliefs might affect their memory for political events. Typically, when people read a text they abstract generalizations from it. Lehnert (1981) suggests that such generalizations are often based on stereotyped interpersonal relationships which people use to interpret the interactions of actors in a story. These stereotyped relationships have been called plot units.

It seems likely that people with different political beliefs may see different plot units as being applicable to interpreting the behavior of a political actor. For instance, a liberal Democrat and conservative Republican may see the relationship of Russia to the U.S. very differently. As a result, they may apply very different plot units to interpreting Russia's actions on the world stage. One way to study this is to look at how people summarize various events. Several authors have suggested that such summaries are based on the generalizations people abstract from a text. By examining people's summaries of events we should be able to relate their differing generalizations to the different knowledge structures they use.

The above considerations suggest that if one wants to know whether people's beliefs will affect their memory for political events then we first need to know two things. First, precisely how will those beliefs affect people's representation for the event? Second, what role will those beliefs play in the retrieval of the events?

CONCLUSIONS

In this chapter we have attempted to integrate work done in the psychology of text comprehension as well as that in artificial intelligence. In so doing, we developed the filter model as a framework in which to understand a wide variety of findings. We have also tried to indicate some ways in which this framework might provide a useful way of thinking about work in social cognition. We end with a restatement of our original assumption. Stories are about social behavior and social interactions. It is important that social and cognitive psychologists demonstrate more than tacit awareness of this fact.

REFERENCES

Abbott, V., & Black, J. B. *A comparison of the memory strength of alternative text relations.* Paper presented at the 1982 Meeting of the American Education Research Association, New York, 1982.

Abbott, V., Black, J. B., & Smith, E. E. *The representation of scripts in memory.* Paper submitted for publication, 1982.

Abelson, R. P. Does a story understander need a point of view? In R. C. Schank & B. L. Nash-Webber (Eds.), *Theoretical issues in natural language processing.* Washington, D.C.: Association for Computational Linguistics, 1975.

Abelson, R. P. Psychological status of the script concept. *American Psychologist,* 1981, *36,* 715–729.

Anderson, J. A. *Language memory and thought.* Hillsdale, N.J.: Lawrence Erlbaum Associates, 1976.

Bartlett, F. C. *Remembering.* New York: Cambridge University Press, 1932.

Berman, J. S., Read, S. J., & Kenney, D. A. *Processing inconsistent social information.* Paper submitted for publication, 1982.

Black, J. B. Point of view and causal inferences in story understanding. *Cognitive Science Technical Report # 18,* Yale University, 1982.

Black, J. B., & Bern, H. Causal coherence and memory for events in narratives. *Journal of Verbal Learning and Verbal Behavior*, 1981, *20*, 267–275.

Black, J. B., & Bower, G. H. Episodes as chunks in narrative memory. *Journal of Verbal Learning and Verbal Behavior*, 1979, *18*, 309–318.

Black, J. B., & Bower, G. H. Story understanding as problem-solving. *Poetics*, 1980, *9*, 223–250.

Black, J. B., Turner, T. J., and Bower, G. H. Point of view in narrative comprehension, memory and production. *Journal of Verbal Learning and Verbal Behavior*, 1979, *18*, 187–198.

Bower, G. H. Experiments on story comprehension and recall. *Discourse Processing*, 1978, *1*, 211–232.

Bower, G. H., Black, J. B., & Turner, T. J. Scripts in memory for text. *Cognitive Psychology*, 1979, *11*, 177–220.

Bransford, J. D., & Johnson, M. K. Contextual prerequisites for understanding: Some investigations of comprehension and recall. *Journal of Verbal Learning and Verbal Behavior*, 1972, *11*, 717–726.

Brewer, W. F., & Lichtenstein, E. H. Event schemas, story schemas and story grammars. In J. Long & A. Baddeley (Eds.), *Attention and Performance IX*. Hillsdale, N.J.: Lawrence Erlbaum Associates, 1981.

Cantor, N., & Mischel, W. Prototypes in person perception. In L. Berkowitz (Ed.), *Advances in Experimental Social Psychology*, Vol. 12. New York: Academic Press, 1979.

Carbonnell, J. G. Subjective Understanding: Computer models of belief systems. *Computer science technical report 150*, Doctoral Dissertation, Yale University, 1979.

Craik, F. I. M., & Tulving, E. Depth of processing and the retention of words in episodic memory. *Journal of Verbal Learning and Verbal Behavior*, 1975, *11*, 671–684.

Cullingford, R. E. Script application: Computer understanding of newspaper stories. *Computer science technical report 116*, Doctoral Dissertation, Yale University, 1978.

Dyer, M. G. In-depth understanding: A computer model of integrated processing for narrative comprehension. *Computer science technical report 219*, Doctoral Dissertation, Yale University, 1982.

Galambos, J. A. *The mental representation of common events*. Unpublished Doctoral Dissertation, University of Chicago, 1981.

Galambos, J. A. *Question answering and the plan structure of routine activities*. Paper presented to the American Educational Research Association Annual Meeting. New York, March 1982. (a)

Galambos, J. A. Normative studies of six characteristics of our knowledge of common activities. *Cognitive science technical report 14*, Yale University, 1982. (b)

Galambos, J. A., & Black, J. B. Getting and using context: Functional constraints on the organization of knowledge. *Proceedings of the Fourth Conference of the Cognitive Science Society*. Ann Arbor, Michigan, 1982.

Galambos, J. A., & Rips, L. J. Memory for routines. *Journal of Verbal Learning and Verbal Behavior*, 1982, *21*, 260–281.

Glenn, C. G. The role of episodic structure and of story length in children's recall of simple stories. *Journal of Verbal Learning and Verbal Behavior*, 1978, *17*, 229–247.

Graesser, A. C. *Prose comprehension beyond the word*. New York: Springer-Verlag, 1981.

Graesser, A. C., Gordon, S. E., & Sawyer, J. D. Memory for typical and atypical actions in scripted activities: Test of a script pointer + tag hypothesis. *Journal of Verbal Learning and Verbal Behavior*, 1979, *18*, 319–332.

Graesser, A. C., Woll, S. B., Kowalski, D. J., & Smith, D. A. Memory for typical and atypical actions in scripted activities. *Journal of Experimental Psychology: Human Learning and Memory*, 1980, *6*, 503–515.

Greenwald, A. G., & Sakamura, J. S. Attitudes and selective learning: Where are the phenomena of yesteryear? *Journal of Personality and Social Psychology*, 1967, *7*, 387–397.

Grice, H. P. William James Lectures, Harvard University, 1967. Published in part as "Logic in Conversation" in P. Cole & J. L. Morgan (Eds.), *Syntax and semantics*, Vol. 3, *Speech Acts*. New York: Academic, 1975.

Haberlandt, K. Story grammars and the reading time of story constituents. *Poetics*, 1980, *9*, 99–116.

Haberlandt, K., & Bingham, G. Verbs contribute to the coherence of brief narrative passages: Reading related and unrelated sentence triplets. *Journal of Verbal Learning and Verbal Behavior*, 1978, *17*, 419–425.

Hastie, R. Memory for behavioral information which confirms or contradicts a general impression. In R. Hastie, T. M. Ostrom, E. B. Ebbesen, R. S. Wyer, D. L. Hamilton, & D. E. Carlston (Eds.), *Person memory: The cognitive basis of social perception*. Hillsdale, N.J.: Erlbaum, 1980.

Hastie, R., & Kumar, P. A. Person memory: Personality traits as organizing principles in memory for behaviors. *Journal of Personality and Social Psychology*, 1979, *37*, 25–38.

Jones, E. E., & Aneshansel, J. The learning and utilization of contravalent material. *Journal of Abnormal and Social Psychology*, 1956, *53*, 27–33.

Jones, E. E., & Kohler, R. The effects of plausibility on the learning of controversial statements. *Journal of Abnormal and Social Psychology*, 1958, *57*, 315–320.

Jones, E. E., & Nisbett, R. E. The actor and the observer: Divergent perceptions of the causes of behavior. In E. E. Jones, D. E. Kanouse, H. H. Kelley, R. E. Nisbett, S. Valins, & B. Weiner (Eds.), *Attribution: Perceiving the causes of behavior*. Morristown, N.J.: General Learning Press, 1971.

Kintsch. W. *The representation of meaning in memory*. Hillsdale, N.J.: Erlbaum, 1974.

Kintsch, W., & van Dijk, T. A. Toward a model of test comprehension and production. *Psychological Review*, 1978, *85*, 363–394.

Latane, B., & Darley, J. M. *The unresponsive bystander: Why doesn't he help?*. New York: Appleton, 1970.

Lehnert, W. G. Plot units and narrative summarization. *Cognitive Science*, 1981, *5*, 293–331.

Lehnert, W. G., Black, J. B., & Reiser, B. J. Summarizing narratives. *Proceedings of the 7th International Joint Conference on Artificial Intelligence*, Vancouver, BC, 1981.

Levine, J. M., & Murphy, G. The learning and forgetting of controversial material. *Journal of Abnormal and Social Psychology*, 1943, *38*, 510–517.

Lichtenstein, E. H., & Brewer, W. F. Memory for goal-directed events. *Cognitive Psychology*, 1980, *12*, 412–445.

Malpass, R. S. Effects of attitude on learning and memory: The influence of instruction-induced sets. *Journal of Experimental Social Psychology*, 1969, *5*, 441–453.

Mandler, J. M. A code in the node: The use of a story schema in retrieval. *Discourse Processes*, 1978, *1*, 14–35.

Mandler, J. M., & Johnson, N. S. Remembrance of things parsed: Story structure and recall. *Cognitive Psychology*, 1977, *9*, 111–151.

Mandler, J. M., & Johnson, N. S. On throwing out the baby with the bathwater: A reply to Black and Wilensky's evaluation of story grammars. *Cognitive Science*, 1980, *4*, 305–312.

Mio, J. S., & Black, J. B. *Attribution inferences in story comprehension*. Unpublished manuscript, University of Illinois, Chicago, 1979.

Newell, A. Production systems: Models of control structures. In W. C. Chase (Ed.), *Visual information processing*. New York: Academic Press, 1973.

Newtson, D. A. Foundations of attribution: The perception of ongoing behavior. In J. H. Harvey, W. J. Ickes, & R. F. Kidd (Eds.), *New directions in attribution research*, Vol. 1. Hillsdale, N.J.: Erlbaum, 1976.

Newtson, D. A., Engquist, G., & Bois, J. The objective basis of behavior units. *Journal of Personality and Social Psychology*, 1977, *35*, 847–862.

Nisbett, R. E., Borgida, E., Crandall, R., & Reed H. Popular induction: Information is not always informative. In J. S. Carroll & J. W. Payne (Eds.), *Cognition and Social Behavior,* Vol. 2, 1976, 227–236.

Picek, J. S., Sherman, S. J., & Shiffrin, R. M. Cognitive organization and coding of social structure. *Journal of Personality and Social Psychology,* 1975, *31,* 758–768.

Read, S. J., & Rosson, M. B. Rewriting history: The biasing effects of attitudes on memory. *Social Cognition,* in press.

Reiser, B. J., Black, J. B., & Lehnert, W. G. Thematic knowledge structures in the understanding and generation of narratives. *Cognitive Science Technical Report 16,* Yale University, 1982.

Riesbeck, C. K. Conceptual Analysis. In R. C. Schank (Ed.), *Conceptual information processing.* New York: American Elsevier, 1975.

Rumelhart, D. E. Notes on a schema for stories. In D. G. Bobrow & A. M. Collins (Eds.), *Representation and understanding: Studies in cognitive science.* New York: Academic Press, 1975.

Rumelhart, D. E. Understanding and summarizing brief stories. In D. LaBerge & S. J. Samuels (Eds.), *Basic processes in reading: Perception and comprehension.* Hillsdale, N.J.: Lawrence Erlbaum Associates, 1977.

Schank, R. C. The structure of episodes in memory. In D. G. Bobrow & A. M. Collins (Eds.), *Representation and understanding: Studies in cognitive science.* New York: Academic Press, 1975.

Schank, R. C. Identifications of conceptualizations underlying natural language. In R. C. Schank & K. M. Colby (Eds.), *Computer models of lanuage and thought.* San Francisco: Freeman, 1973, 187–247.

Schank, R. C. *Dynamic memory.* New York: Cambridge University Press, 1982.

Schank, R. C., & Abelson, R. P. *Scripts, plans, goals and understanding.* Hillsdale, N.J.: Lawrence Erlbaum Associates, 1977.

Seifert, C. M., Robertson, S. P., & Black, J. B. On-line processing of pragmatic inferences. *Proceedings of the Fourth Annual Conference of the Cognitive Science Society,* Ann Arbor, Mi., 1982.

Sharkey, N. E., & Mitchell, D. C. *New primes for old: Passive decay versus active suppression of scripts in working memory.* Paper presented to the British Psychological Society, Plymouth, September, 1981.

Smith, E. E., & Collins, A. M. Use of goal-plan knowledge in understanding stories. *Proceedings of the Third Annual Conference of the Cognitive Science Society,* Berkeley, Calif., 1981.

Spiro, R. J. Accommodative reconstruction in prose recall. *Journal of Verbal Learning and Verbal Behavior,* 1980, *19,* 84–95.

Srull, T. K. Person memory: Some tests of associative storage and retrieval models. *Journal of Experimental Psychology: Human Learning and Memory,* 1981, *7,* 440–463.

Stein, N. L. The definition of a story, *Pragmatics,* in press.

Stein, N. L., & Glenn, C. G. An analysis of story comprehension in elementary school children. In R. O. Freedle (Eds.), *New directions in discourse processing,* Vol. 2. Norwood, N.J.: Ablex, 1979.

Stein, N. L., & Trabasso, T. What's in a story: Critical issues in story comprehension. In R. Glaser (Ed.), *Advances in the psychology of instruction,* Vol. 2. Hillsdale, N.J.: Lawrence Erlbaum Associates, in press.

Taylor, S. E., & Crocker, J. C. Schematic bases of social information processing. In E. T. Higgins, P. Herman, & M. P. Zanna (Eds.), *The Ontario symposium on personality and social psychology,* Vol. 1. Hillsdale, N.J.: Lawrence Erlbaum Associates, 1980.

Taylor, S. E., & Fiske, S. T. Salience, attention and attribution: Top of the head phenomenon. In L. Berkowitz (Ed.), *Advances in experimental social psychology,* Vol. 11. New York: Academic Press, 1978.

Thorndyke, P. W. Cognitive structures in comprehension and memory of narrative discourse. *Cognitive Psychology*, 1977, *9*, 77–110.

Trabasso, T., Seco, T., & van den Broek, P. Causal cohesion and story coherence. In H. Mandl, N. L. Stein, & T. Trabasso (Eds.), *Learning and comprehension of text*. Hillsdale, N.J.: Lawrence Erlbaum Associates, in press.

Tyler, S. W., & Voss, J. F. Attitude and Knowledge Effects in Prose Processing. *Journal of Verbal Learning and Verbal Behavior*, 1982, *21*, 524–538.

Waly, P., & Cook, S. N. Attitude as a determinant of learning and memory: A failure to confirm. *Journal of Personality and Social Psychology*, 1966, *4*, 280–288.

Weldon, D. E., & Malpass, R. S. Effects of attitudinal cognitive and situational variables on recall of biased communications. *Journal of Personality and Social Psychology*, 1981, *40*, 34–52.

Wilensky, R. *Understanding goal-based stories. Computer Science Technical Report 140*, Doctoral Dissertation, Yale University, 1978.

Winograd, T. *Understanding natural language*. New York: Academic Press, 1972.

Woodworth, R. S., & Schlosberg, H. *Experimental psychology*. New York: Holt, Rinehart and Winston, 1954.

Wyer, R. S., & Srull, T. K. The processing of social stimulus information: A conceptual integration. In R. Hastie, T. M. Ostrom, E. B. Ebbesen, R. S. Wyer, D. L. Hamilton, & D. E. Carlston (Eds.), *Person memory: The cognitive basis of social perception*. Hillsdale, N.J.: Lawrence Erlbaum Associates, 1980.

Zadny, J., & Gerard, H. B. Attributed intentions and informational selectivity. *Journal of Experimental Social Psychology*, 1974, *10*, 34–52.

3 Communication and Social Cognition

Robert E. Kraut
Bell Laboratories

E. Tory Higgins
New York University

Contents

As many of the papers in the current volume indicate, the recent study of social cognition is only marginally social. The emphasis is on the asocial determinants of cognitions about social phenomena, for example, those underlying social judgments, person perception, person memory, stereotypes, and attitudes.

Relatively little work in social psychology has been done on communication, a potentially rich intersection of the cognitive and the social. Indeed, it is our belief, which we hope to illustrate in this chapter, that the construction of communication is the major way that social cognition manifests itself in daily life. To understand communication, one must study social cognition, and to understand the most important aspects of social cognition one must study communication.

Communication and social cognition are joined in many ways. Clearly, conversation is inherently social in that it involves the transmission of messages between at least two people. And it is inherently cognitive in that the messages are the result of cognitive activity within the communicators. But conversation is more than the sequential joining of two independent processes—individualistic cognition and social communication. For one thing, the media of conversation—language and communication conventions—are themselves social, being products of a language community. Moreover, conversation often involves the exchange of social information, for example, gossip about other people or influence attempts. Finally, conversation is the basic tool people use to achieve their various social goals.

While these are important aspects of the relation between social cognition and communication, from the perspective of a handbook on social cognition, communication and social cognition are related in two additional, supremely important ways. First, in order to converse, communicators must plan, to varying degrees, what they will say to each other. At the basis of their planning is their ability to know what their partners already know and what their partners need to know so that the communication will be effective (cf., Clark, in press). That is, a basis for communication (i.e., knowing what a partner knows) is also a central topic in social cognition (i.e., person perception). Second, when speakers enact their plans, the messages they produce often influence what they themselves subsequently know, believe, and remember. In sum, social cognition—beliefs about others—is at the root of communication and communication itself can influence social cognition.

The goals of the present chapter are to explore the levels of planning communicators perform in order to converse, to explore the ways that they coordinate their message with their partners' knowledge, and to examine the influence of their message on their own subsequent cognitions.

Communication is embedded in more general social interaction. It is the most important of the interactional tools that people use to further their more general goals for interaction. One can think of human life as motivated by a deeply nested hierarchy of goals. At each level, subordinate goals are the means through which people achieve their superordinate ones (Miller, Galanter, & Pribram, 1960). Social psychologists have been concerned with intermediate-level goals, such as selling a candidate or being socially engaging. These, in turn, are achieved through lower-level goals, such as being persuasive or presenting a good impression, which are mediated by even lower level social interaction techniques such as presenting information clearly or creating consistency among aspects of performance, setting, and demeanor (Goffman, 1955).

To understand social phenomena one must keep in mind the goals at a level or two above and below one's focus. In particular, to understand most social psychological processes, we need to understand the conversation through which many of them are mediated. And to understand conversation we need to consider explicitly both the social goals of communication, at more general levels, and the mechanisms of sequencing interaction, constructing sentences, and developing propositions, at more detailed levels.

To achieve their higher-level social goals people engage in conversations, adopting some general conversational goals. Among the most important are: (1) the exchange of information, (2) persuasion, and (3) enjoyment. (See Higgins, Fondacaro, & McCann, 1981, for a summary and discussion of communication goals.) In the service of these general conversational goals, speakers adopt a large number of subsidiary conversational goals, such as introducing a topic, telling a story, or answering a question. Like all goals, conversational goals imply that speakers have a desired end-state in mind, and that they compare their current state with the end-state and make modifications in their behavior to try to decrease the discrepancy between the two (Heider, 1958; Miller et al., 1960).

The goals in conversation are nested. Speakers must decide on the effect they want to achieve in their listeners and then the general outline of the discourse that would achieve this effect, including the high-level constituents such as greetings, narratives, arguments, or illustrations of which discourse is composed. At a lower level, speakers must plan the speech acts or intended effects of small chunks of speech, sentences, and the constituents of sentences, such as phrases and words.

The process of achieving any of these subsidiary goals is a mixture of both *premeditation* and nonpremeditated *interaction*. In a premeditated mode, when planning their speech, speakers take into account their knowledge of the language, the topic they are addressing, and characteristics of their listeners, including what they already know. In an interactional mode, speakers also adapt what they are saying to their own prior speech and to their partners' contributions. Each of the subgoals we have mentioned above can be planned non-interactively, as speech writers and novelists do, relying solely on their general knowledge of the topic at hand and the intended audience, without direct feedback from that audience. On the other hand, plans can be modified during the course of the conversation on the basis of explicit feedback from conversational partners.

This chapter surveys some of the constraints on communicators as they use language to achieve their social goals and considers some of the consequences of such language use. In the interests of brevity, we concentrate on the speaker's role in conversation, and on goals, constraints, and consequences that have the most social psychological flavor. We recognize our oversimplification in treating speaker and listener as separate roles, since in any one conversation interactants switch roles frequently. Even while they are speaking, speakers receive both verbal and nonverbal communication from their listeners. Conversely, listeners provide feedback to speakers even while they themselves are planning their own speech. Similarly, our emphasis on topics such as the cooperation between the speaker and listener, conversational implicatures, and speech acts, rather than on the details of semantic memory or syntax tells only part of the story of conversation. We believe, however, that these are the areas of most interest to social psychologists and the areas where social psychology can offer most to the study of language.

In the sections below we present a more detailed examination of some of these areas of planning that we have outlined here. Our strategy is to start with general constraints on conversation (i.e., conversational maxims), move to the largest units of conversational planning (e.g., discourse and narratives), consider smaller units of analysis (e.g., speech-acts and word choice), and finally treat the role of conversational partners on the organization and production of speech (e.g., audience effects and explicit feedback).

GENERAL CONVERSATIONAL MAXIMS

Conversationalists are constrained by some general conventions of speech, as well as by the particular social effects they wish to achieve. Speakers and listeners follow a set of conversational maxims (e.g., Clark & Clark, 1977) or general rules of the communication game (Higgins, 1981). According to Grice (1975), the basic rule in conversation is that speakers and listeners try to cooperate with each other. More specifically, speakers and listeners adopt several conventions about the way in which speech will be used, and then they both cooperate, the speaker by observing the conventions and the listener by interpreting what the speaker says in light of these conventions. According to Grice and other writers on discourse (cf. Austin, 1962; Cushman & Whiting, 1972; Delia, 1976; Gumperz & Hymes, 1972; Rommetveit, 1974; van Dijk, 1977; see Higgins, 1981 and Clark & Clark, 1977 for useful summaries) speakers in conversation follow rules such as the following:

1. *Maxim of quantity:* speakers should make their contribution as informative as required, providing neither too much nor too little information.
2. *Maxim of quality:* speakers should convey the truth as they see it.
3. *Maxim of relation:* speakers should produce a message that is appropriate to their communicative intent or purpose.
4. *Maxim of relevance:* speakers should produce a message that is relevant to the context and circumstances.
5. *Maxim of manner:* speakers should try to be clear, coherent, comprehensible, and concise.
6. *Maxim of sensitivity:* speakers should adapt their messages to their listeners' characteristics, including what they believe their listeners know.

Listeners assume that speakers are following these rules and interpret the conversation as if they were. In addition, they have a parallel set of rules that they follow themselves (see Higgins et al., 1981). For example, they pay attention to the message, try to determine the speaker's communicative intent, take the context and the speaker's characteristics into account when making interpretations, and provide feedback to the speaker about their interpretation or understanding of the message.

Speakers' adherence to the cooperative principle and the conversational maxims forms the basis for many of the "authorized inferences" (Clark, 1977) that listeners make in conversation. That is, this adherence allows listeners to go beyond what a speaker literally says to infer an indirect meaning that the speaker intended the listener to infer. We discuss the concept of indirect meaning more fully in our section on speech acts, below. Here, we simply wish to note that when speakers say something that appears to violate a conversational maxim, listeners assume that speakers are indeed adhering to the cooperative principle and interpret the utterance consistent with the maxim. For example, in a Thurber (1965) story one character asks another, "What's after you?" in a context in which everyone knows that nothing is following the addressee. In order to make the question follow the maxims of quality and relevance, the addressee (and the reader) compute the indirect meaning of the question as "Why are you in such a rush?" Similarly, for example, in the face of the mandate that speakers be truthful, listeners can interpret a "Gee, that's good" in response to blatantly nauseating food as sarcasm or irony.

The clear discrepancy between the direct meaning of the speaker's words and the situation to which they apply should be sufficient to indicate to listeners the speaker's indirect and intended meaning. But to insure that listeners judge them to be truthful, speakers will often augment the interpretation that could be conveyed on pragmatic grounds alone with nonverbal signals, such as a mock look of disgust, or with paralinguistic signals, such as a sarcastic tone of voice, that help to communicate the desired message. The precise conditions under which speakers augment spoken language with these other channels, however, remains to be described.

DISCOURSE STRUCTURE

While the cooperative principle provides the most general constraint on conversation, rules about the structure of discourse provide additional, high-level constraints. Conversation, like scripts (Bartlett, 1932; Schank & Abelson, 1977), generally provides a general structure for communicators to follow, while leaving room for plot and stylistic variation. The prescribed structure undoubtedly depends on the conversational genre (e.g., debate, instruction, small-talk), the subject matter (e.g., politics, cooking, vacations), and the host of factors that influence or are related to the communicator's social goals (e.g., relative status, setting, reinforcements). Thus, one can debate a wide range of topics for a wide range of reasons, and the structure of the debate is probably determined jointly by the fact of the debate, by the topic being debated (Weiner & Goodenough, 1977), and by what one hopes to achieve from it.

Openings, Closings, and Coherence

Among the problems in structuring a conversation, three seem fundamental, regardless of genre or subject: how to start it, how to end it, and how to achieve coherence among the topics, turns, and propositions it contains.

Openings.   In starting a conversation, speakers must announce their intentions and insure that listeners will participate with them. Conversations generally start with a summons-answer sequence (Schegloff, 1968). The summons catches listeners' attention and allows them to indicate their willingness to participate. In telephone conversations, the summons is the ringing of the phone and the answer is the first words uttered by the person who picks it up (e.g., "hello?" or "yeah" or "Macy's"; Schegloff, 1968). When the answering party doesn't respond to the ring-summons, the summoning party typically reiterates the summons verbally until the listener responds (e.g., "Hello, hello, is anyone there?"). In face-to-face conversation the summons may be any number of linguistic devices (e.g., "You know what?" or "Mommy!" or "Excuse me.") and nonlinguistic devices (e.g., establishing eye-contact or co-orientation; Kendon & Ferber, 1973) that the initiator uses to get the other's attention and signal the desire for conversation.

Closings.   Following the summons-answer sequence, conversationalists have more or less structured talk, and then close the conversation in a conventional way. The devices for closing a conversation include bounding a topic (e.g., ". . . and so that's what I told him."), offering an invitation to close (e.g., "Ok, I'll let you get back to your work now."), and the actual termination of the interchange (e.g., Anne: "Ok" Bob: "Ok" Anne: "Bye" Bob: "Bye") (Knapp, Hart, Friedrich, & Shulman, 1973; Schegloff & Sachs, 1973).

Coherence.   Between the opening and the closing, conversations have varying amounts of structure, depending on the level of analysis one chooses. We have seen above that one of the conversational maxims is relevance; speakers should say what is relevant to context and circumstances. The context includes the linguistic context: speakers should be relevant to both their own and their partners' preceding speech. In being relevant, speakers strive for two goals. First they need to demonstrate relevance, per se, to what has gone before. And second, they need to show the nature of the relevance, i.e., the relationship between the current topic, speaking turn, sentence, or phrase, and previous ones.

In order to demonstrate relevance or cohesion, speakers use a variety of techniques. Children as young as 3 years old typically repeat a prior utterance to show that what they are saying is related to what went before (Keenan, 1974). Older children and adults demonstrate coherence both syntactically and semantically (Halliday & Hasan, 1976). Syntactically, conjunctions and other connectives both show that two linguistic elements are relevant to each other and show the nature of their relations. For example, in describing a cowboy movie (Kraut, Lewis, & Swezey, 1982) a speaker said, "The mayor tries to have the hero killed, gets one of his ruffians to shoot him. *But* the hero managed to shoot his way out of the hotel." The *but* signifies that the two sentences are related, and that the second violates an expectation set up by the first.

Speakers also use semantic coherence to demonstrate the relatedness between linguistic units. They have a range of techniques through which they semantically refer back to previous material. For example, speakers interweave the semantics of sentences through anaphoric reference, in which nouns are referred to in other forms. Consider this fragment from an interview with Aaron Pryor, the boxer, discussing how he rode the bulls in the stockyards of Cincinnati.

> I wanted to fantasize. I tried it and I liked it. It was the same thing I had about hopping trains, catching a train going 30 or 40 miles an hour. It was just doing things your parents tell you not to. Them bulls, they'd throw me off, and I'd have to run not to get gored. But I'd climb back on and start whuppin' them in the head.

These forms include pronouns (e.g., whuppin' *them* in the head), definite articles (e.g., *them* bulls), verbal substitution (e.g., *hopping trains* versus *catching a train*), and ellipsis (I'd climb back on [the bulls]; Halliday & Hasan, 1976).

In addition to demonstrating that two linguistic units are related, speakers are also under an obligation to show the nature of the relationship. Consider the case of speech topics. Conversations are often divided up into topics, with rules for the transition between them (e.g., Keenan & Schieffelin, 1976; Nofsinger & Boyd, 1979; Planalp & Tracy, 1980; Schank, 1977; Sullivan, 1970; Vuchinich, 1977). A topic is the underlying theme of a group of possibly noncontiguous utterances. The topic can be developed by a single speaker independently or jointly by several speakers, across speaking turns. It is developed through what Reichman (1978) calls context spaces, groups of utterances that refer to a single issue (e.g., "Abortion is immoral" or "John's new car") or a single event (e.g., "My trip to the shore" or "The meeting in Denver") and the relations among them.

The relations joining these context spaces or subthemes include *illustration, generalization, digression and return, new topic shift* (Reichman, 1978), *equivalence, alternative, causation,* and *summarization,* among others (Grimes, 1975; Kraut & Lewis, in press). A word like "because" communicates a causal relationship between the current sentence and preceding ones. Similarly, a phrase like "On the other hand" communicates an alternative relationship between two sentences or clauses, in which the ideas in the second linguistic unit oppose those in the first.

One might argue that these *relationship communicators* express the relationship between linguistic units only as a side-effect of creating that relationship.

Under these assumptions, the word "because" creates the causal relationship and, as a consequence, communicates it. Communicating the relationship, however, is conceptually independent of creating it. A phrase such as "Let me change the topic" does not, by itself, change the topic. For example, in the following, despite the phrase, the topic doesn't change.

> Ann: We're thinking about vacationing in the Bahamas this winter.
> Bob: Let me change the topic. We'll spend our vacation at home.

Rather, the topic is changed when speech dosen't refer back to preceding material, either in terms of its content or its syntactic construction. As an aside, new topic shifts appear to occur when speakers cannot get a partner to take over the speaking turn (Maynard, 1980). A relationship communicator seems to mark the relationship between linguistic units, not necessarily create it.

Relationship communicators also serve other functions. In addition to being parsing aids, letting listeners know what relationship among ideas to expect, they also illustrate to listeners that speakers are self-aware of the relations among their ideas. In the extreme, when speakers violate the relevance principle by changing topic, they need to inform their audience that they know what they are doing and, in essence, to apologize in advance for the breach.

Narrative

Many two-person conversations are well-structured, but the structure of discourse is easiest to illustrate in extended, single-topic discourse. Consider the construction of a narrative. A narrative is more stereotyped and structured than many chunks of extended discourse; still, the problems that speakers must solve to produce a narrative illustrate many of the problems in discourse production generally. Narratives are interesting in their own right. Although a narrative is often used in the context of a complex conversation as a single speech-act, it may at other times comprise the major part of a conversation. We discuss narratives here, however, primarily to illustrate some techniques speakers use to solve the problems of openings, closings, and coherence.

Following Labov and Fanshel (1977), we consider a narrative as a means of representing past experience by a sequence of ordered sentences that present the temporal sequence of the events by the order of the sentences. Like other types of discourse, narratives have a hierarchical and recursive structure. Narratives may be decomposed into *settings* (which specify time, locale, and the like) and *episodes*. Episodes can be decomposed into *events* and *reactions*. Events, in turn, can be decomposed recursively into episodes, changes of state, actions, or events. (For a more formal statement of these relations, see Rumelhart, 1975, 1977.)

The decomposition of narratives and their recursive nature can be illustrated with narratives that Chafe (1977) collected. Chafe had people describe a problem that they had with a bureaucratic office. Embedded in many of these narratives was an incident that Chafe calls "a run-around," in which the protagonist is shunted from functionary to functionary without accomplishing his or her intended task. The "run-around" in turn is composed of several components: a purpose or the task that the protagonist wanted accomplished, a deflection, in which the protagonist is prevented from accomplishing the task (repeated one or more times), and a resolution. Verbal schemata, such as deflections, can be further broken down. For example, deflections consist of a protagonist's arrival at an office, waiting for some time, the protagonist's request to a functionary, the functionary's response, the protagonist's remonstration to the functionary, and the functionary's reiterated responses, with some of these components being optional. The similarity between Chafe's notion of verbal schema and Shank and Abelson's event scripts (1977) is strong.

Openings. A speaker who starts a narrative is confronted with three problems. The speaker must show the relation between the story and the preceding conversation, orient listeners to the story, and reserve some conversational space for telling the story. To integrate the story with the ongoing conversation, speakers use many of the coherence techniques we've discussed earlier. When the story isn't topically relevant, speakers use other techniques to display a relation between the story and the prior conversation and thus account for telling the story and propose its appropriateness. To show that they know that the story is off the topic, speakers often use *disjunct markers* such as "oh, that reminds me," "incidentally," "as a matter of fact," and the like. To show their listeners what in the prior conversation triggered the story, they use *embedded repetition* to refer back (e.g., they use phrases like "Speaking about Christmas," or "Saying Rasputin reminds me" as well as the lexical coherence devices we referred to above; see Jefferson, 1976 for a fuller discussion.)

Settings are often used to introduce a narrative. They provide the listener with orienting information about the particular events they introduce. They are also a device to reserve conversational space so that the speaker can develop a sustained narrative. In this way, at least, they are functionally similar to a summons that introduces conversation. Speakers typically signal that they are starting a narrative by referring to time, place, persons, and behaviors characteristic of a situation in a way that clearly differentiates the occasions referred to from the present time of speaking. Adverbs of time are typical (e.g., Labov, 1972; Labov & Fanshel, 1977; Labov & Waletzky, 1967). Thus "Once upon a time" and "Do you remember when I went to the Cape for vacation? Well, let me tell you . . ." both orient the listener and protect the speaker from interruption.

Settings, however, are not the only discourse structure that introduces the narrative and orients the listener. A statement of the general proposition that the narrative illustrates, which Labov and Fanshel (1977) call the *abstract,* is also frequently used. For example, in Kraut, Lewis, and Swezey (1982) speakers summarized a cowboy movie to listeners. Speakers typically started their summaries by providing setting information, introducing the main characters and their general situation (e.g., settlers on a wagon train to Oregon). But a substantial minority of the speakers introduced their narrative with an abstract. In most cases this abstract had the form of a statement of what they intended to do (e.g., "Now I'm going to summarize the movie, 'Bend of the River' "). Rarely did the abstract convey the moral of the movie (e.g., "It's about how men can change"), although this was occasionally used as a closing device to bound the summary.

Coherence.   After introducing the narrative, speakers must get down to the business of telling the story. The sequencing of uninterrupted narratives tends to preserve the order of the events depicted (Labov & Fanshel, 1977); that is, speakers use the sequence of utterances to indicate the sequence of events. Children learn this rule even before they know the words "before" and "after" (e.g., Clark, 1970).

In several instances adults do not preserve this order. Telling of an event out of order may be used as a stylistic device. For example, a speaker may introduce a crucial event early on, or may hold it in abeyance, because that event is the point or punchline of the narrative. On the other hand, out of order events may result from a failure of adequate planning. Thus, a speaker may introduce an event out of sequence, only when its causal significance is needed to explain another event. For example, in Kraut et al. (1982) speakers typically failed to mention an arrow wound that the heroine received during an Indian attack when it happened, but introduced it much later when they needed to explain why she had not traveled with the rest of the settlers.

Of course, in a narrative, speakers cannot possibly reproduce all of the detail that occurred in the situation they are describing. In deciding which details to include in the narrative and which to exclude, they seem to follow what might be called a *consequence rule*: they only mention events that have consequences (Rumelhart, 1977). For example, in the movie-summarization experiment (Kraut et al., 1982), speakers generally failed to mention a dramatic killing, because no other actions in the story followed from it; its purpose in the movie was only to illuminate the villain's character.

In condensing, speakers also tend to follow an *ends rule*: they mention only ends and goals and omit means by which these are reached (Rumelhart, 1976). In the cowboy movie summaries, for example, every speaker mentioned that the hero escaped from a town with needed supplies, but few mentioned how this was accomplished. Similarly, most subjects menioned that the heroes killed the bad guys, but many fewer mentioned that this was by means of an ambush. In a related vein, speakers follow a *script-rule*: they omit explicit mention of details that should be obvious to their listeners because they were required by the story script (cf. Schank & Abelson, 1977). For example, in the cowboy movie summaries few speakers mentioned that the heroes rode their horses into town to retrieve their supplies, since horse riding is required in the cowboy-movie script. Many more mentioned the heroes rode away from town on a steam-boat, because it couldn't be predicted from the cowboy movie script itself. If speakers were exclusively following the ends-rule, however, they would have failed to mention both styles of transportation equally.

Closing.   In closing a narrative, speakers are faced with two problems. First, when a narrative is being used as a single speech act, speakers must ensure that the listeners have understood the point being made. And second, they must ensure that the listeners know the narrative is over and interactive conversation is to resume. A closing signal is important for many types of extended discourse, and especially important for narratives, since narratives are accounts of indeterminate length and require a closing bracket before a listener knows the speaker is through. Speakers can solve both of their problems by summarizing the main point of the narrative and expressing it abstractly.

In addition, speakers have a number of other devices at their disposal to wrap up a narrative and bring the listener back to the present (Labov & Fanshel, 1977). In the cowboy movie summaries, speakers typically summarized the moral of the movie (e.g., "[They] realize that . . . men can change"), used highly conventionalized ending signals (e.g., "Glen and Laura kissed, and they lived happily ever after"), or baldly stated that they were finished. Except for the few speakers who were cut off when they ran out of time, every speaker used some obvious method to indicate when the summary was over.

SPEECH ACTS

We have discussed the ways that speakers plan the overall structure or outline of what they have to say and then decide how to fill in some of the details. At a lower level of abstraction, speakers also plan speech acts. Conversations as a whole fulfill social functions or goals. Their components, such as sentences, do as well. According to Austin (1962) and Searle (1970, 1976), speakers utter a sentence for some social end and to achieve some social effect. Speech acts are sentences used to perform social actions, in which the action is performed by virtue of the speaker's utterance. For example, in the clergy's utterance "I hereby pronounce you husband and wife," the pronouncement itself transforms a couple's status from unmarried to married. Speakers use their sentences to assert, question, beg, apologize, threaten, announce, bet, and perform many other actions. If a performative verb X fits comfortably in the frame "I hereby X you . . . ," X probably introduces a speech action (Clark & Clark, 1977).

Taxonomies.   Basing their taxonomies primarily on analytic considerations, Austin (1962), Vendler (1972), and Searle (1975) have attempted to classify actions that speakers perform when they utter sentences. For example, Searle identified five basic speech act classes, based on variations that sentences show on three primary dimensions:

1. The purpose of an act (e.g., commands get someone to do something; assertions represent how something is).
2. The direction of fit between words and the world (e.g., assertions mirror the way the world is; orders or promises attempt to change the world).
3. The psychological states expressed (e.g., assertions express a belief; apologies express a regret; promises express an intention).

Searles' basic categories include *representatives* such as stating, deducing, and asserting, *directives* such as ordering, requesting, and permitting, *commissives* such as promising and committing, *expressives* such as apologizing, condemning, and congratulating, and *declaratives* such as quitting, nominating, and grading.

In their extensive analysis of 15 minutes of a therapy session, Labov and Fanshel (1977) developed a speech act taxonomy that partially overlaps with earlier work. Expanding on the work of Austin, Searle, and Vendler, Labov and Fanshel explicitly acknowledge the interactive nature of the relationship between speakers and listeners. They, therefore, organized their speech act classes in terms of actions oriented around a speaker's initiative and performed by both speakers and listeners. (See also Dore, 1977, for another example of a speech act taxonomy that takes social roles and obligations into account.) They identified four groups of speech acts that their subjects used:

1. Metalinguistic speech acts, such as *initiating, interrupting, repeating,* or *ending,* have to do with the regulation of speech itself.

2. Representations, such as *giving information* or *expressing emotion,* are concerned with events. The truth of some representations is indisputable, in that speakers have private knowledge. In this case all that listeners can do is *acknowledge* or *reinforce* the previous speech act. The truth of other events is disputable, for example, when speakers are *asserting, giving evaluations,* or *giving interpretations.* The listener can then *deny, agree, give support,* or *reinterpret* what the speaker said.

3. Speech acts that concern the speakers' requests, such as *requests* themselves, *mitigations, acknowledgments, reinstatements,* or *renewals,* are a third class. Here, the listeners' response may be to *carry out the request, put it off,* or *refuse it* with or without an explanation.

4. Acts that concern challenges are a fourth class. These include *challenges* and *questions,* as well as *retreats* and *mitigations,* on the part of speakers, and *defenses* and *admissions* on the part of listeners.

Labov and Fanshel present a methodological and theoretical tour de force in their detailed analysis of the workings of a therapy session. On the theoretical level they have documented the nested nature of speech acts and the extent to which what is said in discourse is conveyed through indirect speech acts. The next section develops their theoretical contribution more fully.

Indirect Speech-acts

A number of linguists and psycholinguists have distinguished between direct and indirect speech acts (e.g., Austin, 1962; Searle, 1970, 1975). Direct speech acts are those expressed by constructions specifically designed for those acts. Indirect speech acts express the same acts with constructions specifically designed for different acts. Thus, for example, the direct command ''I hereby command you to get me a drink'' and its elliptical form ''Get me a drink'' can also be expressed indirectly by constructions designed for questions (''Could you get me a drink?''), for assertions (''I'm thirsty''), or for apologies (''I'm sorry to have to ask you for a drink now'').

Labov and Fanshel note that understanding what goes on in an interaction requires peeling layers of meaning from what on the surface appears to be simple conversation. For example, Rhoda, the client in the therapy session that Labov and Fanshel studied, recounts that she asked her mother, ''When do you plan t'come home?''. The analysis of this simple utterance reveals a cascade of speech acts, each dependent for its meaning on the one before. Thus, this sentence is a direct request to her mother for information, an indirect request to her mother that she come home, and an indirect request to her mother for help, since that would be the purpose of her mother's return. In addition, this request for help is further an admission to her mother and her therapist that Rhoda needs help, a demonstration to her therapist that Rhoda has learned from him to be direct about her feelings, and an implicit criticism of her mother for not helping earlier.

It is an open question whether these layers of meaning, which Labov and Fanshel believe are *available* in most discourse, are actually intended by a speaker and typically understood by a listener during the course of their conversation, without the extensive micro-analysis that the researchers performed in Rhoda's case to extract meaning.

The availability of indirect meaning raises both dangers and benefits for speakers. On the one hand, listeners may over-interpret a communication, reading in meaning which was not intended, or they can under-interpret it, failing to notice intended meanings. On the other hand, as Goffman (1955, 1959) has noted, speakers can express socially unacceptable meanings through indirect meaning, while at the same time being able to deny them, claiming responsibility only for the direct meaning.

In addition to the theoretical points they make, on the methodological level, Labov and Fanshel's analysis shows what can be learned from a small piece of interaction when the analysts systematically combine all they know about the situation, its history, verbal behavior, nonverbal behavior, and general rules of interaction. Especially interesting to social psychologists is the attempt to link an analysis of conversation with an examination of personal change and a developing social relationship.

Implications for Person Perception

In addition to the direct, propositional content that they possess, speech acts help listeners form impressions of speakers. Most current work on social cognition is concerned with the ways that information about other people is conserved or transformed in a principled way. The goal is to develop models of or rules through which these transformations occur. A major deficiency in much of this work is its neglect of the first step in the cognitive process: the conversion of sensory information into symbolic form so that it can be manipulated using the rules of social cognition (cf. Higgins, 1981; Kraut & Poe, 1980).

Speech acts provide an entry-point into the cognitive system. They are one way of describing a complex and important social stimulus, discourse, in ways that have clear implications for listeners' impressions of speakers. For example, D'Andrade and Wish (1981; Wish, D'Andrade, & Goodnow, 1980) present data showing the relation between their speech act coding categories and some central dimensions of person perception and relationship perception. They analyzed conversations from National Educational Television's documentary, *The American Family*. This documentary presented a candid view of the naturally occurring communication that members of a middle-class California family had with each other and their associates. In their data, when the speaker expressed an approval reaction, he or she was judged both friendly and emotional. Refusing to comply with a request, expressing a disapproval reaction, evaluating a listener negatively, making a forceful assertion, and making a forceful request all led to the judgment that the speaker was hostile. All but the first of these speech acts also led to judgments that the speaker was dominant and emotional. (See also Davis & Holtgraves, 1982.)

Whether the speaker decides to perform the speech act directly or indirectly also has some important social consequences. Direct and indirect speech acts with the same propositional content, that is with the "same" meaning, differ in force, directness, politeness, and other social attributes. Thus, for example, women's speech with its greater proportion of indirect speech acts, especially indirect questions and requests, is judged to be less forceful. As a result, according to D'Andrade and Wish's analysis, women using this style should be judged less hostile, but also less dominant (cf. Lakoff, 1973, 1975, 1979; McConnell-Ginet, 1979; Thorne & Henley, 1975).

More specific theories exist explaining why different forms of the "same" speech-act differ in the impressions they inspire. For example, the perceived politeness of various requests can be explained in terms of a cost-benefit analysis of the direct meaning of an indirect request (Brown & Levinson, 1978; Clark & Schunk, 1980). The theory holds that requests are more polite as they incur less cost for the addressee. These costs include both the effort and expense of fulfilling the request and the loss of status and face (Goffman, 1955) that comes from following another person's orders. So, the indirect request "Would you get me a drink?" is judged more polite than the direct "Get me a drink." because the indirect request lowers the addressee's status less. Similarly, ability requests like "Could you get me a drink?" are judged more polite than commitment requests like "Would you get me a drink?" because the ability request gives the addressee more grounds for refusing and, therefore, saves more face (Clark & Schunk, 1980).

SENTENCES AND WORDS

We can think of the production of speech as the filling in of a nested series of flexible frames, from discourse, to speech-act, to sentence, to word. We have argued that conversation in general and some very high-level chunks of conversation, such as narratives, are well-structured. Each of these chunks of speech themselves can be broken down into increasingly smaller chunks, many of which, in turn, are well-structured.

At some point, the speaker must arrive at chunks that are small enough to be expressed in sentences (what Chafe, 1977 calls framing). Sentences express one or more propositions. The nouns in sentences play roles such as agent, object, experiencer, patient, location, and goal (Fillmore, 1968). These roles or cases are slots that speakers instantiate with particular words. The sentence and the word are the lowest levels of abstraction of general interest to social psychologists. Through word choice, speakers demonstrate the way they think about others. For this reason, and because the process of word choice sheds light on general issues of categorization, we consider this instantiation process in more detail.

The Meaning of Meaning

Word choice is akin to categorization. It is the application of a linguistic label to entities (e.g., objects, actions, events, states, or disposition) in the real or imagined world. As Brown (1958) has pointed out, we often speak of the name of a thing as if there were just one name. An entity, however, may have many potential names, depending how speakers categorize it and which aspects of it they wish to emphasize. Because naming is the matching of linguistic labels to meaning, it would be useful here to distinguish among different aspects of meaning.

Naming, Meaning, and Knowledge.   First, we distinguish between the information a person uses in applying labels to entities (i.e., naming), and the storehouse of facts and generalizations a person has about these entities—that person's encyclopedic knowledge about named categories. The linguistic or lexical meaning of a label is the subset of a person's total knowledge about categories that is used to classify or label instances as a member of some category. When people use a label, they are indicating what part of their encyclopedic knowledge about the category (e.g., physical appearance, functional attributes) is pertinent to the category membership assertion they are trying to make (cf. Miller & Johnson-Laird, 1976).

Entities need not have defining characteristics for speakers to name them (e.g., Rosch, 1973; Rosch & Mervis, 1975). Some entities are good examples or prototypes of a category and, therefore, have "natural" names (Rosch, 1973; Rosch & Mervis, 1975; Wittgenstein, 1953). For example, most kitchen and dining room chairs share enough physical, functional, and other qualities that they are easily categorized and named as chairs. On the other hand, as Brown and Lenneberg (1954) noted about colors, as Labov (in press) noted about cups, and as Chafe (1977) noted about jungle-gyms, some particular objects or entities do not share the prototypical qualities and are not easily categorized or named. Objects that are not highly codable are named either with longer words or with phrases rather than with single words. Moreover, they take longer to name, show less agreement in naming between subjects, and are less consistently named by a single subject (e.g., Berlin, 1972).

Even when an object is highly codable and could be named by its "natural" name, speakers often give a "non-natural" name because they are trying to emphasize non-prototypical attributes of the object. In the *Chaneysville Incident,* the protagonist, who is a historian, builds a small blaze made of pencils, index cards, and kindling. The novelist calls this a pyre rather than a fire. By using this word, he is emphasizing death, a break with the past, and a veneration of the past as well as the heat, light, and destructive force typical of fires (Bradley, 1981).

Metaphorical use of language, in which names are used to highlight some of an entities' innumerable characteristics, is common. Any theory of meaning that fails to account for it and what Clark (1981) calls the nonce sense of words (i.e., new meanings whose sense depends on the context) is inadequate.

Referent and Reference.   We can also usefully distinguish between the linguistic meaning of a label and the label's referent and reference (see Ogden & Richards, 1968). The *referent* of a label is the set of things in the real or imaginary world to which the label can apply. The *reference* of a label is the stored mental representation of the information about the referent. The reference of a label includes more of the speaker's total knowledge about the category to which the label applies and about the particular instance of that category than does the linguistic meaning of the label. For example, when calling a person "brother" the target's gender and relation to the speaker are basic to the linguistic meaning. The referent is the particular person designated, and the reference contains the speaker's knowledge of brothers in general and his own brother in particular.

Change of Meaning and Impression Formation.   These distinctions among meaning, referent, and reference shed light on the formation of impressions from verbal descriptions and on the effects of labeling on memory and on action.

Change-of-meaning.   Consider, for example, the debate in the impression formation literature about "change-of-meaning"—whether the meaning of a word varies as a function of the words with which it is combined. Asch (1946) proposed that impression formation is a gestalt-like process in which the elements are perceived in their dynamic interrelations, and that, therefore, an accurate understanding of impression formation cannot be obtained from the individual elements alone. This "holistic" approach to impression formation has been associated with the position that the meaning of a word varies across linguistic contexts (cf., Hamilton & Zanna, 1974; Wyer, 1974). The alternative point of view is that knowledge of the importance and value of each element considered in isolation is sufficient to allow an accurate prediction of the outcome of the impression formation process (cf. Anderson, 1971, 1974; Kaplan, 1971; Osgood, Suci, & Tannebaum, 1957). This "elementistic" approach to impression formation has been associated with the position that "change-of-meaning" is restricted to words with more than one precise meaning (i.e., homonyms).

With the earlier distinctions in mind, however, it is possible to take a "holistic" approach to impression formation without positing "change-of-meaning." Consistent with current psycholinguistic accounts of comprehension (cf. Clark & Clark, 1977), Higgins and Rholes (1976) suggest that the linguistic meaning of each term in a phrase and the grammatical relations among terms are used to form an integrated, holistic representation that forms a basis for evaluating the phrase as a whole.

Although the linguistic meaning of the terms does not generally change when combined with other terms, the reference of terms often changes across different linguistic contexts (cf. Higgins & Rholes, 1976). For example, the linguistic, color-meaning of "green" remains constant in the phrases "green lettuce" and "green bread." But once the linguistic meanings of the words have been combined to form a reference, the references that the phrases bring to mind are different. The reference for green lettuce is fresh lettuce and the reference for green bread is stale and moldy bread. Similarly, although the linguistic meaning of "casual" remains the same when associated with different roles (i.e., more nonchalant than the average role occupant), the implications of its reference in "casual surgeon" and "casual professor" are very different. In fact, even though "casual" and "surgeon" are each evaluated very positively when considered in isolation, their combination is evaluated very negatively.

Evaluative Meaning.   These distinctions are also useful in considering a related issue in the impression formation literature; namely, whether people's evaluative judgments from person descriptions are based upon the word's emotive and evaluative meaning or whether it is based on the word's linguistic meaning. Even those who have taken the holistic approach to impression formation have assumed that impressions are based upon the emotive meaning of person descriptions (e.g., Hamilton & Zanna, 1974). If words had an emotive meaning distinct from their linguistic meaning and from their reference, one might expect that people would simply combine the independent emotive meanings of the words to form an evaluation of another person. We need a holistic account, however, because people's evaluations are based on the reference constructed from the integration of the linguistic meanings of words—not their emotive meaning (cf. Higgins & Rholes, 1976). As Weinreich (1958) pointed out, the semantic meaning of a verbal description *as a whole* determines how it is evaluated, and not the evaluative or emotive meaning of its constituents. The positive evaluation of "The wicked witch is dead" is not due to some averaging of the emotive meanings of the individual words.

Labeling, Assertions, and Memory

The distinction between meaning and reference also leads us to reconsider how labeling can influence memory. Previous research on labeling effects has typically considered the effects of using different labels to describe the same stimulus (e.g., Carmichael, Hogan, & Walter, 1932; Kelley, 1950; Kraut, 1973; Loftus & Palmer, 1974; Thomas, DeCapito, Caronite, La Monica, & Hoving, 1968). For example, in Carmichael, Hogan, & Walter's (1932) classic study, subjects saw a series of ambiguous shapes. In different conditions, these stimuli had different labels or no labels attached to them (e.g., "curtains in a window" or "a diamond in a rectangle"; "eyeglasses" or "dumbbells"). When subjects subsequently had to draw what they had seen, their reproductions were strongly influenced by the labels attached to the stimuli. Thus, subjects who were exposed to the label "eyeglasses" drew pictures that were more like actual eyeglasses than did subjects exposed to the "dumbbell" label for the same stimulus. If we assume that people over time increasingly use their prior labeling of a stimulus as a basis for reconstructing the original stimulus information (cf., Bartlett, 1932; Higgins & Rholes, 1978; Neisser, 1967), then they should remember the stimuli differently to the extent that the encoding labels differ in meaning.

The distinction between meaning and reference, however, suggests another way that labeling can affect memory, namely, the case in which the meaning of an assertion remains the same but the reference for the assertion varies. To trace this effect, however, we must consider in more detail what it means to make an assertion. Our discussion focuses on trait assertions, which are frequently studied in the person perception literature.

The two statements "The Count is evil" and "The Count behaves in an evil manner" on first inspection appear to make basically the same assertion, once about the Count and once about his behavior. The linguistic and psycholinguistic literatures suggest, however, that these statements are different. (See also Wyer & Srull, 1980.) The statement that "A behaves in an X manner" asserts that A's behavior is an instance of the X category of acts. Thus, when we say "The Count behaves in an evil manner," we are asserting that his behavior shows sufficient malevolence, nastiness, and remorselessness to be classified as an instance of the category of evil acts. In contrast, the trait statement that "A is an X" asserts that A is more X than some standard or norm (cf., Clark, 1969; Huttenlocher & Higgins, 1971; Lyons, 1968; Vendler, 1968). Thus, saying "The Count is evil" is to assert that he is more evil than some standard.

In this analysis, one must then identify both the standard and the basis for comparison that is being talked about. For example, Jones and Davis (1965) suggest that for trait assertions the standard is that of the average or typical person and the basis of comparison is the magnitude (i.e., the intensity or extremity) of an action. In Kelley's (1967) covariation model, the standard is still the typical person, but the basis of comparison is the frequency of acts and their generality across situations. But these are not the only standards or bases of comparison. The standard may be the norm of some superordinate class of which the target of the assertion is a member. For example, the meaning of "Tom is fast" depends on whether he is a boy or a horse.

When there is a context available, the standard is often given by the context, which could be linguistic or extralinguistic. For example, in the comparative statement "Daniel is brighter than his classmates," the standard of intelligence is the linguistically mentioned classmates. It is likely that a teacher saying "Daniel is bright" would have in mind the implicit standard of the classmates, even if they weren't explicitly mentioned.

Although both the psycholinguistic and social psychological literatures suggest that the trait assertions are comparative, there are some problems with this account. A major one is that native speakers believe that the majority of the population possesses each of a large number of traits (i.e., that the majority of people are friendly, aggressive, energetic, and intelligent; Higgins & Winter, 1982). This suggests that to some extent speakers must also use a threshold criterion when applying some trait assertions. Thus, Roderick may still be judged friendly if he smiles often and pets little dogs, even if he does so less than the average person. To this extent, the assertion that Roderick is friendly and the assertion that he acts in a friendly way are based on more similar, absolute criteria than is classically assumed. (See Higgins, 1977a, for further discussion of when trait assertions are interpreted in more absolute terms.) Nevertheless, the fundamental property of trait assertions is that they involve an implicit comparison to some standard.

To the extent that trait assertions do involve such a comparison, this could cause an additional effect of labels on memory as well as raising problems for communication generally. The mental representation of the labeled person depends on the particular standard the perceiver has in mind. Thus, if the standard differs for different perceivers or if it changes over time for a particular perceiver, then the reference of the label may be different even though the label's linguistic meaning is the same.

Let us consider the case in which the standard changes over time. For example, Frank, a young juvenile delinquent has labeled Hank "tough," meaning tougher than the typical juvenile delinquent Frank has come in contact with. When Frank goes to prison and meets hardened criminals, his standards for assessing toughness change. When he returns to his neighborhood, he still remembers Hank as tough. Now this means very tough indeed, since Hank is still remembered as tougher than the standard toughness, but Frank's standard has shifted upward. (Higgins and Lurie [in press] found results consistent with this reasoning.)

The case in which two people, one a speaker and one a listener, have different standards is likely to lead to miscommunication. Imagine that Carol, a community college student tells Phil, a Ph.D. student from a prestigious school, that a friend is smart. If neither Carol nor Phil is aware of the other's background and, hence, are not aware of the other's different standards of comparison, Phil is likely to receive an inflated estimate of the friend's IQ. According to the cooperative principle and the maxim of sensitivity, speakers who are aware of differences in standards should modify their trait descriptions to highlight these differences. Thus, Carol should say "He's smart, for someone from my school." Similarly, if listeners are aware of the differences in standards, attribution theorists would argue that they should discount the trait description. Speakers' production of ritual insults such as "He's pretty smart . . . (pause) . . . for an aggie" show that people are capable of understanding these distinctions. There is as yet no evidence, however, that speakers and listeners actually perform such modifications.

The Role of Context

The context of communication has a major impact on both the production and the comprehension of messages. As stated earlier, for example, the standard involved in trait assertions is often provided by the linguistic or extralinguistic context. More generally, language use is interwoven with the accompanying activities and context, and both the appropriateness and the meaning of a speech event is dependent on the surrounding linguistic and non-linguistic context (cf. Applegate & Delia, 1980; Bolinger, 1975; Ervin-Tripp, 1969; Hintikka, 1973; Hymes, 1974; Wittgenstein, 1953). Different speech styles are appropriate for different physical settings, culturally defined occasions, topics, genres, communication modalities, and social relationships (Fondacaro & Higgins, in press; Hymes, 1974; Trudgill, 1974).

Context can influence trait assertions and labeling in a variety of ways. It can determine the words applied to a constantly conceived stimulus (i.e., a word-choice effect). The impact of context on word choice is especially evident in the literature on referential communication. Many studies have found that people will vary their labeling of a stimulus as a function of the context in which it appears (cf. Glucksberg, Krauss, & Higgins, 1975; Manis & Armstrong, 1971; Olson, 1970; Rosenberg & Cohen, 1966). Of course, variation in context could also directly influence a communicator's cognitive representation of the stimulus person, as well as influencing the trait or label applied to a constantly represented stimulus. In this case, differential labeling depending on context would reflect a cognitive contrast effect of context per se, rather than a word choice effect (cf. Krantz & Campbell, 1961; Simpson & Ostrom, 1976).

A study by Higgins and Lurie (in press) examined the ways in which context influences word choice and trait assertions. In this study, subjects read about the sentencing decisions of a target trial judge in the context of other trial judges who consistently gave either higher sentences or lower sentences than the target judge. As expected, the context influenced how they described the target: subjects were more likely to describe the target judge as lenient in the context of harsh judges and vice versa. This effect, however, was not due to a cognitive contrast effect that changed subjects' cognitive representation of the target. Although subjects' verbal labeling of the target (i.e., the trait assertion) was strongly influenced by context, their immediate recall of the target's sentencing decisions was not influenced by the context. That is, in this case context was influencing the way subjects used language and not the mental representation they had of the target.

AUDIENCE EFFECTS

In planning all aspects of discourse, from structure to word choice, speakers need to shape or tailor their message to suit their audience's attributes. In order to achieve their social goals with particular audiences, speakers must plan their speech with those audiences in mind. They make inferences about their audiences' mental states that are relevant to the achievement of their goals. The inferences are based on their prior knowledge of the audiences, many of the audience's observable social characteristics, and the situation that the speakers and listeners find themselves in.

Adjusting one's speech to a target is not simply a fillip appended to a pre-formed and otherwise asocial message. Instead, as Mead (1934) argued, this ability is at the core of communication and at the core of being social. Communication requires speakers' ability to infer what listeners already know so that speakers can phrase the message they provide. As Clark (in press) has persuasively argued, adjustment or coordination—"the idea that speakers attempt to coordinate what they say with the interpretations their addressees impute to what they say"—"is central at all levels of language—from individual words to conversations and narratives."

The concept of coordination is so central to communication, that researchers may be tempted to dismiss it or overlook it because of its obviousness. "Of course," one might protest, "people cannot communicate unless they agree on a common language, with a common vocabulary and syntax." We argue, however, that the challenge to researchers in social cognition is to go beyond Mead's proclamation of the centrality of coordination and trace both the mechanisms through which people manage to coordinate communication and the cognitive and social consequences of the coordination. Researchers in social cognition, with a heritage in social and cognitive psychology, are uniquely suited to the study of communication; the study of communication should be at the heart of their concerns.

The sections below present a sampling of the work needed to understand the coordination of communication. This sampling is intended to illustrate both the importance of the problem as well as some approaches to solving it. For a more systematic and theoretical account of this topic, see Clark (in press).

Mutual Knowledge

As we have said, coordination is basic to communication. Chafe (1975) argues that many basic distinctions in language use, for example, the distinctions between new and given information, between definite and indefinite reference, or between subject and comment, are all based on the speakers' assessment of what addressees know or can be expected to know (see also Clark & Clark, 1977).

The New-given Distinction.   Consider the distinction between new and given information in a sentence. New information is that which speakers want listeners to be aware of, and given information is the information that speakers assume to be activated in the listeners' consciousness (Clark & Haviland, 1977). For example, if a speaker saw someone admiring a picture on his wall, he might say, "I bought it last week." In English, and perhaps all languages, given information is conveyed in a weaker and more attenuated form than new information (Chafe, 1975; Li, 1975). In this example, the idea of the picture is treated as given and hence pronounced with low pitch and weak stress, as well as being pronominalized as "it."

Definite Reference. Speakers may also use definite or indefinite pronouns and noun phrases, depending on whether they assume that the addressee is able to identify the referent. Thus, speakers would say "Shall I buy it?" rather "Shall I buy anything?" and "Shall I buy the camera?" rather than "Shall I buy a camera?" depending on whether they think their listeners will understand which "it" and "camera" they are talking about. The basic principle underlying the web of rules for pronoun reference (Chafe, 1974; Cole, 1974; Halliday & Hasan, 1976; Langacker, 1969; Ross, 1967) seems to be that pronouns should be used only when the referent is in the listener's consciousness (Chafe, 1974), either when the referent is physically present in the situation surrounding the speech or linguistically present in the surrounding speech (Halliday & Hasan, 1976).

Clark and Marshall (1981) have considered the issue of definite reference in more detail. They argue that to use definite reference correctly, speakers must be aware of what the listener is aware of, including the listener's knowledge of the speaker's knowledge of the listener, ad infinitum. They consider why the establishment of mutual knowledge—conversationalists' shared knowledge of the world, including each other's knowledge of the world—does not become an infinite regress, in which neither party can be sure what the other knows, thus dragging speech to a halt.

Clark and Marshall argue that speakers solve the problem through a "copresence" heuristic. Speakers assume that when they, the addressee, and the referent of the object or situation which they are talking about are all present simultaneously, the mutual knowledge regress has been solved. The simultaneous presence can be physical, as when both speaker and listener are present in the same place as the object; it can be linguistic, as when the object has been introduced recently in the conversation; or it can be indirect. In the indirect case, speakers assume that the social and historical background which they and the addressee share means that they also have common beliefs about the object and they have the knowledge that they share these beliefs.

According to Clark and Marshall, these different methods of establishing mutual knowledge lead to speakers' using different linguistic forms to express their meanings. Regardless of the validity of the details of their positions, both Chafe's and Clark and Marshall's main point is important. In order to communicate to another and use appropriate linguistic forms during the communication, speakers must establish with some accuracy the current state of their listeners' consciousness.

Audience Characteristics

Speakers can use some aspects of their listeners' relatively stable characteristics to help them to develop appropriate communication. These include characteristics such as age, race, sex, social class, relationship to the speaker, attitudes, intelligence, and occupation. Which attributes of listeners are relevant to the speakers' planning depends to a large degree on the speaker's social goals.

Global Audience Characteristics.   Some audience attributes that influence communication seem generally relevant if the speaker wishes to communicate at all. Factors like age, fluency, mental disabilities, and hearing disabilities have implications for the extent to which listeners can apprehend and comprehend speech. Thus, for example, many writers have noted the vocabulary and syntax shifts that occur in speech when adults talk to young children; they talk more in the here and now, and use simpler vocabulary and simpler and better formed syntax (e.g., Gelman & Shatz, 1977; Holtzman, 1972; Newport, 1976; Sachs & Devin, 1976; Shatz & Gelman, 1973; Snow, 1972). In the extreme their speech is cast in the highly distinctive ''baby-talk'' register (Ferguson, 1977). Normal speakers also use a varient of baby-talk when describing objects to retarded adults and foreigners as well, presumably because the listeners' characteristics are cues to their ability to understand conversation (Coleman, 1982).

Modification of speech to adapt it to listeners' characteristics is very general. Even young children can adapt their communication to a listener's lack of a common visual perspective (e.g., Maratsos, 1973), lack of common knowledge (Menig-Peterson, 1975), age (Sachs & Devin, 1976; Shatz & Gelman, 1973), social status (Shatz & Gelman, 1977), linguistic level (Masur, 1978), and communicative responsiveness (Masur, 1978; see Schmidt & Paris, 1981, and Shatz, 1983 for reviews).

Social Goals.   Other adjustments that speakers make to their conversation on the basis of listeners' characteristics seem more closely tied to the speakers' specific social motives. We have stressed that speakers use conversation to meet their social goals. How they do this depends jointly on the goal and on the audience.

For example, in a conversation to inform another, what speakers say must depend on what they believe addressees know. In a recent study, Higgins, McCann, and Fondacaro (1982) examined whether communicators would modify their message about stimulus person information as a function of the amount of topic-related information they and their listeners held in common (see also Flavell, Botkin, Fry, Wright, Jarvis, 1968; Higgins, 1977b). The communicators read an essay describing the behaviors of a stimulus person whom they were to describe to a partner. When the communicators believed that their addressee had different information about the stimulus person they were more likely to ''stick to the facts'' (i.e., less distortion, deletion, and polarization) than when they believed that their addressee had received similar information. Thus, communicators took into account what their addressee knew in constructing messages. They probably reasoned that relatively uninformed addressees couldn't be expected to correct misimpressions speakers might generate. If speakers' intentions were to deceive, however, uninformed addressees would place fewer constraints on them and, hence, lead to more flamboyant lying.

In another example, speakers' use of different vocabulary, syntax, and intonational patterns helps to establish what have been labeled "casual," "intimate," or "deferential" speech registers. Which speech register they adopt depends on the social relationship they have or wish to develop with their conversational partner. The social relationship depends, in turn, on who the partner is. This point is illustrated by the dilemma some speakers find themselves in when they have to satisfy simultaneously two audiences with whom they have different social relationships. For example, when a husband calls his wife at her office, he can often tell if she has a stranger in the office because she adopts a formal style in response to his small-talk instead of her normal intimate style.

Speakers' goals for a conversation often are based on personal motives. They can, however, be based on a general goal orientation derived from social group membership, such as social class, cultural or ethnic membership, or sex. Bernstein (1970), for example, has argued that working class speech emphasizes social relationship goals more than does middle class speech. These goals, combined with a working class social world that is more homogeneous than is the middle class world, lead to a working class speech style that is characterized by a "restricted code." In this speech style "orders of meaning are particularistic, . . . principles are linguistically implicit, . . . and . . . much of the meaning is embedded in the context and may be restricted to those who share a similar contextual history" (Bernstein, 1970). Compared to an "elaborated code," Bernstein describes the restricted code as having such features as repetitive use of conjunctions, individual qualification implicit in sentence organization, frequent requests that a previous speech sequence be reinforced (e.g., "Wouldn't it?", "You know."), and use of idiomatic phrases. (But see Labov, 1970, and Higgins, 1976a, for alternative viewpoints.)

In a similar vein, many writers have asserted that women are more motivated by social relationship goals than are men. If this assertion is correct, it may help explain why women's speech is less assertive than men's (see Lakoff, 1973, 1975, & 1979). Language use can also be dictated by group-identity goals. Bourhis, Giles, Leyens, and Tajfel (1979), for instance, found that Flemish students were more likely to switch from English to Flemish in an English language lab when confronted with a non-Flemish questioner who was unsympathetic toward the Flemish language.

One frequent way in which speakers modify their message to suit their audiences is by changing their speech to agree with the audiences' beliefs, attitudes, and evaluations. For example, communicators modify their message about an issue to suit the recipients' position on the issue (Higgins, 1981; Manis, Cornell, & Moore, 1974; Newtson & Czerlinsky, 1974). Similarly, communicators modify their description of a target person to agree generally with the recipient's attitude toward the target (Higgins & Rholes, 1978). And, significantly, communicators do not take into account sufficiently the influence of the audience on their message content when they subsequently use the message to reconstruct the original stimulus information and evaluate the target, which causes distortions in their subsequent judgments and memory of the target (e.g., Higgins & Rholes, 1978).

The tendency to adapt one's speech to fulfill one's social goals with a particular audience can also be influenced by the communicator's personality and the social relationship between the communicator and the audience. Higgins and McCann (in press), for example, have found that high authoritarians modify their message toward their audience's attitude to a greater extent than do low authoritarians. This effect occurs when the audience has higher status than they do but not when the audience has equal status. There is also evidence that high self-monitors, who carefully attend to cues from others about the way they should behave, modify their messages to suit the audience more than do low self-monitors (McCann & Hancock, 1983).

Functions of Speech Adjustment.   Why do speakers make these modifications in their speech to suit the audiences they talk to? The dominant assumption is that these adjustments make speech more appropriate to audiences' needs and thereby improve the communication, in the sense of helping speakers achieve their social goals.

Surprisingly little research has tested whether speech generated for a particular audience improves communication to that audience over others and helps speakers reach their social goals. Instead, the typical research attempts to show that speakers change their speech according to the audience, examines the nature of these changes, and then makes *prima facie* arguments about the appropriateness of the changes. For example, Freedle, Naus, and Schwartz (1977) demonstrated that when adults retold stories for other adults or for children, a judge could identify the audiences from the stories alone and the stories differed in vocabulary and other transformations. Yet this research did not explicitly examine whether adults better understood the stories meant for them than the stories meant for children (see also Gelman & Shatz, 1977).

The improvement-in-communication argument is most tenable when applied to the simplified, baby-talk-like registers spoken to young children, foreigners, and the retarded. Here the simplified vocabulary and syntax, redundancy, and extended explanations probably simplify a too-complex message, and the higher pitch and intonational variability heighten interest, so that the child can pay attention to, understand, and respond to the message (Gelman & Shatz, 1977; Newport, 1976).

The argument may also apply to speakers' modification of their expressed attitudes and evaluations to appear consistent with their audience's beliefs. This change is likely to lead to greater liking between speakers and listeners (Byrne, 1961) and to avoid social conflict. It may also make communication more persuasive, since it is likely to be in the audiences' lattitude of acceptance (e.g., Sherif & Hovland, 1961). Since affiliation and attitude change are two of the major goals for which conversation is a tool, in these cases speech adjustment is likely to increase goal attainment.

The role of speech adjustment in increasing communication and social goal attainment is less obvious for other types of audience adjustments, however. For example, the simplified registers used for lovers, pets, the elderly, and the sick do not seem to serve the goal of simplifying language. They are used to fulfill some social relationship goals—to express concern and affection—but the form of the speech seems related to these uses only through convention. Similarly, the formal speech used in classroom lectures and professional presentations decreases communication by making the vocabulary and syntax more complex (Brown & Fraser, 1979). Here, however, it may enhance self-presentational goals, giving an academic talk the veneer of competence, even if no one understands it.

Krauss, Vivekananthan, and Weinheimer (1968) have demonstrated that, in the extreme, the adjustments one speaker makes for different audiences improve communication with each audience. That is, speakers communicate more accurately when they are shaping their speech for other people rather than for themselves. In their research, communicators described colors for themselves (nonsocial message) or for another person (social message). Communicators later served as recipients of the messages, identifying colors based on their own nonsocial messages, another communicator's non-social messages, and another communicator's social messages. Accuracy in identifying colors was greatest for names that communicators themselves had supplied, intermediate for others' social messages, and lowest for others' non-social messages. Communicators used their own color names with equal accuracy, regardless of whether the names had been given under social or nonsocial instructions. (But see also Danks, 1970.)

Krauss' work shows that social communication is indeed more communicative than is non-social communication. But we have found no research demonstrating that speech modification improves communication for audience differences less extreme than self versus others. For example, Kraut and Gomez (in preparation) had expert, intermediate, and novice cooks describe recipes in an indexing task so that either expert cooks or novice cooks could locate them on the basis of the descriptions. Although communicators describing for experts tended to use more esoteric language, there was no evidence that the language directed toward one type of audience was more appropriate for that audience. For example, it did not overlap more with the language that the particular audience produced when in the role of communicator.

Consequences of Speech Adjustment. Although some of the causes of speech adjustment remain unclear, it is clear that these modifications can have both social and individual consequences. For example, as mentioned earlier, speakers' memories, impressions, and attitudes after communication tend to be consistent with the information that they communicated even though this information was biased by the communicative context (See Higgins, 1981 and Mc-Cann & Higgins, in press, for reviews). When the communication situation caused speakers to provide inaccurate or incomplete descriptions of a target, their own memories of the target also became inaccurate and incomplete. In some ways, this research is reminiscent of work on counterattitudinal advocacy, which also found that communicators' advocacy of a position caused changes in the communicators' own attitudes (Festinger, 1952; Janis & King, 1954; Wicklund & Brehm, 1976).

The literature on person perception suggests that some speech adjustments could have large effects on how speakers are perceived, regardless of the adjustments' effects on the effectiveness of the communication or the achievement of other social goals. For example, the verbal components of being polite, including tag questions (e.g., . . . , don't you?), qualifiers (e.g., sort of), and compound requests (e.g., Won't you close the door?) lead to judgments that the speaker is warmer and less assertive as well as more polite (Erickson, Lind, Johnson, & O'Barr 1978; Giles, 1979, Newcombe & Arnkoff 1979). Similarly, the adjustments majority speakers make when speaking to minority members often give the impression that the speaker is patronizing and distant and, in turn, affect the recipients' behavior and conversational style (e.g., Erickson, 1979; Word, Zanna, & Cooper, 1974).

Feedback

To this point we have concentrated on mechanisms through which communicators enact their plans for their speech through internal, cognitive processes. For example, speakers rely on their personal knowledge of the discourse structure they are planning and their anticipations of how their communication performance will influence their audience.

But of course speakers also get almost continuous feedback from their listeners' verbal, paralinguistic, and nonverbal behavior. This feedback provides them with information about the listeners' cognitive and affective states that helps speakers form and reform their speech. These mechanisms are important for social psychology, both because they are central to communication and because they provide an interesting arena for the study of person perception. In addition to forming their speech, speakers are engaged in online judgments of their partners' transient states that have immediate consequences for their own behavior.

The ability to take the perspective of the audience towards one's own speech, which Mead (1934) and others have identified as the central component of being social, is at best a semi-social activity. The problem of course is that planning speech with an audience in mind is performed in relation to an imaginary audience that may not match any real one. As a result, the communication may not have been adapted appropriately for the audience for whom it was intended.

The problem of misexecuting a communication further compounds the problem of misplanning a communication for a particular audience. Linguists and psycholinguists have identified a large number of syntactic, semantic, and pragmatic rules that speakers must obey in order to perform skilled speech. While native speakers of the language are presumed to have the competence to follow the rules, their actual performances show large numbers of violations (e.g., Maclay & Osgood, 1959). For example, consider the example presented by Halliday and Hasan (1975):

Child: Why does THAT one come out?
Parent: That what?
Child: THAT one.
Parent: That what?
Child: That ONE!
Parent: That one what?
Child: That lever there that you push to let the water out.

This example represents a failure of a child to accommodate her discourse to the perspective of a parent. This is not to say that children cannot accommodate to a particular audience's knowledge, for we have seen above that they can. But the process is hard and mistakes are inevitable.

Adults frequently make similar mistakes, for example, not clarifying which part of a nested construction the indefinite pronoun "that" refers to. While Clark and Marshall (1981) have pointed out the importance of mutual knowledge in the conduct of conversation (i.e., the speaker's and listener's knowledge of what they are mutually aware of), they have not emphasized the frequent difficulty for both parties in determining what each is aware of. The well-known tendency to overgeneralize applies here: we all assume that others are more similar to ourselves than they actually are (Nisbett & Ross, 1980; Ross, 1977). In particular, speakers tend to assume that what they know is also clear to listeners. While this may be the cause of numerous errors in communication, little research with adults has addressed the issue, although this issue has received considerable attention in the developmental literature (see Glucksberg et al., 1975, for a review).

Speakers can sometimes catch and correct their planning and execution errors, simply by evaluating their own productions from the perspective of the language community. From a face-saving perspective, they would generally prefer to make the correction themselves rather than be corrected by a partner (Schegloff, Jefferson, & Sacks, 1977). But given the difficulty of the task, they may not be able to perform as much self-correction as they need.

In summary, while speakers can plan conversational constituents, both their planning and their execution may lead to communication problems. The difficulties of simultaneously planning future speech, executing current speech, and evaluating past speech mean that speakers frequently cannot catch all their miscalculations and mistakes through self-evaluation. By using feedback from actual listeners, speakers can modify their plans and repair their execution based on evidence of the communication outcome of the conversation.

Semantically Meaningful Feedback.   What evidence do we have that speakers attend to the feedback they get from their listeners and modify their speech accordingly? We can distinguish between two types of feedback that audiences provide speakers. First is the semantically meaningful speech that listeners provide when they take up the speaking turn. Almost everything that one speaker says in response to the other informs the original speaker about the responder's understanding, agreement with, and interest in the original remark. These responses may not be intended to provide feedback; the simple requirement that conversationalists be relevant to the context and the topic at hand, however, means that a speaker can often glean a listener's reaction from the listener's response.

The means through which conversationalists maintain discourse coherence (i.e., make sequential speaking turns appropriate and relevant to each other) also serve the feedback functions we have been discussing. For example, imagine that Ralph says "We used to live on the highway. When we first moved up there, it was terrible sleeping because of all those semis." When Norton responds "Yeah, I'm sympathetic; we had them too," his answer and his use of the pronoun "them" provides evidence that he understood the gist of the comment and understood the problematic "semis" as semi-tractor trailer trucks (cf. Schegloff et al., 1977).

Adjacency pairs are the especially strong links between successive speaking turns. For example, they include questions and answers, summons and responses (Schegloff, 1968), requests and grants (Clark & Clark, 1977), and apologies and acknowledgments (Goffman, 1971). They provide an interesting case of feedback mechanism. Because the second member of the pair is obligatory rather than optional, a failure to offer it constitutes evidence that the speech is inadequate and must be repaired. As a result, speakers use adjacency pairs as conversational devices to elicit a response from a partner (Bloom & Lahey, 1978), in part to test their partners' comprehension. Indeed, in the eavesdropping research described earlier (Kraut et al., 1982), listeners used this device to discover if their speech was getting through to their partners. In this research about one third of subjects who were eavesdropping on a conversation between two others discovered that their own microphones had been disconnected. Almost all subjects who discovered this, did so by asking a question or making some other comment that *required* a contingent response from a partner.

Back Channel Feedback.   Speakers also rely on back channel responses (Yngve, 1970) to gauge their audience's reaction. Listener responses or back channel communications are the small visual and auditory comments an auditor makes while a speaker is talking, without taking over the speaking turn. Unlike general nonverbal reactivity (e.g., eye-contact) or full semantic responses (i.e., a listener's taking over the speaking turn), back channel responses seem to be specialized communication devices to provide feedback to speakers during conversation. They occur frequently in conversation, and seem to have little function other than to inform a speaker of a listener's mental state. Back channel responses include clarifying questions, brief verbal responses such as "yeah," "m-hmm," and the like, head nods, brief smiles, repetitions of the speaker's words, and brief sentence completions (Duncan, 1974). The boundary between them, however, and actual exchanges of a speaking turn is not sharp.

During the course of their conversation, speakers periodically indicate to their listeners that they need feedback about whether their partners are paying attention to what they are saying, are interested in it, are understanding it, and are agreeing with it. Kraut and Bricker (1981) have shown that speakers can use all modalities to invite feedback from their partners. In this research, judges agreed reliably about occasions when they thought listeners' feedback would be appropriate, and their judgments were correlated moderately with occasions when listeners actually gave feedback.

Research by Duncan and his colleagues (e.g., Duncan, 1974), by Dittman (e.g., Dittmann & Llewellyn, 1968), and by Kendon (e.g., 1967) shows many of the ways speakers invite listener feedback. The speaker's shift in head direction toward the partner, completion of a grammatical phrase (Duncan & Fiske, 1977), and the termination of a phonemic clause (Dittmann & Llewellyn, 1968) are examples of such signals. While listeners' back channel responses overwhelmingly occur following these speaker behaviors, the invitational signals appear to allow an optional response. Other results in Kraut and Bricker's research (1981) show that speakers provide many more opportunities for listeners to offer listener responses than listeners actually take advantage of.

Although many writers have speculated that variations of listener responses indicate to speakers the degree to which listeners are paying attention, are understanding points being made, or are agreeing with them (e.g., Yngve, 1970; Rosenfeld, 1978), research to date has been more suggestive than definitive. For example, Leathers (1979) suggested that judges of verbal and nonverbal feedback signals can reliably interpret them as messages about the responder's involvement, state of confusion, thoughtfulness, and affective reaction to what had previously been said.

Kraut and Lewis (Kraut et al., 1982; Kraut & Lewis, in press) have demonstrated that speakers' attention to feedback changes the quality of their communication and have examined some of the mechanisms through which feedback influences communication. For example, in a study by Kraut et al. (1982), speakers tried to describe a movie so that listeners could in turn summarize it. A subject either engaged in a two-way conversation with the speaker (participant-listener) or eavesdropped on a conversation between a speaker and a participant-listener. As speakers received more feedback from their partners, their communication improved. Both listeners who provided the feedback and listeners who eavesdropped on the conversation understood the movie better as their speaker received more feedback. This finding implies that feedback from any listener provides speakers with information about what the speech community as a whole needs in order to understand the communication better. The research also showed that feedback individuates speech, making it especially suited to the person providing feedback; listeners who provided the feedback understood the movie better than listeners who merely eavesdropped on the identical conversation.

Many studies have shown that speakers who receive feedback talk more than speakers who do not (e.g., Kraut & Lewis, in press; Kraut et al., 1982; Matarazzo, Wiens, Sastow, Allen, & Weitman, 1964), and yet feedback does not seem to regulate communication through a traditional reinforcement mechanism. Indeed, on a micro-level, feedback abbreviates speech rather than lengthens it. For example, Krauss and Weinheimer (1964) found that when speakers got feedback as they were describing objects, they used the feedback to confirm that their partners had understood the ad hoc, shorthand expressions they were developing to describe the objects. As a result, they tended to shorten their descriptions over time, unlike speakers who received no feedback. Similarly, Kraut and Lewis (in press) found that immediately after listeners provided feedback, speakers tended to finish talking about a topic and to move up a level of abstraction in developing a theme.

Some listener responses such as "What?" or "Huh?" provide direct information about listeners' comprehension. At other times speakers may interpret listener responses as conventional attentional signals with little specific meaning. Following these signals, speakers may continue with their pre-planned speech. On the other hand, if they fail to receive a listener response when one was appropriate and when they called for one, they may interpret this failure as an implicit signal that the listeners did not understand or agree with a point. To test this hypothesis, Kraut and Bricker (in preparation) developed techniques to identify occasions when invited listener responses failed to occur. They then examined what speakers did when listeners had provided or failed to provide listener responses at appropriate or inappropriate times. Contrary to expectation, speakers did not change the information density of their next utterances following the presence or absence of listener responses, regardless of whether they were appropriate or not. The results suggest that minimal back channel feedback, of the head nod and "m-hmm" variety, may indicate little more than attention, rather than indicating understanding.

GENERAL CONCLUSIONS

The purpose of this chapter has been to provide a brief introduction to and overview of interpersonal communication from the perspective of the social interactional goals that drive it and the social conventions and constraints that shape it. This perspective emphasizes the inherently social nature of communication, which should be of special interest to social psychologists. We believe that communication should be a central topic in social psychology for a number of reasons.

First, communication is itself a major type of social behavior that reflects the impact of important social factors, such as social interactional goals, interpersonal orientation, the social definition of a situation, personality, social roles, and cultural values and conventions. Second, communication mediates many other types of interpersonal behavior and relations, including friendship, interpersonal attraction, aggression, interpersonal conflict, helping, and social influence. Thus, a familiarity with the nature of interpersonal communication should enrich our understanding of these interpersonal domains. Third, even for social psychological areas that typically have not been conceptualized or examined in terms of social interaction, such as impression formation, communication variables can play a significant role, as we have seen. In fact, investigating person perception in the context of communicative interaction would enhance its external validity and generalizability and yield new insights into its complex, interdependent nature. Fourth, conducting research in social psychology necessarily involves various kinds of communication. Therefore it is important for researchers to be sensitive to the ways their choice of communication situations might influence their findings.

The determinants and consequences of interpersonal communication also play a significant role in social cognition. We have reviewed various ways in which communication influences the verbal encoding and representation of people and social events. Not only is this an important aspect of the general process of encoding and representing social stimuli, but it also provides an especially well-articulated and well-developed model of this process. In addition, we have provided examples of the ways such encoding and representation influence people's subsequent judgments, evaluations, and memory of social stimuli. Thus, the area of communication provides both an avenue for studying the cognition of social psychology (i.e., the cognitive mediators of social behavior) and an especially useful way of examining the social psychology of cognition (i.e., the social or interpersonal determinants of information processing). By using this window on the pragmatics of social cognition, social psychologists can shed new light on the nature of social information processing and behavior.

ACKNOWLEDGMENT

This research was supported by NSF grants BNS-07963 and BNS-8141319 to Robert Kraut, and by a National Institute of Mental Health Grant, RO1MH31427, to E. Tory Higgins.

REFERENCES

Anderson, N. H. Two more tests against change of meaning in adjective combinations. *Journal of Verbal Learning and Verbal Behavior*, 1971, *10*, 75–85.

Anderson, N. H. Cognitive algebra: Integration theory applied to social attribution. In L. Berkowitz (Ed.), *Advances in experimental social psychology*. New York: Academic Press, 1974.

Applegate, J. L., & Delia, J. G. Person-centered speech, psychological development, and the contexts of language use. In R. St. Clair & H. Giles (Eds.), *The social and psychological contexts of language*. Hillsdale, N.J.: Lawrence Erlbaum Associates, 1980.

Asch, S. E. Forming impressions of personality. *Journal of Abnormal and Social Psychology*, 1946, *41*, 258–290.

Austin, J. *How to do things with words*. Oxford: Oxford University Press, 1962.

Bartlett, F. *Remembering*. Cambridge: Cambridge University Press, 1932.

Berlin, B. Speculations on the growth of ethnobotanical nomenclature. *Language in Society*, 1972, *1*, 51–86.

Bernstein, B. *Theoretical studies towards a sociology of language*. Routledge & Kegan Paul, 1970.

Bloom, L., & Lahey, M. *Language development and language disorders*. New York: Wiley, 1978.

Bolinger, D. *Aspects of language (2nd ed.)*. New York: Harcourt Brace Jovanovich, 1975.

Bourhis, R., Giles, H., Leyens, J., & Tajfel, H. Psycholinguistic distinctiveness: Language divergence in Belgium. In H. Giles & R. St. Clair (Eds.), *Language and social psychology*. Oxford: Blackwell, 1979.

Bradley, D. *Chaneysville Incident*. New York: Harper and Row, 1981.

Brown, P., & Levinson, S. Universals in language usage: Politeness phenomena. In E. Goody (Ed.), *Questions and politeness*. Cambridge: Cambridge University Press, 1978.

Brown, P., & Fraser, C. Speech as a marker of situation. In K. Scherer & H. Giles (Eds.), *Social markers in speech*. New York, Cambridge University Press, 1979.

Brown, R. How shall a thing be called? *Psychological Review*, 1958, *65*, 14–21.

Brown, R., & Lenneberg, E. A study in language and cognition. *Journal of Abnormal and Social Psychology*, 1954, *19*, 454–462.

Byrne, D. Interpersonal attraction and attitude similarity. *Journal of Abnormal and Social Psychology*, 1961, *67*, 713–715.

Carmichael, L., Hogan, H., & Walter, A. An experimental study of the effects of language on the reproduction of visually perceived form. *Journal of Experimental Psychology*, 1932, *15*, 72–86.

Chafe, W. L. Language and consciousness. *Language*, 1974, *50*, 111–133.

Chafe, W. L. Givenness, contrastiveness, definiteness, subjects, topics, and point of view. In C. Li (Ed.), *Subject and topic*. New York: Academic Press, 1975.

Chafe, W. L. Creativity in verbalization and its implications for the nature of stored knowledge. In R. Freedle (Ed.), *Discourse production and comprehension*. Norwood, N.J.: Ablex, 1977.

Clark, E. How young children describe events in time. In G. B. Flores d'Arcais & W. J. Levelt (Eds.), *Advances in psycholinguistics*. Amsterdam: North-Holland Publishing, 1970.

Clark, H. Linguistic processes in deductive reasoning. *Psychological Review*, 1969, *76*, 387–404.

Clark, H. Inferences in comprehension. In D. LaBerge & S. Samuels (Eds.), *Basic processes in reading: Perception and comprehension*. Hillsdale, N.J.: Lawrence Erlbaum Associates, 1977.

Clark, H. Making sense of nonce sense. In G. B. Flores d'Arcais & R. Jarrelle (Eds.), *The process of understanding language*. New York: Wiley, 1981.

Clark, H. Language use and language users. In G. Lindzey & E. Aronson (Eds.), *Handbook of social psychology (3rd Ed.)*. Reading, Mass.: Addison-Wesley, in press.

Clark, H., & Clark, E. *Psychology and language*. New York: Harcourt Brace Jovanovich, 1977.

Clark, H., & Haviland, S. Comprehension and the given-new contract. In R. Freedle (Ed.), *Discourse production and comprehension*. Norwood, N.J.: Ablex, 1977

Clark, H., & Marshall, C. Definite reference and mutual knowledge. In A. Joshi, I. Sag, & B. Webber (Eds.), *Elements of discourse understanding*. Cambridge: Cambridge University Press, 1981.

Clark, H., & Schunk, D. Polite responses to polite requests. *Cognition*, 1980, *8*, 111–143.

Cole, P. Indefiniteness and anaphoricity. *Language*, 1974, *50*, 665–674.

Coleman, L. *Co-occurring features in speech registers*. Unpublished manuscript. University of Michigan, Ann Arbor, Michigan, 1982.

Cushman, D., & Whiting, G. An approach to communication theory: Toward consensus on rules. *Journal of Communication*, 1972, *22*, 217–238.

D'Andrade, R., & Wish, M. *Speech act theory in quantitative research on interpersonal behavior*. Unpublished manuscript. University of California at San Diego and Bell Laboratory, 1981.

Danks, J. Encoding of novel figures for communication and memory. *Cognitive Psychology*, 1970, *1*, 179–191.

Davis, D., & Holtgraves, T. *Perceptions of unresponsive others: Attributions, attraction, understandability, and memory of their utterance*. Unpublished manuscript. University of Nevada, 1982.

Delia, J. G. A constructivist analysis of the concept of credibility. *Quarterly Journal of Speech*, 1976, *62*, 361–375.

Dittmann, A., & Llewellyn, L. Relationship between vocalizations and head nods as listener responses. *Journal of Personality and Social Psychology*, 1968, *9*, 79–84.

Dore, J. Children's illocutionary acts. In R. Freedle (Ed.), *Discourse production and comprehension*. Norwood, N.J.: Ablex, 1977.

Duncan, S. On the structure of speaker-auditor interaction during speaking turns. *Language in society*, 1974, *2*, 161–180.

Duncan, S., & Fiske, D. *Face-to-face interaction: Research methods and theory*. Hillsdale, N.J.: Lawrence Erlbaum Associates, 1977.

Erickson, B., Lind, E., Johnson, B., & O'Barr, W. Speech style and impression formation in a court setting: The effects of ''powerful'' and ''powerless'' speech. *Journal of Experimental Social Psychology*, 1978, *14*, 266–279.

Erickson, F. Talking down: Some cultural sources of miscommunication in interracial interviews. In A. Wolfgang (Ed.), *Nonverbal behavior: Applications and cultural implications*. New York: Academic Press, 1979.

Ervin-Tripp, S. Sociolinguistics. In L. Berkowitz (Ed.), *Advances in experimental social psychology*. New York: Academic Press, 1969.

Ferguson, C. Baby talk as a simplified register. In C. Ferguson & C. Snow (Eds.), *Talking to children: Language input and acquisition*. Cambridge: Cambridge University Press, 1977.

Festinger, L. *A theory of cognitive dissonance*. Stanford: Stanford University Press, 1952.

Fillmore, C. The case for case. In E. Bach & R. Harms (Eds.), *Universals of linguistic theory*. New York: Holt, Rinehart, & Winston, 1968.

Flavell, J., Botkin, P., Fry, C., Wright, J., & Jarvis, P. *The development of role-taking and communication skills in children*. New York: Wiley, 1968.

Fondacaro, R., & Higgins, E. T. Cognitive consequences of communication mode: A social psychological perspective. In D. Olson, A. Hildyard, & N. Torrance (Eds.), *The nature and consequences of literacy*. Hillsdale, N.J.: Lawrence Erlbaum Associates, in press.

Freedle, R., Naus, M., & Schwartz, L. Prose processing from a psychological perspective. In R. Freedle (Ed.), *Discourse processes: Advances in research and theory. Vol. I*. Norwood, N.J.: Ablex, 1977.

Gelman, R., & Shatz, M. Appropriate speech adjustments: The operation of conversational constraints on talk to two-year-olds. In M. Lewis & L. Rosenblum (Eds.), *Interaction, conversation, and the development of language*. New York: Wiley, 1977.

Giles, H. Ethnicity markers in speech. In K. Scherer & H. Giles (Eds.), *Social markers in speech*. New York: Cambridge University Press, 1979.

Glucksberg, S., Krauss, R., & Higgins, E. T. The development of referential communication skills. In F. Horowitz, E. Hetherington, S. Scarr-Salapatek, & G. Siegel (Eds.). *Review of child development research (Vol. 4)*. Chicago: University of Chicago Press, 1975.

Goffman, E. On face-work: An analysis of ritual elements in social interaction. *Psychiatry*, 1955, *18*, 213–231.

Goffman, E. *The presentation of self in everyday life*. Garden City, N.Y.: Doubleday, 1959.

Goffman, E. *Relations in public*. New York: Harper & Row, 1971.

Grice, H. Logic and conversation. In P. Cole & J. Morgan (Eds.), *Syntax and semantics, Vol. 3: Speech acts*. New York: Academic Press, 1975.

Grimes, J. *The thread of discourse*. The Hague: Mouton, 1975.

Gumperz, J., & Hymes, D. (Eds.), *Directions in sociolinguistics: The ethnography of communication*. New York: Holt, Rinehart, & Winston, 1972.

Halliday, M. A. K., & Hasan, R. *Cohesion in English*. London: Longman, 1976.

Hamilton, D., & Zanna, M. Context effects in impression formation: Changes in connotative meaning. *Journal of Personality and Social Psychology*, 1974, *29*, 649–654.

Heider, F. *The psychology of interpersonal relations*. New York: Wiley, 1958.

Higgins, E. T. Social class differences in verbal communicative accuracy: A question of "which question?" *Psychological Bulletin*, 1976, *83*, 695–714. (a)

Higgins, E. T. Effects of presupposition on deductive reasoning. *Journal of Verbal Learning and Verbal Behavior*, 1976, *32*, 125–132. (b)

Higgins, E. T. The varying presuppositional nature of comparatives. *Journal of Psycholinguistic Research*, 1977, *6*, 203–222. (a)

Higgins, E. T. Communication development as related to channel, incentive, and social class. *Genetic Psychology Monographs*, 1977, *96*, 75–141. (b)

Higgins, E. T. The 'communication game': Implications for social cognition and persuasion. In E. T. Higgins, C. P. Herman, & M. P. Zanna (Eds.), *Social cognition: The Ontario Symposium, Volume 1*. Hillsdale, N.J.: Lawrence Erlbaum Associates, 1981.

Higgins, E. T., Fondacaro, R., & McCann, D. Rules and roles: The "communication game" and speaker-listener processes. In W. Dickson (Ed.), *Children's oral communication skills*. New York: Academic Press, 1981.

Higgins, E. T. & Lurie, L. Context, categorization, and recall: The "change-of-standard" effect. *Cognitive Psychology,* in press.

Higgins, E. T., & McCann, C. D. Social encoding and subsequent attitudes, impressions, and memory: "Context-driven" and motivational aspects of processing. *Journal of Personality and Social Psychology,* in press.

Higgins, E. T., McCann, C. D., & Fondacaro, R. The "communication game": Goal-directed encoding and cognitive consequences. *Social Cognition,* 1982, *1,* 21–37.

Higgins, E. T., & Rholes, W. Impression formation and role fulfillment: A "holistic reference" approach. *Journal of Experimental Social Psychology,* 1976, *12,* 422–435.

Higgins, E. T., & Rholes, W. S. "Saying is believing": Effects of message modification on memory and liking for the person described. *Journal of Experimental Social Psychology,* 1978, *14,* 363–378.

Higgins, E. T., & Winter, L. *Normative beliefs about traits and trait-related behaviors.* Unpublished manuscript, New York University, 1982.

Hintikka, J. *Logic, language-games, and information.* London: Oxford University Press, 1973.

Holtzman, M. The use of interrogative forms in the verbal interaction of three mothers and their children. *Journal of Psycholinguistic Research,* 1972, *1,* 311–336.

Hornby, P. A. Surface structure and presupposition. *Journal of Verbal Learning and Verbal Behavior,* 1974, *13,* 530–538.

Huttenlocher, J., & Higgins, E. T. Adjectives, comparatives, and syllogisms. *Psychological Review,* 1971, *78,* 487–504.

Hymes, D. *Foundations in sociolinguistics: An ethnographic approach.* Philadelphia: University of Pennsylvania Press, 1974.

Janis, I., & King, B. The influence of role-playing on opinion change. *Journal of Abnormal and Social Psychology,* 1954, *49,* 211–218.

Jefferson, G. Sequential aspects of storytelling in conversation. In J. Schenkein (Ed.). *Studies in the organization of conversational interaction.* New York: Academic Press, 1976.

Jones, E. E., & Davis, K. E. From acts to dispositions: The attributional process in person perception. In L. Berkowitz (Ed.), *Advances in experimental social psychology* (Vol. 2). New York: Academic Press, 1965.

Kaplan, M. F. Context effects in impression formation: The weighted average versus the meaning-change formulation. *Journal of Personality and Social Psychology,* 1971, *19,* 92–99.

Keenan, E. Conversational competence in children. *Journal of Child Language,* 1974, *1,* 163–183.

Keenan, E., & Schieffelin, B. Topic as a discourse notion: A study of topic in the conversations of children and adults. In C. Li (Ed.), *Subject and topic.* New York: Academic Press, 1976.

Kelley, H. H. The warm-cold variable in first impressions of persons. *Journal of Personality,* 1950, *18,* 431–439.

Kelley, H. H. Attribution theory in social psychology. In D. Levine (Ed.), *Nebraska symposium on motivation,* 1967, *15,* 192–238.

Kendon, A., & Ferber, A. A description of some human greetings. In R. Michael & J. Crook (Eds.), *Comparative ecology and behavior of primates.* London: Academic Press, 1973.

Kendon, A. Some functions of gaze-direction in social interaction. *Acta Psychologica,* 1967, *26,* 22–63.

Knapp, M., Hart, R., Friedrich, G., Shulman, G. The rhetoric of goodbye: Verbal and nonverbal correlates of human leave taking. *Speech Monographs,* 1973, *40,* 182–198.

Krantz, D. L., & Campbell, D. T. Separating perceptual and linguistic effects of context shifts upon absolute judgments. *Journal of Experimental Psychology,* 1961, *62,* 35–42.

Krauss, R., Vivekananthan, P. S., & Weinheimer, S. Inner speech and external speech: Characteristics of communication effectiveness of socially and nonsocially encoded messages. *Journal of Personality and Social Psychology,* 1968, *9,* 295–300.

Krauss, R., & Weinheimer, S. Changes in the length of reference phrases as a function of social interaction: A preliminary study. *Psychonomic Science,* 1964, *1,* 113–114.

Kraut, R. E. Effects of social labeling on giving to charity. *Journal of Experimental Social Psychology,* 1973, *9,* 551–562.

Kraut, R. E., & Bricker, P. *The appropriateness of listener feedback.* Bell Laboratories, Technical Memorandum TM-81-11229-23, 1981.

Kraut, R. E., & Bricker, P. *The consequences of appropriate and inappropriate listener feedback.* Bell Laboratories, In preparation.

Kraut, R. E., & Gomez, L. *Human communication through computers: The problem of fuzzy language.* Bell Laboratories, In preparation.

Kraut, R. E., & Lewis, S. H. Some functions of feedback in conversation. In H. Applegate & J. Sypher (Eds.), *Understanding interpersonal communication: Social cognitive and strategic processes in children and adults.* Beverly Hills, CA: Sage Publications, in press.

Kraut, R. E., Lewis, S. H., & Swezey, L. Listener responsiveness and the coordination of conversation. *Journal of Personality and Social Psychology,* 1982, *43,* 718–731.

Kraut, R. E., & Poe, D. Behavioral roots of person perception: Deception judgments of customs inspectors and laymen. *Journal of Personality and Social Psychology,* 1980, *39,* 784–798.

Labov, W. The logic of non-standard English. In F. Williams (Ed.), *Language and poverty: Perspectives on a theme.* Chicago: Markham, 1970.

Labov, W. *Language in the inner city.* Philadelphia: University of Pennsylvania Press, 1972.

Labov, W. (Ed.), *Quantitative analysis of linguistic structure.* New York: Academic Press, in press.

Labov, W., & Fanshel. *Therapeutic discourse: Psychotherapy as conversation.* New York: Academic, 1977.

Labov, W., & Waletzky, J. Narrative analysis: Oral versions of personal experience. In *Essays on the verbal and visual arts.* Seattle: University of Washington Press, 1967.

Lakoff, R. Language and woman's place. *Language in Society,* 1973, *2,* 45–79.

Lakoff, R. *Language and woman's place.* New York: Harper & Row, 1975.

Lakoff, R. Stylistic strategies within a grammar of style. In J. Orasanu, M. Slater, & L. Adler. *Language, sex, and gender: Does la différence make a difference? Annals of the New York Academy of Science,* 1979, *327,* 53–80.

Langacker, R. Pronominalization and the chain of command. In D. Reibel & S. Schane (Eds.), *Modern studies in English.* Englewood Cliffs, N.J.: Prentice-Hall, 1969.

Leathers, D. The information potential of the nonverbal and verbal components of feedback responses. *The Southern Speech Communication Journal,* 1979, *44,* 331–354.

Li, C. (Ed.), *Subject and topic.* New York: Academic Press, 1975.

Loftus, E., & Palmer, J. Reconstruction of automobile destruction: An example of the interaction between language and memory. *Journal of Verbal Learning and Verbal Behavior,* 1974, *13,* 585–589.

Lyons, J. *Introduction to theoretical linguistics.* London: Cambridge University Press, 1968.

Maclay, H., & Osgood, C. Hesitation phenomena in spontaneous English speech. *Word,* 1959, *15,* 19–44.

Manis, M., & Armstrong, G. Contrast effects in verbal output. *Journal of Experimental Social Psychology,* 1971, *7,* 381–388.

Manis, M., Cornell, S., & Moore, J. Transmission of attitude-relevant information through a communication chain. *Journal of Personality and Social Psychology,* 1974, *30,* 81–94.

Maratsos, M. Nonegocentric communication abilities in preschool children. *Child Development,* 1973, *44,* 697–700.

Masur, E. F. Preschool boys' speech modification: The effects of listeners' linguistic levels and conversational responsiveness. *Child Development,* 1978, *49,* 924–927.

Matarazzo, J., Wiens, A., Sastow, G., Allen, B., & Weitman, M. Interviewer mm-hmm and interviewee speech duration. *Psychotherapy: Theory, Research, and Practice,* 1964, vol. 1, 109–114.

Maynard, D. Placement of topic changes in conversation. *Semiotica,* 1980, *3/4,* 263–290.

McCann, C. D., & Hancock, R. D. Self-monitoring in communicative interactions: Social cognitive consequences of goal-directed message modification. *Journal of Experimental Social Psychology,* 1983, *19,* 109–121.

McCann, C. D., & Higgins, E. T. Individual differences in communication and labeling: Social cognitive determinants and consequences. In H. Sypher & J. Applegate (Eds.), *Understanding interpersonal communication: Social cognitive and strategic processes in children and adults.* Beverly Hills, CA: Sage Publications, in press.

McConnell-Ginet, S. Our father tongue: Essays in linguistic politics. *Diacritics,* 1979, 44–50.

Mead, G. *Mind, self, and society.* C. Morris, (Ed.), Chicago: University of Chicago Press, 1934.

Menig-Peterson, C. The modification of communicative behavior in preschool-aged children as a function of the listener's perspective. *Child Development,* 1975, *46,* 1015–1018.

Miller, G. A., Galanter, E., & Pribram, K. H. *Plans and the structure of behavior.* New York: Holt, 1960.

Miller, G., & Johnson-Laird, P. *Language and perception.* Cambridge, Mass.: Harvard University Press, 1976.

Neisser, U. *Cognitive psychology.* New York: Appleton-Century-Crofts, 1967.

Newcombe, N., & Arnkoff, D. B. Effects of speech style and sex of speaker on person perception. *Journal of Personality and Social Psychology,* 1979, *37,* 1293–1303.

Newport, E. Motherese: The speech of mother to young children. In N. Catellan, D. Pisoni, & G. Potts (Eds.), *Cognitive theory. Vol. II.* Hillsdale, N.J.: Lawrence Erlbaum Associates, 1976.

Newtson, D., & Czerlinsky, T. Adjustment of attitude communications for contrasts by extreme audiences. *Journal of Personality and Social Psychology,* 1974, *30,* 829–837.

Nisbett, R., & Ross, L. *Human inference: Strategies and shortcomings of social judgment.* Englewood Cliffs, N.J.: Prentice-Hall, 1980.

Nofsinger, R. Jr., & Boyd, W. *Topic management procedures: Executing tactics and displaying adherence to rules.* Paper presented at the annual meeting of the Western Speech Communication Association, Los Angeles, California, 1979.

Offir, C. E. Recognition memory for presuppositions of relative clause sentences. *Journal of Verbal Learning and Verbal Behavior,* 1973, *12,* 636–643.

Ogden, C. K., & Richards, I. A. *The meaning of meaning.* New York: Harcourt Brace Jovanovich, Inc., 1968.

Olson, D. Language and thought: Aspects of a cognitive theory of semantics. *Psychological Review,* 1970, *77,* 257–273.

Osgood, C., Suci, G., & Tannenbaum, P. *The measurement of meaning.* Urbana: University of Illinois Press, 1957.

Planalp, S., & Tracy, K. Not to change the subject but . . . : A cognitive approach to the management of conversation. In D. Nimmo (Ed.), *Communication Yearbook 4.* New Brunswick, N.J.: Transaction, 1980.

Reichman, R. Conversational coherency. *Cognitive Science,* 1978, *2, 283–327.*

Rommetveit, R. *On message structure: A Framework for the study of language and communication.* New York: Wiley, 1974.

Rosch, E. On the internal structure of perceptual and semantic categories. In T. Moore (Ed.), *Cognitive development and the acquisition of language.* New York: Academic Press, 1973.

Rosch, E., & Mervis, C. Family resemblances: Studies in the internal structure of categories. *Cognitive Psychology,* 1975, *7,* 573–605.

Rosenberg, S., & Cohen, B. Referential processes of speakers and listeners. *Psychological Review,* 1966, *73,* 208–231.

Rosenfeld, H. Conversational control functions of nonverbal behavior. In A. Siegman & S. Feldstein (Eds.), *Nonverbal behavior and communication*. Hillsdale, N.J.: Lawrence Erlbaum Associates, 1978.

Ross, J. On the cyclic nature of English pronominalization. In *To honor Roman Jakobson: Essays on the occasion of his 70th birthday*. The Hague: Mouton Publishers, 1967.

Ross, L. The intuitive psychologist and his shortcomings: Distortions in the attribution process. In L. Berkowitz (Ed.), *Advances in experimental social psychology (Vol. 10)*. New York: Academic Press, 1977.

Rumelhart, D. Notes on a schema for stories. In D. Bobrow & A. Collins (Eds.), *Representations and understanding: Studies in cognitive science*. New York: Academic Press, 1975.

Rumelhart, D. Understanding and summarizing brief stories. In D. LaBerge & S. Samuels (Eds.), *Basic processes in reading: Perception and comprehension*. Hillsdale, N.J.: Lawrence Erlbaum Associates, 1977.

Sachs, J., & Devin, J. Young children's use of age-appropriate speech styles in social interaction and role-playing. *Journal of Child Language*, 1976, *3*, 81–98.

Schank, R. Rules and topics in conversation. *Cognitive Science*, 1977, *1*, 421–444.

Schank, R., & Abelson, R. *Scripts, plans, goals, and understanding*. Hillsdale, N.J.: Lawrence Erlbaum Associates, 1977.

Schegloff, E. Sequencing in conversational openings. *American Anthropologist*, 1968, *70*, 1075–1095.

Schegloff, E., Jefferson, G., & Sacks, H. The preference for self-correction in the organization of repair in conversation. *Language*, 1977, *53*, 361–382.

Schegloff, E., & Sacks, H. Opening up closings. *Semiotica*, 1973, *8*, 289–327.

Schmidt, C. R., & Paris, S. G. The development of children's verbal communication skills. In H. Reese & L. Lipsitt (Eds.), *Advances in child development and behavior. (Vol. 15)*. New York: Academic Press, in press.

Searle, J. *Speech acts: An essay in the philosophy of language*. Cambridge: Cambridge University Press, 1970.

Searle, J. A classification of illocutionary acts. *Language in Society*, 1976, *5*, 1–23.

Shatz, M. Communication. In P. H. Mussen (Ed.), *Handbook of child psychology, Volume 3: Cognitive development*. New York: Wiley, 1983.

Shatz, M., & Gelman, R. The development of communication skills: Modifications in the speech of young children as a function of listener. *Monographs of the Society for Research in Child Development*, 1973, *38*, Serial No. 152.

Shatz, M., & Gelman, R. Beyond syntax: The influence of conversational constraints on speech modifications. In C. Ferguson & C. Snow (Eds.), *Talking to children: Language input and acquisition*. Cambridge: Cambridge University Press, 1977.

Sherif, M., & Hovland, C. I. *Social judgment: Assimilation and contrast effects in communication and attitude change*. New Haven, Conn.: Yale University Press, 1961.

Simpson, D., & Ostrom, T. Contrast effects in impression formation. *Journal of Personality and Social Psychology*, 1976, *34*, 625–629.

Snow, C. Mothers' speech to children learning language. *Child Development*, 1972, *43*, 549–565.

Snyder, M. Self monitoring of expressive behavior. *Journal of Personality and Social Psychology*, 1974, *30*, 526–537.

Sullivan, H. S. *The psychiatric interview*. New York: Norton, 1970.

Thurber, J. The catbird seat. In *55 Short Stories from the New Yorker*. New York: Simon and Schuster, 1965.

Thorne, B., & Henley, N. (Eds.). *Language and sex: Difference and dominance*. Rowley, Mass.: Newbury House, 1975.

Trudgill, P. *Sociolinguistics: An introduction*. Harmondsworth, Middlesex, England: Penguin Books, 1974.

Thomas, D., DeCapito, C., Caronite, A., La Monica, G., & Hoving, L. Mediated generalization via stimulus labeling: A replication and extension. *Journal of Experimental Psychology,* 1968, *78,* 531–533.

van Dijk, T. Context and cognition: Knowledge frames and speech act comprehension. *Journal of Pragmatics,* 1977, *1,* 211–232.

Vendler, Z. *Adjectives and nominalizations.* Mouton, The Hague, 1968.

Vendler, Z. *Res cognitans: An essay in rational psychology.* Ithaca: Cornell University Press, 1972.

Vuchinich, S. Elements of cohesion between turns in ordinary conversation. *Semiotica,* 1977, *20,* 229–257.

Weiner, S., & Goodenough, D. A move toward a psychology of conversation. In R. Freedle (Ed.), *Discourse processes: Advances in research and theory.* Norwood, N.J.: Ablex, 1977.

Weinreich, U. Travels through semantic space. *Word,* 1958, *14,* 346–366.

Wicklund, R. A., & Brehm, J. W. *Perspectives on cognitive dissonance.* Hillsdale, N.J.: Lawrence Erlbaum Associates, 1976.

Wish, M., D'Andrade, R., & Goodnow, J. II. Dimensions of interpersonal communication: Correspondences between structures for speech acts and bipolar scales. *Journal of Personality and Social Psychology,* 1980, *39,* 848–860.

Wittgenstein, L. *Philosophical investigations.* New York: MacMillan, 1953.

Word, C., Zanna, M., & Cooper, J. The nonverbal mediation of self-fulfilling prophecies in interracial interaction. *Journal of Experimental Social Psychology,* 1974, *10,* 109–120.

Wyer, R. Changes in meaning and halo effects in personality impression formation. *Journal of Personality and Social Psychology,* 1974, *29,* 829–835.

Wyer, R., & Srull, T. The processing of social stimulus information: A conceptual integration. In R. Hastie, E. B. Ebbesen, T. Ostrom, R. Wyer, D. Hamilton, & D. Carlston (Eds.), *Person memory: The cognitive basis of social perception.* Hillsdale, N.J.: Lawrence Erlbaum Associates, 1980.

Yngve, V. On getting a word in edgewise. In *Papers from the sixth regional meeting, Chicago Linguistics Circle.* Chicago: Chicago Linguistics Circle, 1970.

4 The Self

Anthony G. Greenwald
Ohio State University

Anthony R. Pratkanis
Carnegie-Mellon University

Contents

1. INTRODUCTION

> One of the oddest events in the history of modern psychology is the manner in which the ego (or self) became sidetracked and lost to view. (Allport, 1943, p. 451)

This chapter is written in the spirit of two prior reviews—William James's (1890) chapter on "The Consciousness of Self" in his *Principles of Psychology*, and Gordon W. Allport's 1943 article, "The ego in contemporary psychology." Like James and Allport, we have set out to shape a usable, psychological concept of the self by mixing conceptual analysis and empirical review. Also, like them, we find it convenient to subdivide our treatment into several aspects, or functions of the self. For each of these subdivisions of the topic, we start by summarizing the relevant positions of James and Allport. We then review subsequent developments in theory and research—most of these achieved within the last decade—with the aim of extending and revising James's and Allport's conclusions.

To anticipate the end of this review, we hope to convince the reader that some issues that have long been considered mysterious—even beyond the realm of scientific psychology—are theoretically and empirically tractable. We shall conclude by defining the self as a complex, person-specific, central, attitudinal schema. But, before proceeding, we start by summarizing the two prior reviews that have defined the major issues with which our review is concerned.

William James (1890)

James's chapter on the self occupies 111 pages in Volume 1 of his *Principles* (pp. 291–401). The chapter divides treatment of the normal self into major sections on "The Empirical Self or Me" (291–329) and "The Pure Ego" (329–373). A third section, which we do not review here, concerns "The Mutations of the Self" (373–400), including phenomena of multiple personality, fugue, amnesia, hypnosis, and trance.

The empirical self is the self as an object of perception and knowledge—what today is called the *self-concept*. James divides the empirical self into the *material* self, the *social* self, and the *spiritual* self. The material self includes not only one's body, but also clothes, family, home, and property. The social self is the impression that one gives to significant others. (James said that "a man has as many social selves as there are distinct groups of persons about whose opinion he cares" [p. 294].) The spiritual self is one's "inner or subjective being, . . . psychic faculties or dispositions [such as] moral sensibility and conscience, . . . indomitable will," and "ourselves as thinkers" (p. 296).

After thus describing the material, social and spiritual "constituents" of the empirical self, James proceeds to treat self-feeling, self-seeking, conflict of the different selves, and self-love. Distributed through these four subsections are James's treatment of individual differences in self-related affect ("self-estimation") and conation ("self-seeking"). Table 4.1 is adapted from James's own summary table of the affective and conative aspects of self (p. 329). We have added a row to his table, to include the cognitive or perceptual-object aspect of self.

The long section on the "pure ego" gives James's analyses of personal identity and unity of the stream of thought (330–342), and his detailed critiques of alternative philosophical formulations (342–370). James considers that personal identity and unity are properties of the empirical self. He identifies three

TABLE 4.1
James's Analysis of the Empirical Self[a]

	Subdivisions of the Empirical Self		
	Material Self	*Social Self*	*Spiritual Self*
CONSTITUENTS (COGNITIVE COMPONENT)	Body, clothes, family, home, possessions	Recognition from persons one loves; liking by peers; fame, honor	Inner or subjective being; psychic faculties, dispositions, will; a portion of the stream of thought
SELF-ESTIMATION (AFFECTIVE COMPONENT)	Personal vanity, modesty, pride of wealth, fear of poverty	Social and family pride, vainglory, snobbery, humiliation, shame	Sense of moral or mental superiority, purity, sense of inferiority or guilt
SELF-SEEKING (CONATIVE COMPONENT)	Bodily appetites and instincts; love of adornment, foppery, acquisitiveness, constructiveness, love of home	Desire to please, be noticed, admired; sociability, emulation, envy, love, pursuit of honor, ambition	Intellectual, moral and religious aspiration, conscientiousness

[a]Based on James (1890), p. 329.

varieties of a contrasting, "pure ego," theory—that is, theories that consider identity and unity *not* as functions of the empirical self. These are (i) theories of the soul, defined as immaterial substance (for example, the unextended mental substance postulated by Descartes); (ii) the associationist theory, which treats identity and unity as unexplained, emergent properties of associated collections of ideas; and (iii) the transcendental ego (especially Kant's) theory, in which identity and unity are innate properties of mind. James shows little patience with these nonempirical theories—for example, characterizing the transcendental ego as "simply nothing; as ineffectual and windy an abortion as Philosophy can show" (p. 365). We return later to the question of the possibility of empirical interpretations of the self as knower.

Gordon Allport (1943)

Allport introduces his review by lamenting the disappearance of the self from psychology, noting that it was perhaps legitimately banished by a behaviorist positivism that would not tolerate a concept dwelling "on the unenlightening plane of dialectics" (p. 452). He credited psychoanalysis with preserving "the study of certain functions of the self that postivistic psychology had consigned to oblivion" (p. 453). The aim of Allport's review was to regain the "admittance of the ego to good standing in psychology" (p. 476).

The first of two major sections, "Main Conceptions of the Ego" (453–459), reviews eight senses of ego (or self—Allport used the two terms interchangeably). The following summary of Allport's eight senses of ego includes some of our observations on relationships with James's analysis:

1. *Ego as knower* designates the experiencing agent, corresponding to the philosophers' "pure ego," and to the functions that James attributed to the spiritual portion of the empirical self.
2. *Ego as object of knowledge* is the bodily self, which was a part of James's material self.
3. *Ego as primitive selfishness* corresponds to James's *material* self-seeking (see Table 4.1, above).
4. *Ego as dominance drive* refers to "that portion of the personality that demands status and recognition" (p. 455), corresponding to James's *social* self-seeking.
5. *Ego as a passive organization of mental processes* was Allport's acknowledgement of Freud's concept of ego, a neutral arbitrator among the conflicting forces of id, superego, and environment.
6. *Ego as a fighter for ends* corresponds to James's *spiritual* self-seeking, and to the dynamic view of ego in psychoanalytic thinking since Hartmann (1939/1958).
7. *Ego as a behavioral system* designated the Gestalt-psychological concep-

tion of a central region of personality, found in the work of Koffka (1935) and Lewin (1936).

8. *Ego as the subjective organization of culture* refers to the self as a residue of socialization experience, a system of social values.

The second major section of Allport's paper, "Experimental Evidence" (pp. 460–472), contains his presentation of evidence in support of the point that

> ego-involvement, or its absence, makes a critical difference in human behavior. When a person reacts in a neutral, impersonal routine atmosphere, his behavior is one thing. But when he is behaving personally, perhaps excitedly, seriously committed to a task, he behaves quite differently. In the first condition his ego is not engaged; in the second condition . . . one finds that the ego is acting in several, if not all, of the eight capacities I have listed. In other words, *ego-involvement* is, as the phrase implies, a condition of total participation of the self—as knower, as organizer, as observer, as status seeker, and as socialized being. (p. 459)

This justification for the concept of ego-involvement was the core of Allport's argument for the acceptability of the self in psychology. Allport's eight senses of ego didn't provide as neat a classification as did James's earlier (Table 4.1) analysis. Indeed, Allport later attempted to improve his classification (Allport, 1955, 1961). By 1961, Allport had concluded that the self as knower did not belong in psychology, and was better left to philsophy.

In 1943 Allport was confident that the time was ripe for psychology to take up the self. Despite the presence of other advocates (Hilgard, 1949; Rogers, 1942; Sherif & Cantril, 1947), no sustained programs of research developed. One can attribute this, retrospectively, to a lack of successful research procedures. Now, 40 years later, it appears that a variety of research procedures for studying the self have at last established their usefulness. Accordingly, and with the clarity of vision afforded by at least 5 years of hindsight, it seems time to conclude that the self *has* attained good standing in psychology.

2. THE SELF AS KNOWER

William James (1890) devoted over 40 pages to his own and others' attempts to explain the self's subjectivity, its function as the agent of experience, its role as knower. His own explanation treated these as properties of the stream of thoughts. "Each later Thought," he said, "knowing and including . . . the Thoughts which went before, is the final receptacle . . . of all that they contain" (p. 339). To amplify this unusual idea, he used a variety of analogies, among them "a long succession of herdsmen coming rapidly into possession of the same cattle" (p. 339). Just as each passing herdsman is successively the owner of the cattle, so "the passing Thought then seems to be the Thinker" (p. 342). James's hypothesis that the current thought bears the properties of the self as knower was intended to keep the self's subjectivity within the empirical self (part of its spiritual constituent—see Table 4.1, above). However, his hypothesis does not appear to have gained adherents, nor does it have apparent testable implications. In short, it may not be distinguishable from the "pure ego" theories that James so vigorously criticized.

In the context of James's review and Allport's (1961) abandonment of the self as knower, perhaps the most remarkable advances that are reported in this chapter are recent empirical treatments of the self as knower. We consider this progress in two areas, self as a memory system and biases in self-relevant judgment, and then summarize implications for a conception of the self as knower.

Self as a Memory System[1]

> The phenomenon of Self and that of Memory are merely two sides of the same fact. We may, as psychologists, set out from either of them, and refer the other to it.
> (James Mill, *Analysis of the Human Mind*, 1829)

As the quote from James Mill indicates, the idea of a connection between self and memory is not a novel development. In the nineteenth century and through most of the twentieth century, the best empirical evidence for this connection was in pathologies, such as amnesia and multiple personality, that showed simultaneous disorders of memory and in the sense of personal unity—specifically, amnesia, fugue, and multiple personality. Edouard Claparède (1911/1951) identified the amnesia of Korsakoff syndrome as another self/memory disorder, presaging much modern attention to memory in Korsakoff patients (e.g., Butters & Cermak, 1980; Jacoby & Witherspoon, 1982).

> If one examines the behavior of such a patient, one finds that everything happens as though the various events of life, however well associated with each *other* in the mind, were incapable of integration with the *me* [ego] itself. (Claparède, 1911/1951, p. 71)

Kurt Koffka (1935) devoted more than 60 pages of his major work, *Principles of Gestalt Psychology,* to making a case for the function of ego as a memory system. However, the evidence he reviewed was not difficult to accommodate equally within theories of memory organization that did not appeal to a self (especially Bartlett's, 1932). After Koffka, the self-memory relation lay dormant

---

[1]This section summarizes and updates a recent review by the first author (Greenwald, 1981).

until a burst of research was initiated by Rogers, Kuiper, and Kirker's (1977) report of the *self-reference effect*. Greenwald (1981) summarized the results of this recent research activity, drawing it together with previous more isolated findings, to identify three "self/memory" effects.

1. *The self-generation effect.* Material that is actively generated by the learner is retrieved more easily than is material passively encountered (Bobrow & Bower, 1969; Erdelyi, Buschke, & Finkelstein, 1977; Greenwald & Albert, 1968; Jacoby, 1978; Slamecka & Graf, 1978).

2. *The self-reference effect.* Material that is encoded with reference to self is more easily retrieved than is material otherwise encoded (Bower & Gilligan, 1979; Brenner, 1973; Hull & Levy, 1979; Keenan & Baillet, 1980; Kuiper & Rogers, 1979; Lord, 1980; Markus, 1980; Owens, Dafoe, & Bower, 1977; Rogers, 1981; Rogers et al., 1977; Ross & Sicoly, 1979).

3. *The ego-involvement effect.* Material that is associated with a persisting task is more easily retrieved than is material associated with a completed task (Aall, 1913; Bjork, 1972; d'Ydewalle, Degryse, & DeCorte, 1981; Epstein, 1972; Jacoby, Bartz, & Evans, 1978; Nuttin, 1953; Nuttin & Greenwald, 1968; Zeigarnik, 1927, 1938).

In the few years since Greenwald's review, a fourth self/memory finding—the second-generation effect—has appeared, and several researchers have actively investigated the self-reference effect.

The Second-generation Effect.   Greenwald, Banaji, Pratkanis, and Breckler (1981) gave subjects a generation task for each of 20 nouns ("targets")—to produce a sentence that contained both the target noun and a specific person's name. After an involving filler task, subjects received an unexpected test for recall of the 20 nouns. In a condition that produced a very high level of incidental recall, the names used in sentences (along with the target nouns) had themselves been produced by a generation task—specifically, the task of producing a list of names of friends. (In a comparison condition that produced significantly lower recall, these names were ones of unfamiliar people.) The beneficial effect of the additional, or second, generation task explains the description of the result as a "second-generation effect." This effect has been replicated by Banaji (1982) and by Greenwald and Banaji (1983).

Recent Studies of the Self-reference Effect

In the original procedure of Rogers et al. (1977), subjects judged whether each of a series of trait adjectives (for example: friendly, shy) was self-descriptive or not. On a later unexpected recall test, subjects recalled more trait words that had been incidentally encountered in this task than of ones encountered in other tasks.

Variant Self-reference Effects.   Several researchers have modified the procedures of the self-reference experiment in a search for the conditions that
control the effect. Bower and Gilligan (1979) obtained equivalently strong recall
with a different self-reference task in which subjects were asked to retrieve
personal experiences (episodes) relevant to the trait words. Friedman and
Pullyblank (1982), Bellezza (1983), and Banaji, Devine, and Greenwald (1983)
have similarly found strong memory benefits of tasks involving the retrieval of
personal experiences. Banaji, Devine, and Greenwald (1983) reported another
self-reference-like effect—imaging objects in personal settings (such as the location of their home telephone) produced better recall of the objects than imaging
them in impersonal settings (such as a pay telephone booth). Bellezza (1983)
reported two variant self-reference effects—recall was enhanced when nouns
were associated with parts of one's body, and also when nouns were integrated
into a fabricated story about the self.

Self-reference Versus Other-reference.   Several studies have compared the
effect on subsequent recall of making judgments relevant to the self versus
making judgments relevant to others. Findings have varied between superior
recall for self-reference (Keenan & Baillet, 1980; Kuiper & Rogers, 1979) and
comparably strong recall for self- and other-reference (Bower & Gilligan, 1979;
Friedman & Pullyblank, 1982). In a study that varied familiarity of the other
persons on whom judgment tasks focused, Keenan and Baillet (1980) reported
that incidental recognition improved in an orderly fashion with increases in the
familiarity of the other. Chew (1983) and Claeys (1983) have since replicated
this orderly relationship between familiarity of the other and memory, using
incidental recall measures.

Modifications that Eliminate the Self-reference Effect.   In their second experiment, Keenan and Baillet (1980) found that the task of judging whether
anatomical features were possessed by self and others did *not* yield a superiority
for features judged in terms of self. They suggested that the self-reference effect
might occur only for evaluative judgments. Relevant to this, Ferguson, Rule, and
Carlson (1983), and also Friedman and Pullyblank (1982), found that judgments
of the evaluative character of trait words facilitated memory as much or nearly as
much as did judging their self-descriptiveness. Lord (1980; replicated by Karylowski, 1983) found that recall of object names was worse for the task of
imaging oneself together with each of the objects than for the task of imaging
another person in interaction with them. He suggested that imagery of the self
was not part of the self as a memory structure. Maki and McCaul (1982) noticed
that both Keenan and Baillet's and Lord's conditions that did not produce self-
reference effects involved nouns (rather than trait adjectives) as the target stimuli. In their own studies, Maki and McCaul found a self-reference effect with the
usual self-descriptiveness judgment task for trait adjectives, but not with either of

two judgment tasks in which the target items were nouns, nor with the task of judging whether trait adjectives were used in speech on a daily basis.

Part-of-speech, Evaluation, and Imagery are not Critical. Three empirical hypotheses can be derived from the empirical variations that have eliminated the self-reference effect: (i) that the self-reference effect occurs only with trait adjectives (and not with nouns), (ii) that it occurs only when an evaluative judgment task is used, or (iii) that it does not occur in tasks using imagery. These three hypotheses, however, can be discounted on the basis of other findings in which variant self-reference effects (see above) have been obtained in tasks using nouns, using nonevaluative encoding tasks, and using imagery (Banaji, Devine, & Greenwald, 1983; Bellezza, 1983).

Theoretical Interpretation of Self-reference Effects

The most successful theoretical accounts of the self-reference effect have interpreted it in terms of either effective *encoding processes* or effective use of *existing cognitive structures*.

Encoding processes. This type of interpretation has been advocated by Bower and Gilligan, Keenan and Baillet, and Friedman and Pullyblank. They note that judgment tasks vary in the degree of elaboration (or richness or complexity) of associative processes that occur during initial encounter with to-be-recalled items (Anderson & Reder, 1979; Craik & Tulving, 1975). Self-reference tasks, they assume, produce more elaborate associative encodings than do the tasks with which they are compared (for example, other-reference or semantic judgment tasks). More elaborate associations, in turn, provide a larger set of associative paths that can be used later to retrieve the encoded items. A minor difficulty for the elaboration hypothesis stems from the fact that self-relevance judgments are often made more rapidly than other-reference or semantic judgments (Keenan & Baillet, 1980; Rogers et al., 1977). In order to preserve the elaboration hypothesis, one has to sacrifice (as did Craik & Tulving, 1975) the intuitively attractive notion that degree of cognitive elaboration in a judgment task is proportional to the time taken to do the task.

Existing Cognitive Structure—Prototype. One cognitive structure explanation for the self-reference effect treats self as a prototype (Rogers, 1981). In this interpretation, the task of judging trait adjectives for self-relevance makes salient their relation to the self-prototype. Later, the (assumed) pre-existing prototype structure can be used to guide recall of the set of judged items. Prior research on cognitive prototypes has shown that (i) items are judged rapidly as being members of a category to the extent that they resemble a prototype, or model instance, from which category members have been generated (e.g., Posner & Keele, 1968), and (ii) false recognition responses occur for not-previously-presented items that correspond closely to such a prototype (e.g., Bransford & Franks,

1971). Accordingly, the prototype interpretation is supported by findings of (i) relatively rapid judgments for the self-reference task and (ii) high false alarm rates in recognition tests for unpresented self-descriptive adjectives (Breckler & Greenwald, 1981; Chew, 1983; Kuiper & Rogers, 1979; Lord, Gilbert, & Stanley, 1982; Rogers, Rogers, & Kuiper, 1979). The prototype interpretation is further supported by the finding of superior recall of items judged as self-relevant compared to ones judged not self-relevant (Kuiper & Rogers, 1979; replicated by Breckler & Greenwald, 1981). At the same time, the prototype hypothesis is not well-suited to account for some of the variant self-reference effects that have been reported—especially ones that have used an episode-retrieval task (Banaji et al., 1933; Bellezza, 1983; Bower & Gilligan, 1979; Friedman & Pullyblank, 1982).

Existing Cognitive Structure—Internal Cues.   A second cognitive structure hypothesis treats the self as an organized system that is capable of providing mnemonically useful cues, as in Greenwald's (1981) self/memory system and Bellezza's (1983) internal cuing hypothesis. In these hypotheses, material that is experienced in a self-relevant setting becomes associated with (ordinarily) covert or internal cues produced by the hypothesized cuing structure. Later recall is facilitated by using the cuing structure again, at the time of retrieval, to re-produce the cues earlier used in encoding. Both Bellezza and Greenwald have observed that this interpretation can be related to the operation of familiar mnemonic strategies (see Bellezza, 1981). The internal cuing hypothesis is sup-ported by the (variant) self-reference effect findings of Bellezza (1983) and by the second-generation effect studies of Greenwald and Banaji (1983) and Green-wald et al. (1981).

Overview

Three interpretations—encoding elaboration, self-as-cognitive-prototype, and internal cuing—have been used successfully in explaining results of various self-reference experiments. The viability of three interpretations suggests that we should refer, not to *the* self-reference effect but, rather, to self-reference effect*s*. The original self-reference finding of Rogers et al. (1977), using judgments of trait words, seems to be best explained by the self-as-cognitive-prototype hy-pothesis. Findings based on the encoding task of retrieving personal episodes (e.g., Bower & Gilligan, 1979), however, are better explained in terms of encoding elaboration. The third interpretation for self-reference effects—use of an internal cuing structure—fits well with the results of studies that have made self-produced cues overt (e.g., Bellezza, 1983). Far from being distressing, the viability of three explanations for self-reference effects helps to justify the con-cluding that relating information to self is a highly effective strategy for remem-bering.

Biases in Self-Relevant Judgment

> And nothing, not God, is greater to one than one's self is.
> (Walt Whitman, *Song of Myself*)

> We can all benefit from seeing ourselves as we appear to others.
> (Poor modern rendition of Robert Burns, *To a Louse*)

The Totalitarian Ego

In a recent review, Greenwald (1980) summarized evidence concerning the pervasiveness of three biases in self knowledge of the average normal adult of (at least) North American culture. These cognitive biases are (i) *egocentricity,* the tendency for judgment and memory to be focused on self, (ii) *beneffectance,* the tendency for self to be perceived as effective in achieving desired ends while avoding undesired ones, and (iii) *cognitive conservatism,* the tendency to resist cognitive change. The constellation of these three biases was labeled the "totalitarian ego," acknowledging that the biases match ones that are considered to be characteristic of the information control apparatus of a totalitarian dictatorship. The unattractive epithet, totalitarian, was intended to be provocative—a challenge to understand why biases that are disparaged in a political system may be just the ones that are used to manage the personal flow of information. A brief overview of the evidence for each of the three biases follows.

Egocentricity.   The egocentric character of knowledge is indicated, in part, by the self/memory effects just reviewed. Information that is related to self apparently has a privileged position in memory. A second type of evidence for cognitive egocentricity is the tendency to insert self into perceived causal sequences, either as influencing agent (cf. Langer's, 1975, illusion of control) or as influenced object (Jervis, 1976, Chapter 9; Fenigstein, 1983; Zuckerman, Kernis, Guarnera, Murphy, & Rappoport, 1983).

Beneffectance.   This term, which designates the bias of seeing the self as effective and competent, was compounded from beneficence (doing good) and effectance (competence). It was coined as an umbrella term to cover phenomena previously labeled as self-serving, egocentric, egotistic, and ego-defensive attributions by other writers. Four lines of research have demonstrated the pervasiveness of this bias in the normal personality. These are (i) the tendency to recall successes more readily than failures (Glixman, 1949; Rosenzweig, 1943); (ii) the acceptance of responsibility for successes but not for failures on individual or group tasks (Johnston, 1967; Miller & Ross, 1975; Schlenker & Miller, 1977; Snyder, Stucky, & Higgins, in press; Wortman, 1976; Weary [Bradley, 1978]); (iii) denial of responsibility for harming others (Harvey, Harris, &

Barnes, 1975); and (iv) the tendency to identify with victors and to disaffiliate with losers ("basking in reflected glory"—Cialdini et al., 1976; Tesser & Campbell, 1983). Interestingly, the beneffectance bias is absent in depressives, who have been shown to perceive themselves more objectively or realistically (Alloy & Abramson, 1979; Lewinsohn, Mischel, Chaplin, & Barton, 1980). Evidently—and contrary to Robert Burns's famous poem that is paraphrased above—seeing ourselves as others see us is not necessarily a welcome gift.

Cognitive Conservatism.   Conservatism, in general, is the disposition to preserve what is already established. In perception, basic skills such as *object conservation* (perceptual constancy) and *assimilation* (reuse of existing categories) illustrate cognitive conservatism. Such conservative processes are widely regarded as functioning in the service of veridical knowledge. Two other conservative (change-resisting) processes, *confirmation bias* and *rewriting of memory,* appear to serve the interests of accuracy less well. Confirmation bias is apparent in (i) information-seeking strategies that selectively confirm initial hypotheses (Snyder & Swann, 1978; see also Darley & Gross, 1983; Swann, 1983); (ii) selective recall of information that confirms previously established beliefs (Mischel, Ebbesen, & Zeiss, 1976; Pratkanis, 1983; Snyder & Uranowitz, 1978; Swann & Read, 1981); (iii) selective generation of arguments that support opinions under attack (Greenwald, 1968; Petty, Ostrom, & Brock, 1981); and (iv) researchers' selective evaluation of their own data as a function of the data's agreement with their hypotheses (Greenwald, 1975). Rewriting of memory is evident in (i) systematic misrecall of prior opinions so as to obscure the occurrence of opinion change (Bem & McConnell, 1970; Goethals & Reckman, 1973); (ii) believing that newly acquired facts have had lengthy residence in memory (Fischhoff, 1977; Loftus, Miller, & Burns, 1978); and (iii) overestimating the validity of inaccurate memories (Trope, 1978). Rewriting of memory has the interesting characteristic of allowing the content of memory actually to change (for example, opinions may change or new facts may be learned), even while the larger system maintains an illusion of no change.

Functions of the Totalitarian Ego Biases

Greenwald (1980) observed that the egocentricity, beneffectance, and conservatism biases are found not only in totalitarian information control and in normal human cognition, but also in the development of effective theoretical paradigms in "normal" science (Kuhn, 1970). The association of these biases with the human self is made plausible by findings indicating that the biases are typically increased in strength by procedures that have been identified as "ego-involving" (Greenwald, 1980, pp. 610–611), and by the success with which Epstein (1973) and Loevinger (1976) used the metaphor of scientific theory in their discussions of the self. These arguments led to the following conclusion about the function of the egocentricity and conservatism biases.

The cognitive biases of a successful scientific paradigm or of an established total-itarian system presumably function to preserve organization. It follows that the corresponding biases in ego may similarly function to protect the integrity of ego's organization of knowledge. In particular, by coding much information in relation to self, the egocentricity bias ensures that the self-system maintains wide scope; this information-assimilating activity preserves organization in the same way that a library's maintenance depends on a continuing program of acquisitions. By retain-ing previously used cognitive categories, the conservatism bias ensures that similar information encountered at different points in time is encoded into the same catego-ries; as with the library, such consistency of encoding over time preserves access to already stored information in a growing organization of knowledge. (Greenwald, 1980, p. 613)

Greenwald was unable to link beneffectance directly to the function of pre-serving organization, noting rather that this bias appeared to be "associated with effective performance in situations in which preservance might be the critical determinant of effectiveness" (p. 614; cf. Bandura's, 1977, concept of self-efficacy). It remains possible, however, that further research on the relationship between affect and cognition (Isen, this volume) will indicate that affectively positive self-regard serves a critical role in maintaining or expanding an organi-zation of knowledge. (What we have in mind here is a possible intrapsychic analog of political phenomena such as the relation between nationalism and imperialism, or between nationalism and governmental stability.)

Implications for a Conception of the Self as Knower

Our decision to discuss memory strategies and cognitive biases under the heading of the *self as knower* was made without initially drawing attention to it. Howev-er, it would have been possible to consider these topics as manifestations of the *self as an object of knowledge*. That is, both the memory and cognitive bias results could have been treated as manifestations of the self as a data structure. One cannot, of course, avoid assuming that this data structure is used by some processes or activities, but it is not necessary to identify those activities with the self. The self could be identified just with the "passivities" of the data structure.

The question therefore arises: On what basis should one choose between attributing some cognitive function (such as the egocentricity of memory or the beneffectance bias) to structure rather than process? (The reader should be warned that the remainder of this section concerns issues that some will regard as more philosophical than psychological. It will become clear, however, that we find no basis for drawing a sharp line between the [philosphical?] self as knower and the [empirical/psychological?] self as object of knowledge.)

A Computer Metaphor

Our view on the allocation of function between self as knower and self as object of knowledge reflects two strong influences: (i) the distinction, made by students of cognitive science and artificial intelligence, between procedural and declarative knowledge (e.g., Anderson, 1976, pp. 116–119), and (ii) the evolutionary epistemology analysis of knowledge (Campbell, 1974, 1979; Popper, 1935/1959).[2] From the perspective we adopt, the distinction of process versus structure interpretations is related to the interesting question of introspective access to mental functioning—a question that has been debated recently by Nisbett and Wilson (1977) and Ericsson and Simon (1980). A frequently stated position on the question of introspective access is that we have access to the products of cognitive process, but not to the workings of cognitive process (e.g., Mandler, 1975; Neisser, 1967; Nisbett & Wilson, 1977, p. 232). The view just stated is plausibly extended to say that we have access to the input and output of cognitive processing, in other words, to mental *data*. The cognitive processes to which we lack access, in the computer metaphor that we are falling into, correspond to the computer's *program*.

We propose to identify the self as knower with the program aspect of the computer metaphor, and the self as object of knowledge with data stored in the computer's memory. However, it remains to justify the metaphor. Let us start by appearing to undermine it. A problem with the metaphor is that the program/data distinction is not a sharp one. Because both program and data are represented by elements in the same medium (for example, bits in random access memory), program elements can be read as data. However, far from being a problem with the metaphor to self, the fuzziness of the program versus data distinction captures, as will be seen, an essential aspect of the distinction between self as knower and self as object of knowledge.

The computer metaphor is developed further in Table 4.2. By means of this metaphor, we identify the *subjective* aspects of the self with the self as cognitive *process* and hence with the *program* component of the computer. We identify the self as *object of knowledge* with the *content* of cognitive processes and hence with the (input, output, and stored) *data* aspect of the computer metaphor. Further, we shall use the customary assumption of lack of access to cognitive process to *define* cognitive process. Cognitive process (or the subjective aspect of the self, self as knower) is thus defined as those aspects of cognitive function to which we do not have introspective access. It remains for us to clarify the notion of introspective access.

If we could sort the cognitive domain sharply into introspectively accessible and inaccessible portions, our process/content distinction would also be sharp. However, we cannot, because the accuracy of introspection cannot be well-defined. That is, the accuracy of introspection can be defined only in terms of the extent to which introspective reports agree with psychological theory about the

---

[2]The procedural-declarative distinction and evolutionary epistemology are, themselves, products of many earlier influences that we shall not attempt to review. However, see the sources cited for references to earlier literature.

TABLE 4.2
Division between Self as Subject and Self as Object

	Self as Subject	Self as Object
COGNITIVE SCIENCE CATEGORIES	Procedural Knowledge	Declarative Knowledge
TERMS IN THE COMPUTER METAPHOR	Program	Input, Output, and Stored Data
COGNITIVE FUNCTIONS OF SELF	Egocentric Memory and Judgment	Self-Concept, Self-Image
INFORMAL TERMS	Mental Process Unconscious Skills	Mental Content Conscious Experience
PHILOSOPHICAL CATEGORIES	Self as Knower, I	Empirical Self, Me

corresponding functions. The accuracy assessment involves, in other words, a comparison between theories contained in self-report (the "naive" psychology of the subject) and those considered valid on the basis of psychological research. Neither of these theoretical endeavors—neither the naive nor the scientific—can be capable of certain knowledge. Accordingly, the boundary between mental process and content—like the boundary between computer program and data—is inherently fuzzy.

If, as psychologists, we had complete theories of memory and cognition, we should be able to regard the self fully as an object or structure—in other words, as legible, accessible mental content. We would not then be inclined to sort out some aspects of the self and declare them to be manifestations of a special entity, the self as knower. However, our understanding of the mental skills that produce (say) the egocentricity of memory and the totalitarian ego biases is decidedly imperfect. Accordingly, we (psychologists and nonpsychologists alike) experience a dichotomy or duality within the self. On the one hand are those aspects of the self that appear to be understood, that we can describe verbally to others— these we identify as the empirical self, the self-concept, or the self as an object of knowledge. On the other hand are those aspects of the self that we don't understand—for these the phrases, self as subject and self as knower, indicate our lack of comprehension. Table 4.2 summarizes the groupings of terms that we assimilate, respectively, to the subjective and objective aspects of the self.

Sensible Metaphors for the Self

The subject/object duality of self has long been an enigma to philosophers and psychologists. This enigma has sometimes found expression in a mirror metaphor. Interestingly, although mirrors have had productive use in recent empirical investigations of the self (e.g., Gallup, 1977; Lewis & Brooks-Gunn, 1979; Wicklund, 1975), the metaphorical use of a mirror to represent subject/object duality has only been confusing, a point that was well expressed by Hilgard (1949):

> [The] self-evident character of self-awareness is in fact most illusive. You presently find yourself as between the two mirrors of a barber-shop, with each image viewing each other one, so that as the self takes a look at itself taking a look at itself, it soon gets all confused as to the self that is doing the looking and the self which is being looked at. (p. 377)

Recently, cognitive scientists have taken an interest in the self's paradoxical duality. Hofstadter (1979), in particular, has provided several new metaphors for the self, each more substantial and more stimulating than the mirror. Hofstadter's metaphors are characterized by complex self-reference, such as the DNA molecule that contains instructions for its own replication and Godel's theorem that asserts its own unprovability. Hofstadter's metaphors share the mirror metaphor's property of not clearly representing a separation between subjective and objective aspects of the self. A consequence is that they leave the experienced duality of the self a mystery, and thereby encourage the suspicion that the self as subject/knower is beyond the domain of scientific treatment. Our use of the program/data metaphor, interpreting these conceptually in terms of mental process versus content and procedural versus declarative knowledge, serves (we hope) to bring the self as knower within the domain of empirical psychology.

3. COGNITIVE ASPECTS OF SELF

In his 1943 review Allport wrote that "the existence of one's own self is the one fact of which every mortal—every psychologist included—is perfectly convinced" (p. 451). What is the nature of this self-concept that we all so certainly possess? James had divided the known self into three parts—material, social, and spiritual selves. Allport presented somewhat varying descriptions of the self in 1943, 1955, and 1961. Nevertheless, he was convinced of the uniqueness and the special importance of the self-concept. In this section we update James's and Allport's descriptions of the self as known, and we address two questions about the self-concept. First, what are its contents? Second, how are data about the self organized in memory? The attention we give to these questions reflects the emphasis in much recent research on cognitive models of the self. At the end of this section on cognitive aspects of self, we comment on the relation of the recent work on which our review focuses to the extensive body of earlier work.

Contents of the Self-Concept

McGuire and his associates (McGuire & McGuire, 1980, 1981, 1982; McGuire, McGuire, Child, & Fujioka, 1978; McGuire, McGuire, & Winston, 1979; McGuire & Padawer-Singer, 1976) have investigated the contents of the spontaneous self-concept, by categorizing responses to the query, "Tell us about yourself." This open-ended probe does not constrain the subject's response. Accordingly, the specific items of self-description elicited should represent the range and relative prominence of different categories of content in the self-concept. Among the responses to "Tell us about yourself," McGuire and Padawer-Singer (1976) found that children most frequently mentioned activities, significant others, and attitudes; to a lesser extent they included demographic characteristics, self-evaluations, and physical features. The obtained self-descriptions provided support for a distinctiveness principle—attributes that distinguish the self from others, either in the general population or in the specific testing environment, were especially likely to be mentioned.

Others have used more reactive techniques to assess individual differences in cognitive content of the self-concept. Markus has investigated individual differences in speed of judgments and accessibility of information on dimensions such as independence, gender role, and body weight, finding that efficiency of processing varies with the importance of the dimension to the subject (Markus, 1977; Markus, Crane, Berstein, & Siladi, 1982; Markus, Hamill, & Sentis, 1980). Kuiper and Rogers (1979) have similarly shown that information consistent with one's self-concept is judged and retrieved efficiently. Kuiper and his associates (reviewed in Kuiper & Derry, 1981) have applied these principles to demonstrate that the content of depressed persons' self-concepts, in contrast with that of normals, consists of data supporting a negative self-image. Linville (1982) reported that persons with complex self-concepts (that is, self-concepts having many distinct aspects) are more resistant to negative feedback and exhibit less variability of mood than do persons with cognitively simple self-concepts.

This recent research establishes that the cognitive content of the self varies across persons. However, that point hardly needed to be made. The major import of the recent research of McGuire, Markus, Kuiper and others is, rather, its development of techniques for assessing both the content of individual differences in self-concept and the cognitive function of those differences.

Models of the Cognitive Organization of Self

Self as a Central Structure

The psychic centrality of the self has been a frequent theme in theoretical discussions. Cooley (1902/1964) gives this description of the self's centrality:

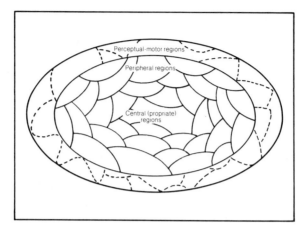

FIG. 4.1.   Allport's conception of the self-concept as the central region of personality (from Allport, 1961).

"I", then, is not all of the mind, but a peculiarly central, vigorous, and well-knit portion of it, not separated from the rest but gradually merging into it, and yet having a certain practical distinctiveness, so that a man generally shows clearly enough by his language and behavior what his "I" is as distinguished from thoughts he does not appropriate. It may be thought of . . . under the analogy of a central colored area on a lighted wall. It might also, and perhaps more justly, be compared to the nucleus of a living cell, not altogether separate from the surrounding matter, out of which indeed it is formed, but more active and definitely organized. (p. 182)

Claparède (1911/1951) similarly placed the self ("le moi") in the center of the psyche, as did Koffka (1935), both crediting the self with achieving the coherence of experience and the persistence of personal identity through time. Combs and Snygg (1949/1959) state: "It [the self] provides the central core around which all other perceptions are organized" (p. 122). Figure 4.1 presents Allport's (1961) diagram of personality (developed from Lewin, e.g., 1936) as a series of regions with the central region being the proprium (Allport's term for the self or ego).

Recent Models—Schemata, Hierarchies, Prototypes, Networks, Spaces

Self as Schema.   Markus (1977; Markus & Sentis, 1982; Markus & Smith, 1981) views the self as a system of schemata. In this conceptualization, the self is a memory structure that consists of a collection of schemata, such as those suggested by the ellipses in Figure 4.2. Note that some of the schemata in Figure 4.2 (such as Ladders and Rentagrams) are not connected to the self. In other words, the person is aschematic for these concepts. Other schemata (such as

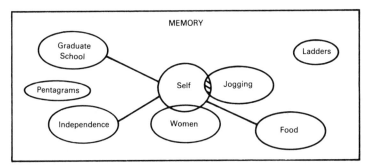

FIG. 4.2.   A hypothetical system of self-schemata (from Markus & Sentis, 1982).

Jogging and Independence) are related to the self in varying degrees (as indicated by their closeness to the self), meaning that the person is schematic on these characteristics.

In Markus's analysis, each schema is a generalization about the self and contains person-specific information about past experiences and personal characteristics. The specific organization of knowledge within a self-schema is not specified by Markus, although her definition of schema is based on Neisser (1976), who wrote:

> a schema is like a *format* in a computer-programing language. Formats specify that information must be of a certain sort if it is to be interpreted coherently. Other information will be ignored or will lead to meaningless results. . . . A schema is not merely like a format; it also functions as a *plan*. . . . Perceptual schemata are plans for finding out about objects and events, for obtaining more information to fill in the format. . . . The schema is not only the plan but also the executor of the plan. It is a pattern *of* action as well as a pattern *for* action. (pp. 55–56)

The conception of the self as a system of schemata provides a welcome means of accommodating the self as knower alongside the self as object of knowledge. (See discussion of the subject/object distinction in Section 2.)

Self as Hierarchical Category Structure.   Rogers (1981), using a conceptualization based on Rosch (1978) and Cantor and Mischel (1979), views the self as a cognitive category with internal hierarchical organization.

> the elements . . . are self-descriptive terms such as traits, values, and possibly even memories of specific behaviors and events. These terms are ordered hierarchically, becoming more concrete, distinctive, specific, and less inclusive, with increasing depth into the hierarchy. Making a self-referent decision involves comparing the stimulus item with [this structure] to determine if it "fits" into the structure. (p. 196)

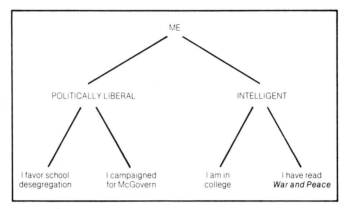

FIG. 4.3.   Illustration of a hypothetical fragment of a hierarchical model of the self.

Figure 4.3 presents a hypothetical instance of a fragment of the model suggested by Rogers. As an aside, we should note that Rogers uses the term ''prototype'' to describe this model. We have avoided using that term here, in keeping with a more generally accepted definition of a prototype as a model example for a cognitive category. Such a model example is sometimes considered as a unit, or as an unordered collection of features, and is not necessarily hierarchical in structure (Smith & Medin, 1981). Other hierarchical conceptions of the self have been offered by Epstein (1973) and by Carver and Scheier (1981).

Self as Prototype.   Various researchers have sought to demonstrate that latency and memory effects associated with judgments concerning cognitive prototypes occur also with judgments concerning one's self. Kuiper (1981), Breckler (1981), and Lord, Gilbert, and Stanley (1983) have found that self-referent judgments are made more rapidly for words extremely high or low in self-descriptiveness. This inverted-U effect resembles results found for judgments of similarity to best exemplars of a variety of cognitive categories (Rosch, 1973, 1975; Schnur, 1977; Smith, 1976). Rogers, Rogers, and Kuiper (1979) and Breckler (1981) have found that subjects give false alarm recognition responses to highly self-descriptive adjectives, again resembling an effect found in other domains for novel stimuli that resemble a prototype from which previously presented stimuli have been generated (Cantor & Mischel, 1977; Posner & Keele, 1970). These findings support the conclusion that the self-concept functions as a cognitive prototype—a category central tendency with which novel stimuli can be compared.

Self as Associative Network.   Bower and Gilligan (1979) have presented a model of the self-concept based on associative network models such as HAM

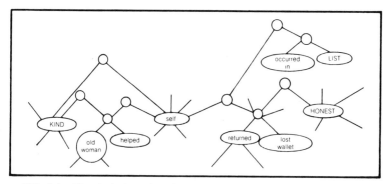

FIG. 4.4.   Hypothetical portion of an associative network model of the self-concept (from Bower & Gilligan, 1979).

(Anderson & Bower, 1973) and ACT (Anderson, 1976). Figure 4.4 shows a portion of such an associative memory network that can be identified with the self-concept. Information is stored in the form of propositions (represented by small circles in Fig. 4.4) that relate subject (in this case the self) and predicate (specific episodes and generic information about the self). Links (lines) represent logical relations among concepts and propositions (nodes). For example, a self-schematic trait of kindness is represented by a link between the self and the node for the concept, kind. A self-nonschematic trait is represented by the absence of a direct link between the self and the trait concept (for example, honest in Fig. 4.4).

Self as Multidimensional Space.   Breckler and Greenwald (1982) have developed a technique for representing the self in a multidimensional cognitive space. In their method a multidimensional trait space is first constructed, using trait similarity ratings for a group of subjects. Next, subjects are individually located in the trait space by placing them near traits that they rate as self-descriptive and distant from nondescriptive traits. Figure 4.5 presents a two-dimensional trait space that has a general evaluative dimension (horizontal) and an intellectual good/bad dimension (vertical). Persons are represented by open circles and are scattered through the space, representing individual differences in self-concepts relative to these dimensions. The location of self in this space has been related both to personality measures, such as self-esteem, and to differences in cognitive processing (see Breckler, Pratkanis, & McCann, 1983).

The Current Picture of the Self-Concept

The several models that we have reviewed provide structural descriptions with little, and sometimes no, specification of how the structure is used by judgment and memory processes. Such partially specified models readily survive empirical

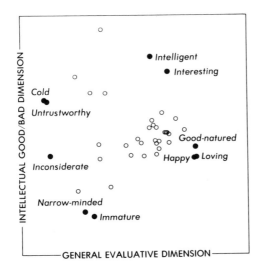

FIG. 4.5. The self in multidimensional cognitive (trait) space, with open circles indicating person locations (from Breckler, Pratkanis, & McCann, 1983).

tests because of the ease with which processing assumptions can be added to accommodate diverse findings. As a consequence, the various attempts at describing the microstructure of the self-concept are for the present equally viable. This situation should not be regarded as distressing. The enterprise of testing theories of mental representation is in its infancy. The situation of a diversity of viable model representations of the self is similar to that for conceptual representations in other knowledge domains (Smith & Medin, 1981).

As a specific example of the current indeterminacy of microstructural models of the self, consider the attempt to use the "fan" effect as a basis for thinning the ranks of such models. A familiar prediction of associative network models, using a spreading activation concept, is that the more items of knowledge attached to a given point (node) in memory, the slower should be judgments or memory retrievals for which that node is an intermediary. (Judgment time is positively related to the spread, or fan, of links from a node used in the judgment— Anderson & Bower, 1973.) In associative network models, the self is considered to be a very richly connected node (Bower & Gilligan, 1979; Keenan & Baillet, 1980). Accordingly, Rogers (1981) suggested that associative network models of the self should be rejected, because the rapidity with which self-referent judgments are made is in direct opposition to this expected "fan effect." Despite this observation, it is not the case that network models of the self have failed. Anderson (1981) has provided a patch for the network model to handle a related point concerning the speed of expert judgments, raised by Smith, Adams, and Schorr (1978). The debate awaits further research (see Kihlstrom & Cantor, in press).

Despite the present indeterminacy of cognitive models of the self, recent modeling efforts have the virtue of having inspired research in several laboratories, providing several new techniques for empirically investigating the self-concept. The accumulating results are producing a collection of specifications that a viable model of the self will have to meet.

As noted earlier, this review has ignored the voluminous research and theory on the self-concept that preceded very recent interest in cognitive models. Excellent reviews of earlier work can be found in Gergen (1971), Wylie (1974, 1979), Rosenberg (1979), Smith (1980), and Gecas (1982). Perhaps the most significant novel feature of the recent cognitive approach is the tendency to replace the notion of self-concept with that of self-schema. Whereas the self-concept is typically regarded as a passive data structure, consisting of the characteristics of the self, the self-schema is an active information processing structure. Compare, for example, Rosenberg's (1979) description of the self-concept—"the totality of the individual's thoughts and feelings having reference to himself as an object" (p. 7)—with Rogers et al.'s (1977) description of the self-schema as "deeply involved in the processing, interpretation, and memory of personal information" (p. 677). Epstein's (1973) interpretation of the self-concept as an active, information-gathering *theory* of the person's involvement in the world can be seen, in retrospect, as an early indication of the transition from self-concept to self-schema language.

4. AFFECTIVE ASPECTS OF THE SELF

Our remoter spiritual, material, and social selves, so far as they are realized, come also with a glow and a warmth.
(William James, 1890, p. 333)

Since 'I' is known to our experience primarily as a feeling, or as a feeling-ingredient in our ideas, it cannot be described or defined without suggesting this feeling. There can be no final test of the self except the way we feel; it is that toward which we have the 'my' attitude.
(C. H. Cooley, 1902/1964, p. 172)

Nothing, it is said, is ultimately sacred except the beloved ego.
(Gordon Allport, 1937, p. 169)

The observation that the self engenders strong feelings—ones often characterized by passionate warmth—has been made not only by the writers quoted above, but also by contemporary students of the self (Epstein, 1973; Markus & Sentis, 1982; C. Rogers, 1951; T. B. Rogers, 1981). This self-feeling is, apparently, of great significance in guiding social interaction. As a small sample of the accumulated research that indicates relationships between self-esteem and social behavior: Aronson (1980, Chapter 7) and Tesser and Campbell (1983) have shown that social attraction choices are very frequently made in a manner that maintains or enhances one's self-esteem; Costanzo (1970) has shown that persons high in self-esteem tend to resist conformity pressure; and Shrauger and Sorman (1977) and McFarlin and Blascovich (1982) have demonstrated that high self-esteem is associated with persistence at difficult tasks.

In this section we develop the view (advocated previously by Sherif & Cantril, 1947, and Rosenberg, 1967) that the prominent feeling component of self-regard justifies conceiving the self as an attitude object. We support this view by considering the important functions of the (usually positive) self-attitude and by pointing out the substantial parallels between self-relevant and attitude-relevant cognition. We conclude by noting that a conception of the self as an attitude object can be applied in the measurement of self-esteem.

The Self-Regarding Attitude

A Thought Experiment

Imagine that you are paralyzed from the neck down, but that, fortunately, you own a marvelous robot that responds to your spoken commands. It carries you from place to place, reaches for and picks up objects on your command, types messages as you speak them, dials the telephone, feeds you, and (thank heavens) even disposes of the resulting digestive wastes. Would you do whatever you could to make sure that your robot stayed in good working order? (More properly, and interestingly, would you have *it* do what is needed to keep it in good working order?) Would you be upset to learn that others have robots that work better than yours? Would you develop a liking for the robot?

Perhaps you wouldn't expect yourself to take care of the robot, wouldn't be upset at attacks on its virtuosity, and wouldn't feel warmly toward it—*if* newer and better replacement models were available just for the asking. But, let's suppose that these robots are issued for life—if you lose or damage yours, you'll have to do (rather, not do) without it. The answers are now clear. You'd be a fool not to have the robot spend a substantial fraction of its time in self-maintenance. Also, because it is most unwelcome to hear that your robot is inferior, you might develop strategies for avoiding such reports, or for convincing yourself that any such reports must be in error. (For example, you might believe that the reports were originated by others jealous of your robot.) And you might well feel fondly toward your robot, although it's not yet clear what difference that might make.

Of course, this is only a thought experiment. You don't have such a robot—but you do have a much better device! Your body does everything that the robot does (and more) and is equally irreplaceable. Among the extra features of your body is its ability to "read your mind," and to upgrade itself by acquiring capabilities that weren't built in. Some of these skills are so remarkable that they are given the special name, "mental" abilities. The whole package, physical and mental, is called your "self."

This thought experiment is intended to make it reasonable that people take care of their selves and have reason to think better of their selves than others may. But we wish to make the further point that self-regard has the properties of an attitude. Understanding this attitudinal function will help to explain the affective aspect of self-regard, the warmth of self-feeling that was remarked by James, Cooley, and Allport.

Attitudinal Properties of Self-Regard

The attitudinal nature of self-regard can be established by identifying parallel findings in attitude research and research on the self. The search for such parallels is hampered by the fact that different problems have been studied and different research designs have been used in the two areas. Nevertheless, the evidence that does exist establishes several parallels, and provides a basis for expecting that additional research will reveal more.

Parallels Between Attitudinal and Self-Relevant Judgment Latencies. As noted in Section 3, several studies have shown that, in judging traits for self-descriptiveness, the most rapid judgments occur at the rating extremes—an inverted-U effect for judgment times as a function of degree of self-descriptiveness (Breckler, 1981; Kuiper, 1981; Kuiper & Derry, 1981; Lord et al., 1983). Judd and Kulik (1980) have reported the same pattern of results with attitude statements—more rapid responses for judgments of high or low agreement than for moderate agreement.

Parallels Between Attitudinal and Self-Relevant Memory. In some of the above studies of judgment latencies, unexpected tests for recall or recognition of the previously judged items have been administered. For attitudinal judgments, Judd and Kulik (1980) found that this incidental recall was better for items at the extremes of agreement and disagreement. Similarly, Dutta and Kanungo (1967) have reported that both affectively positive and affectively negative items are remembered better than neutral items. These bipolar results are paralleled by Breckler and Greenwald's (1981) finding of more false alarm recognition responses for traits that were at the self-descriptiveness extremes (as determined by judgments made after the recognition test). However, bipolar facilitation effects are not the rule. A unipolar false alarms effect, focused on highly self-descriptive traits, was found by Rogers, Rogers, and Kuiper (1979). Breckler and Greenwald (1981) also found that false alarms were greater for highly self-descriptive than for highly nonself-descriptive traits. In the attitude literature, the unipolar effect has also been found (e.g., Jones & Kohler, 1958; Levine & Murphy, 1943; Pratkanis, 1983; Read & Rosson, 1982). Another parallel occurs in the discovery that the tasks of judging traits for their evaluative (i.e., attitudinal) qualities or for their descriptiveness of well-liked others (themselves objects of a positive attitude) produce incidental memory effects comparable in strength to those obtained with self-descriptiveness judgments (Ferguson, Rule, & Carlson, 1983; Friedman & Pullyblank, 1982). In a related finding, Pratkanis (1983) found that an attitude-reference judgment task produces results parallel to the self-reference task. That is, judging whether a word is relevant to an attitude topic yields better subsequent incidental recall in subjects who have an attitude on the topic than among subjects who have no attitude. As a final parallel, the technique of spontaneous retrieval from memory has been successful in producing assessments of both the self-concept (e.g., Markus, 1977; McGuire & McGuire, 1982) and attitudes (Cullen, 1968; Greenwald, 1968).[3]

Parallels Between Cognitive Defense of Attitudes and of Self-Concept. In attitude research a listed-thought technique has been used to examine subjects' cognitive reactions to persuasive communications. A very reliable finding is that the evaluative content of these reactions can be well predicted from knowledge of the subject's existing attitude on the communication's topic (Greenwald, 1968). Cognitive reactions to a communication, in other words, defend the existing attitude. A parallel exists in research that examines subjects' explanations (attributions) for a successful or unsuccessful performance. Normal subjects, who have favorable self-regard, attribute the failure to bad luck or to external factors such as the actions of others or the poor quality of a test, deftly avoiding the implication that the failure reveals a defect of the self (see Snyder et al., in press, for a recent review of this excuse-making process). This cognitive defense of the self is remarkable for its absence in depressives, who apparently do not have a positive self-concept to defend (Alloy & Abramson, 1983).

Summary. Perhaps, in citing the parallels between attitude and self-concept research, we have strained to establish a point that is self-evident. After all, social psychologists have long treated persons other than the self as attitude objects and have considered ego-involved attitudes as a particularly important topic of investigation (Ostrom & Brock, 1968; Sherif & Hovland, 1961). Why not treat the most ego-involved object/person, one's self, also as an attitude object? Perhaps the only remaining problem in declaring that the self is an attitude object is to define that object. Consider that, in discussing attitudes, one ordinarily treats the attitude object as a consensually shared category that is not in

---

[3]Despite these parallels, other tests of selective recall hypotheses in the self-concept and attitude domains have produced complex findings that have yet to be encompassed within a well-organized explanatory framework. In the area of self-relevant memory, problems have long been apparent in the confusing data on recall of successes and failures for ego-involved performances (see, e.g., Greenwald, 1982a). The attitude literature contains reports of both bipolar and unipolar facilitation effects, along with findings of no attitude facilitation of recall (e.g., Greenwald & Sakumura, 1967; Waly & Cook, 1966).

need of definition—whether it be a person, an ethnic group, a commercial product, or a policy issue. Such implicit definition of the attitude object, however, will not do for the self. As established in Sections 1 and 3 (and also in Section 5, below) the self-concept is complex in content and varies from person to person. Thus, although we can identify the self as an attitude object, it is a decidedly uncommon one that is different for each person.

Why is Self-Regard (Or Any Other Attitude) Affective?—Affective Heuristics

Three Components of the Self-Attitude.   The purpose of the thought experiment that opened this section was to establish that maintenance and protection of one's body is sensible from a biological perspective; traits that achieve these effects should be selected in evolution because they increase the likelihood of survival to reproductive age. This reasoning suggests a plausible basis for behavioral self-care such as grooming, exercising, and feeding. It also provides a justification for behavioral and cognitive strategies that permit anticipation and avoidance of stress. These "self" defenses may reasonably be interpreted as behavioral and cognitive components of an attitude toward the self. But, in the familiar three-component definition of attitude, the central component of an attitude is the remaining one, affect or feeling. In the case of the self-attitude, also, affect is obviously present (see quotes at the beginning of this section).

Why Affect?   What is the function of self-feeling? It is hard to credit affect directly with any maintenance or protection function and, therefore, difficult to understand why affect is so prominent in self-regard (or, for that matter, in other attitudes). That is, if we properly care for and protect ourselves and the other important persons and objects in our environment, why should it matter whether or not we have warm feelings toward them? In order to answer this question we appeal to, and extend, the controversial arguments of Zajonc (1980). (See Lazarus, 1982 and Mandler, 1982, for some of this controversy.) Zajonc reviewed a variety of evidence indicating that affective reactions to stimuli occur very rapidly and appear not to be mediated by knowledge retrieval or judgment. As he put it—and this was the controversial point—"preferences need no inferences."

Adaptive Significance of Affect.   When an affect-arousing stimulus is encountered, this stimulus controls attention (Deutsch & Deutsch, 1963) and therefore leaves little capacity available for judgment. In this situation, immediately elicited affect may help to guide an adaptive response. Affect, that is, may serve as an efficient, or heuristic, guide to behavior. In suggesting this hypothesis, we are guided by the influential work of Tversky and Kahneman (1974) and Nisbett and Ross (1980) on cognitive heuristics. Affective reactions to persons or objects, we propose, guide behavior by assigning the object either to a positive class, for which a favoring heuristic (approaching, helping, protecting) is applicable, or to a negative class, for which a disfavoring heuristic (avoiding, neglecting, harming) is used. Affective heuristics very likely extend to thought, such that object-relevant knowledge seeking, interpretation, retrieval and imagination fall into distinct patterns as a function of the positive or negative affective reaction to the object (or person). However, such affective guidance of cognition, even though a topic of long interest to psychologists (see Isen, this volume; Rapaport, 1942/1971), is not yet understood well enough to permit confident delineation of such heuristics.

Implications for Measuring Self-Esteem

The enterprise of measuring affective self-regard, or self-esteem, has been broadly criticized for inattention to conceptual underpinnings, psychometric technique, and empirical validation (Wylie, 1974, 1979). At the same time, several self-esteem measures have been used successfully in research—that is, they have yielded interpretable correlations (for example, Coopersmith, 1967; Helmreich, Stapp, & Ervin, 1979; Janis & Field, 1959; Rosenberg, 1965; see also the capsule review of measures in Robinson & Shaver, 1973). Our analysis suggests the wisdom of applying the well-established technology of attitude measurement (e.g., Edwards, 1957; Fishbein, 1967) to self-esteem assessment. Of the many existing self-esteem measures, however, only one (Rosenberg, 1965) has made use of the conception of self-esteem as an attitude.

The application of attitude-scaling techniques to self-esteem is, regrettably, not an entirely straightforward matter. Two problems must be dealt with. One is the possibility that subjects may report a more positive self-image than they privately experience, in the hope of producing a favorable impression on the tester. This problem is a routine one in personality measurement. However, it takes a special twist in the case of self-esteem measurement because the wish to present a desirable image to others is, itself, an aspect of self-esteem. The second problem, briefly alluded to earlier in this section, is more troublesome. It is the problem of defining the unique self-concept that serves as the attitude object for each respondent. The problem of identifying the uniqueness of each subject's self in the reactive format of psychometrically based tests is formidable. Thus, it may be a long time before it is possible to improve on test items that simply refer, in a nonspecific way, to "yourself" (or, if in the first person, "myself"), allowing the respondent to provide the necessary person-specific interpretation.

5. CONATIVE ASPECTS OF SELF—SELF AS TASK ORIENTATION

The social self . . . ranks higher than the material self. . . . We must care more for our honor, our friends, our human ties, than for a sound skin or wealth. And the spiritual self is so supremely precious that, rather than lose it, a man ought to be willing to give up friends and good fame, and property, and life itself.
(James, 1890, pp. 314–315)

The employer thinks that wages and security are the dominant desires, whereas in reality the ego-satisfactions are primary. What a different outlook there would be on our economic life if we took firm hold on the issues of status and self-respect in industry, and re-planned our industrial society in a manner that would rescue the worker's ego from oblivion.

(Allport, 1943, p. 472)

James and Allport, as these quotations illustrate, view the self as the focus of motivations that ordinarily outweigh bodily needs and material desires. In this section we take as points of general consensus among theorists of human motivation that (i) the most important endeavors of a normal adult human cannot be explained by reduction to organic or tissue needs, and (ii) these important concerns vary from person to person. The question we then address is whether the concept of self is indeed useful (as James and Allport suggest) in accounting for these "higher" human motives and their variation across persons.

Ego-Involvement

Allport, in 1943, used the concept of ego-involvement to describe the role of self in behavior directed toward important goals. In 1955, he replaced ego-involvement with the term, "propriate striving," to express the conative aspect of self. (Allport had coined "proprium" as a pointed counter to the apparent backward-facing world view of behaviorism's *re*active concepts, such as reflex, response, recognition, and the like. He wanted a *pro*active term to convey the idea that the person is typically forward-looking and future-oriented.) At present it is ego-involvement, not propriate striving, that survives—but with an uncertain status. As observed by Greenwald (1982a), by the early 1960s the concept of ego-involvement had become difficult to use in the main area of research in which it had been applied—memory for experiences of success and failure. Part of the difficulty was that ego-involvement had, apparently, developed three meanings:

Ego-involvement₁. Concern about public impression, or evaluation by others; similar to evaluation apprehension, need for approval.
Ego-involvement₂. Concern about private self-evaluation; similar to need for achievement.
Ego-involvement₃. Personal importance, linkage to central values.

One might imagine that it would be conceptually fatal for a term to vary so in meaning. However, the different senses of ego-involvement may successfully correspond to individual differences in important motivational concerns. Greenwald related the first two senses of ego-involvement to the recently developed concepts of public and private self-awareness/self-consciousness (Buss, 1980; Fenigstein, Scheier, & Buss, 1975; Scheier & Carver, 1981), and set them in a framework for analyzing person-situation interactions, *ego task analysis*. Greenwald and Breckler (in press) extended ego task analysis to include the third type of ego-involvement. We use their scheme to organize a review of recent research on conative aspects of the self.

Ego Task Analysis—Facets of the Self

An ego task is an important, persisting task that provides a basis for self-evaluation. Ego tasks take precedence over other tasks, and are not terminated by successes—they continue to be important because self-evaluation is a lifelong enterprise. Greenwald and Breckler (in press) used ego task analysis to identify four *facets of the self* that may be said to be engaged in ego tasks. These four facets (or subselves) are presented in Table 4.3.

The *diffuse self* is, in some senses, a pre-self, a condition of not distinguishing sharply between self and others, with behavior hedonically guided toward positive affective states. The *public self* is sensitive to the evaluations of others and seeks to win the approval of significant audiences of parents, peers, and authorities. Developmentally, the public self depends upon achievement of a cognitive discrimination between self and others, and an ability to attend to those aspects of one's behavior that are also noticed by others. The ego task of the public self can be described, in part, as social accreditation—that is, earning credit in exchange relationships with others. However, another important aspect of the public self's task is to internalize the evaluative standards of significant others. This self-definition aspect of the public self's task can lead to development of the *private self*. By providing an inner audience for behavior, the private self permits self-evaluation to proceed in the absence of others. We designate the private self's ego task as individual achievement, with ''achievement'' being used, in the sense of McClelland, Atkinson, Clark and Lowell (1953), to indicate guidance by internal standards. As a further developmental step, the goals of groups with which the person is identified (reference groups) become internalized, yielding the *collective self*. The collective self's task is also an achievement task, contributing toward a reference group's attainment of its goals.[4]

Strategies in the Service of Ego Tasks

Winning a Nobel Prize or an Olympic gold medal are, we would guess, strongly satisfying experiences. Perhaps they are so satisfying because they simultaneously serve the interests of a public self, a private self, and a collective self. That is, they simultaneously earn the approval of others, achieve success by personal standards, and signify fulfillment of a reference group's goal. (Perhaps we should have said ''co-winning a Nobel Prize.'') Many everyday achieve-

---

[4]Our speculation that the four facets of self develop in the left-to-right order of Table 4.3 is, we should note, partly at odds with others' suggestions that the private self developmentally precedes the public self (Buss, 1980; Cheek & Hogan, 1983; see Loevinger, 1976, for a broad review of theories of ego development).

TABLE 4.3

Interrelation of Facets of the Self, Ego Tasks, Personality Measures, Experimental Procedures, and Performance Strategies

	Facets of the Self			
	Diffuse Self	*Public Self*	*Private Self*	*Collective Self*
EGO TASK DESIGNATION	hedonic satisfaction	social accreditation; self-definition	individual achievement	collective achievement
BASIS FOR SELF-EVALUATION	attainment of positive affect	approval of others (outer audience)	internal standards (inner audience)	internalized goals of reference group
INDIVIDUAL DIFFERENCE MEASURES OF TASK ORIENTATION		Public Self-consciousness; Need for Approval; high Self-monitoring	Private Self-consciousness; Need for Achievement; low Self-monitoring	
SITUATION INDUCERS OF TASK ORIENTATION	anonymity in group; drug intoxication	minority status in group; solo before audience; camera; public failure	privacy; exposure to performance replay; mirror; private failure	reference group salience; cohesive group; superordinate goals
STRATEGIES IN SERVICE OF TASK	norm violation	conformity; obedience; opinion moderation; basking in reflected glory	independence; defiance; opinion resistance	

ments, similarly, simultaneously serve two or more ego tasks. Examples are being promoted in one's job, earning a college degree, winning in competitive sports, and raising children. If all human endeavors simultaneously pleased inner and outer audiences and achieved group goals, we could be sure that the ego task analysis of Table 4.3 would be useless. But that is not the case. And, interestingly, some of the everyday activities that focus on single ego tasks correspond well to tasks that have been cultivated for use in the social psychological laboratory.

The procedures of experiments on conformity, obedience, and persuasion characteristically put the subject in a dilemma that pits the public self against the private self. That is, concern about approval by an audience pulls behavior in one direction at the same time that the attempt to adhere to personal standards pulls in the opposite direction. In these experiments, the audience pressure often leads the subject to give in to a source of influence that would be resisted with less pressure.

The Diffuse and Collective Selves.   The pattern of entries in Table 4.3 indicates that the facets identified as diffuse and collective selves have been relatively neglected in social psychological research. Nevertheless, there is sufficient evidence to justify their inclusion in Table 4.3, and to encourage further research efforts. The diffuse self has been investigated in research on deindividuation. Previous reviewers' observations about paradoxical aspects of deindividuation (Diener, 1977, 1980; Dipboye, 1977; see also Zimbardo, 1969) were summarized by Greenwald (1982a):

> Deindividuation is sometimes associated with loss of identity but other times with acquisition of identity via a distinctive group (of which one is an indistinguishable member); it is sometimes sought but other times avoided; and it is sometimes associated with chaotic, norm-violating behavior but other times with conforming, uniform behavior. (p. 172)

This paradox can be resolved with the aid of the distinction between the diffuse and the collective selves. All deindividuation procedures, including anonymity, alcohol intoxication, and strong stimulation, reduce the salience of internal standards. However, some deindividuation procedures can make the subject's participation in a reference group salient—for example, being among a crowd of cheering fans at a football contest. These group-salience procedures can engage the collective self, leading to coordinated or norm-adhering behavior. Greenwald suggested that the term "deindividuation" be restricted to procedures that elicit norm-violating behavior—ones that, in Table 4.3's terms, invoke the diffuse self.

The collective self has received relatively little attention from social psychologists, apart from the contributions of Muzafer Sherif and his coworkers. Sherif and Cantril's (1947) description of ego-involvement stressed participation in causes that give the individual "some relative role with respect to other individuals, groups, or institutions" (p. 96). And the famous Robbers' Cave experiment of Sherif, Harvey, White, Hood, and Sherif (1961) stands as a relatively isolated, but nevertheless convincing, plea for the usefulness of collective (superordinate) goals in overcoming intergroup hostility. The concepts of impulsive and institutional aspects of self in the work of the sociologist, Turner (1976), correspond in part to the present analysis's diffuse and collective aspects of self.

Personality and Situation as Determinants of Ego Tasks

Consider an experimental subject who is confronted with the conflicting pressures of outer and inner audiences—perhaps a subject in Milgram's (1963) obedience experiment who has been asked to inflict severe shocks on a participant in a learning experiment. What determines whether this subject will obey or defy the experimenter's authoritative request? One determinant is the relative strength of the subject's *personality* dispositions to engage in the ego tasks of the public and private selves. If the subject is guided more strongly by the standards of others than by internalized standards, then we should expect him to obey. The more the subject is guided by internal standards (which are assumed to include restraints against harming innocent others) the more likely it is that he will defy the experimenter's request.

A second determinant of obedience versus defiance in the obedience experiment is the extent to which the *situation* evokes the ego tasks of the public versus the private self. For example, if the subject is alone, in a room separate from the obedience-requesting authority, the approval of the authoritative experimenter is less salient. This should reduce the tendency for concerns of the subject's public self to be engaged. The expected result is greater defiance, which is in fact observed (Milgram, 1974).

Lastly, we can expect an interaction of features of the situation and characteristics of persons. For example, a subject who is strongly guided by internalized principles may be relatively little affected, in the obedience experiment, by the difference between the authority being immediately present and distant. In contrast, a subject for whom the public self is strong should be very sensitive to this same variation.

Individual Differences in Orientation Toward the Public and Private Selves

Public and Private Self-consciousness. Fenigstein, Scheier, and Buss (1975) developed a scale that provides separate measures of consciousness of the public and private facets of self.[5] Fenigstein et al. define the public self as

---

[5]The analyses of public and private aspects of self by Fenigstein, Scheier, and Buss (1975), Buss (1980), and Scheier and Carver (1981)—based on the earlier self-awareness theory of Duval and

consisting of observable self-produced stimuli, such as physique, clothing, grooming, facial expression and speech; the private self consists of self-produced stimuli that are not publicly observable, such as internal bodily sensations, emotional feelings, thoughts, and self-evaluations (see also Buss, 1980). Fenigstein et al. interpret public and private self-consciousness as predispositions to *attend* to public and private aspects of the self, respectively. In contrast, ego task analysis makes *evaluative orientation* toward outer versus inner audiences central to the public versus private contrast. Perhaps Fenigstein et al.'s Self-consciousness Scales, even though designed to assess attention to public and private aspects of the self, also measure the evaluative orientations toward the ego tasks of the public and private selves—that is, orientation toward the standards of others versus internalized standards. This is plausible, because persons concerned about evaluations of others may attend selectively to the aspects of themselves that are noticed by others, and those guided by internalized standards may be attentive to private stimuli and thoughts.

The usefulness of the Public and Private Self-consciousness Scales as measures of ego task orientations is indicated by the findings of a few studies in which subjects have been put in situations of social pressure, Scheier (1980) found that opinion moderation in anticipation of a discussion was greater for subjects high in Public Self-consciousness than for ones low in Public Self-consciounsess. Scheier and Carver (1980) found that resistance to the opinion change effects of a counterattitudinal role playing procedure was associated with high scores on Private Self-consciousness; in contrast, expression of opinion change in this situation (interpreted as an impression management strategy of maintaining consistency) was associated with high scores on Public Self-consciousness. Froming and Carver (1981) found that subjects high in Private Self-consciousness were more likely to resist group pressure than were those low in Private Self-consciousness (see also Santee & Maslach, 1982). In an experiment in which women subjects were deliberately ignored by two peers holding a conversation, Fenigstein (1979) found that those high in Public Self-consciousness were most sensitive to this rejection.

Self-monitoring.   Snyder's (1974) Self-monitoring Scale may also be relevant to the motivational orientations of the public and private facets of the self. Snyder conceives the high self-monitoring person as one who is attentive to interpersonal cues. The high self-monitor therefore shares the outward orientation of the public self. In support of this interpretation of the high self-monitor is Leary, Silver, Schlenker, and Darby's (1982) identification of a substantial

---

Wicklund (1972; Wicklund, 1975)—have strongly influenced the formulation presented here. We have refrained from citing these sources at every suitable point, only in the interest of an orderly exposition.

portion of the Self-monitoring Scale's items with a factor of public impression management. On the other hand, the low self-monitor is conceived as a "principled self" (Snyder & Campbell, 1982) who is relatively inattentive to interpersonal cues, a characteristic shared with our hypothesized private facet of the self. These interpretations of the Self-monitoring Scale place the public and private facets of the self at opposite ends of the scale. Thus, if the Self-monitoring Scale does assess the public and private ego task orientations, it may do so by assessing the relative strengths of these two orientations, rather than by measuring either separately.

Need for Achievement.   McClelland et al. (1953) formulated the construct of need for achievement as a measure of motivation to excel in relation to internal standards. If need for achievement is indicative of orientation toward an inner audience, then subjects high in need for achievement should, like ones high in Private Self-consciousness, be resistant to group pressure. McClelland et al. reported such a finding (1953, p. 287).

Need for Approval.   Crowne and Marlowe (1964) formulated their Social Desirability Scale as a measure of need for approval, defined as concern about evaluation by others. Strickland and Crowne (1962) reported that high scores on the Social Desirability Scale were associated with responsiveness to a social influence attempt. This is consistent with an interpretation of the Social Desirability Scale as a measure of the motivational orientation of the public self.

Situational Influences on the Public and Private Selves

Being in the presence of an audience, a camera, or a mirror tends to make one self-aware. However, according to both recent self-awareness theory (Buss, 1980; Carver & Scheier, 1981; Scheier & Carver, 1981) and ego task analysis, these states of self-awareness are not all equivalent. An audience or a camera should selectively engage the public facet of the self, whereas a mirror (providing a private reflection of performance) engages the private facet.[6] Therefore, a camera and a mirror should produce opposite effects in social pressure situations. The camera should make subjects more sensitive to the influence of others, whereas the mirror should enhance the guidance of behavior by internalized standards, yielding resistance to influence. Confirmation of these expectations has been obtained by Froming, Walker, and Lopyan (1982), and Scheier and Carver (1980). (See Scheier & Carver, 1983, for a more thorough review of relevant studies.)

---

[6]Buss (1980) suggests that only small mirrors engage the private self, and that large mirrors should, instead, make the public facet salient.

Relative Strength of the Public and Private Facets of the Self

Self-presentation theorists (Baumeister, 1982; Goffman, 1959; Jones & Pittman, 1982; Schlenker, 1980) have stressed the importance of the public facet of the self. Much of what is done in public, they urge, is in the interest of the social accreditation (or impression management) task of the public self. The implication, perhaps clearest in Goffman's treatment, is that the person typically presents to others only a superficial mask, a prettied image that is not believed by the presenter, but (the presenter hopes) will nevertheless be accepted at "face" value. Ego task analysis prompts some hesitation in fully accepting this view. Consider that when people act in interpersonal settings, they remain in the presence of the inner audience (which is quite portable). Therefore, they should be under a continuing constraint to adhere to internal standards, even while trying to win the approval of others. Further, if people believe that *they* typically misrepresent *themselves* to others, they should be unlikely to accept the self-presentations of others at face value, and self-presentations should tend to be ignored. Of course, in some situations self-presentations are indeed received skeptically—for example, in employment interviews (cf. Nisbett & Ross, 1980, p. 290). However, other than in such instances of exceptional pressure to make an impression, self-presentations do seem often to be trusted and trustworthy.

Researchers interested in impression management (e.g., Schlenker, 1980, in press) have been especially concerned that the typically favorable self-descriptions that research subjects provide reflect only a public self, and misrepresent the private facet. Reassuringly, however, three types of evidence indicate that the self-presentations offered by subjects in experiments—self-enhancing though they may be—do often reflect the private self. First, self-presentations obtained in privacy, with assurances of anonymity, tend to be just as self-enhancing as those obtained under public reporting conditions (Arkin, Appleman, & Burger, 1980; Frey, 1978; Greenberg, Pyszczynski, & Solomon, 1982; Schlenker, 1975; Schlenker, Hallam, & McCown, 1983). Second, the strong honesty constraint introduced by Jones and Sigall's (1971) bogus pipeline procedure (see also Quigley-Fernandez & Tedeschi, 1978) does not diminish the self-enhancing quality of self-presentations (Riess, Rosenfeld, Melburg, & Tedeschi, 1981). And, third, the fact that self-favorable judgments tend to be delivered more rapidly than self-unfavorable ones (Breckler & Greenwald, 1981) suggests that subjects are not engaging in deliberate (and presumably time-consuming) efforts at fabrication. (See Greenwald & Breckler, in press, for a more detailed discussion of these findings.)

Implications for the Role of Self in Human Motivation

The case for an important role of the self in human motivation has gained considerably since 1943, when Allport believed that the evidence was already compelling. The argument that the self should figure prominently in accounts of human motivation now has the added support of a recent, massive accumulation of evidence for the conclusion that favorable self-evaluation is an important and enduring goal of human action. Recent research on self-presentation, self-consciousness, ego-involvement, and self-esteem maintenance has established, further, that favorable self-evaluation has multiple roots.

We have attempted to characterize the complexity of the bases of self-evaluation by recognizing four types of ego tasks, and associating each with a distinct facet of the self—the diffuse self, the public self, the private self, and the collective self. Orientations toward the ego tasks of these four subselves vary from person to person, presumably as a function of developmental experiences that have yet to be analyzed fully. Additionally, the temporary strength of each facet of the self varies under the control of situational elements. These person and situation variations have been the focus of recent study, particularly for public and private facets of the self.

6. CONCLUSIONS

In 1890, William James sought to bring the self firmly within psychology by arguing that unity and continuity of experience are aspects of the empirical self—properties of the stream of thought. However, James's argument—more properly, his assertion—was not generally accepted. In 1943, Gordon Allport argued for the self's good standing in psychology by documenting a wide variety of dramatic effects resulting from procedures that made experimental tasks important to subjects. Allport credited these effects to ego-involvement, which he defined as "a condition of total participation of the self." The evidence of history is that academic psychology did not accept Allport's argument. Much as Allport, in 1943, could credit psychoanalytic theory with "having preserved and advanced the study of certain functions of the self that postivistic psychology had consigned to oblivion" (p. 453), so can we now credit a variety of factions within the field of personality theory with having performed a similar function for much of the 40 years since Allport's review.

Perhaps the self would have achieved greater acceptance if its adherents had provided coordinated conceptual definitions and research procedures. However, there has never been much coordination between theory concerning the self and data collection. For example, the research procedure most commonly connected to the idea of self prior to about 1975—the use of skill-test instructions to produce ego-involvement—was never well tied to a theory of the self. The description of the skill-test procedure as ego-involvement had been generally abandoned by the early 1960s, a victim of theoretically irreconcilable conflicts among findings (Greenwald, 1982a; Iverson & Reuder, 1956; Van Bergen, 1968).

Has the situation changed? The best indication of a genuine new direction is the wide variety of recent findings that have been described in terms of newly introduced self-related concepts. Among these new procedures are ones that have been described as self-reference in memory, self-serving attributional bias, self-awareness, self-consciousness, self-verification, self-presentation, spontaneous self-concept, self-schema, and self-monitoring. But the lesson of history is that such research activity is not enough. Without an integrative conceptual scheme, critics will suggest that the "self-" with which these concepts start is merely a distracting speech defect, endemic to social and personality psychologists.

Accordingly, the argument that the self is, at last, ready for good standing in psychology requires an accompanying conceptual integration. Our review has been organized toward this end. The major points of this integration have been distributed among the preceding four sections. We now bring them together, and then conclude by summarizing the answers that this conception provides for several major questions that have traditionally surrounded the idea of a self.

The Self is a Complex, Person-Specific, Central, Attitudinal Schema

The major conclusions of our review has been:

1. The self as a knower is accessible to psychological investigation.
2. The self is a central cognitive structure, a self-concept with content that varies from person to person.
3. The self is a focus of affective regard—in other words, an attitude object.
4. The self is complex, consisting of diffuse, public, private, and collective facets, each providing a distinct basis for self-evaluation. The relative strengths of these facets, or subselves, vary as a function of person and situation.

Perhaps the most prominent feature of the self is the positive affect that is normally attached to one's own actions, attitudes, attributes, and memories. The self is thus the object of an *attitude*. But it is also an active, functioning organization that both acquires and retrieves knowledge. To include these (self-as-knower) properties we conceive the self not simply as an attitude object, but as an attitudinal *schema*.

We describe the self as a *central* attitudinal schema to indicate its importance relative to other schemata, and to acknowledge the many theoretical statements that, although differing in details, have credited the self with a central position in a larger cognitive structure. The self's mixture of cognitive, affective, and conative properties, and its multifacetedness—its mixture of the diffuse, public, private, and collective orientations—warrant its characterization as *complex*. And, lastly, the variable content of the self—individual differences in self-concept, in self-esteem, in motivational orientation, and in cognitive biases—oblige us to characterize the self as *person-specific*.

Our conception of the self as a complex, person-specific, central, attitudinal schema is, itself, complex. But it need not be unmanageably so. The first observation in our final section, just below, is that the self is constructed from *ordinary* materials. Its complexity and variability therefore present obstacles, but not ones so potent as to deter study.

Approaches to Traditional Enigmas of the Self

Is the Self Ordinary or Unique? The main ingredients of our definition of the self are attitude and schema, familiar psychological constructs that are well tied to research operations. We thus view the self as ordinary, but it is also undeniably special. It is unique due to the quantity of knowledge it synthesizes and to its complexity. Among the unique properties that may be credited to the scope and complexity of the self are the abilities to retrieve knowledge of events of the distant past, and to maintain the coherence of personal experience.

How Shall the Subject/Object Duality of the Self be Explained? We have faulted others' tendency to metaphorize the self's subject/object duality in terms of the reflectivity of a mirror. The mirror metaphor is debilitating in its failure to differentiate subject-of-knowledge (self as knower) and object-of-knowledge (self as known) properties. Instead, we suggest treating the subjective aspects of self as knowledge *process* and distinguish this from knowledge *content*. The process-content distinction has become increasingly manageable in recent cognitive psychology, and can be conceived with the aid of metaphors such as an evolving scientific theory or the program/data duality of a computer. The psychological concept of schema has been used recently to merge the duality of process and content into a single concept. Accordingly, we make use of the concept of schema in our definition of the self.

Is the Self Genuine and Stable, or Artificial and Malleable? Commentators on the process of self-presentation have often regarded the self as plastic, situation-dependent, and chameleon-like (Gergen, 1982; Goffman, 1959). Such observations obviously tend to undermine the view of the self as a central cognitive structure. In conceiving the self as a federation of diffuse, public, private, and collective factions, we hope to accommodate the broad evidence of situational influences on self-presentation, while preserving the conception of a stable, central organization. The usefulness of this view of person-situation interaction has already been supported by studies using recently developed individual-difference measures of orientation toward public and private aspects of the self.

Is the Self Unitary or Multiple? We agree with Epstein (1973, 1980) in regarding the self as a primary organizer, responsible for achieving a typically large degree of unity in one's personal knowledge structure. The ordinary unity or coherence of the self is particularly compelling when contrasted with pathologies, such as Korsakoff syndrome and multiple personality, in which coherence and unity appear to be lacking. At the same time, we endorse Allport's (1961) observation that "unity of personality is only a matter of degree, and we should avoid exaggerating it" (p. 386). The distinction among diffuse, public, private, and collective facets of the self provides one way of describing multiplicity without abandoning unity. This view of the self's unity should not be mistaken as an advocacy of the idea of total unity within the person. Rather, we see the self's unity as no more than an island of coherence within a larger psychic sea (Greenwald, 1982b).

Are the Self's Cognitive Biases due to External, Informational Influences or to Internal, Motivational Processes?   This question has been the focus of much published debate in recent years (summarized in Tetlock & Levi, 1982). As observed by Greenwald (1980),

> The motivation-information debate is representative of a pervasive and long-standing paradigm clash between internal-cause and external-cause explanations in psychology, other instances being instinct versus learning, heredity versus environment, nativism versus empiricism, drive theory versus radical behaviorsm, and dissonance versus self-perception. (p. 612)

It may be observed that none of the debates on these issues of organism-internal versus organism-external locus of causation has ever been resolved. Psychologists have tended to treat these debates as theoretical disagreements that are to be resolved by suitable data collection. In fact, these are conflicts between heavily defended paradigms that are no more likely to be destroyed by new data than is the ordinary self likely to dissolve in the face of a series of personal failures. At the same time, paradigms do vary in their usefulness, and they gain or lose adherents accordingly. In making the concept of schema central to the self, we have deliberately sidestepped the internal-external paradigm clash. The concept of schema as an active knowledge structure is rooted in evolutionary reasoning in biology, a systems paradigm that appeals to mutuality of influence between organism and environment.

A Final Comment: The Self as Historically Bound.   The self evolves historically during the lifetime. This evolution is due in part to culturally assisted growth in the self's cognitive content. Because the contribution of culture is free also to evolve, it is certain that the self has evolved greatly in history. Perhaps, indeed, the attainment of diffuse, public, private, and collective orientations within the human lifespan recapitulates a similar evolution that has been spread over thousands of years, as the contribution of culture has become more organized. In the last half-millenium, scientific understanding has become an increasingly potent contributor to culture. In just the present century, understanding based on the works of Freud and Piaget has brought once-mysterious mental processes into the range of ordinary understanding. These contributions, to use the terms of Section 2 of this chapter, have transferred some of the self's process into content. The present wave of interest in the self is certain, also, to produce understanding that will diffuse gradually into culture. (Perhaps knowledge of the self's role in ordinary memory will be the most significant such contribution.) This chapter, then, inevitably takes a step toward altering the picture that it describes.

ACKNOWLEDGMENT

For comments on an earlier draft, the authors thank Steven J. Breckler, Charles S. Carver, Seymour Epstein, William Ickes, Morris Rosenberg, and William B. Swann, Jr. Preparation of this chapter was aided by a grant from National Science Foundation, BNS 82-17006.

REFERENCES

Aall, A. Ein neues Gedachtnisgesetz? Experimentelle Untersuchung uber die Bedeutung der Re-produktionsperspektive. *Zeitschrift fur Psychologie,* 1913, *66,* 1–50.

Alloy, L. B., & Abramson, L. Y. Judgment of contingency in depressed and nondepressed students: Sadder but wiser? *Journal of Experimental Psychology: General,* 1979, *108,* 441–485.

Alloy, L. B., & Abramson, L. Y. Learned helplessness, depression, and the illusion of control. *Journal of Personality and Social Psychology,* 1982, *42,* 1114–1126.

Allport, G. W. *Personality: A psychological interpretation.* New York: Holt, Rinehart & Winston, 1937.

Allport, G. W. The ego in contemporary psychology, *Psychological Review,* 1943, *50,* 451–478.

Allport, G. W. *Becoming.* New Haven, CT: Yale University Press, 1955.

Allport, G. W. *Pattern and growth in personality.* New York: Holt, Rinehart & Winston, 1961.

Anderson, J. R. *Language, memory and thought.* Hillsdale, N J : Lawrence Erlbaum Associates, 1976.

Anderson, J. R. Effects of prior knowledge on memory for new information. *Memory and Cognition,* 1981, *9,* 237–246.

Anderson, J. R., & Bower, G. H. *Human Associative Memory.* Washington, D C : Winston, 1973.

Anderson, J. R., & Reder, L. M. An elaborate processing explanation of depth of processing. In L. S. Cermak & F. I. M. Craik (Eds.), *Levels of processing in human memory.* Hillsdale, N J : Lawrence Erlbaum Associates, 1979.

Arkin, R. M., Appleman, A. J., & Burger, J. M. Social anxiety, self-presentation, and the self-serving bias in causal attribution. *Journal of Personality and Social Psychology,* 1980, *38,* 23–36.

Aronson, E. *The social animal.* (3rd ed.) San Francisco: W. H. Freeman, 1980.

Banaji, M. R. *Cognitive models of the self: Evidence for an encoding centrality principle.* Unpublished M. A. thesis, Ohio State University, 1982.

Banaji, M. R., Devine, P. G., & Greenwald, A. G. *By what means does self-reference facilitate memory?* Unpublished manuscript, Ohio State University, 1983.

Bandura, A. Self-efficacy: Toward a unifying theory of behavioral change. *Psychological Review,* 1977, *84,* 191–215.

Bartlett, F. C. *Remembering: A study in experimental and social psychology.* Cambridge: Cambridge University, 1932.

Baumeister, R. F. A self-presentational view of social phenemena. *Psychological Bulletin,* 1982, *91,* 3–26.

Bellezza, F. S. Mnemonic devices: Classification, characteristics, and criteria. *Review of Educational Research,* 1981, *51,* 247–275.

Belleza, F. *The self as a mnemonic device: The role of internal cues.* Unpublished manuscript, Ohio University, 1983.

Bem, D. J., & McConnell, H. K. Testing the self-perception explanation of dissonance phenomena: On the salience of premanipulated attitudes. *Journal of Personality and Social Psychology,* 1970, *14,* 23–31.

Bjork, R. A. Theoretical implications of directed forgetting. In A. W. Melton & E. Martin (Eds.), *Coding processes in human memory.* Washington, D C : Winston, 1972.

Bobrow, S. A., & Bower, G. H. Comprehension and recall of sentences. *Journal of Experimental Psychology,* 1969, *80,* 455–461.

Bower, G. H., & Gilligan, S. G. Remembering information related to one's self. *Journal of Research in Personality,* 1979, *13,* 420–432.

Bradley, G. W. Self-serving bias in the attribution process: A reexamination of the fact or fiction question. *Journal of Personality and Social Psychology,* 1978, *36,* 56–71.

Bransford, J. D., & Franks, J. J. The abstraction of linguistic ideas. *Cognitive Psychology,* 1971, *2,* 331–350.

Breckler, S. J. *Self-referent cognition and personality.* Unpublished M. A. thesis, Ohio State University, 1981.

Breckler, S. J., & Greenwald, A. G. *Favorable self-referent judgments are made faster than non-favorable ones.* Paper presented at Midwestern Psychological Association, Detroit, MI, 1981.

Breckler, S. J., & Greenwald, A. G. *Charting coordinates for the self-concept in multidimensional trait space.* In symposium, "Functioning and Measurement of Self-Esteem," American Psychological Association, Washington, D C, 1982.

Breckler, S. J., Pratkanis, A. R., McCann, D. *The representation of self in multidimensional cognitive space.* Unpublished manuscript, Ohio State University, 1983.

Brenner, M. The next-in-line effect. *Journal of Verbal Learning and Verbal Behavior,* 1973, *12,* 320–323.

Buss, A. H. *Self-consciousness and social anxiety.* San Francisco: Freeman, 1980.

Butters, N., & Cermak, L. S. *Alcoholic Korsakoff's syndrome: An information processing approach to amnesia.* New York: Academic Press, 1980.

Campbell, D. T. Evolutionary epistemology. In P. A. Schilpp (Ed.), *The philosophy of Karl Popper,* LaSalle, IL: Open Court Publishing Co., 1974.

Campbell, D. T. *Descriptive epistemology: Psychological, sociological and evolutionary.* Unpublished manuscript. Northwestern University, 1979.

Cantor, N., & Mischel, W. Traits as prototypes: Effects on recognition memory. *Journal of Personality and Social Psychology,* 1977, *35,* 38–48.

Cantor, N., & Mischel, W. Prototypes in person perception. In L. Berkowitz (Ed.), *Advances in experimental social psychology* (Vol. 12). New York: Academic Press, 1979.

Carver, C. S., & Scheier, M. F. *Attention and self-regulation: A control-theory approach to human behavior.* New York: Springer-Verlag, 1981.

Cheek, J. M., & Hogan, R. Self-concepts, self-presentations, and moral judgments. In J. Suls & A. G. Greenwald (Eds.), *Psychological perspectives on the self* (Vol. 2). Hillsdale, N J : Lawrence Erlbaum Associates, 1983.

Chew, B. R. *Selective recall of self and other referenced information.* Unpublished doctoral dissertation, Harvard University, 1983.

Cialdini, R. B., Borden, R. J., Thorne, A., Walker, M. R., Freeman, S., & Sloan, L. R. Basking in reflected glory: Three (football) field studies. *Journal of Personality and Social Psychology,* 1976, *34,* 366–375.

Claeys, W. *Private self-consciousness and incidental recall of self- and other-referent information.* Unpublished manuscript, University of Leuven, 1983.

Claparède, E. Recognition and "me-ness." In D. Rapaport (Ed.), *Organization and pathology of thought.* New York: Columbia University Press, 1951. (Original French publication, 1911).

Combs, A. W., & Snygg, D. *Individual behavior: A perceptual approach to behavior.* New York: Harper & Brothers, 1949. (Revised edition 1959).

Cooley, C. H. *Human nature and the social order.* New York: Schocken Books, 1964. (Original publication 1902).

Coopersmith, S. *The antecedents of self-esteem.* San Francisco: W. H. Freeman, 1967.

Costanzo, P. R. Conformity development as a function of self-blame. *Journal of Personality and Social Psychology,* 1970, *14,* 366–374.

Craik, F. I. M., & Tulving, E. Depth of processing and the retention of words in episodic memory. *Journal of Experimental Psychology: General,* 1975, *104,* 268–294.

Crowne, D. P., & Marlowe, D. *The approval motive.* New York: Wiley, 1964.

Cullen, D. M. *Attitude measurement by cognitive sampling.* Unpublished doctoral disseration, Ohio State University, 1968.

Darley, J. M., & Gross, P. H. A hypothesis-confirming bias in labeling effects. *Journal of Personality and Social Psychology,* 1983, *44,* 20–33.

Deutsch, J. A., & Deutsch, D. Attention: Some theoretical considerations. *Psychological Review,* 1963, *70,* 80–90.

Diener, E. Deindividuation: Causes and consequences. *Social Behavior and Personality,* 1977, *5,* 143–155.

Diener, E. Deindividuation: The absence of self-awareness and self-regulation in group members. In P. Paulus (Ed.), *The psychology of group influence.* Hillsdale, N J : Lawrence Erlbaum Associates, 1980.

Dipboye, R. L. Alternative approaches to deindividuation. *Psychological Bulletin,* 1977, *84,* 1057–1075.

Dutta, S., & Kanungo, R. N. *Affect and memory: A reformulation.* Oxford: Pergamon Press, 1967.

d'Ydewalle, G., Degryse, M. & DeCorte, E. Expected time of test and the acquisition of knowledge. *British Journal of Educational Psychology,* 1981, *51,* 23–31.

Edwards, A. L. *Techniques of attitude scale construction.* New York: Appleton-Century-Crofts, 1957.

Epstein, S. The self-concept revisited: Or a theory of a theory. *American Psychologist,* 1973, *28,* 404–416.

Epstein, S. The self-concept: A review and the proposal of an integrated theory of personality. In E. Staub (Ed.), *Personality: Basic issues and current research.* Englewood Cliffs, NJ: Prentice-Hall, 1980.

Epstein, W. Mechanisms of directed forgetting. In G. Bower (Ed.), *The psychology of learning and motivation* (Vol. 6). New York: Academic Press, 1972.

Erdelyi, M., Buschke, H., & Finkelstein, S. Hypermnesia for Socratic stimuli: The growth of recall for an internally generated memory list abstracted from a series of riddles. *Memory and Cognition,* 1977, *5,* 283–286.

Ericsson, K. A., & Simon H. A. Verbal reports as data. *Psychological Review,* 1980, *87,* 215–251.

Fenigstein, A. Self-consciousness, self-attention, and social interaction. *Journal of Personality and Social Psychology,* 1979, *37,* 75–86.

Fenigstein, A. *Self-consciousness and the overperception of self as a target.* Unpublished manuscript, Kenyon College, 1983.

Fenigstein, A., Scheier, M. F., & Buss, A. H. Public and private self-consciousness: Assessment and theory. *Journal of Consulting and Clinical Psychology,* 1975, *43,* 522–527.

Ferguson, T. J., Rule, B. G., & Carlson, D. Memory for personally relevant information. *Journal of Personality and Social Psychology,* 1983, *44,* 251–261.

Fischhoff, B. Perceived informativeness of facts. *Journal of Experimental Psychology: Human Perception and Performance,* 1977, *3,* 349–358.

Fishbein, M. (Ed.). *Readings in attitude theory and measurement.* New York: Wiley, 1967.

Frey, D. Reactions to success and failure in public and private conditions. *Journal of Experimental Social Psychology,* 1978, *14,* 172–179.

Friedman, A.,& Pullyblank. J. *Remembering information about oneself and others: The role of distinctiveness.* Paper presented at Psychonomic Society, Minneapolis, MN, 1982.

Froming, W. J., & Carver, C. S. Divergent influences of private and public self-consciousness in a compliance paradigm. *Journal of Research in Personality,* 1981, *15,* 159–171.

Froming, W. J., Walker, G. R., & Lopyan, K. J. Public and private self-awareness: When personal attitudes conflict with societal expectations. *Journal of Experimental Social Psychology,* 1982, *18,* 476–487.

Gallup, G. G. Self-recognition in primates: A comparative approach to the bidirectional properties of consciousness, *American Psychologist,* 1977, *32,* 329–338.

Gecas, V. The self-concept. *Annual Review of Sociology,* 1982, *8,* 1–33.

Gergen, K. J. *The concept of self.* New York: Holt, Rinehart & Winston, 1971.

Gergen, K. J. From self to science: What is there to know? In J. Suls (Ed.), *Psychological perspectives on the self* (Vol. 1). Hillsdale, N J : Lawrence Erlbaum Associates, 1982.

Glixman, A. F. Recall of completed and uncompleted activities under varying degrees of stress. *Journal of Experimental Psychology,* 1949, *39,* 291–296.

Goethals, G. R., & Reckman, R. F. The perception of consistency in attitudes. *Journal of Experimental Social Psychology,* 1973, *9,* 491–501.

Goffman, E. *The presentation of self in everyday life.* New York: Doubleday, 1959.

Greenberg, G., Pyszczynski, T., & Solomon, S. The self-serving attributional bias: Beyond self-presentation. *Journal of Experimental Social Psychology,* 1982, *18,* 56–67.

Greenwald, A. G. Cognitive learning, cognitive response to persuasion and attitude change. In A. G. Greenwald, T. C. Brock, & T. M. Ostrom (Eds.), *Psychological foundations of attitudes.* New York: Academic Press, 1968.

Greenwald, A. G. Consequences of prejudice against the null hypothesis. *Psychological Bulletin,* 1975, *82,* 1–20.

Greenwald, A. G. The totalitarian ego: Fabrication and revision of personal history. *American Psychologist,* 1980, *35,* 603–618.

Greenwald, A. G. Self and memory. In G. H. Bower (Ed.), *The psychology of learning and motivation* (Vol. 15). New York: Academic Press, 1981.

Greenwald, A. G. Ego task analysis: An integration of research on ego-involvement and self-awareness. In A. Hastorf & A. M. Isen (Eds.), *Cognitive Social Psychology.* New York: Elsevier North Holland, 1982. (a)

Greenwald, A. G. Is any*one* in charge? Personalysis versus the principle of personal unity. In J. Suls (Ed.), *Psychological perspectives on the self* (Vol. 1). Hillsdale, N J.: Lawrence Erlbaum Associates, 1982. (b)

Greenwald, A. G., & Albert, R. D. Acceptance and recall of improvised arguments. *Journal of Personality and Social Psychology,* 1968, *8,* 31–34.

Greenwald, A. G., & Banaji, M. R. *The second generation effect.* Unpublished manuscript, Ohio State University, 1983.

Greenwald, A. G., Banaji, M. R., Pratkanis, A. R., & Breckler, S. J. *A centrality effect in recall.* Paper presented at Psychonomic Society, Philadelphia, 1981.

Greenwald, A. G., & Breckler, S. J. To whom is the self presented? In B. R. Schlenker (Ed.), *The self and social life.* New York: McGraw-Hill , in press,

Greenwald, A. G., & Sakumara, J. S. Attitude and selective learning: Where are the phenomena of yesteryear? *Journal of Personality and Social Psychology*, 1967, *7*, 387–397.

Hartmann, H. *Ego psychology and the problem of adaptation*. New York: International Universities Press, 1958. (Original German publication, 1939).

Harvey, J. H., Harris, B., & Barnes, R. D. Actor-observer differences in the perceptions of responsibility and freedom. *Journal of Personality and Social Psychology*, 1975, *32*, 22–28.

Helmreich, R., Stapp, J., & Ervin, C. The Texas Social Behavior Inventory (TSBI): An objective measure of self-esteem or social competence. *Journal Supplement Abstract Service. Catalog of Selected Documents in Psychology*, 1974, *4*, 79.

Hilgard, E. Human motives and the concept of the self. *American Psychologist*, 1949, *4*, 374–382.

Hofstadter, D. R. *Godel, Escher, Bach: An eternal golden braid*. New York: Basic Books, 1979.

Hull, J. G., & Levy, A. S. The organizational functions of the self: An alternative to the Duval and Wicklund model of self-awareness. *Journal of Personality and Social Psychology*, 1979, *37*, 756–768.

Iverson, M. A., & Reuder, M. E. Ego involvement as an experimental variable. *Psychological Reports*, 1956, *2*, 147–181.

Jacoby, L. L. On interpreting the effects of repetition: Solving a problem versus remembering a solution. *Journal of Verbal Learning and Verbal Behavior*, 1978, *17*, 649–667.

Jacoby, L. L., Bartz, W. H., & Evans, J. D. A functional approach to levels of processing. *Journal of Experimental Psychology: Human Learning and Memory*, 1978, *4*, 331–346.

Jacoby, L. L., & Witherspoon, D. Remembering without awareness. *Canadian Journal of Psychology*, 1982, *36*, 300–324.

James, W. *The principles of psychology*. New York: Holt, 1890.

Janis, I. L., & Field, P. B. A behavioral assessment of persuasibility: Consistency of individual differences. In C. I. Hovland & I. L. Janis (Eds.), *Personality and persuasibility*. New Haven, CT: Yale University Press, 1959.

Jervis, R. *Perception and misperception in international politics*. Princeton, NJ: Princeton University Press, 1976.

Johnston, W. A. Individual performance and self-evaluation in a simulated team. *Organizational Behavior and Human Performance*, 1967, *2*, 309–328.

Jones, E. E., & Kohler, R. The effects of plausibility on the learning of controversial statements. *Journal of Abnormal and Social Psychology*, 1958, *57*, 315–320.

Jones, E. E., & Pittman, T. S. Toward a general theory of strategic self-presentation. In J. Suls (Ed.), *Psychological perspectives on the self* (Vol. 1). Hillsdale, N J : Lawrence Erlbaum Associates, 1982.

Jones, E. E., & Sigall, H. The bogus pipeline: A new paradigm for measuring affect and attitudes. *Psychological Bulletin*, 1971, *76*, 349–364.

Judd, C. M., & Kulik, J. A. Schematic effects of social attitudes on information processing and recall. *Journal of Personality and Social Psychology*, 1980, *38*, 569–578.

Karylowski, J. Manuscript in preparation, 1983.

Keenan, J. M., & Baillet, S. D. Memory for personally and socially significant events. In R. S. Nickerson (Ed.), *Attention and Performance VIII*, Hillsdale, NJ: Lawrence Erlbaum Associates, 1980.

Kihlstrom, J. F., & Cantor, N. Mental representations of the self. In L. Berkowitz (Ed.), *Advances in experimental social psychology* (Vol. 15). New York: Academic Press, in press.

Koffka, K. *Principles of Gestalt psychology*. New York: Harcourt, 1935.

Kuhn, T. S. *The structure of scientific revolutions*. Chicago: University of Chicago Press, 1970.

Kuiper, N. A. Convergent evidence for the self as a prototype: The "inverted-U RT effect" for self and other judgments. *Personality and Social Psychology Bulletin*, 1981, *7*, 438–443.

Kuiper, N. A., & Derry, P. A. The self as a cognitive prototype: An application to person perception and depression. In N. Cantor & J. Kihlstrom (Eds.), *Personality, cognition and social interaction*. Hillsdale, NJ: Lawrence Erlbaum Associates, 1981.

Kuiper, N. A., & Rogers, T. B. Encoding of personal information: Self-other differences. *Journal of Personality and Social Psychology*, 1979, *37*, 499–512.

Langer, E. J. The illusion of control. *Journal of Personality and Social Psychology*, 1975, *32*, 311–329.

Lazarus, R. S. Thoughts on the relations between emotion and cognition. *American Psychologist*, 1982, *37*, 1019–1024.

Leary, M. R., Silver, S. E., Schlenker, B. R., & Darby, B. W. The multidimensionality of self-monitoring. *Replications in Social Psychology*, 1982, *2*, 33–36.

Levine, J. M., & Murphy, G. The learning and retention of controversial statements. *Journal of Abnormal and Social Psychology*, 1943, *38*, 507–517.

Lewin, K. *Principles of topological psychology*. New York: McGraw-Hill, 1936.

Lewinsohn, P. M., Mischel, W., Chaplin, W., & Barton, R. Social competence and depression: The role of illusory self-perceptions. *Journal of Abnormal Psychology*, 1980, *89*, 203–212.

Lewis, M., & Brooks-Gunn, J. *Social cognition and the acquisition of self*. New York: Plenum Press, 1979.

Linville, P. W. Affect consequences of complexity regarding the self and other. In M. S. Clark & S. T. Fiske (Eds.), *Affect and cognition*. Hillsdale, NJ: Lawrence Erlbaum Associates, 1982.

Loevinger, J. *Ego development*. San Francisco: Jossey-Bass, 1976.

Loftus, E. F., Miller, D. G., & Burns, H. J. Semantic integration of verbal information into visual memory. *Journal of Experimental Psychology: Human Learning and Memory*, 1978, *4*, 19–31.

Lord, C. G. Schemas and images as memory aids: Two modes of processing social information. *Journal of Personality and Social Psychology*, 1980, *38*, 257–269.

Lord, C. G., Gilbert, D. T., & Stanley, M. A. *Idiographic self-schema and cognitive efficiency: Associations or affect?* Unpublished manuscript, Princeton University, 1983.

Maki, R. H., & McCaul, K. D. *When does self-reference enhance memory?* Paper presented at Psychonomic Society, Minneapolis, MN, 1982.

Mandler, G. Consciousness: Respectable, useful and probably necessary. In R. Solso (Ed.), *Information processing and cognition: The Loyola Symposium*. Hillsdale, NJ: Lawrence Erlbaum Associates, 1975.

Mandler, G. The structure of value: Accounting for taste. In M. Clark & S. Fiske (Eds.), *Affect and cognition: 17th annual Carnegie symposium on cognition*. Hillsdale, NJ: Lawrence Erlbaum Associates, 1982.

Markus, H. Self-schemata and processing information about the self. *Journal of Personality and Social Psychology*, 1977, *35*, 63–78.

Markus, H. The self in thought and memory. In D. M. Wegner & R. R. Vallacher (Eds.), *The self in social psychology*. New York: Oxford Press, 1980.

Markus, H., Crane, M., Berstein, S., & Siladi, M. Self-schemas and gender. *Journal of Personality and Social Psychology*, 1982, *42*, 38–50.

Markus, H., Hamill, R., & Sentis, K. *Thinking fat: Self-schema for body weight and the processing of weight relevant information*. Paper presented at American Psychological Association, Montreal, 1980.

Markus, H., & Sentis, K. The self in information processing. In J. Suls (Ed.), *Psychological perspectives on the self* (Vol. 1). Hillsdale, NJ: Lawrence Erlbaum Associates, 1982.

Markus, H., & Smith, J. The influence of self-schema on the perception of others. In N. Cantor & J. Kihlstrom (Eds.), *Personality, cognition and social interaction*. Hillsdale, NJ: Lawrence Erlbaum Associates, 1981.

McClelland, D. C., Atkinson, J. W., Clark, R. A., & Lowell, E. L. *The achievement motive*. New York: Appleton-Century-Crofts, 1953.

McFarlin, D. B., & Blascovich, J. *Affective, behavioral and cognitive consequences of self-esteem.*

Paper read at a symposium "Functioning and Measurement of Self-Esteem," American Psychological Association, Washington, DC, 1982.

McGuire, W. J., & McGuire, C. V. Salience of handedness in the spontaneous self-concept. *Perceptual and Motor Skills*, 1980, *50*, 3–7.

McGuire, W. J., & McGuire, C. V. The spontaneous self-concept as affected by personal distinctiveness. In A. Norem-Hebeisen, M. D. Lynch, & K. Gergen (Eds.), *The self-concept.* New York: Ballinger, 1981.

McGuire, W. J., & McGuire, C. V. Significant others in self-space: Sex differences and developmental trends in the social self. In J. Suls (Ed.), *Psychological perspectives on the self* (Vol. 1). Hillsdale, N J : Lawrence Erlbaum Associates, 1982.

McGuire, W. J., McGuire, C. V., Child, P., & Fujioka, T. Salience of ethnicity in the spontaneous self-concept as a function on one's ethnic distinctiveness in the social environment. *Journal of Personality and Social Psychology*, 1978, *36*, 511–520.

McGuire, W. J., McGuire, C. V., & Winston, W. Effects of household composition on the salience of one's gender in the spontaneous self-concept. *Journal of Experimental Social Psychology*, 1979, *15*, 77–90.

McGuire, W. J., & Padawer-Singer, A. Trait salience in the spontaneous self-concept. *Journal of Personality and Social Psychology*, 1976, *33*, 743–754.

Milgram, S. Behavioral study of obedience. *Journal of Abnormal and Social Psychology*, 1963, *67*, 371–378.

Milgram, S. *Obedience to authority.* New York: Harper & Row, 1974.

Miller, D. T., & Ross, M. Self-serving biases in the attribution of causality: Fact or fiction? *Psychological Bulletin*, 1975, *82*, 213–225.

Mischel, W., Ebbesen, E. B., & Zeiss, A. R. Determinants of selective memory about the self. *Journal of Consulting and Clinical Psychology*, 1976, *44*, 92–103.

Neisser, U. *Cognitive psychology.* New York: Appleton-Century-Crofts, 1967.

Neisser, U. *Cognition and reality.* San Francisco: Freeman, 1976.

Nisbett, R. E., & Ross, L. *Human inference: Strategies and shortcomings.* Englewood, NJ: Prentice-Hall, 1980.

Nisbett, R. E., & Wilson, T. D. Telling more than we can know: Verbal reports on mental processes. *Psychological Review*, 1977, *84*, 231–259.

Nuttin, J. *Tâche, réussite, et échec.* Louvain, Belgium: Publications Universitaires, 1953.

Nuttin, J., & Greenwald, A. G. *Reward and punishment in human learning.* New York: Academic Press, 1968.

Ostrom, T. M., & Brock, T. C. A cognitive model of attitudinal involvement. In R. P. Abelson, E. Aronson, W. J. McGuire, T. M. Newcomb, M. J. Rosenberg, & P. H. Tannenbaum (Eds.), *Theories of cognitive consistency: A sourcebook.* Chicago: Rand-McNally, 1968.

Owens, J., Dafoe, J., & Bower, G. H. *Taking a point of view: Character identification and attributional processes in story comprehension and memory.* Paper presented at American Psychological Association, San Francisco, 1977.

Petty, R. E., Ostrom, T. M., & Brock, T. C. (Eds.), *Cognitive responses in persuasion.* Hillsdale, NJ: Lawrence Erlbaum Associates, 1981.

Popper, K. *The logic of scientific discovery.* New York: Basic Books, 1959.

Posner, M. I., & Keele, S. W. On the genesis of abstract ideas. *Journal of Experimental Psychology*, 1968, *77*, 353–363.

Posner, M. I., & Keele, S. W. Retention of abstract ideas. *Journal of Experimental Psychology*, 1970, *83*, 304–308.

Pratkanis, A. R. *Attitudes and memory: The heuristic and schematic functions of attitudes.* Unpublished doctoral dissertation, Ohio State University, 1983.

Quigley-Fernandez, B., & Tedeschi, J. T. The bogus pipeline as lie detector: Two validity studies. *Journal of Personality and Social Psychology*, 1978, *36*, 247–256.

Rapaport, D. *Emotions and memory*. New York: International Universities Press, 1942 (Republished in 1971).

Read, S. J., & Rosson, M. B. Rewriting history: The biasing effects of attitude on memory. *Social Cognition*, 1982, *1*, 240–255.

Riess, M., Rosenfeld, P., Melburg, B., & Tedeschi, J. T. Self-serving attributions: Biased private perceptions and distorted public descriptions. *Journal of Personality and Social Psychology*, 1981, *41*, 224–231.

Robinson, J. P., & Shaver, P. R. *Measures of social psychological attitudes*. Ann Arbor, MI: Institute for Social Research, 1973.

Rogers, C. *Counseling and psychotherapy*. Boston: Houghton-Mifflin, 1942.

Rogers, C. *Client-centered therapy*. Boston: Houghton-Mifflin, 1951.

Rogers, T. B. A model of the self as an aspect of the human information processing system. In N. Cantor & J. Kihlstrom (Eds.), *Personality, cognition, and social interaction*. Hillsdale, NJ: Lawrence Erlbaum Associates, 1981.

Rogers, T. B., Kuiper, N. A., & Kirker, W. S. Self-reference and the encoding of personal information. *Journal of Personality and Social Psychology*, 1977, *35*, 677–688.

Rogers, T. B., Rogers, P. J., & Kuiper, N. A. Evidence for the self as a cognitive prototype: The "false alarms effect." *Personality and Social Psychology Bulletin*, 1979, *5*, 53–56.

Rosch, E. On the internal structure of perceptual and semantic categories. In T. E. More (Ed.), *Cognitive development and acquisition of language*. New York: Academic Press, 1973.

Rosch, E. Cognitive representations of semantic categories. *Journal of Experimental Psychology: General*, 1975, *104*, 192–233.

Rosch, E. Principles of categorization. In E. Rosch & B. B. Lloyd (Eds.), *Cognition and categorization*. Hillsdale, NJ: Lawrence Erlbaum Associates, 1978.

Rosenberg, M. *Society and the adolescent self-image*. Princeton, NJ: Princeton University Press, 1965.

Rosenberg, M. Psychological selectivity in self-esteem formation. In C. W. Sherif & M. Sherif (Eds.), *Attitude, ego-involvement, and change*. New York: Wiley, 1967.

Rosenberg, M. *Conceiving the self*. New York: Basic Books, 1979.

Rosenzweig, S. An experimental study of "repression" with special reference to need-persistence and ego-defensive reactions to frustration. *Journal of Experimental Psychology*, 1943, *32*, 64–74.

Ross, M., & Sicoly, F. Egocentric biases in availability and attribution. *Journal of Personality and Social Psychology*, 1979, *37*, 322–336.

Santee, R. T., & Maslach, C. To agree or not to agree: Personal dissent amid social pressure to conform. *Journal of Personality and Social Psychology*, 1982, *42*, 690–700.

Scheier, M. F. Effects of public and private self-consciousness on the public expression of personal beliefs. *Journal of Personality and Social Psychology*, 1980, *39*, 514–521.

Scheier, M. F., & Carver, C. S. Private and public self-attention, resistance to change, and dissonance reduction. *Journal of Personality and Social Psychology*, 1980, *39*, 390–405.

Scheier, M. F., & Carver, C. S. Public and private aspects of the self. In L. Wheeler (Ed.), *Review of personality and social psychology* (Vol. 2). Beverly Hills, CA: Sage, 1981.

Scheier, M. F., & Carver, C. S. Two sides of the self: One for you and one for me. In J. Suls & A. G. Greenwald (Eds.), *Psychological perspectives on the self* (Vol. 2). Hillsdale, NJ: Lawrence Erlbaum Associates, 1983.

Schlenker, B. R. Self-presentation: Managing the impression of consistency when reality interferes with self-enhancement. *Journal of Personality and Social Psychology*, 1975, *32*, 1030–1037.

Schlenker, B. R. *Impression management*. Monterey, CA: Brooks-Cole, 1980.

Schlenker, B. R. (Ed.). *The self and social life*. New York: McGraw-Hill, in press.

Schlenker, B. R., Hallam, J. R., & McCown, N. E. Motives and social evaluation: Actor-observer differences in the delineation of motives for a beneficial act. *Journal of Experimental Social Psychology*, 1983, *19*, 254–273.

Schlenker, B. R., & Miller, R. S. Egocentrism in groups: Self-serving biases or logical information process? *Journal of Personality and Social Psychology,* 1977, *35,* 755–764.

Schnur, P. Testing the encoding elaboration hypothesis: The effects of exemplar ranking on recognition and recall. *Memory and Cognition,* 1977, *5,* 666–672.

Sherif, M., & Cantril, H. *The psychology of ego-involvements.* New York: Wiley, 1947.

Sherif, M., Harvey, O. J., White, B. J., Hood, W. R., & Sherif, C. W. *Intergroup cooperation and competition: The Robbers' Cave experiment.* Norman, OK: University Book Exchange, 1961.

Sherif, M., & Hovland, C. I. *Social judgment: Assimilation and contrast effects in communication and attitude change.* New Haven, CT: Yale University Press, 1961.

Shrauger, J. S., & Sorman, P. B. Self-evaluations, initial success and failure, and improvement as determinants of persistence. *Journal of Consulting and Clinical Psychology,* 1977, *45,* 784–795.

Slamecka, N. J., & Graf, P. The generation effect: Delineation of a phenomenon. *Journal of Experimental Psychology: Human Learning and Memory,* 1978, *4,* 592–604.

Smith, E. E. Theories of semantic memory. In W. K. Estes (Ed.), *Handbook of learning and cognitive processes* (Vol. 5). Hillsdale, NJ: Lawrence Erlbaum Associates, 1976.

Smith, E. E., Adams, N., & Schorr, D. Fact retrieval and the paradox of inference. *Cognitive Psychology,* 1978, *10,* 438–464.

Smith, E. E., & Medin, D. L. *Categories and concepts.* Cambridge, MA: Harvard University Press, 1981.

Smith, M. B. Attitudes, values, and selfhood. In H. E. Howe & M. M. Page (Eds.), *Nebraska Symposium on Motivation 1979.* Lincoln: University of Nebraska Press, 1980.

Snyder, C. R., Stucky, R. J., & Higgins, R. L. *Excuses: The masquerade solution.* New York: Wiley Interscience, in press.

Snyder, M. Self-monitoring of expressive behavior. *Journal of Personality and Social Psychology,* 1974, *30,* 526–537.

Snyder, M., & Campbell, B. H. Self-monitoring: The self in action. In J. Suls (Ed.), *Psychological perspectives on the self* (Vol. 1). Hillsdale, NJ: Lawrence Erlbaum Associates, 1982.

Snyder, M., & Swann, W. B. Hypothesis-testing processes in social interaction. *Journal of Personality and Social Psychology,* 1978, *36,* 941–950.

Snyder, M., & Uranowitz, S. W. Reconstructing the past: Some cognitive consequences of person perception. *Journal of Personality and Social Psychology,* 1978, *36,* 941–950.

Strickland, B. R., & Crowne, D. P. Conformity under conditions of simulated group pressure as a function of the need for social approval. *Journal of Social Psychology,* 1962, *58,* 171–181.

Swann, W. B. Self-verification: Bringing social reality into harmony with the self. In J. Suls & A. G. Greenwald (Eds.), *Psychological perspectives on the self* (Vol. 2). Hillsdale, NJ: Lawrence Erlbaum Associates, 1983.

Swann, W. B., & Read, S. J. Self-verification processes: How we sustain our self-conceptions. *Journal of Experimental Social Psychology,* 1981, *17,* 351–372.

Tesser, A., & Campbell, J. Self-definition and self-evaluation maintenance. In J. Suls & A. G. Greenwald (Eds.), *Psychological perspectives on the self* (Vol. 2), Hillsdale, NJ: Lawrence Erlbaum Associates, 1983.

Tetlock, P. E., & Levi, A. Attribution bias: On the inconclusiveness of the cognition-motivation debate. *Journal of Experimental Social Psychology,* 1982, *18,* 68–88.

Trope, Y. Inferences of personal characteristics on the basis of information retrieved from one's memory. *Journal of Personality and Social Psychology,* 1978, *36,* 93–106.

Turner, R. H. The real self: From institution to impulse. *American Journal of Sociology,* 1976, *81,* 989–1016.

Tversky, A., & Kahneman, D. Judgments under uncertainty: Heuristics and biases. *Science,* 1974, *185,* 1124–1131.

Van Bergen, A. *Task interruption.* Amsterdam: North-Holland, 1968.

Waly, P., & Cook, S. W. Attitude as a determinant of learning and memory: A failure to confirm. *Journal of Personality and Social Psychology,* 1966, *4,* 280–288.

Wicklund, R. A. Objective self-awareness. In L. Berkowitz (Ed.), *Advances in experimental social psychology* (Vol. 8). New York: Academic Press, 1975.

Wortman, C. B. Causal attribution and personal control. In J. H. Harvey, W. J. Ickes, & R. F. Kidd (Eds.), *New directions in attribution research* (Vol. 1). Hillsdale, NJ: Lawrence Erlbaum Associates, 1976.

Wylie, R. *The self-concept* (Vol. 1). Lincoln: University of Nebraska Press, 1974.

Wylie, R. *The self-concept* (Vol. 2). Lincoln: University of Nebraska Press, 1979.

Zajonc, R. B. Feeling and thinking: Preferences need no inferences. *American Psychologist,* 1980, *35,* 151–175.

Zeigarnik, B. Über das behalten von erledigten und unerledigten handlungen. *Psychologische Forschung,* 1927, *9,* 1–85.

Zeigarnik, B. On finished and unfinished tasks. In W. D. Ellis (Ed.), *A source book of Gestalt psychology.* New York: Humanities Press, 1938.

Zimbardo, P. G. The human choice: Individuation, reason and order versus deindividuation, impulse and chaos. In W. J. Arnold & D. Levine (Eds.), *Nebraska Symposium on Motivation* (Vol. 17). Lincoln: University of Nebraska Press, 1969.

Zuckerman, M., Kernis, M. H., Guarnera, S. M., Murphy, J. F., & Rappoport, L. *The egocentric bias: Seeing oneself as cause and target of others' behavior.* Unpublished manuscript, University of Rochester, 1983.

5 Toward Understanding the Role of Affect in Cognition

Alice M. Isen
University of Maryland

Contents

OVERVIEW

A growing body of literature now indicates that affective states—even mild and even positive affective states—can influence thoughts, cognitive processing, and social behavior in some rather remarkable ways. Moreover, the findings of these studies suggest that this literature may contribute to our understanding not only of affect, but also of cognitive functioning more generally. Eventually this work may also help to illuminate the underlying relationship among affect, cognition, and behavior, as well.

179

In the present chapter, we examine the various types of effects that feelings have been found to have on cognition and behavior. In the course of doing this, we distinguish between powerful emotion and more mundane feeling states, consider the relationship between affect and arousal, note the contrast between the effects of positive versus negative feeling states, and discuss some of the methods that have been used to study affect, considering some implications of the different results obtained with the various techniques used. This chapter cannot hope to present all of the recent work relating to the topic of affect. Its goal is to summarize representative research on the influence of affect on cognition and social behavior, to discuss some central issues that have emerged from this work, and to stimulate further thought and empirical investigation of these issues.

INTRODUCTION

Although affect and cognition are generally thought of as separate spheres, the suggestion that strong emotion can influence thought and behavior is not in itself surprising. Most people are aware that intense affect, especially unpleasant emotion such as fear, anger, or sorrow, can influence their actions and even their thoughts. For example, motivational and physiological psychologists have written about emotion as "disorganizing" (e.g., Young, 1943, 1961; see Arnold, 1970, Easterbrook, 1959, and Leeper, 1948, 1970, for critical discussions of this issue). Thus, to some extent it is appealing to envision emotions as "interrupts" in the normal program of behavior, as Simon (1967) did in his computer simulation. People recognize that strong negative emotion interrupts them when it occurs.

If asked to think about the question, most people would also agree that strong positive emotions also influence behavior, interrupting the flow of ideas and activities. Remember the old television show, "The Millionaire"? If someone came to your door and handed you a check for one million dollars, it would be unlikely that, after that person left, you would simply go back to what you had been doing—wrapping hamburger patties for the freezer, writing a paper, building shelves in the basement. No, more likely you would think about what had just happened, and you might want to tell someone about it. Intense positive emotion, like intense negative emotion, would interrupt you, demand your attention, be expressed, and influence your behavior.

But what about more common feeling states, the kind generated by everyday events such as getting your money back in the coin-return of a public telephone after you've made your call, seeing a friendly smiling "hello" from a coworker or acquaintance, or, on the less positive side, discovering that the morning newspaper is soaking wet and soggy from the night's rain? Do these kinds of things have an influence on thought and behavior? Until recently, people generally did not suppose that such states would affect normal cognitive functions and processes. However, recent research suggests that these small things, and the presumably mild affective states that they induce, do indeed influence not only the content of our thoughts about various topics but also the nature of the thinking process itself.

Thus, it seems that the conception of affect as an "interrupt" in an otherwise goal-directed program provides only part of the picture of affect's influence on thought and behavior. Studies indicate that relatively mild feeling states, too, have a pronounced and pervasive effect on both thought and behavior, even though they may not interrupt or disorganize it. Theirs is a more subtle effect but a particularly intriguing one, and it is on the pervasive influence of these commonly-occurring and seemingly-inconsequential, everyday affective states that this chapter will focus.

What is Affect?

Now we will try to define our subject matter a bit more specifically. This is not as easy as it sounds. A recent chapter (Isen & Hastorf, 1982) has touched upon affect in historical perspective, noting both its relative neglect by scientists over the centuries and the special difficulty of defining it. Let us examine this situation in more detail.

Background.   To begin with, the tripartite division of mind, a conceptualization that dominated psychological thinking for 150 years, held that mind or psychological experience was composed of three components: cognition (roughly, thinking), conation (motivation or will, and action or behavior), and affection (approximately, feeling). To appreciate the severity of affect's definitional problem, however, it should be noted that even its independence as a broad category in this tripartite conceptualization was not clear. Hilgard (1980) points out that affect was proposed as a fundamental component of mind relatively late, added by Moses Mendelssohn (1755) to a dual classification scheme proposed by Christian Wolfe in 1732, which involved only the two spheres, "knowledge" and "desire."

Moreover, in some sense, affect seems to overlap both cognition and conation. "Judgment" and "sensibility" (elements of perception and sensitivity) were often categorized as primarily affective, as is attitude today, even though there might be good reason to consider all of these phenomena as primarily cognitive. On the other side, throughout history, to and including the present day, affect has constantly been confused with motivation. (Consider, for example, the blurring of the distinction between anxiety and arousal or drive that occurred in this century.)

These ambiguities probably stemmed to some extent from a misunderstanding of the tripartite conceptualization, which intended to propose that every event was represented in all three spheres (that is, a thought or event in the cognitive domain would influence thinking, feeling, *and* action; an emotion or feeling would influence thinking, feeling, *and* action; an action or goal would influence thinking, feeling, *and* action). But the problem arose when psychologists tried to classify events as *primarily* influencing one or another sphere—for instance, to say that seeing a butterfly has its primary effect on cognition, while success in having caught the butterfly has its primary effect on affect (for example, see McDougall, 1923). Perhaps the prominence of Faculty Psychology in the last century and the early part of the present one played some role in this subtle but meaningful drift in the use of the three-part classification of psychological experience. In any case, when it became common practice to classify events as primarily cognitive, conative, or affective, affect emerged as the most ambiguous of the three.

Beyond this difficulty of broad categorization, attempts to define affect more specifically have likewise proven very difficult. Some (e.g., Duffy, 1934, 1941) have suggested doing away with the concept of emotion in favor of reduction of affect to more basic processes, such as arousal or interpretation of context. However, as noted by Averill (1982), emotional concepts seem to keep coming back into use. Nonetheless, there is not agreement on how to define these emotional concepts.

Probably one reason for this is that attempts to define affect in terms of physiological arousal have not met with success. Despite some promising leads in the 1950s suggesting that differential patterns of physiological activity might be identified as characteristic of various emotional states (e.g., Ax, 1953), we have not been able to identify independent sets of physiological indicators for the various emotions (Brown & Wallace, 1980; Cannon, 1927; Grossman, 1973; Hassett, 1978; Lacey, 1975; Woodworth & Schlosberg, 1954).

At the same time, attempts to define affect in terms of general arousal or activation (Duffy, 1934; Lindsley, 1951), in accord with Cannon's (1927) formulation, have also been disappointing (Lacey, 1959, 1967, 1975; Lacey, Kagan, Lacey, & Moss, 1963). Proposals that affective states can be understood as generalized arousal coupled with specific labels based on environmental conditions (e.g., Schachter & Singer, 1962) have also come under recent criticism (e.g., Lacey, 1975; Leventhal, 1979; Leventhal, 1980). Thus emotional states have defied physiological definition, and the cognitive labeling hypotheses still have to be refined.

Recent Developments. A promising avenue of investigation is currently being developed by studies of brain function, and especially of the neurochemistry of emotion. These studies seem to suggest that certain emotions do have identifiable underlying neural circuits in the brain, although a great deal of interaction between different neurochemical pathways also seems likely (Brown & Wallace, 1980). For example, four types of aggression in animals have been identified as having at least partly different underlying neural substrates (predatory aggression, fear-induced aggression, irritable or shock-induced aggression, and intermale or spontaneous aggression). However, there is also considerable overlap between these pathways; and in addition, this is not the kind of emotion-specificity one might have expected (for example, distinctions between joy and sorrow or sorrow and anger); and the findings at present pertain specifically to laboratory animals.

In a different way, work on the recently-discovered endorphins and enkephalins, naturally-occurring substances in the human body that have many of the same properties and effects as opiates, has sparked the notion that for humans there may be one specific neural pathway that underlies many kinds of rewarding events. The enkephalins have been found to produce both analgesia and euphoria, just as morphine does, and to occupy the same receptor sites as the opiates (Snyder, 1977). This suggests a rather general mediation of positive affect. Some may be reminded of the notion of a "pleasure center" in the brain, but most researchers today believe that the idea of a "pleasure center" is too simplistic (e.g., Brown & Wallace, 1980). Nonetheless, the suggestion of pathways that underlie many kinds of rewarding events is compatible with recent research results; and the identification of biochemical correlates of positive affect offers promise of aiding substantially in the effort to define and study affect.

It might be noted that the evidence thus far suggests a more general mediation of positive affect, in contrast with the more differentiated patterns mentioned above for aggression. This may indicate that positive and negative affect differ in a fundamental way. But it may be that the two conceptualizations represented in this work are at different levels of analysis (aggression, a type of *behavior*, and euphoria, a type of *feeling state*) and therefore not appropriately compared; or it may be that work on positive affect will reveal more specific differences as it progresses. It may also be, however, that positive and negative affective states actually differ in their degree of internal specificity.

Apart from these kinds of efforts, the study of emotion seems in a relatively early stage of development. It has been slow in passing beyond the stage of sheer description bemoaned almost 100 years ago by William James (1890). Its subject matter is not yet agreed upon, nor are the units of analysis well worked out. Only recently has research on emotional states begun to develop definitions and units other than those rooted in the common language, but some believe that developing alternative units is *not* the best path to follow.

Some systems using the common language terms for emotional states begin by postulating "basic" emotions from which other emotions can be derived. However, there is not agreement on what these basic emotions are, whether it is appropriate at all to consider some emotions more basic than others or whether "basic" emotions can, should, or must be identified before further work can be done. Moreover, there is additional disagreement on how the emotions relate to one another. In some conceptualizations, for instance, joy and sorrow, anger and fear, and disgust and acceptance, are considered "opposites" in a symmetrical system that resembles a color wheel. Yet the basis of these assumptions is not clear,[1] and their adequacy and utility are essentially untested.

Mandler (1975), in contrast, has suggested that there is no reason to expect that the common language terms for emotions will serve as adequate tools for the scientific analysis of affect. These terms may not lead us to the kinds of units and levels of analysis that will allow us to develop powerful formulations. Averill (1982), on the other hand, while agreeing that common-sense categorization of emotions and the postulating of sets of "basic" or "primary" emotions may not be appropriate, argues that the scientific study of affect *should* draw upon investigators' introspections of their experience of affect. The question is even more basic than that of whether "joy" and "sorrow" or "anger" and "fear" or "disgust" and "acceptance" are opposites, as has been proposed. The question is whether such terms as "joy" and "sorrow" are the appropriate ones for analysis.

An example of an alternative, non-intuitive approach is offered by Leventhal (1974, 1979, 1980), whose data suggest that feelings of pleasantness and unpleasantness may be basic perceptual reactions to specific features of a stimulus display, preceding an awareness of emotion or interpretation of context. Likewise, recent work by Zajonc and his colleagues (e.g., Moreland & Zajonc, 1979; Zajonc, 1980) supports the view that affect may develop without awareness and may be defined best in ways other than the conventional, introspective terms.

In this context, it is interesting to note that the promising advances in the neurochemical analysis of affect mentioned above did not grow directly out of work on affect. Enkephalin, for example, was discovered in the study of pain management and narcotics addiction. Perhaps it is too early for the systematization of affect on a grand scale; perhaps more precise definitions will follow, rather than precede, affect's illumination.

How, then, shall we begin to study affect? The best way, for the time being, may be to define the phenomena of interest empirically. This means that, at least at first, we will not have a grand theory integrating our efforts and discoveries: progress will be slow and perhaps particulate—that is, we may learn something about one type of affect, such as low-level feeling states for example, without learning much at all about seemingly-related phenomena, such as strong emotion. Still, this process may contribute to our eventual understanding of affect more generally if we keep in mind that our ultimate goal is to understand the

---

[1]The proposed relationships among the various emotions seem based on intuition in most cases. The conceptualization of anger and fear as opposites has been said to be based on Cannon's stress on the body's preparation for fight or flight. Yet, Cannon's position was that the *same* physiological changes occurred in many emotions, and he would not likely have argued for defining these states as "opposites" on a physiological basis. Moreover, other authors (e.g., Woodworth & Shlosberg, 1954) have suggested that anger and fear, or at least the facial expressions accompanying these states, are seen as closely related rather than "opposites."

more general phenomenon. On the other hand, perhaps these manifestations of affect will be found to be truly distinct in important ways, and if so the empirical approach will have allowed identification of these differences.

A Distinction Between "Feelings" and "Emotions"

Most discussions of emotion(s) focus on the emotion-specific events or consequences of the emotional experience: the way emotions feel, their physiological concomitants, their targets, their associated behavior, and the way in which they interrupt other behavior and are expressed either behaviorally or in facial expression. This chapter, in contrast, focuses on the impact of affective states on *other*, seemingly non-affect-related, behavior and cognitive processes. It may be useful, therefore, to distinguish between two different components of affective reactions, or perhaps two different types of affective states, one being rather specific and affect-goal directed in its effects, and the other being less focused on emotion itself and more pervasive in its effects. These states or components may be identified as "emotions" and "feelings," respectively.

My choice of terms is somewhat arbitrary, since students of emotion have defined these words in various ways, and their meaning in common American language usage is rather overlapping. *Webster's New World Dictionary of the American Language* (1966) lists 10 meanings for the noun, "feeling," and two for "emotion"; and, in general what is said to differentiate them in common usage is that emotions are thought of as (1) more intense, and (2) having physical as well as mental manifestations (neither is thought to be influenced by reason, however). I suggest that the particular term used to represent the component of affect that produces non-emotion-related consequences does not really matter. Rather, what may be important is that we provide ourselves some way of representing this distinction of function. In this chapter, "feelings" or "feeling states," which might also be called "moods," refers to pervasive, global, generalized affective components or states that influence seemingly non-affect-related events. I have chosen to represent this function by the term "feeling" because this term has been used previously in research on the impact of affect on non-affect-related thought and behavior. It also has represented mild, everyday affective experiences, in contrast with intense emotion.

Actually, despite the dictionary definition, and while it is true that feeling states can be induced by relatively small events and can be mild, intensity of affect may not be the most important distinction to be made in this context. It may be more useful to conceptualize the distinction in terms of function—that is, as one of *pervasiveness versus specificity of consequences*. Intensity may be correlated with specificity of effect in many instances, simply because intense emotion demands attention and often signals the need for some specific, emotion-related action. But, intensity, in and of itself, may not be the crucial factor in determining the effect in which we are interested. Feeling states can be produced not only by small things but also by major positive or negative events in our lives, and can be intense. What is distinctive about them is their pervasiveness.

Compare, for example, anger with irritability. While the emotion of anger often has a particular referent or is directed at a particular object which caused the anger, and has sets of behaviors, such as glaring or shouting or hitting or insulting, associated with it, the feeling state of irritability that may accompany the anger and that may even last beyond it is more global in its effects and indicators. This component of angry affect has neither specific targets nor specific behavioral impulses associated with it. For another example, following, or while appreciating, a most joyous event, one may feel generally happy, ready to be gracious and generous to all. "It's a girl—Have a cigar!" These effects may be viewed as resulting from the global component of affective experience that we are identifying as "feelings." In many cases feelings are induced without an episode of strong emotion, but even where they result from intense emotion, this residual feeling state that is more general and pervasive can be distinguished from the emotional state itself.

One reason that it may be useful to distinguish this component of affective experience, or to view feelings in this way, rather than simply in terms of intensity of affect, is that this focus may help us to account for certain phenomena that have been difficult to understand. For example, during a serious argument with someone, one may find many angry thoughts coming to mind, even thoughts that are not exactly appropriate to the present argument or adversary. It may be for this reason that people, sometimes much to their own surprise, often "say things they don't mean" during arguments, or dredge up and recreate past disagreements in the context of a current, different dispute. It may not be crucial to have a separate term for this function, but, on the other hand, it may be helpful at least temporarily.

What has been suggested so far is that feeling states occur quite frequently, often in response to seemingy small everyday occurrences, that they are pervasive rather than specific in their effects, that they can be mild, and that they often seem mild even when they are not. Clearly, they are affective, but there is something about them that seems cognitive, as well. They can occur in the presence of strong emotion and arousal but quite often occur without intense emotion or arousal. (Despite the dictionary distinction between feelings and emotions, it is not clear whether or not feelings are accompanied by physiological response.)

All of this implies that in most cases feelings are not terribly attention-getting—even when they are having a pronounced effect on thought and behavior. Unlike strong emotion, these states do not interrupt our thought and behavior; rather, they gently color and redirect ongoing thoughts and actions, influencing what will happen next but almost without notice and certainly without ostensibly changing the context or basic activity. This makes them particularly intriguing—and important—for study.

THE IMPACT OF FEELING STATES ON COGNITIVE PROCESSES AND BEHAVIOR

In this section the effects of feelings on cognition and social behavior will be described in more detail, and the implications of these relationships will be discussed.

Positive and Negative Affect

Before we proceed, a distinction must be made between the effects of positive versus negative affect. When most people think about the influence of affect on thought and behavior, they think first of negative affect. In the case of emotion, they think of anger or fear, or perhaps sorrow, influencing (interrupting) behavior. In the case of feeling states, they think of depression or anxiety, or perhaps irritability. They almost never think of positive affect—joy, elation, contentment, relaxation, or a sense of well-being—as influencing behavior. Ironically enough, however, research has shown that the effects of positive feeling states are quite pronounced and relatively direct, while the influence of negative feeling states is more complex and harder to predict, at least under some circumstances. This isn't to say that negative feelings have no effect, but rather that the influence of positive affect is more clear and simple (though not utterly simple, as we shall see later). Yet people hardly ever think first of positive feelings influencing what they do and think.

Perhaps the reasons for this are similar to the reasons discussed above that the effects of mild or commonly-experienced affective states often go unnoticed: Positive affect is very common (compare the number of times that you laughed today, with the number of times that you cried, for example). Although we probably could not live without positive affect, as recent literature on coping with stress is beginning to suggest (e.g., Lazarus, Kanner, & Folkman, 1980), it does not seem as urgent as negative affect. Negative affect is more rare, perhaps because we try to keep it away. This may also be the reason that, when it does occur, something has to be done about it. In contrast, nothing needs to be done about positive affect, or so it seems. Among psychologists, the neglect of positive affect may have stemmed, in addition, from the prominence of drive-reduction theories, which implied that uncomfortable or unpleasant states, not pleasant ones, were the motivators of behavior.

The research literature indicates that both positive and negative feeling states can have a marked influence on thinking processes, judgment, and behavior, although most studies suggest that this influence may not be symmetrical for the two types of states. We will discuss the comparison between positive and negative states later in this chapter; for now, let us summarize what has been discovered about the effects of feelings, first positive, then negative, on behavior and cognitive processes.

Some Behavioral Consequences of Positive Affect

A growing body of literature indicates that positive affect can influence social behavior. For example, a substantial number of studies has demonstrated that, for both children and adults, positive affect is generally associated with an increase in the tendency to help others (e.g., Aderman, 1972; Batson, Coke, Chard, Smith, & Taliaferro, 1979; Cunningham, 1979; Fried & Berkowitz, 1979; Isen, 1970; Isen, Horn, & Rosenhan, 1973; Isen & Levin, 1972; Isen, Clark, & Schwartz, 1976; Levin & Isen, 1975; Moore, Underwood, & Rosenhan, 1973; Weyant, 1978). In those studies, affect was induced in a large variety of ways, ranging from receiving a free sample or getting one's dime back in the coin return of a public telephone to success on a task or to thinking about positive or negative events that had occurred in the past.

The general conclusion that can be drawn from this work is that feeling good tends to make one more likely to help others. For example, it was found that persons who had found a dime in the coin-return of a public telephone were more likely to help a stranger who had dropped papers that she was carrying (Isen & Levin, 1972); likewise, randomly selected persons who had received information that they had succeeded on a test of perceptual-motor skills subsequently were more generous in donating to charity and were more helpful to a stranger who dropped her books (Isen, 1970).

More recently, a qualification has been added to the generalization that feeling good leads to helping: A person who is feeling especially good may actually be less willing to help than someone in a neutral state, if she or he has reason to believe that engaging in the helping task will destroy the positive feeling state (Isen & Simmonds, 1978). In one study, subjects who had found a dime in the coin return of a public telephone, relative to a control group, subsequently were more likely to help someone by reading and evaluating statements that they were told would put them in a good mood, but positive-affect subjects were *less* likely than a control group to help by reading statements they were told would put them in a bad mood. A similar finding suggests that people who feel good may be more likely to behave as they please, helping more when they want to help, but helping less when there is a reason that they do not want to help (Forest, Clark, Mills, & Isen, 1979). This, in turn, suggests that positive affect may have separately identifiable influences—a tendency to increase the likelihood of helping in general but a tendency toward mood protection and possibly one also toward personal freedom or independence, which under some circumstances may override the increased likelihood of behaviors such as helping.

People who feel good have been found to be more kind to themselves as well as to others: they tend to reward themselves more than control subjects do (Mischel, Coates, & Raskoff, 1968), and to display a greater preference for positive than negative self-relevant information (Mischel, Ebbesen, & Zeiss, 1973, 1976). However, children who have succeeded do not show lessened ability to resist temptation (Frey, 1975) and delay gratification, as do those who have failed (Schwartz & Pollack, 1977; Seeman & Schwartz, 1974). This suggests that the relative self-indulgence noted in the other studies should not be interpreted simply as loss of self-control or impulsiveness. Rather, all of these results might be interpreted as the products of decisions to behave in ways that are kind to oneself as well as to others.

Positive affect has been found to be associated with a number of other changes in social behavior, as well. Persons who have reason to be feeling good tend to be more willing to initiate conversations with others (Batson et al., 1979; Isen, 1970); express greater liking for others and more positive conceptions of people (Gouaux, 1971; Griffitt, 1970; Veitch & Griffitt, 1976); and may be more receptive to persuasive communication (Galizio & Hendrick, 1972; Janis, Kaye, & Kirschner, 1965).

Some other types of behavior with implications for social interaction have also been found to be influenced by affective state. For example, people who feel happy (as induced by means of the Velten procedure) tend to speak faster than those in an experimentally induced negative state (Natale, 1977). Another example is that persons in whom positive affect has been induced (by means of success on a task or by means of a free 50-cent gift certificate) appear more likely than control subjects to take risks, both social and nonsocial, as long as the risk is slight (Isen, Means, Patrick, & Nowicki, 1982). Where risk is great, however, subjects who are feeling good tend to be more conservative than those in a neutral condition (Isen & Patrick, 1983).

These findings regarding risk-taking are compatible with the hypothesis that a positive affective state is accompanied by an inclination to maintain that state (a tendency toward mood protection) and also by an inclination to exercise one's freedom to behave as one wishes, up to a point (e.g., to take a chance where risk is low). So also are the findings that positive affect increases preference for positive self-relevant information, and those demonstrating that persons in whom positive affect has been induced are *less* likely to help than control subjects when helping is incompatible with maintaining their positive feelings.

In summary, the evidence indicates that positive affect is associated with increased sociability and benevolence to both self and others. From the earliest, studies investigating this phenomenon have also tried to explore the process that might underlie such effects—the means by which feeling good oneself might lead one to be more generous and helpful to others (e.g., Berkowitz, 1972; Isen, 1970; Isen & Levin, 1972). At first, interpretations such as increase in frustration tolerance (Berkowitz, 1972) or increase in perceived resources (Isen, 1970) were proposed. But subsequently the level of analysis changed, and authors became concerned with *how* feeling good might lead to increased frustration tolerance or sense of surplus. This has led some authors to propose cognitive processes which might mediate such effects. Thus, interest in the processes by which happiness leads to helping has produced studies of the influence of affect on decision-making and other cognitive processes.

The Impact of Positive Affect on Cognition

The Influence of Positive Feelings on Memory: Effects at Time of Retrieval.
It has been proposed that positive feelings can serve as a retrieval cue for positive material in memory, influencing what comes to mind, and thus influencing many other cognitive processes such as judgment, evaluation, expectations, decision-making, and behavior that follows from those processes (Isen, 1975; Isen, Shalker, Clark, & Karp, 1978). (This idea is to be distinguished from a "state-dependent-learning" effect, which is discussed below, pp. 193–195.) Tversky and Kahneman (1973) have suggested that judgment may be especially influenced by those ideas that come to mind first or most easily. Likewise, it may be in this way, by affecting the content that becomes accessible and comes to mind when one is in the process of weighing alternatives and deciding on a course of action, that positive feelings can influence judgments and decisions to engage in various behaviors.

For example, Isen et al. (1978) induced a positive feeling state in some randomly selected people in a shopping mall by giving them a free gift. People who had received the free gift, in contrast with a control group, later reported on an apparently unrelated consumer survey that their cars and television sets performed better and had better service records. Other studies have shown that people in whom a positive feeling state has been induced rate slides of ambiguous scenes as more pleasant than do people who are not in a positive feeling state (Forest et al., 1979; Isen & Shalker, 1982); have lower tachistoscopic thresholds for success-related words (Postman & Brown, 1952); and tend to rate ambiguous facial expressions (a surprise/fear blend, for example) as more positive than do control subjects (Schiffenbauer, 1974). Additionally, studies have found that being in a positive feeling state causes people to express expectations of future success (Feather, 1966) as well as other kinds of positive events (Masters & Furman, 1976). All of these results are consistent with the suggestion proposed above, that positive feelings cue positive material, which is then brought to bear on decisions being made.

Specific demonstrations that positive affect can influence memory have also appeared. For example, it has been found that positve affect, induced by victory on a computer game (Isen et al., 1978), induced by adopting the facial expression of happiness (Laird, Wagener, Halal, & Szegda, 1982), induced by the Velten (1968) Mood Induction Procedure (Teasdale & Fogarty, 1979; Teasdale & Russell, 1983; Teasdale & Taylor, 1981), induced by instructions to recall an affect-inducing event of a particular type (Nasby & Yando, 1982), and induced by hypnosis (Bower, 1981; Natale & Hantas, 1982), facilitated the recall of positive material.[2]

In eight of these studies, positive material (e.g., positive trait adjectives or positive life experiences) was more *likely* to be recalled than other words by persons in whom positive affect had been induced, relative to other subjects; in the ninth study, positive experiences were recalled more *rapidly* than other experiences by persons in the positive affect condition. These data, together with those showing improved evaluations by positive affect subjects relative to a control group, have been interpreted as supporting the suggestion that positive affect can serve as a retrieval cue for positive material in memory and thereby can influence both the content of what is recalled and any judgments and decisions that rely on that content (Isen et al., 1978).[3]

The influence of affect on memory and judgment has been related to the concepts of "accessibility" and "priming" (Brown, 1979; Neely, 1976, 1977; Tulving & Pearlstone, 1966). For instance, Tulving and Pearlstone (1966) found that subjects could recall more words (for example, "lawyer") from a list of learned words when presented with the name of the category (for example, "professions") appropriate to those words, than when not given this cue. Those authors interpreted this finding as evidence for the difference between availability of material in memory storage and accessibility of that same material under particular conditions of recall. Material of the category was said to be more accessible under conditions of retrieval in which the category was primed. This is the model that was followed in developing the idea that affective state could serve the same function that a retrieval cue is known to serve (Isen, 1975; Isen et al., 1978).

Several recent studies have shown that people respond more quickly and easily to words that are related to material to which they have recently responded, whether these are category names, category members, or other related words or social concepts (e.g., Higgins & King, 1981; Jacobson, 1973; Loftus,

---

[2]The latter three techniques of affect induction involve rather direct manipulation of cognition, and therefore some questions might be raised about their adequacy to represent affect. However, in many instances, the effects of these inductions parallel those of the more subtle instructions that were designed with ecological validity specifically in mind. Where they do not, a note of caution will be raised.

[3]Recent studies by Bower and his colleagues (Bower et al., 1978; Bower et al., 1981) have failed to obtain specifically retrieval effects of positive affect, but in view of the number of replications of this effect, it is possible that these absences should be attributed to the materials used or the means of affect induction (hypnosis). See also pp. 194–195.

1973; Loftus & Loftus, 1974; Meyer & Schvaneveldt, 1971; Posner & Snyder, 1975; Srull & Wyer, 1979; Warren, 1977). As has already been noted, in similar fashion it was proposed that good feeling might cue positive material in memory. There is now considerable evidence that this is the case, and thus, it seems that affective state can function like category name or other organizing unit as a cue to prime related cognitive material.

An alternative interpretation of these results that might be offered is that they are attributable to response bias, rather than to altered accessibility of positive cognitions. This alternative is not compelling, however, for two reasons. First, it is not immediately obvious what kind of process other than the proposed change in relative accessibility of positive cognitions might underlie such a response bias itself. Second, the data tend to accord with the accessibility formulation rather than with the hypothesis of response biase because they suggest that the effect of feelings on these ratings is most pronounced on ambiguous stimuli (e.g., Isen & Shalker, 1982; Schiffenbauer, 1974). The response-bias hypothesis would suggest that affect should influence the ratings of all stimuli to an equal extent. In contrast, the accessibility hypothesis would imply that the ratings of ambiguous items, about which one is more likely to have both positive and negative material in memory, should be more affected by feeling state than should the rating of strongly valenced items. For example, according to the accessibility hypothesis, a stimulus that is entirely negative—say, pictures of Nazi concentration camps in operation—should not seem any more positive when one is feeling happy than when one is in a neutral condition, because there simply *are no* positive elements to be cued or made accessible in memory about this stimulus. Thus, in this respect the accessibility and response-bias hypotheses make differential predictions, and the response bias interpretation does not seem to account as well for the rating data that have been obtained as does the accessibility interpretation.

The Influence of Positive Feelings on Memory: Encoding.   Subsequently, additional studies of the impact of affective state on memory have suggested that affective state at time of learning (encoding) may also influence recall of material being memorized, independently of affective state at time of recall (i.e., even if subjects are in a neutral state when asked to recall the material). Specifically, affective state at time of encoding has sometimes been found to be associated with superior memory for information compatible with that affective state. Bower, Gilligan, and Monteiro (1981) found that participants recalled more facts about persons described as happy (more facts compatible with a positive state) when they themselves had been happy while learning the material; and that persons who learned material while feeling sad, similarly, showed a superiority of memory for information compatible with the negative affective state. Nasby and Yando (1982), using fifth-grade children as subjects, also found that a positive encoding mood facilitated learning positive trait adjectives; however, they did not find a facilitative effect of sadness at time of encoding. (Sadness at encoding did not improve recall of negative material, but rather impaired recall of positive information; more on this effect below.) These authors did, however, find the encoding effect with anger, in that anger at time of learning improved the later recall of negative information.

The Influence of Positive Feelings on Memory: State-Dependent Learning.
Other work in the area has suggested that under certain circumstances relatively normal feeling states may mediate a "state-dependent-learning effect" similar to that which has been observed for states such as alcoholic intoxication or extreme affective states such as mania (Bower, Monteiro & Gilligan, 1978; Bower et al., 1981; Henry, Weingartner, & Murphy, 1973; Leight & Ellis, 1981; Weingartner & Faillace, 1971; Weingartner, Miller, & Murphy, 1977). The "state-dependent learning effect" is to be distinguished from the more general findings that affective state can play a role in memory. This term refers to the tendency for material—any material—learned when a subject is in a specific state (say, alcoholic intoxication) to be recalled better when the subject is again in that state than at another time. It refers to the facilitation of recall by the *matching of states* at time of learning and recall, not more generally to the tendency of affective states to facilitate or impair recall, nor to their tendency to facilitate or impair recall of a specific type of material (as has been observed in the effect of positive affect on retrieval of positive material). State-dependent learning is conceptually similar to simple situational context effects (not complex context effects having to do with meaning) that have been observed to affect recall; but in this case the crucial context variable of interest is feeling state rather than, say, color of the walls or temperature of the air. Actually, studies in the behavioral tradition suggested similar variables to be important in animal learning. For example, the animal's state of hunger or satiety, or fear because of having been shocked in a given experimental chamber was presumed to serve as a discriminable cue that could be linked to others or to responses.

Such "state-dependent" effects of affect in humans have been observed under conditions where learning mood serves as a distinctive cue for otherwise confusable material. For example, Bower et al., (1978), using hypnosis as the means of affect induction, found recall of a list of words to be better when mood during learning was the same as mood during recall, but only if subjects had learned one list of words while happy and another list while sad. (With a single list, those authors did not obtain mood-state-dependent-learning; nor did Bower et al., 1981, for parallel stimulus material, a one-person vignette, in Study 3.) Using negative and neutral mood states, as induced by the Velten procedure, Leight and Ellis (1981) found state-dependent effects to be limited to delayed recognition of nonsense syllables, but did not observe them with meaningful material.

This finding is compatible with the interpretation offered by Isen et al. (1978) in discussing the absence of a state-dependent-learning effect in the memory study reported in that paper (Study 2): that the material to be learned and recalled was likely encoded according to its semantic meaning rather than according to aspects of the physical context in which the learning occurred. In other words, it is likely that where material has meaning, the material will be experienced and encoded according to its meaning rather than according to details of the experimental context, including one's own affective state. (Since affective state is *both* meaningful and contextual, its effects can be observed in either case, but the material that it will cue will be different, depending on which process is operative.) These findings are also compatible with recent results reported by Eich and Birnbaum (1982), and the interpretation offered by those authors, that it is the accessibility of higher order units such as meaning that determines the occurrence or nonoccurrence of state dependence (where higher order units are accessible, state dependence tends not to be observed).

In addition, other studies have allowed for state-dependent-learning effects in their designs but failed to find such effects, despite diverse techniques of affect induction across the papers. For example, in the study by Isen et al. (1978), positive and negative affect were induced by having subjects win or lose a computer game; more recently, two studies by Nasby and Yando (1982), using the "imagine/remember" technique, also failed to confirm a state-dependent effect of happiness, sadness, or anger (fifth-grade children were the subjects in these experiments).

On the other hand, Bower and his colleagues recently have argued that affect state-dependent-learning is robust and may even be the only basis on which so-called "retrieval" effects of affect occur (Bower et al., 1981). They question whether retrieval effects occur, and whether, when they appear to occur (most usually with memory for life experiences), they aren't actually attributable to state-dependent-learning—that is, to matching affective states at time of learning (in life) and retrieval. Those authors (Bower et al., 1981; Bower et al., 1978) suggest that one should not expect to find facilitation of recall of positive words *learned during the experimental session,* if the subjects are in a positive state at time of recall but were not in the same state at time of learning; and they report that they did *not* obtain such retrieval effects. Thus, despite findings of such retrieval effects by others, these authors suggest that improved recall of affect-compatible material learned during the experimental session does not occur unless affective state at time of recall matches affective state during learning.

Teasdale and Russell (1983) note the argument of Bower and colleagues but try to resolve the conflicting findings by attempting to replicate conceptually the findings of earlier studies that obtained retrieval effects with material learned during the experimental session (e.g., Isen et al., 1978). This they succeed in doing, suggesting that feeling state at time of retrieval *can* cue affectively compatible material, even if that material was studied while the subject was in a neutral affective state. Subsequent to Teasdale and Russell's study, additional studies have appeared in the literature, showing this effect of feelings on material learned during the experimental session (e.g., Laird et al., 1982; Nasby &

Yando, 1982). This is a finding that may benefit from additional attempts at replication; but for the present it is fair to say that retrieval effects (of positive feelings) that are not based on state-dependent learning do occur.

Teasdale and Russell (1983) suggest resolving the discrepancy in the literature regarding retrieval effects by noting the differences in materials used by Bower's group as contrasted with those used by the others. They also suggest that retrieval effects might be interpreted as instances of state-dependent-learning in the "broad view." They speculate that trait adjectives (e.g., kind, helpful) used in most of the studies, in contrast with abstract nouns (e.g., honor, justice) employed by Bower and colleagues, in life may be more often used in situations that are compatible with the affective tone of their meanings, and thus their meanings may be more highly associated with actual instances of a corresponding feeling state. Thus, these authors suggest, it may be possible to view the apparent retrieval effect as state-dependent after all, through the association of experience with meaning.

For the present it seems difficult to say whether viewing retrieval effects as examples of state-dependent learning in the "broad view" (or vice-versa) is advantageous or disadvantageous. This approach seems to obscure the meaning of state dependency and to destroy its uniqueness as an interpretative tool; but perhaps it will provide needed integration at some point. (When such integration is attempted, however, it might be interesting to consider whether it would be more powerful theoretically to consider retrieval effects examples of state-dependent learning in the broad view, or to consider state-dependent learning a special case of retrieval effects.) My own inclination is to view the two phenomena as distinct until we know more about each of them. In the present state of our knowledge there appear to be theoretical advantages in distinguishing between state-dependent learning, on the one hand, and organization or learning based on semantic meaning or other more complex principles, on the other. (These will be discussed further in the section of the chapter devoted to theoretical issues, p. 223 ff.)

Thus, in summary, although some authors have argued that state-dependency is a robust phenomenon and even accounts for apparent effects of positive affect on retrieval, considered together, the results of all of the studies that we have reviewed here seem to suggest that state-dependent-learning as an effect of induced mood is a specialized phenomenon, limited to learning situations where the material to be learned is confusable except for its distinctive association with one particular affective state, where affect is intense or for some other reason especially focal in subjects' attention (as in the hypnotic technique), and where there are not better cues for recall: that is, where affect can be used as a distinctive cue to facilitate learning of material at time of input, and few other such cues are available. These qualifications severely limit the applicability of the state-dependent-learning effect; the implications of this will be discussed in the section of the chapter devoted to theoretical issues.

More generally, in summary of the studies on positive affect and memory (the effects of negative affect are not as clear), despite a few conflicting results that may be attributable to materials used and techniques of affect induction, it can be said that positive affect has been found to facilitate the processing of compatible material. Several studies report an effect at retrieval (e.g., Isen et al., 1978; Laird et al., 1982; Nasby & Yando, 1982; Natale & Hantas, 1982; Snyder & White, 1982; Teasdale & Fogarty, 1979; Teasdale & Russell, 1983; Teasdale & Taylor, 1981), while some others report effects attributable to encoding processes (e.g., Bower et al., 1981; Nasby & Yando, 1982).

The Influence of Positive Affect on the Way in Which Information is Processed.   Let us now turn from studies of memory to studies of more complex cognitive processes. It has been suggested that positive affect influences not only the content of what comes to mind, but also the strategies used to think about and solve problems, and thus, sometimes, the solutions reached or decisions made.

This influence may sometimes lead to improved performance and efficiency, but it has sometimes been associated with incorrect solutions to certain types of problems. Studies by Masters and his colleagues have shown that children who were feeling happy (as induced by the imagine/remember technique) performed more efficiently and were able to recall more than control subjects (Barden, Garber, Duncan, & Masters, 1981; Masters, Barden, & Ford, 1979). In another series of studies, persons in whom positive affect had been induced (by giving them a gift of one dollar or serving refreshments) were more likely to use an intuitive strategy or heuristic, rather than a more taxing logical strategy, in solving two types of problems (a physics problem and a numerical estimation task); but in this case their performance on the task was impaired by this tendency (see Isen et al., 1982).

In a more complex decision-making task, it was also found that persons made to feel good, this time by report of success on a test of perceptual-motor skills, made the decision more quickly and efficiently. In addition, they were more likly than control subjects to use a simplifying strategy similar to the one identified by Tversky (1972) as "Elimination by Aspects" (Isen & Means, 1983). Their performance could not be characterized as impaired, however, because their final decisions did not differ, on the whole, from those of the control group; and evidence obtained from analysis of their decision protocols suggests that their decision process, utilizing the simplifying strategy, in this case would be better described as efficient than as sloppy or impaired.

Four recent studies also indicate that positive affect is associated with increased creativity. In two studies, positive affect, induced by exposure to 5 minutes of a comedy film, facilitated performance on Duncker's (1945) candle task, a task usually considered to require innovation in the way in which the solver views the stimulus materials. In the second pair of studies, positive affect induced either by receipt of refreshments during the experimental session or by giving word associations to ten positive affect words, each resulted in subjects' having relatively unusual first associations to a group of neutral words, a phenomenon also likely related to creativity (Isen, Daubman, & Gorgoglione, in press; Mednick, 1962; Mednick, Mednick, & Mednick, 1964). This may mean that positive affect influences cue utilization or the way in which cognitive material is organized.

In summary, then, of the research on the effects of positive feelings, the evidence indicates that people who feel good tend to have positive material more accessible in memory, tend to be more optimistic, tend to judge things to be a little better than usually, and tend to act accordingly—to be more friendly, open, and giving. They are also likely to behave in ways that will help to maintain their positive feeling states. They go about solving problems differently from those not in a positive affective state, using simplifying strategies and perhaps tending to organize material into broader units.

Some Behavioral Consequences of Negative Affect

But what of people who are experiencing negative affect? Negative affect has already been mentioned in the context of the memory studies. But now we will focus on it in greater detail. As pointed out above, and in earlier papers (Clark & Isen, 1982; Isen et al., 1978), the literature suggests an added degree of complexity in the case of negative feelings. The effects of negative states on behavior and cognition are less consistent than the effects of positive; and second, there is a growing sense that the symmetry that is often assumed between positive and negative feeling states may be more a convention of language than a reflection of the actual impact of the states.

It has already been mentioned that negative states may be more demanding when they occur. In addition, the research literature increasingly suggests a qualitative difference as well. Negative states seem often to trigger conflicting tendencies. On one hand, people in negative states may tend to see the negative side of things and be more pessimistic; but on the other hand, the negative state may stimulate attempts to change or eliminate the unpleasantness, and these attempts may involve engaging in rather positive (affect-incompatible) behavior and thinking. Thus, it is difficult to predict, in the case of negative affect, whether thought and behavior will be affect-compatible or affect-incompatible.

For example, the effects of negative feeling states on judgments and behavior are sometimes the opposite of the effects of positive feeling states and result in such reactions as reduced helping (Cialdini & Kenrick, 1976; Moore et al., 1973; Underwood, Froming, & Moore, 1977; Weyant, 1978), or increased aggression (Baron & Bell, 1976; Berkowitz & Turner, 1974). But sometimes negative states produce the *same* kinds of behavior produced by positive feeling states—for example, increased helping (Cialdini, Darby, & Vincent, 1973; Isen et al., 1973; Weyant, 1978). At other times negative states appear to have no effect at all, even where the influence of comparable positive affect is quite marked (e.g., Isen, 1970; Mischel et al., 1968; Mischel et al., 1976), as if competing tendencies had neutralized one another. (See Isen et al., 1978, for a fuller discussion of this issue.)

Several studies, showing that negative feelings can increase positive behaviors, just as positive feeling states do, have proposed that negative affect gives rise to a tendency toward attempts at mood improvement and that one strategy of mood improvement is to engage in positive or prosocial acts (Cialdini et al., 1973; Isen et al., 1973; Weyant, 1978). Negative feeling states such as guilt or embarrassment, incompetence, anger, and sadness have been shown to increase self-reward, or to be associated with increased helping or compliance with a request (e.g., Carlsmith & Gross, 1969; Cialdini et al., 1973; Cialdini & Kenrick, 1976; Donnerstein, Donnerstein & Munger, 1975; Isen et al., 1973; McMillen, 1971; Regan, 1971; Regan, Williams & Sparling, 1972). It may be that these effects are mediated by an interest in improving one's affective state.

This line of reasoning parallels the notion of a tendency toward mood protection in the presence of positive affect. Yet it makes for a more complex situation in the case of negative affect, at least in the context of a situation where positive behavior is called for, because the tendencies induced in that context are opposing, while those generated in response to positive affect are usually compatible. Thus, on the basis of evidence collected so far, it appears that we cannot make a clear and straightforward prediction of the effect of negative feeling states on social behavior.

However, these asymmetrical findings are quite compatible with self-regulatory models proposed by cognitive social learning theorists such as Mischel (1973) and Bandura (1973, 1977). These principles would suggest that the experiencing of positive affect gives rise to strategies designed to maintain that desirable state, as has been proposed, and that negative affect results in strategies aimed at changing the undesirable state. Thus, one might expect, under normal circumstances, that people who feel bad might employ strategies and engage in behavior designed to alleviate the negative state and this would account for the observed asymmetry.

Negative Affect and Cognitive Processes

Cognitive processes have sometimes been found to be influenced by negative affect, and it may be that such processes mediate the behavioral effects observed. As is the case with resultant behavior, however, the impact of negative affect on cognitive processes such as memory and judgment tends to be more difficult to predict than that of positive affect.

On one hand, it has been suggested that people in negative feeling states have a dim view of the world; and research confirms this characterization. For example, people in whom a negative feeling state has been induced rated ambiguous slides as less pleasant (Isen & Shalker, 1982; Forest et al., 1979). They also have been demonstrated to have lower tachistoscopic thresholds for failure-related words than controls (Postman & Brown, 1952), suggesting improved access for the negative, the mirror image of results with positive affect. Being in a negative feeling state decreases attraction toward others and results in more negative conceptions of others (Gouaux, 1971; Griffitt, 1970; Veitch & Griffitt, 1976), and research has also shown that people experiencing negative feelings show an increased tendency to perceive negative affect in others' ambiguous facial expressions (Schiffenbauer, 1974). In addition, Johnson and Tversky (1983) have recently reported that negative affect resulted in increased, and positive affect in decreased, estimates of the likelihood of several types of disasters and unpleasant events occurring.

On the other hand, some judgments do *not* show these corresponding effects of positive and negative affect. Masters and Furman (1976) found improved expectations among children in that study's positive affect condition, but not more pessimistic expectations among children in the negative affect condition.

The Influence of Negative Affect on Memory.   The influence of negative affect on memory is not entirely clear either, since several studies have yielded differing results, perhaps as a function of mode of affect induction and materials used. As noted previously, Bower and his colleagues (e.g., Bower, 1981; Bower et al., 1981), using hypnosis as the means of affect induction, have reported that sadness at *encoding* facilitated the recall of sad material, just as happiness was found to do for positive material. However, Nasby and Yando (1982), using the imagine/remember technique and studying fifth-grade children, did *not* observe this effect with sadness, either at time of encoding or retrieval, even though they did find an effect of happiness at both encoding and retrieval (though no state-dependent-learning effect), and one of anger at encoding.

Teasdale and Russell (1983) have found symmetrical effects of negative and positive feelings at time of *retrieval,* using a Velten-like procedure (depression-elation).[4] More frequently, however, findings regarding retrieval have tended *not* to reflect symmetry in the effects of positive and negative material—that is, they suggest that positive affect at time of retrieval facilitates recall of positive material but that negative affect at time of retrieval does not facilitate the recall of negative material or does so to a lesser extent than does comparable positive

---

[4]Snyder and White (1982) also reported symmetrical effects for their first measure of recall of positive and negative events, but nonsymmetrical effects on a subsequent measure which asked subjects to list all positive and negative events that had occurred. In addition, because of the design of the experiment and the pattern of results reported, these effects may reflect interference with recall of incompatible material, rather than facilitation of recall of compatible material (see below).

affect (Isen et al., 1978, using failure; Teasdale & Fogarty, 1979, Teasdale & Taylor, 1981, and Teasdale, Taylor, & Fogarty, 1980,[5] using the Velten technique; Nasby & Yando, 1982, using the imagine/remember technique; and Natale & Hantas, 1982, using hypnosis). Bower (1981) has reported that sadness (as well as happiness) at time of recall facilitated remembering of sad (happy) events in subjects' lives (not of affect-compatible material learned under neutral conditions during an experiment), but he and his colleagues have suggested that this not be interpreted as a retrieval effect, per se, but rather as a state-dependent-learning effect (see Bower et al., 1981, and the discussion of state-dependent-learning above).

Another type of effect which has been observed is the tendency of an affective state to *impair* the processing of *incompatible* material, either at encoding or retrieval. For example, Nasby and Yando (1982) found that a sad or an angry mood at encoding resulted later in poorer recall of positive material (although, as noted above, sadness at time of encoding did not facilitate recall of negative material, and neither sadness nor anger did so at the time of retrieval). Natale and Hantas (1982, Table 3, p. 931) report data showing that both positive and negative affect at time of retrieval interfered with the recall of incompatible material (but only positive affect facilitated the recall of compatible memories). Some of the studies reported by Teasdale and colleagues are also open to the interpretation that the induced affective state *impaired* the processing of *incompatible* material, rather than that it facilitated the processing of compatible material, since these studies generally involve comparison between negative and positive material (no neutral material) within a given affect condition and contrasts between induced elation and depression conditions only (no control condition). The pattern of results does not always support this interpretation, however (e.g., Teasdale et al., 1980).

Understanding the Asymmetry between Positive and Negative Affect.   In summary, there are a few studies of the effect of affect on memory that obtain symmetrical results of positive and negative affect, but several studies obtain nonsymmetrical results. One hypothesis that has been proposed to understand this differential impact of positive and negative feelings is that of mood maintenance and mood repair. It should be noted that the studies that report symmetrical effects contain elements that render them not necessarily incompatible with this interpretation. In general, the studies reporting symmetrical effects are those in

---

[5]This paper reports effects of negative affect that are opposite to those found for positive affect. However, closer inspection of the results reveals the effects not to be symmetrical: the impact of negative affect is much attenuated in comparison with that of positive affect; sometimes differences are in the predicted direction but fail to reach significance for negative affect (Teasdale et al., 1980, p. 342), or they have been obtained only with extreme stimuli (p. 343), while these qualifications do not apply in the case of correspondingly induced positive affect.

which subjects may be responding to experimenter demand, explicit or implicit, to maintain their affective states as induced. For example, studies by Bower and his colleagues, using hypnosis to induce affective state, report symmetrical results of positive and negative affect induction; but their technique of mood induction involves instructing hypnotized subjects *to maintain their induced affective states,* both positive and negative, at their initial levels of intensity (Bower, 1981; Bower et al., 1981; Bower et al., 1978). This, then, represents an explicit experimenter demand that subjects not engage in the kinds of mood-repair processes postulated to account for the asymmetry observed with other procedures of affect induction. Occasionally (e.g., Teasdale & Russell, 1983) studies using the Velten or the imagine/remember technique have also found symmetrical effects of positive and negative affect induction on retrieval of information from memory, although more frequently they have not (e.g., Nasby & Yando, 1982; Teasdale & Fogarty, 1979; Teasdale et al., 1980[5]).

The controlled-process, mood-repair interpretation of the asymmetry between the effects of positive and negative affect, grounded in the social-learning theory principle of self-regulation, suggests that, where possible, people try to feel better if they are feeling badly. Such mood improvement processes should be less evident in the studies involving hypnotic suggestion to subjects to maintain their negative state, because the employment of such strategies would run counter to this hypnotically suggested experimental instruction. Thus, hypnotized subjects might also be likely to focus on mood-compatible elements to be memorized, in order to help them comply with this same instruction; and this might account for not only the parallel effects of sadness and happiness when moods are induced in this way, but also the *encoding* effect of sadness, which is also usually obtained under these conditions but not with other techniques.

In addition, discrepancies between studies in the tendency to observe parallel effects of negative and positive affect may be in part attributable to other aspects of the different procedures and materials used in the various studies. Regarding studies that obtained memory effects of positive affect but not of negative, one might argue that this may be attributable to failure to induce negative affect intensely enough. Such interpretations might be viable in the case of one or two studies considered in isolation, but they do not seem appropriate for explaining the now-large literature reporting asymmetric effects of positive and negative feelings.

Most studies that attempt to examine both positive and negative affect at once employ parallel procedures intended to induce positive and negative states of equivalent intensity. Often manipulation checks indicate that the induced negative state is as intense as the induced positive state. Yet the effects of these induced states are most often not parallel. If seemingly parallel procedures fail to induce symmetrical states, or if equally intense states of opposite sign fail to have symmetrical effects, then perhaps there is something truly distinctive about the types of states induced.

The mood-maintenance and mood-repair hypotheses are motivational propositions derived from self-regulatory models within cognitive social learning theory. There are two additional, non-motivational, factors that may contribute to the observed pattern, as well. First, these same kinds of factors may produce purely cognitive effects. For example, negative material may come to be less well elaborated and interconnected in the cognitive system than positive, possibly as a result of habits of mood-repair. This, then, may augment the motivational effects described above, resulting in an attenuated effect of negative material, even where only automatic processes are involved. This possibility is described in more detail in Clark and Isen (1982).

Second, increasing evidence suggests that positive and negative affect, even more specifically happiness and sadness, may be distinct feeling states, with different effects and different behavioral implications, rather than opposite ends of one bipolar dimension. Just as reward and punishment are no longer conceived to have symmetrical effects, so happiness and sadness may also come to be recognized as having different kinds of effects. A consideration of this possibility may also help us to understand certain phenomena that are otherwise perplexing: Reflection on our own experience reminds us that opposite emotions such as happiness and sadness or confidence and fear sometimes seem to occur simultaneously, as for example at events such as weddings, or when embarking on a new venture. Recognizing that these apparently-opposite feelings may actually be independent of one another helps us understand how they might sometimes occur in the presence of one another.

Empirical evidence suggests this possibility as well. Abelson, Kinder, Peters, and Fiske (1982), for example, have reported positive and negative affect about a given political figure to be nearly independent of each other. While the findings of these authors reflect reports of affective states that may cover separate occasions, these states may also be related to current feelings about candidates. If opposite feelings are reported simultaneously, it is also likely that they may exist simultaneously. This would not be possible if happiness and sadness, confidence and anxiety, and so forth, were in each case opposite ends of a single continuum. Thus, a second factor beyond the motivational interpretation of the asymmetry between positive and negative affect is that these states may actually be different and should not be expected to be symmetrical.

A Note on Anger.   Anger appears to have different effects from sadness, and if anger is considered negative affect, then a differentiation should be made here. Nasby and Yando (1982) reported that anger (but not sadness) at time of encoding (but not retrieval) facilitated the later recall of negative material. These findings indicate that the cognitive effects of anger are different from those of sadness. But they, and the data showing that anger (and sadness) impairs the recall of positive material, suggest that anger can reasonably be considered negative affect, nonetheless.

Detailed review of all of the material on frustration, anger, and aggression is beyond the scope of this chapter, but it might be mentioned that several authors have proposed a role for cognitive mediation of anger and aggression. For example, Bandura (e.g., 1973) has shown how memory processes may mediate delayed reactions to witnessed aggression. Berkowitz and his colleagues have proposed that cues to aggression may help to elicit aggressive responses in angered subjects (e.g., Berkowitz & LePage, 1967) and have suggested, further, that "internally represented" aggressive stimuli can promote aggression (Berkowitz, 1974; Berkowitz, Lepinski, & Angulo, 1969; Berkowitz & Turner, 1974). More recently, Turner and Layton (1976), finding greater recall of highly imageable aggressive words, as contrasted with low-imagery words, and increased aggressiveness in response to high-imagery words, suggested that performance of aggressive behavior may be a function of the retrievability of stimuli that cue aggression. Rule, Ferguson and Nesdale (1979) proposed, similarly, that aggressive behavior may be mediated by the accessibility of aggression-inducing or aggression-supporting cognitions. (This is conceptually similar to the suggestion that helping behavior may be mediated by the accessibility of positive cognitions.) Additionally, such increased accessibility of aggression cues may also mediate the effect of pain on aggression, reported recently by Berkowitz, Cochran, and Embree (1981). Finally, it may be of interest to family counselors, mediators, and others, that, as noted in the introductory section of this chapter (p. 186), such a process of reminding may account for certain rather destructive aspects of family quarrels and other disputes.

Negative Affect: Anxiety (Arousal). We have not yet mentioned some classic studies on anxiety, which is often thought of as negative affect. Nor have we yet considered in detail the issue of arousal (often assumed to mean negative arousal). As mentioned earlier, there is a great deal of confusion about the relationship between effect and arousal. For example, while many people equate the two, or use manipulation of affect (anxiety) to represent global arousal, at the same time, others suggest that the two can and must be separated if the effects of affect are not to be explained away as resulting from "mere" arousal.

Let us examine the topic of anxiety briefly and at the same time give some consideration to the issue of arousal. For a long time it has been known that states that might be considered negative affect states, such as anxiety, often have impact on behavior and cognitive processes. The influence of anxiety on achievement or academic performance has received particular attention. Very early it was suggested that academic performance was facilitated by a moderate, as opposed to either a very low or a very high, level of anxiety. This issue was of both theoretical and practical interest, and later the idea was extended to many kinds of performance (e.g., Freeman, 1948; Hebb, 1955; Lindsley, 1957; Malmo, 1959; Schlosberg, 1954; 1966; Yerkes & Dodson, 1908).

For the most part, this work was not conceptualized so much in terms of affect, however, as motivation; and the general conclusion extracted from it was the familiar and important principle that anxiety (arousal or motivation) bears an inverted U-shaped relationship to performance—that performance is facilitated by moderate levels of anxiety (arousal) but debilitated by either extremely low or extremely high levels of anxiety (motivation). Another general conclusion was that arousal improves performance of simple tasks and interferes with performance of complex tasks, a view that was expressed in Hullian terms by saying that *drive* increases the likelihood of the dominant response. Here it can be seen that attention was not focused on the feeling tone of the affective state so much as on the global motivational consequences of the feeling state.

Anxiety was equated with "arousal," and arousal with motivation or derive, often explicitly so. (This is an example of the fuzzy distinction between affect and motivation that was mentioned in the introductory section of this chapter.) What can be said, however, is that the general conclusion was that moderate levels of anxiety (arousal or motivation) are most facilitative of performance. High levels of arousal were found to disrupt performance and also to reduce the range of attention (e.g., Bruner, Matter, & Papanek, 1955). Some researchers did focus on the emotional nature of the arousing situation, and most who did so concluded that emotion was "disorganizing" (e.g., Easterbrook, 1959; Young, 1961; but see Leeper, 1948, 1970, for an alternative view).

Arousal.   Arousal has entered the study of affect in two ways. First, physiological arousal, as a general state, has often been considered a component of emotional or affective state and therefore is considered to be operative whenever an affective state is induced. Second, manipulations intended to produce arousal or motivation have often involved, more or less unintentionally, induction of states that we can recognize as affective states, such as anxiety.

To begin with in discussing arousal, researchers distinguish between two types of physiological arousal, cortical and visceral. Cortical arousal can be measured by EEG and is characterized by faster frequency and lower amplitude brain waves (say, alpha waves, characteristic of relaxed attention, and beta waves, characteristic of greater arousal). It is under the control of the reticular activating system and can occur with or without visceral arousal; it can be induced by mild stimuli and accompanies interest or attention. Visceral arousal, on the other hand, is elicited by strong stimuli and occurs only when high levels of cortical arousal are also present.

Piliavin, Dovidio, Gaertner, and Clark (1982) have recently called attention to the need to define "arousal" more precisely than typically has been done in work on emotion. In this context, they note the distinction between two arousal response patterns identified by Sokolov (1963) as the *orienting response* and the *defense reaction*. Piliavin et al. (1982) summarize the literature, indicating that the orienting response occurs in response to novel stimuli of moderate intensity and involves the following: positive feedback to the reticular activating system, resulting in increased attention to incoming stimulation; decrease in heart rate; increase in skin conductance; peripheral vasoconstriction; pupillary dilation; and feelings of pleasantness. The defense reaction, which occurs in response to sudden or intense stimuli, on the other hand, is subjectively experienced as unpleasant; physiologically, it is characterized by negative feedback to the reticular activating system, resulting in blocking of external stimulation; sympathetic nervous system involvement; increase in heart rate; increase in skin conductance; peripheral vasoconstriction; and pupillary constriction.

This distinction between the orienting and the defense reaction parallels to some extent the one made above between cortical and visceral arousal, especially if one takes the view that visceral arousal occurs in response to stimulation of greater intensity than does cortical arousal alone. However, it has a different emphasis from that of the cortical-visceral distinction: it calls attention to the body's differential response patterns in orienting versus defensive reactions (which might also mean in response to mild versus intense stimulation and pleasant versus unpleasant arousal). In addition, however, since there can be high levels of cortical arousal that do not involve a defense reaction, these two sets of distinctions are both important in understanding the human reaction to arousal.

While cortical arousal has been found to be relatively general (EEG electrodes placed at different points in the scalp will usually yield the same type of wave), visceral arousal has been the topic of much controversy on just this point, as has already been noted (p. 182). Whether people experience differential visceral cues associated with specific physiological states, and the nature of and extent to which such cues serve to define the affective state, are questions that have been asked at least since the time of James (1890). Thus, cortical rather than visceral arousal, being rather general and involving the amount of nonspecific input being sent to the cognitive analyzers, may be seen as relating to the energizing or motivational conceptualization noted above.

Regarding the issue of this general (cortical) arousal and performance, there is general agreement that, as suggested by the inverted U-shaped function, a medium level of arousal is optimal for performance. However, it has also been found that just what this optimal level of arousal is depends on the task to be performed: Each task has its own optimal level of arousal; simple tasks seem to have higher optimal levels of arousal, while complex tasks can be performed better in the presence of lower levels of arousal (Martindale, 1981). This may simply be another way of saying that arousal facilitates the performance of simple tasks and interferes with performance of complex tasks; but this relationship between complexity of the task and the level of arousal that can be tolerated or is optimal may explain why arousal (''drive'') makes the dominant response more likely: In general, the more arousal, the more a simple response is preferred. It also holds implications for the impact of arousal on creativity. But most importantly for present purposes it complicates the picture of the influence of arousal on perfor-

mance. We cannot know whether to predict that arousal (which is often represented or induced by bringing about anxiety or some other negative affect) will
impair or facilitate performance unless we know how complex the task is and
what the person's dominant response is (and possibly what the person's current
level of arousal is).

In addition, if we now attempt to relate the effects of arousal to those of
affect, the situation is further complicated by the fact that arousal itself has
hedonic tone (feeling of pleasantness or unplesantness) inherent in it. People
avoid and dislike both very high and very low arousal states, and, rather, seek a
medium level of arousal (e.g., Berlyne, 1971). In general, the statement can be
made that, up to a point, increasing arousal yields pleasure, but that beyond that
point further increases in arousal are unpleasant. There are differing views of
why this occurs, but there is general agreement that arousal and affect bear a
relationship to one another, known as the Wundt Curve (Martindale, 1981).

The existence of a relationship between affective tone and arousal itself has
hampered attempts to study arousal and affective tone separately. Recently, the
technique of exercise has been used to study arousal (visceral) independently of
affect. From the beginning of such efforts, there were objections that exercise did
not represent well the concept of "arousal"; but these objections probably
stemmed from the fact that exercise seemed to have no affective (anxiety or
anger) component, which people had come to equate with "arousal," as the term
is used in common language. However, for researchers interested in studying the
influence of affect and arousal separately, this was seen as an advantage rather
than as a failing in the technique.

More troubling for these researchers may have been the criticism that exercise
deals with visceral arousal rather than cortical, and that measures such as heart
rate, which are typically used as indicators of "arousal," are of unclear relationship to cortical arousal. Since high levels of visceral arousal are accompanied by
high levels of cortical arousal (though the reverse relationship is *not* true),
exercise may also induce cortical arousal. However, perhaps a measure of cortical arousal, rather than heart rate (or some indication of the relationship between
cortical arousal and heart rate) should be reported in the studies under discussion,
if this point is to be made.[6]

Now there is an even more difficult problem facing the use of exercise as a
means to induce affectless "arousal": Recently there have been questions raised

---

[6]In fact, heart rate may be especially inappropriate as an indicator of arousal because it has been
found to decrease in the orienting response (which occurs in situations of novel stimulation, of mild,
pleasant arousal) but to increase in the defense response (which occurs in situations of sudden or
intense stimulation). Thus, heart rate does not bear a direct, nor even unidirectional, relationship to
arousal; and in some situations, as intensity of arousal increases from zero, heart rate might be
expected first to decrease and then to increase (if a defense response occurs). This situation renders
heart rate espeically problematic as an indicator of arousal.

about whether exercise is affectively neutral. Studies have reported finding increased levels of enkephalin accompanying exercise, and there have been reports of phenomena such as "addiction" to exercise ("runner's high"). If exercise is fun, as a growing number of people attest, separate study of arousal and feelings of pleasantness and unplesantness may prove difficult indeed. Actually, this is not surprising in view of the curvilinear relationship between arousal and affect itself. These considerations imply that arousal should not always be equated with negative affect such as anxiety, nor with affectless motivation, as has sometimes been done. Sometimes arousal is fun.

Moreover, it is now clear that there can be negative affect states that involve very low levels of arousal. In this context, it is instructive to note that the negative state of sadness or depression, which is the prototype of negative affect, typically identified as the opposite pole to happiness, is associated, not with arousal, but with *slowed* movement, functioning, and thought processes.

Negative Affect: Depression.   Thus far, we have considered some effects of sadness on behavior and cognition, but we have not included reference to the vast literature that exists regarding depression. Clearly, detailed study of all that is known about the clinical phenomena of depression is beyond the scope of this chapter. Yet some mention of recent positions that offer a cognitive interpretation of depression (e.g., Beck, 1967, 1976), and of findings that create a bridge between the clinical and social literatures on the topic (e.g., Alloy & Abramson, 1979) is probably in order.

Beck and his associates have developed a therapy based on a cognitive interpretation of depression. It suggests that the negative affect characteristic of depressed individuals (or depressed state) results from negative cognitions (and a resulting negative bias in the coding and processing of a broad range of stimuli). In the terms that we have been using in this chapter, one might say that depression may involve increased accessibility of negative material. Moreover, negative material may also be more extensive or better integrated with other material than is the case for normal individuals (or at times of nondepression). Beck's therapy, like efforts by so-called "cognitive behavior modifiers" such as Meichenbaum and Goldfried, but unlike more traditional psychotherapeutic approaches, attempts to help patients to break the cycle of negative thoughts by intervening directly in the cognitive process.

Another set of findings that has been particularly stimulating, and that may also aid us in understanding the effects of negative affect that have been observed, is the work that began by focusing on the influence of depression on perception of control (perception of contingency between one's own actions and events that occur). This work stemmed from the assumption in the Learned Helplessness theory of depression (Seligman, 1975) that a major problem in depression was that people had lost the ability to see their behavior as effective, to see the contingency between their actions and subsequent events or outcomes.

The findings, in contrast with those which would be predicted by the Learned Helplessness theory, have been that depressives tend to be *more* realistic than normal control subjects in estimating their degree of control over outcomes (e.g., Alloy & Abramson, 1979; Gollin, Terrell, & Johnson, 1977). Researchers have extended this work into the topic that now has been called, more generally, "depressive realism."

For example, Nelson & Craighead (1977) found that depressives were more accurate than normal controls in estimating the frequency of negative feedback on a laboratory task; Lewinsohn, Mischel, Chaplain, and Barton (1980) reported that depressives' ratings of their social competence agreed with observers' ratings of them, while nondepressed psychiatric patients and normal control subjects rated themselves more positively than did observers; and studies of the attribution process of depressed college students and children have reported findings consistent with the results mentioned above: nondepressed people were more likely than depressed to attribute negative outcomes to external, unstable, and specific causes (Klein, Fencil-Morse, & Seligman, 1976; Kuiper, 1978; Rizley, 1978; Seligman, Abramson, Semmel, & von Baeyer, 1979).

In general, taken together, these findings suggest that, relative to normals, depressives tend to exhibit a self-derrogating bias, making relatively negative judgments of themselves and tending to attribute negative outcomes to themselves but positive outcomes to external factors. However, it should be emphasized that this tendency can be described as "biased" only relative to the behavior of normals. Abramson and Alloy (1981) and others have argued that depressives are actually more realistic and that it is normal people whose judgments and attributions are biased in a way that might be called self-serving or subject to an "illusion of control," involving attribution of positive outcomes to themselves but negative outcomes to external factors (e.g., Langer, 1975; Miller & Ross, 1975).

Most recently, Schwartz (1981) has challenged some of the conclusions drawn from this work, suggesting that the apparent errors and biases of normals may be attributable to the particular materials used and conditions of testing in the laboratory studies. He suggests a motivational interpretation of depressives' apparent lack of self-serving bias, centering on the effect pointed out by Reber (1967, 1976) of attempts to infer rules (attempts to infer rules cause filtering of information). Further, Abramson and Alloy (1981) have acknowledged that the content domain of the materials used in their studies may hinder attempts to generalize from their findings, and most recently it has been suggested that depressives' apparent resistance to the "illusion of control," or their apparent accuracy in estimating (lack of) contingency of (positive) events, may be limited, as well, to situations which involve themselves (e.g., Martin, Abramson, & Alloy, in press). It may be that depressives only seem more accurate than normals in attributing control in some studies because the tasks have involved controllable bad events and uncontrollable good events. The unflattering pattern of attribution which is required in order to be accurate in perception of control on these tasks is one to which depressives, but not normal persons, are accustomed. Thus, because depressed persons are more willing than are normal individuals to attribute negative outcomes to themselves, and less willing to attribute positive outcomes to themselves, in a situation where negative events are controllable and positive are not, the depressed will appear more accurate than the control group. In contrast, normals, who usually *are* responsible for good things rather than bad, may not be accustomed to expect such situations. As Abramson and Alloy (1981) have suggested, it may be that normals would adapt over time to the changed reality, come to have such expectations, and appear more accurate, if they had more experiences in which they were responsible for negative outcomes.

To summarize these developments, it appears that depressives are more likely to accept responsibility for negative outcomes than are normals. This difference may be attributable to an accurate reflection of reality on the part of both groups, given their own particular environments and life situations; or it may be attributable to a breakdown among the depressed in the motivation to maintain self-esteem (Abramson & Alloy, 1981; Schwartz, 1981). Where problems are posed in such a way that in order to be accurate subjects must attribute contingency or responsibility for bad events to themselves, depressives may thus appear more accurate than normals. The difference between depressives and normals may also be attributable to depressives' lessened interest in the task and fewer attempts to grapple with it, which inadvertently may lead to less filtering of information and more accurate perception of contingency (Schwartz, 1981). In any case, because these findings indicate that depressives tend to perceive contingency between their own actions and events, they present something of a challenge to cognitive theories of depression that postulate and depend on depressives' underestimation of their own control or of contingency between their actions and events, in relatively negative situations (e.g., Learned Helplessness).

Finally, it should be noted that all that has been found in this literature suggests that it should be difficult to make a normal person depressed (Abramson & Alloy, 1981; Schwartz, 1981) and perhaps also to keep a temporarily depressed normal person depressed. This suggestion is compatible with the data that have been presented regarding the attenuated impact of sadness on memory, the asymmetry that has been noted between the effects of positive and negative affect on both cognition and behavior, and the interpretation that has been offered for this asymmetry—that, where possible, people try to avoid depression (not necessarily irrationally so) and naturally try to make themselves feel better if they become depressed. As we have seen, it is not necessary to postulate any irrational, unconscious "defense mechanisms" to account for this effect.

The recent theoretical work of Beck and his colleagues, together with the findings discussed in this chapter, suggest that a useful approach to the study of depression may be to attempt to identify the cognitive patterns that differentiate depressive (or depressed) individuals from normals. These patterns may involve relatively stable differences between persons, since cognitive habits may be developed. Observation of such stable differences between persons would be compatible with the literature in two ways: Cognitive patterns are known to be more stable than many so-called personality characteristics (Mischel, 1968); and depression is often seen to characterize individuals. Yet the same approach allows for situational variability, which also accords with the episodic nature of affective disorders such as depression. It may be that depression can be understood as involving increased accessibility for negative material, and/or a more extensive or elaborated or better interconnected network or schema of negative material than characterizes normal individuals or the normal state.

SOME METHODOLOGICAL CONSIDERATIONS

In this section, we focus on some of the ways in which affect has been induced, and its impact measured, in experiments. The fact that certain procedures have been successful in altering affect may say something about the nature of affect, and we examine these implications. On the other hand, we also consider the extent to which some of the procedures themselves may have directly influenced the results obtained. In addition, we address some technical issues such as ways of verifying that affect has been manipulated (the "manipulation-check" issue). In this context, we also consider whether it is appropriate to speak broadly of "positive" and "negative" affect, as is frequently done, and even whether it is useful to postulate the unseen intervening variable of "affective state" at all in accounting for the findings that have been obtained.

Affect has been induced in experiments in a wide variety of ways, ranging from finding money, to hypnosis. Experimenters have sought to make people feel good or bad by providing a report of success or failure on a task, by arranging for subjects to find a dime in the coin return of a public telephone, by giving out free samples, by providing refreshments, by having subjects wait in hot and crowded conditions as opposed to comfortable conditions, by playing relaxing music, by providing an unexpected bonus of one dollar or a fifty-cent certificate good toward purchase of a hamburger, by having subjects adopt the facial expression of various emotional states, by asking subjects to remember or imagine a happy, sad, or angering event, by having subjects read statements designed to put them into a good or bad mood (the Velten Procedure), and by post-hypnotic suggestion of emotional state to hypnotized persons. These procedures vary in many respects, including the naturalness of the settings in which they can be employed, the extent to which events like them are likely to be encountered in everyday life, their receptiveness to checks on the manipulation of affect, and the degree to which they involve direct—rather than indirect— manipulation of cognition. Each of these issues will be considered in turn.

Several of the studies which employed finding money or receipt of free samples were conducted at shopping centers, airports, and train stations, using subjects who did not know that they were participants in an experiment. These features of those studies add to the external validity of their findings: that is, events of the kind arranged by the experimenter are likely to happen during the course of people's daily lives, and the observed reactions of the subjects are quite likely to be genuine, uninfluenced by experimenter effects, evaluation apprehension, and so on. (See Rosenthal & Rosnow, 1969, for discussions of these and related issues.) Thus, one has the sense that in these studies one has observed effects as they may occur in life.

On the other hand, it is fair to ask of these, as well as other studies of affect, whether the manipulations employed in the studies actually induced the particular affective state intended by the experimenters. Thus, I turn now to a brief consideration of the use of "manipulation checks" and alternatives to them.

Laboratory studies of affect have tended to use so-called "manipulation checks" on the induction of affect—usually questionnaires asking subjects about their current affective states. However, the correspondence between subjects' feeling states and their checkmarks on these rating scales has not itself been established, and therefore these responses are difficult to interpret. Difficulty of interpretation arises not only because of the potential influence of experimenter demand or subject expectation on the responses obtained, but also because people may not be willing, or able, to express their feelings accurately in terms of ratings on a scale.

Because of these kinds of considerations, some studies have opted for more indirect assessments of affect such as ratings of neutral material. Such ratings have been shown to be influenced by manipulations that were designed to induce affective state and that were found to affect social behavior in the predicted ways (e.g., Forest et al., 1979; Isen, Daubman, & Gorgoglione, in press; Isen & Shalker, 1982).

In addition, several studies, especially field studies such as those described above, have relied on converging operations and discriminant validation over a series of studies, to verify the manipulation of affect conceptually (e.g., Isen & Levin, 1972. See Campbell & Fiske, 1959; Garner, Hake, & Eriksen, 1956, for a discussion of this and related issues). For example, it has gradually been established that positive affect induced by different events (but events that all converge on the concept of positive affect), such as success on a task of perceptual-motor skills (Isen, 1970), being offered a cookie while studying in a library (Isen & Levin, 1972), finding a dime in the coin return of a telephone booth (Isen & Levin, 1972), reading statements designed to induce good mood (Aderman, 1972), receiving a free sample (Isen et al., 1976), hearing pleasant music (Fried & Berkowitz, 1979), and the weather (Cunningham, 1979), all produce helpful and charitable behavior (in some cases measured by the same dependent measure, e.g., helping someone pick up dropped items). Moreover, some studies have indicated that the effect of these manipulations is to promote helpful behavior in particular rather than simply to promote all kinds of behavior equally (e.g.,

Isen & Levin, 1972). Thus, there is growing conceptual validation that positive affect has been induced and has influenced helping behavior.

Such convergent and discriminant validation has also enabled authors in many cases to rule out potential alternative interpretations of their findings. Not only do these procedures help to establish that affect was manipulated as intended, but they also make less plausible the possibility that the observed effect of feelings in any given case was attributable to extraneous side-effects associated with the particular way in which affect was induced in the case at hand (i.e., that something *in addition* to affect was induced and caused the observed effect).

Moreover, the use of varying methods of affect-induction across many studies has provided another benefit. It demonstrates the utility of, and the justification for, postulating a nonobservable intervening variable such as affective state. There are some who would argue that behavior can better be understood by reference only to the conditions and stimuli that "produced" it, without reference to nonobservable internal states or cognitive processes. What has emerged from a decade of research on the impact of affective states on social behavior and cognition, however, is one more demonstration of the power of explanatory constructs, coupled *with* behavioral analysis, to predict behavior and to direct research in important ways.

In illustration, since we now know something about the way in which a person's tendency to help others responds to positive feeling state as induced by finding a dime in the coin return of a public telephone, receiving a free sample, learning of success on a task, and so forth, a behavioral account might propose that the concept of feeling state is superfluous and that the behavior can be understood in terms of the operations alone. Yet, without the concept of affective state, why would one have expected these diverse stimuli and situations to produce similar behavior? The only a priori similarity among them is in the unobservable way that they make people feel. In some, but not all, cases an operant description might be able to account for the effects observed, after the fact; but it would not have predicted them. For example, perhaps the principle of generalization might be employed to account for the similar effects of the affect manipulations; but without the concept of "feeling good," one would not have predicted that such diverse situations would have produced similar behavior, because the dimension along which to generalize would not have been apparent.

Additional results have been obtained that would not have been predicted without the concept of affective state (and its tendency to be maintained). For example, in the study by Isen and Simmonds (1978), divergent behavior was observed in a single situation simply as a function of the feeling tone of the experimental task to be performed: persons who had found a dime agreed to help more than a control group where the helping task involved reading positive-mood-inducing (maintaining) statements, but such persons, were *less* willing than control subjects to help in a situation where helping would have involved their reading statements designed to induce negative mood, destroying their positive state. Nor would an operant account have predicted the variety of effects (on interpersonal behavior, memory, performance, decision-making, risk-taking, and the like) that were predicted and have been observed to result from a given operation (success, for example).

Thus, summarizing the findings of a broad range of studies employing diverse methods of affect induction, one can conclude that affect has been manipulated and found to influence social behavior and cognition as described. It is instructive that such diverse techniques of affect induction have produced similar effects, such as increased helpfulness. Clearly, there must be differences among the affective states induced by, say, success, finding money, and remembering a happy event; and attempts to distinguish among them in either quality or effects might prove fruitful. But the literature that demonstrates similar effects of these various manipulations implies that there is something unitary about positive affect, or at least that some component of it is similar across inductions.

This view accords with the point made by Leventhal, that the general quality of positivity or negativity of a stimulus plays an important role in determining response to it and may be innately perceived. It is also compatible with the argument made by Zajonc for an immediate and general affective response to affective stimuli, and with the data suggesting that the neurochemical mediation of positive affect also may be rather general.

Nonetheless, distinctions are to be found among affective states even of the same general tone. In addition, distinctions might be made among methods of affect induction. In particular, a distinction needs to be made between manipulations that involve rather direct intervention in cognitive processes (such as those instructing subjects to think about events that made them happy) and those whose effect on cognitive processes is more indirect (such as those in which subjects received a free sample). It is this issue to which we turn next.

When we give subjects a free sample or a success experience and then discover that they are more helpful than control subjects and that their cognitive processes are influenced by such treatments—they make more positive judgments about a broad range of topics or items, memory for positive material is enhanced, and they go about solving problems in a different way—we find this noteworthy. It teaches us that affective experience can influence cognitive processing (and social behavior). On the other hand, if we manipulate affect by *directing* subjects to think about certain kinds of experiences or thoughts, or even by reading certain kinds of statements, any effects observed on cognition seem somehow less surprising and instructive. Effects on social behavior would still be interesting; but effects on cognition seem less so, because the latter may be entirely attributable to our initial instruction. This is one problem that has arisen in considering several of the ways currently employed to manipulate affect in experiments—techniques such as hypnosis, instructions to recall or imagine affect-inducing events, and instructions to read a set of affect-inducing statements—that cognitive changes in response to instructions that directly manipulate cognitions are not really very remarkable.

A similar interpretation of the more indirect methods (e.g., free gift) of affect induction has also been offered, but in an attenuated form. It is that the affect-induction procedure—the procedure itself, and not any affective state induced—cues the relevant cognitions which then produce the other effects observed. This has led some investigators to attempt to establish that in studies involving affect manipulation it is the feeling, rather than only the topic or affect-inducing procedure, that has produced the various results obtained (e.g., Teasdale & Taylor, 1981; Laird et al., 1982; Snyder & White, 1982).

It should also be noted, as was described above regarding an operant analysis of this literature, that such an interpretation of the findings (i.e., that the effects are due not to the feeling state induced but rather to direct cueing of a certain set of cognitions by the operations designed to induce affect) would have difficulty in accounting for the similar results obtained with varied modes of affect induction (success, receipt of a free sample, refreshments, finding money). It would also have an especially difficult time accounting for the interactions observed in several studies described earlier (Forest et al., 1979; Isen & Levin, 1972; Isen & Patrick, 1983; and Isen & Simmonds, 1978). In those studies, subjects who had been offered cookies were more willing to help by aiding a fellow student, but less willing to help by annoying a fellow student; those who found a dime were more willing to help by reading positive-affect-inducing statements but less willing to help by reading negative-affect-inducing statements; and subjects who were given a fifty-cent gift certificate for a fast-food product were more willing to take a low-risk bet but less willing to make a high-risk bet.

The manipulations of affect by cognitive intervention are more vulnerable to such interpretations; and in addition, they face a second challenge, that their effects are attributable to experimenter demand: That is, that the manipulation constitutes a demand of subjects that they behave in an obviously expected way, that the results obtained fit the description of the expected behavior, and that thus the results may be the product of this experimenter demand. Such objections have been countered by the proponents of the various techniques (e.g., Bower, 1981, for hypnosis; Velten, 1968, for the Velten statements); yet concern about this possibility does not seem to subside (e.g., Buchwald, Strack, & Coyne, 1981; Polivy & Doyle, 1980). The problem with attempts to dispel such interpretations is that if a technique is vulnerable to experimenter demand effects, the fact that such an interpretation may be ruled out or seen as unlikely in one case does not address the issue for any other particular study reported, unless the same point is being made. That is, *each time* hypnosis or the Velten procedure, or the imagine/remember technique is used, it is open to the effect of experimenter demand; and experimenters must take precautions against this influence and demonstrate that, because of the particular way in which the given study was conducted, the "demand" interpretation cannot account for the new effects obtained.

The Velten statements (Velten, 1968) have been in the literature the longest of any of these techniques, and have been the subject of the most analysis. Thus, more is known about the effects of this technique, but it has also encountered additional criticism. In this technique, subjects are asked to read a set of 50 positive, negative, or neutral statements, printed one to a card or page. The positive and negative statements describe bodily states or expressions of self-concept appropriate for the affective state to be induced (for example, "I'm getting tired out. I can feel my body getting exhausted and heavy," or "I've doubted that I am a worthwhile person"; "I'm full of energy and ambition—I feel like I could go a long time without sleep," or "My judgment about most things is sound"). The neutral statements have nothing to do with either somatic well-being or sense of accomplishment and capability (for example, "At the end appears a section entitled 'bibliographic notes' "). Both the positive and negative batteries of items have been shown to induce behavior compatible with the desired state (e.g., Velten, 1968). However, recent research has suggested that the effect of the negative Velten statements is attributable primarily to their somatic component—that is, to the statements referring to slowed movement and tiredness (Frost, Graf, & Becker, 1979). While tiredness and somatic symptoms are acknowledged components of clinical depression, this factor may not always be the one that researchers would wish to manipulate in studies of mood.

More problematic for use of the Velten technique in research on affect are the results of recent studies indicating that the effect of the statements, especially of the positive statements, may not last long enough beyond the manipulation check to influence the dependent measure of interest (Frost & Green, 1982; Isen & Gorgoglione, 1983). Thus, the effects of the Velten procedure seem somewhat unpredictable and unstable, a factor which may render them especially vulnerable to experimenter demand or which may undermine confidence in the use of that technique of affect induction.

Hypnosis as a means of inducing affect also merits some discussion. The implicit-experimenter-demand interpretation seems especially plausible with this technique, because hypnosis itself is thought to involve hypnotist (experimenter) suggestion ("demand") coupled with subject suggestibility or receptiveness or ability to immerse oneself in such demand (but see Bower, 1981, for an argument against the experimenter-demand interpretation of his findings). As has already been noted, these studies also involve an explicit experimenter demand that subjects maintain their affective states at the initial level at which they were induced, a feature which has implications for the interpretation of certain patterns of data obtained using this technique.

Another problem for studies employing hypnosis as the means of affect induction is the fact that use of this technique results in a subject population that is highly selected (for hypnotic-suggestibility), since only a small portion of the student population meets the hypnotic-suggestibility criterion necessary for them to participate. This factor not only may tend to limit the generalizability of the findings obtained in these studies, but it also serves to reduce drastically the size of the subject pool from which samples can be drawn, with the result that the *same* subjects may participate in many studies (see, for example, Bower et al.,

1978, and Bower et al., 1981). This is not necessarily an insurmountable barrier to use of hypnosis as a technique of affect induction, but it does sound a note of caution.

Thus, in order to establish the utility of this potentially convenient, but at present controversial, method of affect induction, it will be very important to compare the results obtained in studies using hypnosis with those found in studies using other techniques of affect induction. To the extent that these studies tend to confirm one another's findings, we can have increased confidence in all of the manipulations used.

The discussion of methodological considerations has focused thus far on validation and other matters relating to induction of affect. It should be mentioned that similar methodological issues also surround the dependent measures studied, for example, altruism or helping, judgments or rating data of various kinds, and memory processes.

We have touched on one of these issues, the validation of helping or altruistic behavior as a result of positive affect, in the discussion of discriminant validation of affect induction: positive affect has been found to promote helpful and kindly behavior specifically, in distinction from other types of behavior such as that which is harmful or annoying (e.g., Isen & Levin, 1972). This is not to say that positive affect might not also promote other kinds of behavior in addition to the helpful (e.g., Batson et al., 1979), but it is clear that positive feelings do not simply "energize" all behavior indiscriminatly (Forest et al., 1979; Isen & Levin, 1972; Isen & Simmonds, 1978). Going even further in studying the dependent variable, Batson and his colleagues have focused on developing a paradigm to distinguish experimentally between altruistically motivated helping and other acts that might appear helpful but that are more egoistic in motivation (e.g., Batson, Duncan, Ackerman, Buckley, & Birch, 1981; Toi & Batson, 1982).

Likewise, regarding the dependent measures of judgment, rating data, and memory processes, similar methodological issues might be raised. For example, we have already noted that these kinds of data may sometimes be subject to an interpretation in terms of response bias, rather than differential retrieval effects. For example, Bellezza and Bower (1981), applying signal detection theory to the forced-choice data of a person-memory study have shown that some findings of apparently superior memory for stereotype-consistent information could be accounted for by guessing bias. (In the case of the affect-memory studies, however, this interpretation is less plausible, as has already been noted, because of the designs of the experiments and the patterns of results obtained.)

Another methodological/theoretical issue in memory studies is whether the effects of feelings are attributable to an influence at time of encoding, time of retrieval or to a state-dependent-learning effect. Sometimes, studies using memory as the dependent measure but proposing effects on encoding or cognitive organization may be subject to the alternative interpretation that the results instead reflect the influence of retrieval processes and therefore cannot always speak unequivocally to the questions of encoding or organization of material.

One way that has recently been proposed for dealing with this potential problem is to utilize a technique involving *priming* as a means of studying organization of cognitive material (Isen & Daubman, 1983), as has been suggested by McKoon and Ratcliff (1980). The priming technique involves determining whether a given word serves as an effective prime (that is, reduces reaction time when presented prior to the target word in, for example, a memory task or a lexical decision task) for target words. This may permit us to study cognitive organization independently of retrieval strategy because it may indicate which words or concepts function as related to one another.

This discussion of the methods used in studying the impact of affect on cognition and behavior has revealed several methodological concerns. Yet it has also shown that considerable advance and refinement have been made in studying affect and its influence on non-affective cognitive processes and behavior. Some of the methodological concerns and advances that we have considered also hold theoretical implications, and it is to this fundamental matter that we now turn our attention.

MODELS OF THE PROCESSES BY WHICH AFFECT INFLUENCES BEHAVIOR: THEORETICAL IMPLICATIONS

Recent work investigating the influence of affect on cognition and behavior has begun to explore the processes which enable or are responsible for the effects that have been observed, and we have already been introduced to some of the models (such as accessibility of compatible material) that have been proposed to account for these effects. This section of the chapter addresses such underlying processes in more detail. It describes some of the conceptualizations that have been offered for understanding the impact of affective states on cognition and behavior. It also points out some implications that these interpretative models may have for the next level of analysis—cognitive structure and organization.

Accessibility, Affect, and Cognitive Organization and Structure

As has been noted, a substantial body of evidence now suggests that positive affect can serve as a retrieval cue, influencing the material or the aspects of material in memory that come to mind. What is currently known about the organization of affect in memory does not allow us to say anything specific, however, about *how* affect is linked to other material nor about the underlying structure of memory, even as regards affective material. For example, discovering that positive affective state can serve as a retrieval cue for positive material in memory does not allow one to say that affect functions as a node in a network, according to an associative theory of memory. The accessibility hypothesis is compatible with both associative network and contextualist or "schema" theoretical positions regarding the underlying structures, processes, and organization of memory. (The concept of priming was developed in the context of the associative network and spreading activation view of memory, and therefore references to priming or increased accessibility may seem to imply assumption of the network and spreading activation model. This is not necessarily the case, however.) On the other hand, these findings do imply that affective tone may be an important dimension of cognitive organization, and this has enormous consequences for our concepts of both cognition and affect.

If affect can serve as a retrieval cue, then affect must constitute an organizational "concept" or unit or at least component of a unit. The "encoding specificity" principle indicates that material will be accessible by means of a given cue only if it was initially encoded, or is now stored, as relevant to that cue (Tulving & Thompson, 1973). Thus, if feeling state serves as a retrieval cue, then material in memory must be encoded according to how that material makes one feel, perhaps episodically, perhaps semantically, or perhaps both.[7] This suggests a much more intimate relationship between affect and cognition than was ever suspected previously; and it also suggests some interesting possible extensions of cognitive theory. There is nothing about this which is necessarily incompatible with current views of cognitive processing, but, at the same time, the idea that feeling may be a unit of cognitive organization may possibly suggest alternative conceptualizations and some new directions of research.

Ways in which the influence of affect may be conceptualized according to existing models in cognitive psychology have recently been suggested in detail (Bower, 1981; Bower et al., 1981; Clark & Isen, 1982). For example, both Bower (1981) and Clark and Isen (1982) have indicated how affect might fit into an associative network and "spreading activation" theory. Clark and Isen (1982) have also noted how the Storage Bin model proposed by Wyer and Srull (1981) might account for the observed findings; and they have also utilized the distinction between automatic and controlled processes (e.g., Hasher & Zacks, 1979; Posner & Snyder, 1975; Schneider & Shiffrin, 1977) to understand the observed effects of feelings on cognitive processes and behavior. In addition, Isen et al. (1978) have found the framework of the contextualist position in cognitive psy-

---

[7]One other possibility is that the relationship between the feeling state and the cognitions made accessible is not this direct, but rather that feeling state cues the cognitive category of, say, "things relevant to positive feelings," and that this then makes certain items more accessible. This would still imply affect as a cognitive unit, but it omits the experiential component inherent in the alternate phrasing. Whether the feeling state and the cognitive category can be differentiated and, if so, whether feeling itself constitutes a separate (additional) cue are now topics of interest among psychologists (e.g., Laird et al., 1982; Snyder & White, 1982; Teasdale & Taylor, 1981).

chology useful in understanding these findings. The way in which an associative network theory of memory can be used to understand the influence of affect on cognition has been illustrated several times recently (e.g., Bower, 1981; Bower et al., 1981; Clark & Isen, 1982) and therefore will not be undertaken here again. However the utility of the concept of automatic and controlled processes, and the usefulness of some of the views associated with the contextualist position in understanding the processing of affect are less well known and will be briefly described below.

Automatic and Controlled Processing

"Automatic" processes may be defined as those cognitive processes that occur without conscious awareness, without intention, without effort, and without interfering with other mental activities (Posner & Snyder, 1975); they produce thoughts or feelings that seem to intrude upon us rather than come to us as the result of our effort. Such processes have been of increasing interest among cognitive psychologists recently, and Clark and Isen (1982) have suggested that affect may be processed at least in part automatically, and that certain other social phenomena that involve affect may be attributable to automatic processes. For example, apparently nonreflective evaluations and decisions in person perception, discussed by Schneider, Hastorf, and Ellsworth (1980) as "snap judgments," may be mediated by affect and may be the result of automatic processes. The findings of Zajonc and his colleagues (e.g., Zajonc, 1968), that mere exposure to a stimulus increases the positivity of judgments about that stimulus, may also be attributable to the automatic processing of affect.

Clark and Isen (1982) suggest that automatic processing contributes to many of the effects that feelings have been found to have on cognition and behavior; but they go on to propose a role for controlled processes, as well, in these effects. Controlled processes, in contrast with automatic, are those that do involve time, effort, and at least some degree of conscious awareness in order to be performed. They can vary in complexity, and include everything from complicated strategies to simple "set" to perceive or react (Posner, 1978). Their distinguishing characteristic is that, because they require at least some effort, they are thought to drain the limited capacity information processing system.

It seems likely that such processes play a role in the behavior that accompanies affective states. Both folk knowledge and experimental evidence indicate that people attempt to control feelings, especially negative feelings, and that often such efforts are successful. "Whistling past the graveyard" refers to a strategy for coping with fear; and the words to two familiar songs illustrate how children may be taught to cope cognitively with fear and sadness: "Whenever I feel afraid, I hold my head erect and whistle a happy tune, so no one will suspect I'm afraid. . . . Make believe you're brave and the trick will get you far. You may be as brave as you make believe you are." (Rodgers & Hammerstein, 1951,

p. 16), and ". . . when the dog bites, when the bee stings, when I'm feeling sad, I simply remember my favorite things and then I don't feel so bad . . ." (Rodgers & Hammerstein, 1959, p. 27).

Experimental evidence confirms that such actions and strategies can influence emotional experience. For example, recent studies have shown that direct manipulation of cognitions can improve mood in both depressed and nondepressed persons (Hale & Strickland, 1976; Raps, Reinhard & Seligman, 1980; Strickland, Hale, & Anderson, 1975; Teasdale & Bancroft, 1977). Schneider et al. (1980) summarize the literature showing that "putting on a happy face" can make one feel happier (e.g., Kleck et al., 1976; Laird, 1974; but see also Tourangeau & Ellsworth, 1979, and Buck, 1980); and Laird et al., (1981) have recently shown that such techniques can also influence recall of affectively-toned material from memory.

As has already been proposed, affective states may give rise to strategies (controlled processes) of mood-maintenance and mood-repair. Clark and Isen (1982) suggested some of the implications of the differences between automatic and controlled processes and of the fact that they can be expected to act together to produce the observed effects of feelings on behavior. Given that affect is subject to controlled processes as well as automatic, and given that positive and negative states might be expected to be associated with differing strategies for dealing with affect, one should not be surprised to observe asymmetry between positive and negative feeling states in their effects on behavior and cognitive processing. Moreover, as noted earlier, the habitual use of certain strategies for dealing with affect may influence the actual pattern of relationships among cognitions, so that automatic processes as well as controlled may come to contribute to this asymmetry.

In addition, the fact that controlled processes require effort has implications for the circumstances under which they will be used most effectively. For example, one might expect the effects of controlled processes to be less apparent at times of weakness or cognitive preoccupation and, as Hasher and Zacks (1979) have suggested, in childhood, old age, times of depression, and times of fatigue. Further, where automatic and controlled processes give rise to opposing tendencies, in both thought and behavior, as in the case of sad affect for example, such conditions that influence cognitive capacity may be expected to influence the cognitive and/or behavioral outcome, because they will play a role in the extent to which controlled processes will likely be employed.

One further implication of this interpretation of the asymmetry between the effects of positive and negative states is that strategies are for the most part learned and therefore their effects should not be as apparent in young children as they are in older children or adults. Affect should produce more symmetrical effects on behavior among very young children. The findings reported by Cialdini and Kenrick (1976), which intended to examine this issue in the context of helping behavior, lend some support to this proposition. This study found that for very young children (6–8 years of age), but not for older children (10–12), negative affect was associated with decreased helping. One possible interpretation of these findings is that helping in response to negative affect results from employing a strategy for mood improvement, and that young children tend not to help under these circumstances because they have not yet learned this strategy for mood-improvement. In partial support of this argument (the component suggesting that children have learned these strategies by the age of 10), Nasby and Yando (1982), also studying fifth-grade children, found asymmetric effects of positive and negative affect, this time on memory. Their results do not speak directly to the issue of whether these effects should be attributed to learned strategies, but they do confirm that, if so, the strategies are learned early.

Theoretical Issues to be Resolved and Opportunities to Extend Existing Theories

Not all of the findings regarding the influence of affect on cognitive processes have turned out to be quite as compatible with existing cognitive theories, especially associative network theory, as they might be; and these, then, may provide opportunities for extension of existing theory, at least as regards affect.

(How) Does Activation (of Affect) Really Spread? Taking off on the title used by Ratcliff and McKoon (1981) to question the viability of the Spreading Activation theory, I wish now to mention results recently reported by Johnson and Tversky (1983) that have implications regarding a "spreading activation" model for understanding the processing of affect. Those authors found that induction of a negative affective state by exposure to a brief account of a tragedy affected (increased) subjects' perceptions of the frequency of many different kinds of negative events occurring. Working only with negative situations, Johnson and Tversky (1983) also found that positive affect was associated with a perception of reduced risk of these events occurring. The most interesting theoretical point raised by these results is that although the various potential tragedies whose frequency was to be judged varied in their similarity to the affect-inducing stimulus, the impact of the stimulus on subjects' judgments did not vary as a function of this similarity.

A theory such as one proposing "spreading activation" within a network would expect something akin to a generalization gradient in the effect of the tragic story on people's estimates of the likelihood of the various risks. According to the theory, activation travels out from a node, along the network, and material more closely related to the node receives more activation, and receives activation sooner, than less centrally located or related material. Thus, in the paper by Johnson & Tversky (1983), risks that were closely linked to the target should have been influenced more than unrelated risks. But this is not what Johnson & Tversky (1983) found. Subjects' estimates of the likelihood of lung cancer were greater in the experimental than in the control condition, regardless of whether the negative-affect-inducing paragraph that they had read had been about someone dying of cancer or someone dying in a fire. One might summarize the four studies in the Johnson & Tversky (1983) paper by saying that reading about, say, dying of cancer increased subjects' estimates of the likelihood of being struck by lightning or losing their jobs, as much as of the likelihood of, say, dying of heart disease.

As Johnson and Tversky suggest, these results seem to pose a problem for associative network theories employing the notion of spreading activation. Proponents of the spreading-activation view might argue that if the negative-affect-inducing event was arousing enough, it could have activated the entire network, but Johnson and Tversky point out that the affect-inducing event was mild. (If the proponents of spreading-activation theory would suggest that activation of the entire network happened quite readily and frequently, or that this is more likely to happen with affective nodes or affective activation, then the network concept would lose much of its explanatory and predictive power, at least as concerns affect.)

There is another factor that presents something of a problem for the suggestion that the impact of affect on cognitive processes can be understood in terms of a spreading activation theory of memory. This is the concept of "cue-overload" (e.g., Watkins, 1979), or the "fanning effect," as Bower and his associates have called it (Anderson & Bower, 1973), that is part of the spreading activation theory. Studies have shown that the more stimuli that there are associated with a given cue, the less effective that cue is in activating any single one of those elements. Thus, if a given cue, say the color of white walls or affective state, is associated with thousands of events and associated memories, the effectiveness of that cue as a retrieval cue for any given memory should be slight. The white walls of your living room should not remind you of any particular event because this cue is associated with so many stimuli.

A spreading-activation view of affect's influence on cognition would suggest that affect functions as this kind of context cue and that thus experientially (or state-dependent related) material would be associated with affective state in memory. However, on this basis alone there is no way of predicting that some stimuli experienced at the same time as the state would be associated with it while others would not. This is a problem because, for most individuals, an affective state such as happiness as a simple context cue must be associated with thousands of events or stimuli, and thus it would be difficult to explain, in terms of this conception alone, the activation of certain memories by means of affective state.

On the basis of this view proposed by spreading-activation theory, one might predict that affect might facilitate recall of a compatible event over incompatible memories, if the subject were asked to recall *any* event from his or her past; but, using this model, it would be hard to understand how affective state could facilitate the recall of a *specific* event or item learned while in a positive state. Since positive feelings *have* been found to cue specific positive material in memory, perhaps some other conceptualization, such as that provided by schema theory, will be more appropriate to understanding the influence of affect on cognitive processes.

An Alternative Suggested by Schema or Contextualist Theory.   The difficulty in obtaining state-dependent-learning effects of feelings, and the existence of memory-affect effects that are not state-dependent, such as an influence of affect at time of retrieval alone, are sets of results that may be problematic or simulating for traditional cognitive theory as it has been proposed to account for the effects of feelings on memory. Associative network theory, for example, is not incompatible with these results, but it may have to bend a bit more to accommodate the affect findings than if state-dependent-learning explained the entire phenomenon.

To illustrate, consider that from the perspective of associative network theory, state-dependent-learning would be the simplest way to incorporate the effects of feelings, with the least accommodation on the part of the theory. State-dependent-learning can be viewed as a simple context effect; and thus, affect too might be seen as having a quite simple impact on cognitive processes, as a simple context effect. As we have seen, however, state-dependent-learning as a function of feeling state appears to occur only under a limited range of conditions. Moreover, the "cue-overload" proposition of associative network theory places a cap on the utility of interpretations in terms of context effects in cases such as those involving specific memory facilitated by common affective states.

In addition, other effects of feelings on cognition have been observed, effects that cannot be subsumed under the state-dependent-learning rubric. The fact that positive feeling state has been found to serve as an effective retrieval cue independently of affective state at time of encoding (that is, even where subjects were not in the same affective state at time of learning and time of recall, and thus a state-dependent-learning effect is not compelling) is, likewise, problematic for this kind of interpretation.

Rather than maintaining that these effects be understood as examples of a broad view of state-dependent-learning, perhaps we should consider alternative ways of fitting what is being discovered about the effects of feelings with what is already known about cognitive processing. What does it mean if the impact of affect on cognition requires more than the state-dependent-learning interpretation in order to be understood? First, it may be that no new conceptualization is required, but that affect's place isn't *only* as a simple context effect.

The framework of the contextualist position in cognitive psychology (e.g., Bransford, 1979; Bransford, McCarrell, Franks, & Nitsch, 1977; Jenkins, 1974) may help us to understand the findings regarding the ways in which feelings influence cognitive processes and behavior, including certain apparent anomalies in the data, such as failures to obtain the state-dependent-learning effect of mood states. According to the contextualist view, the conditions of learning or stimulus features of the physical surroundings (external or internal) of learning are not the only, nor even the most usual, basis for encoding of material. Thus, one would not usually expect state-dependent-learning effects, especially where material is meaningful. If the meaning of the stimulus material or the way in which it is experienced is assumed to be the most important determinant of its subsequent accessibility, then the subject's state at time of learning may make only a small contribution to the way in which material is encoded. It may sometimes be observed to be of importance, but it may often be lost, overridden or obscured by other factors, such as the semantic meaning of the words to be learned or the way in which the words are interpreted by the subject.

Perhaps affect's role in cognitive processing is more similar to that of meaning than that of context. The data (for example, the retrieval data) suggest that feeling functions to some extent like semantic meaning in influencing cognition. This is not to say that the meaning of the affect term is separate from the feeling, nor that the meaning without the feeling would be as effective as the feeling state itself, nor that affect categories are simply semantic categories. Rather, I am suggesting that feeling—actual feeling—may function like meaning and thus lead to the kind of encoding that has been said to involve a "deeper" level of organization (e.g., Craik & Lockhart, 1972) or a more "elaborated" representation (Craik & Tulving, 1975).

On the other hand, intuitively affect *seems* so much like context; it is an experience—it feels like an experience, and its role in memory feels like that of place or time, which also are experiential. In addition, there are the data suggesting instantaneous processing of affect (Leventhal, 1979; Zajonc, 1980; Moreland & Zajonc, 1979). Perhaps affect is both semantic and experiential (episodic), functioning like both simple context cues and semantic meaning simultaneously. This might account for the effects that have been observed so far.

Most complexly of all, perhaps these two functions of affect interact to produce new or additional meaning units. It is possible that at least some stimuli mean different things when one is feeling good from what they mean in a neutral state, or when one is feeling bad. This, of course, is the most speculative interpretation of the findings that has been offered so far. But it is not supernatural.

Actually, this interpretation of the impact of feelings on cognition—that they may change the relationship among cognitions or result in multiple encodings of material—is compatible with what contextualists have been saying all along (e.g., Bartlett, 1932), and what social psychologists have proposed since the time of Gordon Allport, if not Oswald Külpe. Külpe and his students (Ach, Meyer, Orth, & Watt) had observed that set and context altered the images that they had in response to stimuli (see Isen & Hastorf, 1982, for a discussion of the importance of these findings for social and cognitive psychology). That is, that context—not context in the associationist sense of context cues, but context in the sense that setting may give rise to differing goals, perception of meaning, contingencies, or expectations among subjects—influences the actual meaning of the stimuli.

Recently, a similar view has been expressed by an increasing number of cognitive psychologists (e.g., Bransford, 1979; Barclay, Bransford, Franks, McCarrell, & Nitsche, 1974; Medin, 1975; Medin & Schaffer, 1978). Bransford and his colleagues have pointed to the way in which the meaning context in which a word appears influences the way in which that word or sentence is processed, and Medin and his colleagues have suggested, further, for discrimination learning and classification judgments, that such context effects may operate by providing access to exemplar information—information about stimuli similar to the context cue (Medin, 1975; Medin & Schaffer, 1978; Smith & Medin, 1981). Another example may be available in the work of the schema theorists (e.g., Rumelhart & Ortony, 1977; Schank & Ableson, 1978), who suggest that ideas or concepts may be grouped in experiential units, rather than, or as well as, in semantic units.

This conception implies a flexible, possibly multiple, and probably changing organizational structure of material in memory, dependent in part on organizational or retrieval cues present at time of recall. Whether this formulation is new or old, it should not be surprising if affect produced *this* kind of context effect, since feelings, unlike most other stimuli, contain not only meaning associates, experiential (episodic) associates, and stimulus properties, but also a reward value and motivational effects (both general, as in the tendency to energize or retard behavior, and specific, as in the tendency to maintain or to change the state) inherent in them. And, in fact, the results of recent studies investigating the impact of affect on cognitive organization suggest that affect may influence the way in which stimuli are grouped, organized, and related to one another (Isen & Daubman, 1983; Isen et al., 1983).

One problem that might be raised regarding this interpretation is that, if affect influences even the meaning and associative networks of stimuli, then state-dependent effects might be expected to be especially pronounced. That is, if even meaning or interpretation is changed by affective state, then one might expect that encoding of material to be learned might be truly distinct while in an affective state, and only retrievable when one is again in that same state, and therefore that state-dependent-learning effects should be the rule. However, it is very unlikely that material would be learned in so limited and inflexible a way. Rather, at least in the case of positive affect, it is likely that both usual and unusual ways of encoding, usual and unusual senses of meaning and of stimuli, might be available for use. In fact, the view that fits best with schema theory is that material is simultaneously multiply encoded and therefore multiply retrievable. (Negative affect—depression, at least—may not result in the same processes because of the overall cognitive deficiency associated with that state.)

This would suggest that people should be more efficient (but also possibly more distractable) when they are happy, because they would be theorized to have multiple cues or encoding and retrieval devices as a function of happiness. It is apparent that the particular stimuli or material to be learned must make a crucial difference in whether such effects will be observed; nonetheless, increased efficiency and improved performance, as well as greater distractability or tendency to be misled, *have* sometimes been found as a function of positive affect (Barden et al., 1981; Isen et al., 1982; Masters et al., 1979).

Negative affect should not be expected to have the same effect on efficiency as positive, because the former tends to be so demanding, focusing of attention, and, in the case of depression, associated with slowed thought and behavior. Negative affect was not found to promote efficiency in the studies by Masters and his colleagues. However, recalling the work on arousal (anxiety) and performance, there probably are situations under which such effects might be observed; but there should be systematic differences in the kinds of circumstances under which positive, as opposed to negative, affect will promote efficiency. These and related topics remain for investigation.

AFFECT AND COGNITION

In this chapter I have summarized evidence showing the influence of feelings on thought and behavior. As we have seen, feeling states are so pervasive—they color almost everything that we experience and do—that they seem to involve as part of their definition the cognitive processes whereby they tend to cue compatible thought and behavior. That is, perhaps this cognitive effect is a process by which feelings are maintained and have influence on other ongoing thought and behavior, and is then in an important sense a defining characteristic of feeling states.

This possibility suggests that cognition may play a crucial role in the experience of affect or even in what affect is. The point being made is different from the one involved in the debate over the role of interpretation in the generation, definition, and maintenance of affect. Although the present proposal suggests a cognitive process in the definition of affect, it does not suggest that feelings involve a *reasoning* process such as is implied by the concept of interpretation. Unlike the positions that suggest complex cognitive mediation, such as attributional, labeling, or interpretive processes (e.g., Schachter & Singer, 1962; Weiner, 1980), this suggestion is perfectly compatible with the positions of those who argue for a more direct and immediate generation of affective experience (Leventhal, 1974, 1979; Wilson, 1979; Zajonc, 1980).

Complex processes such as interpretations may surely play a role in affective experiences under some circumstances, but simple, automatic ones may be responsible for much of what we feel, a good part of the time. Current research suggests that feelings relatively automatically tend to lead to compatible thought and behavior, particularly in the case of positive feelings, and that this process tends to prolong the affective state and may mediate other cognitive and behavioral effects, as well.

The suggestion that affect may involve cognitive changes (even simple, automatic ones) at its very base, does imply that affect and cognition might be viewed, even defined, in a single framework. For example, this conceptualization suggests that feeling states consist in the cueing of compatible ideas, feelings, and behavior sequences, in thinking related thoughts and having easy access to a substantial amount of additional compatible material in memory.

To some, this may seem a peculiarly cognitive way to view affect. Yet, it may turn out that the tradition that we have developed of viewing affect and cognition (and behavior) as distinct may not be a productive one, and that this seemingly radical step of viewing affect in cognitive terms will account best for the data that are accumulating. As suggested in an earlier chapter (Isen & Hastorf, 1982), this may also prove a useful step in integrating our knowledge of all types of processes. For, the accumulating data also indicate that cognition itself is profoundly affected by feelings, even mild feelings.

It may also be, thus, that the view proposed above—that feeling states consist in the cueing of compatible material—is not particularly cognitive. Rather, it may simply be a description of process, focusing on the accessibility or association between certain kinds of material, cognitive, conative, and affective. The process may seem "cognitive" because the process of "accessibility" has been studied primarily in the context of cognition. Yet it may be that accessibility applies equally to other realms, perhaps under other names, as when behaviors are made salient and/or selected for performance based on their association with other stimuli or expected consequences (as illustrated in the literature of both classical and instrumental conditioning, dating back to the work of Pavlov and Thorndyke).

It remains for scientists to establish empirically whether feelings and cognitions can be separated, for example, in terms of their effects. In the meantime, it is proving helpful to investigate the extent to which affective states may enjoy the same process mechanisms that have been discovered for cognition. Whether examination of such similarities will eventually indicate that affect and cognition (and behavior) are inseparable reflections of one single whole, are parallel subcategories within a single superordinate class, or are completely distinct (though interacting) systems that only happen to share process mechanisms, is a matter for future study. For now, it remains a puzzle.

ACKNOWLEDGMENT

The author wishes to express appreciation to C. Daniel Batson, Frank Bellezza, Leonard Berkowitz, William G. Graziano, Lowell D. Groninger, Colin Martindale, Thomas K. Srull, John D. Teasdale, and Robert S. Wyer, Jr., for their helpful comments on the manuscript, and to Madelon Kellough for her help and skill in typing it.

REFERENCES

Abelson, R. P., Kinder, D. P., Peters, M. D., & Fiske, S. T. Affective and semantic components in political person perception. *Journal of Personality and Social Psychology*, 1982, *42*, 619–630.

Abramson, L. Y., & Alloy, L. B. Depression, nondepression, and cognitive illusions: Reply to Schwartz. *Journal of Experimental Psychology: General*, 1981, *110*, 436–447.

Abramson, L. Y., Seligman, M. E. P., & Teasdale, J. Learned helplessness in humans: Critique and reformulation. *Journal of Abnormal Psychology*, 1978, *87*, 49–74.

Aderman, D. Elation, depression and helping behavior. *Journal of Personality and Social Psychology*, 1972, *24*, 91–101.

Alloy, L. B., & Abramson, L. Y. Judgment of contingency in depressed and nondepressed students: Sadder but wiser? *Journal of Experimental Psychology: General*, 1979, *108*, 441–485.

Anderson, J. R., & Bower, G. H. *Human associative memory*. Washington, D.C.: Winston, 1973.

Arnold, M. B. Perennial problems in the field of emotion. In M. B. Arnold (Ed.), *Feelings and emotion*. New York: Academic Press, 1970.

Averill, J. Emotion: What is the proper unit of analysis? Paper presented at the symposium, "Current issues in theories of the emotions," L. deRivera, Chair. Meeting of the American Psychological Association, Washington, D.C., 1982.

Ax, A. F. The physiological differentiation between anger and fear in humans. *Psychosomatic Medicine*, 1953, *15*, 433–442.

Bandura, A. *Aggression: A social learning analysis*. Englewood Cliffs, N.J.: Prentice Hall, 1973.

Bandura, A. Self-efficacy: Toward a unifying theory of behavioral change. *Psychological Review*, 1977, *84*, 191–215.

Barden, R. C., Garber, J., Duncan, S. W., & Masters, J. C. Cumulative effects of induced affective states in children: Accentuation, innoculation, and remediation. *Journal of Personality and Social Psychology*, 1981, *40*, 750–760.

Barclay, J. R., Bransford, J. D., Franks, J. J., McCarrell, N. S., & Nitsch, K. Comprehension and semantic flexibility. *Journal of Verbal Learning and Verbal Behavior*, 1974, *13*, 471–481.

Baron, R. A., & Bell, P. A. Aggression and heat: The influence of ambient temperature, negative affect, and a cooling drink on physical aggression. *Journal of Personality and Social Psychology*, 1976, *33*, 245–255.

Bartlett, F. C. Remembering: A study in experimental and social psychology. NY: Cambridge, 1932.

Batson, C. D., Coke, J. S., Chard, F., Smith, D., & Taliaferro, A. Generality of the "Glow of goodwill": Effects of mood on helping and information acquisition. *Social Psychology Quarterly*, 1979, *42*, 176–179.

Batson, C. D., Duncan, B. D., Ackerman, P., Buckley, T., & Birch, K. Is empathic emotion a source of altruistic motivation? *Journal of Personality and Social Psychology*, 1981, *40*, 290–302.

Beck, A. T. *Depression: Clinical, experimental, and theoretical aspects*. New York: Harper & Row, 1967.

Beck, A. T. *Cognitive therapy and the emotional disorders*. New York: International Universities Press, 1976.

Berlyne, D. E. *Aesthetics and psychobiology*. New York: Appleton Century Crofts, 1971.

Bellezza, F., & Bower, G. H. Person stereotypes and memory for people. *Journal of Personality and Social Psychology*, 1981, *41*, 856–865.

Berkowitz, L. Social norms, feelings, and other factors affecting helping and altruism. In L. Berkowitz (Ed.), *Advances in experimental social psychology, 6*. New York: Academic Press, 1972.

Berkowitz, L. Some determinants of impulsive aggression: Role of mediated associates with reinforcements for aggression. *Psychological Review*, 1974, *81*, 165–176.

Berkowitz, L., Cochran, S. T., & Embree, M. C. Physical pain and the goal of aversively stimulated aggression. *Journal of Personality and Social Psychology,* 1981, *40,* 687–700.

Berkowitz, L., & LePage, A. Weapons as aggression-eliciting stimuli. *Journal of Personality and Social Psychology,* 1967, *7,* 202–207.

Berkowitz, L., Lepinski, J., & Angulo, E. Awareness of our own anger level and subsequent aggression. *Journal of Personality and Social Psychology,* 1969, *11,* 293–300.

Berkowitz, L., & Turner, C. W. Perceived anger level, instigating agent, and aggression. In H. London & R. E. Nisbett (Eds.), *Thought and feeling: Cognitive alteration of feeling states.* Chicago: Aldine, 1974.

Bower, G. H. Mood and memory. *American Psychologist,* 1981, *36,* 129–148.

Bower, G. H., Gilligan, S. G., & Montiero, K. P. Selectivity of learning caused by affective states. *Journal of Experimental Psychology: General,* 1981, *110,* 451–473.

Bower, G. H., Montiero, K. P., & Gilligan, S. G. Emotional mood as a context for learning and recall. *Journal of Verbal Learning and Verbal Behavior,* 1978, *17,* 573–585.

Bransford, J. D. *Human cognition.* Belmont, Ca.: Wadsworth, 1979.

Bransford, J. D., McCarrell, N. S., Franks, J. J., & Nitsch, K. E. Toward unexplaining memory. In R. E. Shaw & J. D. Bransford (Eds.), *Perceiving, acting and knowing.* Hillsdale, N.J.: Lawrence Erlbaum Associates, 1977.

Brown, A. Priming effects in semantic memory retrieval processes. *Journal of Experimental Psychology: Human Learning and Memory,* 1979, *5,* 65–77.

Brown, T. S., & Wallace, P. M. *Psychological psychology.* New York: Academic Press, 1980.

Bruner, J. S., Matter, J., & Papanek, M. L. Breadth of learning as a function of drive-level and mechanization. *Psychological Review,* 1955, *62,* 1–10.

Buchwald, A. M., Strack, S., & Coyne, J. C. Demand characteristics and the Velton Mood Induction Procedure. *Journal of Consulting and Clinical Psychology,* 1981, *49,* 478–479.

Buck, R. Nonverbal behavior and the theory of emotion: The facial feedback hypothesis. *Journal of Personality and Social Psychology,* 1980, *38,* 811–824.

Campbell, D. & Fiske, D. Convergent and discriminant validation. *Psychological Bulletin,* 1959, *56,* 81–105.

Cannon, W. B. The James-Lange theory of emotions: A critical examination and an alternative. *American Journal of Psychology,* 1927, *39,* 106–124.

Carlsmith, J. M., & Gross, A. Some effects of guilt on compliance. *Journal of Personality and Social Psychology,* 1969, *11,* 240–244.

Cialdini, R. B., Darby, B., & Vincent, J. Transgression and altruism: A case for hedonism. *Journal of Experimental Social Psychology,* 1973, *9,* 502–516.

Cialdini, R. B., & Kenrick, D. T. Altruism as hedonism: A social development perspective on the relationship of negative mood state and helping. *Journal of Personality and Social Psychology,* 1976, *34,* 907–914.

Clark, M. S., & Isen, A. M. Toward understanding the relationship between feeling states and social behavior. In A. H. Hastorf & A. M. Isen (Eds.), *Cognitive social psychology.* New York: Elsevier, 1982.

Craik, F. I. M., & Lockhart, R. S. Levels of processing: A framework for memory research. *Journal of Verbal Learning and Verbal Behavior,* 1972, *11,* 671–684.

Craik, F. I. M., & Tulving, E. Depth of processing and the retention of words in episodic memory. *Journal of Experimental Psychology,* 1975, *104,* 268–294.

Cunningham, M. R. Weather, mood, and helping behavior. *Journal of Personality and Social Psychology,* 1979, *37,* 1947–1956.

Donnerstein, E., Donnerstein, M., & Munger, G. Helping behavior as a function of pictorially induced moods. *Journal of Social Psychology,* 1975, *97,* 221–225.

Duffy, E. Emotion: An example of the need for reorientation in psychology. *Psychological Review,* 1934, *41,* 184–198.

Duffy, E. An explanation of "emotional" phenomena without the use of the concept of "emotion." *Journal of General Psychology*, 1941, *25*, 282–293.

Duncker, K. On problem-solving. *Psychological Monographs*, 1945, *58* (whole No. 5).

Easterbrook, J. A. The effect of emotion on cue utilization and the organization of behavior. *Psychological Review*, 1959, *66*, 183–201.

Eich, J. E., & Birnbaum, I. M. Repetition, cueing, and state-dependent memory. *Memory and Cognition*, 1982, *10*, 103–114.

Feather, N. T. Effects of prior success and failure on expectations of success and subsequence performance. *Journal of Personality and Social Psychology*, 1966, *3*, 287–298.

Forest, D., Clark, M. S., Mills, J., & Isen, A. M. Helping as a function of feeling state and nature of the helping behavior. *Motivation and Emotion*, 1979, *3*, 161–169.

Fried, R., & Berkowitz, L. Music hath charms . . . and can influence helpfulness. *Journal of Applied Social Psychology*, 1979, *9*, 199–208.

Frey, P. S. Affect and resistance to temptation. *Developmental Psychology*, 1975, *11*, 466–472.

Frost, R. O., Graf, M., & Becker, J. Self-devaluation and depressed mood. *Journal of Consulting and Clinical Psychology*, 1979, *47*, 958–962.

Frost, R. O., & Green, M. L. Duration and post-experimental removal of Velten Mood Induction procedure effect. *Personality and Social Psychology Bulletin*, 1982, *8*, 341–342.

Galizio, M., & Hendrick, C. Effect of musical accompaniment on attitude: The guitar as a prop for persuasion. *Journal of Applied Social Psychology*, 1972, *2*, 350–359.

Garner, W. R., Hake, H. W., & Eriksen, C. W. Operationism and the concept of perception. *Psychological Review*, 1956, *63*, 149–159.

Gollin, S., Terrell, T., & Johnson, B. Depression and the illusion of control. *Journal of Abnormal Psychology*, 1977, *86*, 440–442.

Gouaux, C. Induced affective states and interpersonal attraction. *Journal of Personality and Social Psychology*, 1971, *20*, 37–43.

Griffitt, W. B. Environmental effects on interpersonal affective behavior: Ambient effective temperature and attraction. *Journal of Personality and Social Psychology*, 1970, *15*, 240–244.

Grossman, S. P. *Essentials of physiological psychology*. New York: Wiley, 1973.

Hale, W. D., & Strickland, B. R. Induction of mood states and their effect on cognitive and social behaviors. *Journal of Consulting and Clinical Psychology*, 1976, *44*, 155.

Hasher, L., & Zacks, R. T. Automatic and effortful processes in memory. *Journal of Experimental Psychology: General*, 1979, *108*, 356–388.

Hassett, J. *A primer of psychophysiology*. San Francisco, Calif.: Freeman, 1978.

Hebb, D. O. Drives and the C.N.S. (Conceptual Nervous System). *Psychological Review*, 1955, *62*, 243–253.

Henry, C. M., Weingartner, H., & Murphy, D. L. Influence of affective states and psychoactive drugs on verbal learning and memory. *American Journal of Psychiatry*, 1973, *130*, 966–971.

Higgins, E. T., & King, G. Accessibility of social constructs: Information processing consequences of individual contextual variability. In N. Cantor & J. F. Kihlstrom (Eds.), *Personality, cognition, and social interaction*. Hillsdale, N.J.: Lawrence Erlbaum Associates, 1981.

Hilgard, E. R. The trilogy of mind: Cognition, affection and conation. *Journal of the History of the Behavioral Sciences*, 1980, *16*, 107–117.

Isen, A. M. Success, failure, attention and reactions to others: The warm glow of success. *Journal of Personality and Social Psychology*, 1970, *15*, 294–301.

Isen, A. M. Positive affect, accessibility of cognitions, and helping. Paper presented at symposium, "Directions in Theory on Helping Behavior" (J. Piliavin, Chair), *Eastern Psychological Association* Convention, April, 1975.

Isen, A. M., Clark, M., & Schwartz, M. F. Duration of the effect of good mood on helping: "Footprints on the sands of time." *Journal of Personality & Social Psychology*, 1976, *34*, 385–393.

Isen, A. M., & Daubman, K. A. The influence of object on categorization. Manuscript, 1983.

Isen, A. M., Daubman, K. A., & Gorgoglione, J. M. The influence of positive affect on cognitive organization. In R. Snow & M. Farr (Eds.), *Aptitude, learning and instruction: Affective and conative processes.* Hillsdale, N.J.: Lawrence Erlbaum Associates, in press.

Isen, A. M., & Gorgoglione, J. M. Some specific effects of four affect-induction procedures. *Personality and Social Psychology Bulletin,* 1983, *9,* 136–143.

Isen, A. M., & Hastorf, A. H. Some perspectives on cognitive social psychology. In A. H. Hastorf & A. M. Isen (Eds.), *Cognitive social psychology.* New York: Elsevier, 1982.

Isen, A. M., Horn, N., & Rosenhan, D. L. Effects of success and failure on children's generosity. *Journal of Personality and Social Psychology,* 1973, *27,* 239–247.

Isen, A. M., & Levin, P. F. The effect of feeling good on helping: Cookies and kindness. *Journal of Personality and Social Psychology,* 1972, *21,* 384–388.

Isen, A. M., & Means, B. Positive affect as a variable in decision making. *Social Cognition,* 1983, *2,* 18–31.

Isen, A. M., Means, B., Patrick, R., & Nowicki, G. Some factors influencing decision-making strategy and risk-taking. In M. S. Clark & S. T. Fikse (Eds.), *Affect and cognition: The 17th annual Carnegie Symposium on Cognition.* Hillsdale, N.J.: Lawrence Erlbaum Associates, 1982.

Isen, A. M., & Patrick, R. The effect of positive feelings on risk-taking: When the chips are down. *Organizational Behavior and Human Performance,* 1983, *31,* 194–202.

Isen, A. M., & Shalker, T. E. The influence of mood state on evaluation of positive, neutral, and negative stimuli: When you "accentuate the positive," do you "eliminate the negative"? *Social Psychology Quarterly,* 1982, *45,* 58–63.

Isen, A. M., Shalker, T., Clark, M., & Karp, L. Affect, accessibility of material in memory and behavior: A cognitive loop? *Journal of Personality and Social Psychology,* 1978, *36,* 1–12.

Isen, A. M., & Simmonds, S. F. The effect of feeling good on a helping task that is incompatible with good mood. *Social Psychology* (now *Social Psychology Quarterly*), 1978, *41,* 345–349.

Jacobson, J. Z. Effects of association upon masking and reading latency. *Canadian Journal of Psychology,* 1973, *27,* 58–69.

James, W. *Principles of psychology,* New York: Dover, 1890.

Janis, I. L., Kaye, D., & Kirschner, P. Facilitating effects of "eating while reading" on responsiveness to persuasive communications. *Journal of Personality and Social Psychology,* 1965, *11,* 181–186.

Janis, I. L., & Mann, L. *Decision making.* San Francisco: Freeman, 1976.

Jenkins, J. J. Remember that old theory of memory? Well, forget it! *American Psychologist,* 1974, *29,* 785–795.

Johnson, E., & Tversky, A. Affect, generalization, and the perception of risk. *Journal of Personality and Social Psychology,* 1983, *45,* 20–31.

Kleck, R. E., Vaughan, R. C., Cartwright-Smith, J., Vaughan, K. B., Colby, C. Z., & Lanzetta, J. T. Effects of being observed on expressive, subjective, and physiological responses to painful stimuli. *Journal of Personality and Social Psychology,* 1976, *34,* 1211–1218.

Klein, D. C., Fencil-Morse, E., & Seligman, M. E. P. Depression, learned helplessness, and the attribution of failure. *Journal of Personality and Social Psychology,* 1976, *33,* 508–516.

Kuiper, N. A. Depression and causal attributions for success and failure. *Journal of Personality and Social Psychology,* 1978, *36,* 236–246.

Lacey, J. I. Psychophysiological approaches to the evaluation of psychotherapeutic process and outcome. In E. A. Rubenstein & M. B. Parloff (Eds.), *Research in psychotherapy.* Washington, D.C.: American Psychological Association, 1959.

Lacey, J. I. Somatic response patterning and stress: Some revisions of activation theory. In M. H. Appley & R. Trumbul (Eds.), *Psychological stress: Issues in research.* New York: Appleton-Century-Crofts, 1967.

Lacey, J. I. Psychophysiology of the autonomic nervous system. In J. R. Nazarro (Ed.), *Master lectures on physiological psychology.* Washington, D.C.: American Psychological Association, 1975.

Lacey, J. E., Kagan, J., Lacey, B., & Moss, H. A. The visceral level: Situational determinants and behavioral correlates of autonomic response patterns. In P. H. Knapp (Ed.), *Expressions of the emotions in man.* New York: International Universities Press, 1963.

Laird, J. Self-attribution of emotion: The effects of expressive behavior on the quality of emotional experience. *Journal of Personality and Social Psychology,* 1974, *29,* 475–486.

Laird, J. D., Wagener, J. J., Halal, M., & Szegda, M. Remembering what you feel: The effects of emotion on memory. *Journal of Personality and Social Psychology,* 1982, *42,* 646–657.

Langer, E. J. The illusion of control. *Journal of Personality and Social Psychology,* 1975, *32,* 311–328.

Latane, B., & Darley, J. *The unresponsive bystander: Why doesn't he help?* New York: Appleton Century Crofts, 1970.

Lazarus, R. S., Kanner, A. D., & Folkman, S. Emotions: A cognitive phenomenological analysis. In R. Plutchik & H. Kellerman (Eds.), *Theories of emotion* (Vol. 1 of *Emotion: Theory, research and experience*). New York: Academic Press, 1980.

Leight, K. A., & Ellis, H. C. Emotional mood states, strategies, and state-dependency in memory. *Journal of Verbal Learning and Verbal Behavior,* 1981, *20,* 251–266.

Leeper, R. W. A motivational theory of emotion to replace "emotion as disorganized response." *Psychological Review,* 1948, *55,* 5–21.

Leeper, R. W. The motivational and perceptual properties of emotions indicating their fundamental character and role. In M. B. Arnold (Ed.), *Feelings and emotions.* New York: Academic, 1970.

Leventhal, H. A. Emotions: A basic problem for social psychology. In C. Nemeth (Ed.), *Social psychology: Classic and contemporary interactions.* New York: Rand McNally, 1974.

Leventhal, H. A. A perceptual-motor processing model of emotion. In R. Pliner, K. R. Blankenstein, & I. M. Spigel (Eds.), *Advances in the study of communication and affect,* Vol. 5. New York: Plenum, 1979.

Leventhal, H. A. Toward a comprehensive theory of emotion. In L. Berkowitz (Ed.), *Advances in Experimental Social Psychology,* Vol. 13. NY: Academic, 1980, 139–207.

Levin, P. F., & Isen, A. M. Something you can still get for a dime: Further studies on the effect of feeling good on helping. *Sociometry,* 1975, *38,* 141–147.

Lewinsohn, P. M., Mischel, W., Chaplain, W., & Barton, R. Social competence and depression: The role of illusory self-perceptions? *Journal of Abnormal Psychology,* 1980, *89,* 203–212.

Lindsley, D. B. Emotion. In S. S. Stevens (Ed.), *Handbook of experimental psychology.* New York: Wiley, 1951.

Loftus, E. F. Activation of semantic memory. *American Journal of Psychology,* 1973, *86,* 331–337.

Loftus, G. R., & Loftus, E. F. The influence of one memory retrieval on a subsequent memory retrieval. *Memory and Cognition,* 1974, *2,* 467–471.

Mandler, G. *Mind and emotion.* New York: Wiley, 1975.

Martin, D. J., Abramson, L. Y., & Alloy, L. B. The illusion of control for self and others in depressed and nondepressed college students. *Journal of Personality and Social Psychology,* in press.

Martindale, C. *Cognition and consciousness.* Homewood, Ill.: Dorsey, 1981.

Masters, J. C., Barden, R. C., & Ford, M. E. Affective states, expressive behavior, and learning in children. *Journal of Personality and Social Psychology,* 1979, *37,* 380–390.

Masters, J. C., & Furman, W. Effects of affect states on noncontingent outcome expectancies and beliefs in internal or external control. *Developmental Psychology,* 1976, *12,* 481–482.

McDougall, W. *Outline of psychology.* New York: Scribner, 1923.

McKoon, G., & Ratcliff, R. Priming in item recognition: The organization of propositions in memory for text. *Journal of Verbal Learning and Verbal Behavior,* 1980, *19,* 369–386.

McMillen, D. L. Transgression, self-image, and compliant behavior. *Journal of Personality and Social Psychology*, 1971, *20*, 176–179.

Medin, D. L. A theory ot context in discrimination learning. In G. H. Bower (Ed.), *The psychology of learning and motivation* (Vol. 9). New York: Academic Press, 1975.

Medin, D. L., & Schaffer, M. M. Context theory of classification learning. *Psychological Review*, 1978, *85*, 207–238.

Mednick, S. A. The associative basis of creative process. *Psychological Review*, 1962, *69*, 220–232.

Mednick, M. T., Mednick, S. A., & Mednick, E. V. Incubation of creative performance and specific associative priming. *Journal of Abnormal and Social Psychology*, 1964, *69*, 84–88.

Mendelssohn, M. Letters on sensation, 1755. Referenced in J. E. Erdmann, *A history of philosophy*, Vol. 2. London: Swan Sonnenschein, 1892.

Meyer, D. W., & Schvaneveldt, R. W. Facilitation in recognizing pairs of words: Evidence of a dependence between retrieval operations. *Journal of Experimental Psychology*, 1971, *90*, 227–234.

Miller, D. T., & Ross, M. Self-serving biases in the attribution of causality: Fact or fiction? *Psychological Bulletin*, 1975, *82*, 213–225.

Mischel, W. *Personality and assessment.* New York: Wiley, 1968.

Mischel, W. Toward a cognitive social learning reconceptualization of personality. *Psychological Review*, 1973, *80*, 252–283.

Mischel, W., Coates, B., & Raskoff, A. Effects of success and failure on self-gratification. *Journal of Personality and Social Psychology*, 1968, *10*, 381–390.

Mischel, W., Ebbesen, E., & Zeiss, A. Selective attention to the self: Situational and dispositional determinants. *Journal of Personality and Social Psychology*, 1973, *27*, 129–142.

Mischel, W., Ebbesen, E., & Zeiss, A. Determinants of selective memory about the self. *Journal of Counseling and Clinical Psychology*, 1976, *44*, 92–103.

Moore, B. S., Underwood, B., & Rosenhan, D. L. Affect and altruism. *Developmental Psychology*, 1973, *8*, 99–104.

Moreland, R., & Zajonc, R. Exposure effects may not depend on stimulus recognition. *Journal of Personality & Social Psychology*, 1979, *37*, 1085–1089.

Nasby, W., & Yando, R. Selective encoding and retrieval of affectively valent information. *Journal of Personality and Social Psychology* 1982, *43*, 1244–1255.

Natale, M. Effects of induced elation-depressed on speech in the initial interview. *Journal of Counseling and Clinical Psychology*, 1977, *45*, 45–52.

Natale, M., & Hantas, M. Effects of temporary mood states on memory about the self. *Journal of Personality and Social Psychology*, 1982, *42*, 927–934.

Neely, J. H. Semantic Priming and retrieval from lexical memory: Evidence for facilitatory and inhibitory processes. *Memory and Cognition*, 1976, *4*, 648–654.

Neely, J. H. Semantic priming and retrieval from lexical memory: Roles of inhibitionless spreading activation and limited-capacity attention. *Journal of Experimental Psychology: General*, 1977, *106*, 226–254.

Nelson, R. E., & Craighead, W. E. Selective recall of positive and negative feedback, self-control behaviors, and depression. *Journal of Abnormal Psychology*, 1977, *86*, 379–388.

Piliavin, J. A., Dovidio, J. F., Gaertner, S. L., & Clark, R. D., III. Responsive bystanders: The process of intervention. In V. J. Derlaga & J. Grzelak (Eds.), *Cooperation and helping behavior*. New York: Academic Press, 1982.

Piliavin, I. M., Rodin, J., & Piliavin, J. A. Good samaritanism: An underground phenomenon? *Journal of Personality and Social Psychology*, 1969, *13*, 289–299.

Polivy, J., & Doyle, C. Laboratory induction of mood states through the reading of self-referent mood statements: Affective changes or demand characteristics? *Journal of Abnormal Psychology*, 1980, *89*, 286–290.

Posner, M. I. *Chronomatic explorations of the mind*. Hillsdale, N.J.: Lawrence Erlbaum Associates, 1978.

Posner, M. I., & Snyder, C. R. R. Attention and cognitive control. In R. L. Solso (Ed.), *Information processing and cognition: The Loyola symposium*. Hillsdale, N.J.: Lawrence Erlbaum Associates, 1975.

Postman, L., & Brown, D. R. Perceptual consequences of success and failure. *Journal of Abnormal and Social Psychology*, 1952, *47*, 213–221.

Raps, C. S., Reinhard, K. E., & Seligman, M. E. P. Reversal of cognitive and affective deficits associated with depression and learned helplessness by mood elevation in patients. *Journal of Abnormal Psychology*, 1980, *89*, 342–349.

Ratcliff, R., & McKoon, G. Does activation really spread? *Psychological Review*, 1981, *88*, 454–462.

Reber, A. S. Implicit learning of artificial grammars. *Journal of Verbal Learning and Verbal Behavior*, 1967, *6*, 855–863.

Reber, A. S. Implicit learning of synthetic languages: The role of instructional set. *Journal of Experimental Psychology: Human Learning and Memory*, 1976, *2*, 88–94.

Regan, J. W. Guilt, perceived injustice and altruistic behavior. *Journal of Personality and Social Psychology*, 1971, *18*, 124–132.

Regan, D. T., Williams, M., & Sparling, S. Voluntary expiation of guilt: A field experiment. *Journal of Personality and Social Psychology*, 1972, *24*, 422–445.

Rizley, R. Depression and distortion in the attribution of causality. *Journal of Abnormal Psychology*, 1978, *87*, 32–48.

Rodgers, R., & Hammerstein, O. II. *The King and I*. New York: Williamson Music Co., Inc., 1951.

Rodgers, R., & Hammerstein, O. II. *The Sound of Music*. New York: Williamson Music Co., Inc., 1959.

Rosenthal, R. & Rosnow, R. *Artifact in Behavioral Research*. New York: Academic Press, 1969.

Rule, B. G., Ferguson, T. J., & Nesdale, A. R. Emotional arousal, anger, and aggression: The misattribution issue. In P. Pliner, K. R. Blankstein, & I. M. Spigal (Eds.), *Perception of emotions in self and others*. New York: Plenum, 1979.

Rumelhart, D. E., & Ortony, A. The representation of knowledge in memory. In R. C. Anderson, R. J. Spiro, & W. E. Montagne (Eds.), *Schooling and the acquisition of knowledge*. Hillsdale, N.J.: Erlbaum, 1977.

Schachter, S., & Singer, J. L. Cognitive, social, and physiological determinants of emotional state. *Psychological Review*, 1962, *69*, 379–399.

Schank, R. C., & Abelson, R. P. *Scripts, plans, goals, and understanding*. Hillsdale, N.J.: Lawrence Erlbaum Associates, 1977.

Schiffenbauer, A. Effect of observer's emotional state on judgments of the emotional state of others. *Journal of Personality and Social Psychology*, 1974, *30*, 31–35.

Schneider, D. J., Hastorf, A. H., & Ellsworth, P. C. *Person perception*. Reading, Mass.: Addison-Wesley, 1980.

Schneider, W., & Shiffrin, R. M. Controlled and automatic human information processing: I. Detection search, and attention. *Psychological Review*, 1977, *84*, 1–66.

Schwartz, B. Does helplessness cause depression, or do only depressed people become helpless? Comment on Alloy and Abramson. *Journal of Experimental Psychology: General*, 1981, *110*, 429–435.

Schwartz, J. C., & Pollack, P. R. Affect and delay of gratification. *Journal of Research in Personality*, 1977, *11*, 147–164.

Seeman, G., & Schwartz, J. C. Affective state and preference for immediatee versus delayed reward. *Journal of Research in Personality*, 1974, *7*, 384–394.

Seligman, M. E. P. *Helplessness: On depression, development, and death*. San Francisco: Freeman, 1975.

Seligman, M. E. P., Abramson, L. Y., Semmel, A., & von Baeyer, C. Depressive attributional style. *Journal of Abnormal Psychology,* 1979, *88,* 242–247.

Simon, H. A. Motivational and emotional controls of cognition. *Psychological Review,* 1967, *74,* 29–39.

Smith, E. E., & Medin, D. L. *Categories and concepts.* Cambridge, Ma.: Harvard University Press, 1981.

Snyder, S. H. Opiate receptors and internal opiates. *Scientific American,* 1977, *236,* 3, 44–56.

Snyder, M., & White, P. Moods and memories: Elation, depression, and remembering the events of one's life. *Journal of Personality,* 1982, *50,* 149–167.

Sokolov, E. N. *Perception and the conditioned reflex.* Oxford: Pergamon, 1963.

Srull, T. K., & Wyer, R. S. The role of category accessibility in the interpretation of information about persons: Some determinants and implications. *Journal of Personality and Social Psychology,* 1979, *37,* 1660–1672.

Strickland, B. R., Hale, W. D., & Anderson, L. K. Effect of induced mood states on activity and self-reported affect. *Journal of Consulting and Clinical Psychology,* 1975, *43,* 587.

Teasdale, J. D., & Bancroft, J. Manipulation of thought content as a determinant of mood and corrugator electromyographic activity in depressed patients. *Journal of Abnormal Psychology,* 1977, *86,* 235–241.

Teasdale, J. D., & Fogarty, S. J. Differential effects of induced mood on retrieval of pleasant and unpleasant events from episodic memory. *Journal of Abnormal Psychology,* 1979, *88,* 248–257.

Teasdale, J. D., & Russell, Differential aspects of induced mood on the recall of positive, negative, and neutral words. *British Journal of Clinical Psychology,* 1983.

Teasdale, J. D., & Taylor, R. Induced mood and accessibility of memories: An effect of mood state or of induction procedure? *British Journal of Clinical Psychology,* 1981, *20,* 39–48.

Teasdale, J. D., Taylor, R., & Fogarty, S. J. Effects of induced elation-depression on the accessibility of memories of happy and unhappy experiences. *Behavior Research and Therapy,* 1980, *18,* 339–346.

Toi, M., & Batson, C. More evidence that empathy is a source of altruistic motivation. *Journal of Personality and Social Psychology,* 1982, *43,* 281–292.

Tourangeau, R., & Ellsworth, P. C. The role of facial response in the experience of emotion. *Journal of Personality and Social Psychology,* 1979, *37,* 1519–1531.

Tulving, E., & Pearlstone, Z. Availability versus accessibility of information in memory for words. *Journal of Verbal Learning and Verbal Behavior,* 1966, *5,* 381–391.

Tulving, E., & Thompson, D. M. Encoding specificity and retrieval processes in episodic memory. *Psychological Review,* 1973, *80,* 352–373.

Turner, C. W., & Layton, J. F. Verbal imagery and connotation as memory-induced mediators of aggressive behavior. *Journal of Personality and Social Psychology,* 1976, *33,* 755–763.

Tversky, A. Elimination by aspects. *Psychological Review,* 1972, *79,* 281–299.

Tversky, A., & Kahneman, D. Availability: A heuristic for judging frequency and probability. *Cognitive Psychology,* 1973, *5,* 207–232.

Tversky, A., & Kahneman, D. The framing of decisions and the psychology of choice. *Science,* 1981, *211,* 453–458.

Underwood, B., Froming, W. J., & Moore, B. S. Mood, attention, and altruism. *Developmental Psychology,* 1977, *13,* 541–542.

Veitch, R., & Griffitt, W. Good news—bad news: Affective and interpersonal affects. *Journal of Applied Social Psychology,* 1976, *6,* 69–75.

Velten, E. A laboratory task for induction of mood states. *Behavior Research and Therapy,* 1968, *6,* 473–482.

Warren, R. E. Time and the spread of activation in memory. *Journal of Experimental Psychology: Human Learning and Memory,* 1977, *4,* 458–466.

Watkins, M. J. Engrams as cuegrams and forgetting as cue overload. In C. R. Puff (Ed.), *Memory organization and structure.* New York: Academic Press, 1979.

Webster's *New World Dictionary of the American Language.* Cleveland: World, 1966.

Weiner, B. A cognitive (attribution)-emotion-action model of motivated behavior: An analysis of judgment of help-giving. *Journal of Personality and Social Psychology,* 1980, *39,* 186–200.

Weingartner, H., & Faillace, L. A. Alcohol state-dependent learning in man. *Journal of Nervous and Mental Disease,* 1971, *153,* 395–406.

Weingartner, H., Miller, H., & Murphy, D. L. Mood-state-dependent retrieval of verbal associations. *Journal of Abnormal Psychology,* 1977, *86,* 276–284.

Weyant, J. M. Effects of mood states, costs, and benefits of helping. *Journal of Personality and Social Psychology,* 1978, *36,* 1169–1176.

Wilson, W. R. Feeling more than we can know: Exposure effects without learning. *Journal of Personality and Social Psychology,* 1979, *37,* 811–821.

Woodworth, R. S., & Schlosberg, H. *Experimental psychology.* New York: Holt, 1954.

Wyer, R. S., Jr., & Srull, T. K. Category accessibility: Some theoretical and empirical issues concerning the processing of social stimulus information. In E. T. Higgins, C. P. Herman & M. P. Zanna (Eds.), *Social cognition: The Ontario Symposium* (Vol. 1). Hillsdale, N.J.: Lawrence Erlbaum Associates, 1981.

Young, P. T. *Emotions in man and animal.* New York: Wiley, 1943.

Young, P. T. *Motivation and emotion.* New York: Wiley, 1961.

Zajonc, R. B. The attitudinal effects of mere exposure. *Journal of Personality and Social Psychology Monograph Supplement,* 1968, *9*(2, pt. 2), 1–27.

Zajonc, R. B. Feeling and thinking: Preferences need no inferences. *American Psychologist,* 1980, *35,* 151–175.

6 Output Processes in Judgment

Harry S. Upshaw
University of Illinois at Chicago

Contents

"Judgment" is a term with many meanings. It can refer to an opinion, an estimate, a criticism, a summons, or a punishment. Clearly, under the broadest definition of the term, any topic with which this *Handbook* is concerned could qualify for inclusion in a chapter on judgment. The aspirations for the present chapter are much more modest than that. In fact, the primary rule that has governed inclusion in this chapter is that the topic refers to some aspect of judgment that is probably not covered extensively in other chapters of the book.

All judgments have objects. In making a judgment, the person encodes information about the object, integrates that information with previous knowledge, arrives at some conclusion about the object, and renders a response that conveys the conclusion (cf. Burnstein & Schul, 1982; Wyer, 1980; Wyer & Srull, 1981). Much of the material throughout this *Handbook* may be viewed as an elaboration of the encoding and integration facets of judgment. Accordingly, the present chapter focuses upon the last two processes in the chain: the conclusion that a person draws after information is encoded and integrated with prior knowledge, and the response that is delivered in order to communicate that conclusion. Together, these processes constitute the output phases of judgment.

Judgment has been viewed as a task (Galanter, 1962). The many different meanings of the term, however, suggest that there are different judgmental tasks that are particularly relevant to the output phases of judgment. The many types of conclusions that may be made about an object suggest corresponding judgmental processes. They also imply characteristic purposes and intentions which, in turn, suggest that judgment often is an intermediate activity in a goal-directed sequence. That sequence exposes the judge to an assortment of objects in addition to the ones that are explicitly judged. Accordingly, it is appropriate to consider the effects of context on judgments as well as the mediating function of judgment in other aspects of life.

To summarize, this chapter is focused upon drawing conclusions about objects and communicating those conclusions. These output processes are discussed in the context of five particular judgmental tasks. The effects of context upon judgments are also reviewed, and the mediating function of judgment is discussed.

JUDGMENT AS A TASK

Five experimental tasks that have been studied in the general psychology of judgment are stimulus detection, recognition, identification, discrimination, and scaling. These tasks are readily distinguished in social psychology. The *detection* task is that of determining whether a member of a particular object class is present (e.g., Is there an adult at the party?). *Recognition* is the task of determining whether the object is familiar (e.g., Have I seen that person before?). *Identification* is the task of determining to which class of objects a particular one belongs (e.g., Is Mary British or Australian?). *Discrimination* is the task of determining whether one object has more of some attribute than does another (e.g., Is Mrs. Smith friendlier than Mr. Jones?). Finally, *scaling* is the task of estimating the magnitude of a property that the object possesses (e.g., To what extent is Charles responsible for his heavy drinking?).

Detection, identification, discrimination, and scaling are traditionally distinguished in the psychophysical literature (see, for example, Galanter, 1962). In the psychophysical literature, however, the identification task is sometimes referred to as "recognition" (e.g., Luce & Green, 1974). Neglecting the distinction implies no desire to differentiate between the tasks of determining whether an object is merely familiar or whether it is an exemplar of a particular class. Considering the topics that cognitive social psychologists are currently investigating (as manifested in this volume), it seems appropriate here to retain the distinction. Accordingly, we shall use the term "recognition" as it is traditionally used in the literature on verbal learning and memory (cf. Mandler, 1980).

The Detection Task

Psychophysical research on detection is typically focused on what was once known as the problem of the absolute threshold—the problem of establishing the smallest stimulus on a sensory continuum that a person is capable of noticing. Of course, that threshold is not a fixed point for all people, nor even for the same person for all occasions. In order to study its determinants, experiments are conducted to manipulate variables such as the magnitude of the stimulus, the relative frequency with which a stimulus (versus no stimulus) is presented, the incentive for making a correct response, the nature of previous stimulation, and the familiarity of the particular stimulus that is under investigation (Galanter, 1962). All of these factors, and more, have been shown to affect a person's "absolute" sensitivity to physical energy.

The impetus for most of the recent research in this area has been the theory of signal detectability that was formulated by Tanner and Swets (1954; see also Luce & Green, 1974). According to that theory, detection is essentially a task of deciding in a given instance whether a stimulus event (a signal) has occurred or not. The theory assumes that repeated presentations of either the "signal" or "noise" give rise to a distribution of subjective processes. The noise distribution is analogous to the null distribution in statistical inference, and the signal to the alternative distribution. In arriving at a judgment, the person is imagined to perform as an intuitive statistician by choosing which distribution was sampled. An important feature of the approach is that it focuses attention on the possibility that some judgmental phenomena represent truly perceptual (i.e., input) processes whereas others result from response (output) processes. More will be said about this distinction in a later section. For the present, it is sufficient to note the distinction. Remembering that this chapter is restricted to consideration of output processes in judgment, it is noteworthy that signal detection studies have generally established that response or output processes in detection are affected by factors such as the intentions and motives of the judge and characteristics of the response language (Upmeyer, 1981).

Detection as an issue in social cognition seldom concerns the sensitivity of the organism to physical stimuli. More often it is a question of noticing some social cue, such as a friendly overture, or searching for members of a group. Fortunately, the theory of signal detectability is in no way restricted to the sensory domain. It is more a methodological approach than a substantive theory. Although it nicely accommodates social psychological concerns, the theory has some potential for confusion if its indicators of input and output processes are interpreted uncritically.

In psychophysical applications, an input process is considered to be one that refers to sensory or memorial events, whereas output processes refer to response generalization, response bias, and the setting of a response criterion (Luce & Green, 1974). In cognitive applications, on the other hand, the theory applies at two levels simultaneously. The stimulus which is to be detected or not has sensory properties like any other stimulus, and for that reason a straightforward psychophysical analysis of signal detection is appropriate. At the same time, the stimulus has social meaning. The locus of meaning in such complex situations is not at all clear. In order to communicate with other people, we adapt our responses to our anticipation of their interpretations. Reflecting upon this presumed fact of social life leads one to despair of a precise separation of input and output functions. Cognitive input seems inextricably confounded with output.

The Recognition Task

Recognition is a judgment of familiarity. It is the task that confronts us when we pass someone in the corridor and we must decide whether a greeting is appropriate. Mistakes are, of course, of two kinds. We may falsely assume prior exposure, or fail to remember the earlier experience. Clearly, the recognition task entails a challenge at the input level of overcoming confusion among stimuli, and at the output level, confusion among possible responses. It is equally clear that the same types of variables that affect detection are relevant to recognition. Indeed, the signal detection approach is frequently applied in modified form to recognition experiments (Luce & Green, 1974). In addition to this basic psychophysical approach, a number of models have been suggested in the context of verbal learning (e.g., Juola, Fischler, Wood, & Atkinson, 1971; Mandler, 1980; Wolford, 1971).

The Identification Task

Identification requires detection and recognition, but it also requires something more. The judge must assign each stimulus to one of several alternative classes. Viewed from the perspective of the signal detection paradigm, identification involves multiple stimuli (as is the case with recognition) and multiple responses (as distinguished from recognition, which implies only two).

Perhaps the most fruitful approach to the study of identification has been that of information theory (Shannon & Weaver, 1949). Much of the research has been reported by Attneave (1959) and by Miller (1953, 1956). The well-known generalization from this work is that the human organism is a rather poor identifier. When the stimuli to be identified are unidimensional, five to nine identifications seems to be nearly maximum performance (Miller's [1956] "magical number seven plus or minus two"). The amount of transmitted information tends to be substantially increased for multidimensional stimuli. Thus, the more different contexts in which an object is known, and the larger the number of its attributes that are observed, the greater the likelihood of a correct identification (and presumably, the shorter the response latency, greater confidence, and so forth).

Much of the psychological research dealing with identification seems to imply that all of the interesting phenomena associated with the task takes place at the input level. A suggestion to the contrary derives from studies by Upmeyer and Layer (1974). Their subjects matched from memory a set of trait adjectives to a set of labels that were presented a pair at a time. Based upon a signal detection analysis, a "response bias" effect was observed in the identification of the labels.

The Discrimination Task

In ordinary language, the term "discrimination" means to notice a difference, to distinguish, or to differentiate among stimulus objects. Traditionally, however, psychophysicists studied the discrimination of stimuli that differ in a single physical attribute. With such stimuli the sole basis for discrimination is a difference in the amounts of the attribute which characterizes each. Thus, early research focused on the ability of human subjects to detect small differences in levels of stimulation in various stimulus modalities. The challenge was to calculate the value of the noticeably different stimulus for each physical continuum. It is well-known that Weber believed the value of the just noticeable difference (j.n.d.) to be a constant function of the prevailing level of stimulation. Fechner (1860) assumed that equally-often noticed differences are psychologically equal, and based upon that proposition, formulated an influential "law" for accomplishing the measurement of subjective representations of physical quantities. Later, Thurstone (1927) challenged Fechner's Law, contending that the j.n.d. is not an appropriate unit for a scale of experience. He offered as a substitute what he labeled the "discriminal dispersion" of an arbitrarily chosen stimulus.

According to Thurstone, exposure to a stimulus gives rise to a "discriminal process" which can be represented by a number. The discriminal processes associated with each stimulus constitute random variables. The standard deviations of the distributions of these processes that result from repeated exposure to the stimuli are called "discriminal dispersions."

In Thurstone's view, the judge in the discrimination task in effect samples randomly from the distributions of discriminal processes for the pair of comparison stimuli. The probability that one stimulus is judged to be greater than the other depends upon the modal discriminal process of each, and upon the standard error of the difference of their discriminal processes.

An important feature of Thurstone's model of discrimination is its complete independence of the physical continuum. It should be noted that the signal detection model incorporates this and other essential features of the Thurstone approach. In all applications of signal detectability theory two or more distributions of discriminal processes are assumed. Within this approach detection, recognition, identification, as well as discrimination depend critically upon the degree of confusion among unidimensional stimuli (or between a stimulus and "noise").

The task of discriminating stimuli that are not ordered on a single continuum is that of deciding whether they are the same or different. Discrimination "errors" are, of course, of two kinds, those of omission and those of commission. The latter seem especially likely to result from output processes reflecting response incentives and similar factors. Errors of omission with multifaceted stimuli might result from failure to perceive the critical stimulus input. Alternatively, especially in social and cognitive applications, failure to discriminate truly different complex stimuli is possibly the result of some conscious classification scheme on the part of the judge. Hence, a person might judge fox terriers and Alaskan huskies as equivalent in that they are both dogs, while being totally aware of their differences. This example suggests Bruner's (Bruner, Goodnow, & Austin, 1956; Bruner & Tajfel, 1961; Pettigrew, 1958, 1982) concept of "equivalence range" or "category width." This concept has led to a body of interesting literature which has remained separate from psychophysical work on discrimination. In bringing the two traditions under a single rubric, we should note that a judgment of equivalence could result from an input process, that is, failing to perceive a physical difference. More likely, however, it results from an output process whereby the judge classifies objects for purposes of thought and communication.

Multidimensional scaling (Schiffman, Reynolds, & Young, 1981) appears to be a suitable method for studying many of the research issues that arise with respect to discrimination, both for unidimensional and multidimensional stimuli. Shepard (1978) described several highly creative analyses of hue and pitch discriminations based upon nonmetric multidimensional scaling. Research designs based upon Guttman's (1954) concepts and their associated methods of assessment seem particularly promising for discrimination problems. Although the discrimination task is involved in many social and psychophysical phenomena, surprisingly little attention appears to have been focused on its fundamental properties except in the case of unidimensional stimuli.

The Scaling Task

Scaling is the report of perceived magnitude. Obviously, any report of absolute magnitude confounds the psychological experience with the language of the report. This confounding by the judge of experience and report has been matched by a confounding by investigators of phenomenon and theory. As indicated earlier, Fechner believed the Weber ratio to be the basis of the psychological experience of physical magnitude. The familiar logarithmic relationship of stimulus to judgment that defines Fechner's "law" reflects his theory as much as it reflects a fact of nature. Stevens (1970), among others, disputed Fechner's assumption that stimulus confusion has something to do with perceptual magnitude. Stevens believed that people attend to the ratios among stimuli in performing the scaling task. Both Fechner and Thurstone assumed that differences rather than ratios were critical in that task. Which theory is confirmed in an experiment seems to depend upon the response language that is specified for the subject. Fechner and Thurstone do better when categorical judgments are elicited, and Stevens does better when subjects are instructed to judge stimulus ratios (see Birnbaum, 1982).

The Stevens theory of scaling holds that the subjective magnitude of stimuli is a power function of their physical values. A power function is linear when both variables are transformed logarithmically. This fact led Ekman (1964) to suggest that the Stevens power law is a special case of Fechner's logarithmic law. Similar thought seems to underlie a suggestion by Attneave (1962) that both the input and output phases of the scaling task are amenable to perceptual analysis. In other words, scaling consists of matching elements of one sensory dimension with those of another. Therefore, the transformation function that maps a subjective stimulus onto a response is as important to consider as that function which maps a physical stimulus onto its subjective counterpart. Rule and Curtis (1982) developed Attneave's suggestion into a theory of scaling that has produced an impressive literature.

COMPLEX JUDGMENT AS ORGANIZED SUBTASKS

The judgment task, subjectively defined, represents what the judge hopes to accomplish. In some instances the task is completed when a conclusion has been reached about an object. In others, an overt response is required in order to inform someone of that conclusion. In these latter instances, the problem of separating input and output effects poses a serious methodological problem which has already been described in part, and which is dealt with in greater detail in a later section. For the present, it is sufficient to recognize that the problem exists. It is also important to recognize that the experimenter-defined judgment tasks specify outcome rather than process. In order to arrive at a judgmental conclusion and/or a response, whatever the particular task, the judge must implement some plan or script of the sort that Schank and Abelson (1977) described. In defining the experimental task, the investigator seldom, if ever, specifies the details of that plan or script.

A task analysis of judgment emphasizes the goal-direction of the entire process. In pursuit of the major judgmental goal, many sub-goals are likely to emerge. Consider, for example, how one might estimate the likelihood of rain on the day of the long-planned picnic. A skyward glance in search of a gray cloud initiates a detection subtask. If the sky looks darker in the west than in the east (a discrimination subtask), that judgment may instigate an identification subtask by means of which the aspiring picnicker tries to decide whether the gloom is a natural or industrial phenomenon. In arriving at a conclusion about the likelihood of rain (a scaling task) the judge might compare the darker part of the sky with a remembered standard in order to determine how much lighter or darker it appears (a scaling subtask in support of another scaling task). Of course, there are many alternative ways of arriving at a judgment of the likelihood of rain. (One could bypass much of what has been described here by consulting a public weather service, but even then the credibility of the information obtained from it might be evaluated as an adjunctive judgmental task.) The point is that almost any judgmental task is likely to be organized into a series of subtasks.

The structuring of judgment into subtasks occurs in the laboratory as well as in other locales. Asked only to judge whether an auditory signal is present, the subject may invoke a script or plan that includes as subtasks identification or perhaps recognition. Discrimination is probably often a component of both identification and scaling. Which twin is Mary and which is Martha (an identification task) may be resolved on the basis of who is taller (discrimination). Estimating the height of a particular basketball player (scaling) may be based on whether the player is taller than some other player who serves as a standard for the class of very tall people (discrimination).

A probable consequence of the judge's ad hoc structuring of a judgmental task into a chain of subtasks is the fact that some experimental findings appear to be inconsistent with the task that was prescribed by the experimenter. For example, Parducci (1963) found that judges tend to employ response categories with equal frequency in what was formally prescribed as a scaling task. This bias implies a judge's plan to equate discrimination among the stimuli, even though that is not a requirement of the experimental task. Similarly, Tajfel (1957) noted what appears to be an intrusion of either identification or discrimination into the scaling task. He observed that there is a greater separation in scale values for stimuli when a correlated stimulus dimension is salient. This phenomenon suggests that judges utilize the peripheral stimulus dimension to distinguish among the stimuli. Another likely example of the modification of an experimental task by judges' scripts or plans is provided by signal detection research which shows that familiar signals are more quickly and reliably detected than are unfamiliar ones (Galanter, 1962).

JUDGMENT AS A MAPPING OPERATION

Stevens (1966) analyzed the judgment process as the conjoining of a stimulus and a response dimension. Alternatively it may be described as a subjective measurement operation by which objects or events are mapped onto quantitative responses (Upshaw, 1969). Such analyses undoubtedly give an overly simple account of a complex judgmental process. However, they call attention to an important aspect of judgment that seems at times to be overlooked: *all judgment tasks ultimately refer to entire sets of objects, rather than isolated stimuli*. The intellectual work that leads to a conclusion about one object permits a related conclusion about all other objects in the set. After a criterion has been established for deciding whether a signal is present, it is available for judging every stimulus in the set. Similarly, the plans that are invoked for any single familiarity, identification, discrimination, or scaling judgment can be readily applied to judge other stimuli as well.

Although in a particular instance interest may center on the judgment of a limited number of objects, the rules that govern this judgment could be readily applied to all other objects in the relevant set. Any judgment of a single object implies a comparison of that object with all others in the set in terms of the underlying attributes. A person who judges his or her political liberal-conservatism, for example, presumably does so by formulating and applying some rule that is just as appropriate for judging the positions of other people as it is for judging one's own position.

It would be wondrously efficient for judges to recall and apply previously formulated rules whenever they undertake judgment of new stimuli in a reference set. Once again subjects do not behave as experimenters might wish and expect them to. There is abundant evidence that subjects reformulate rules, taking into account the particular sample of reference objects that are salient at the moment. The reformulation of rules is manifested in what has come to be known as "context effects." Much of the research on context effects has been reviewed by M. Sherif and Hovland (1961), Eiser and Stroebe (1972), Birnbaum (1982), and Parducci (1974, 1982). At the input level, context probably affects judgments by means of category accessibility (cf. Wyer & Srull, 1981). Its effect on output, however, is most likely on mapping rules, which is indicated by the fact that entire distributions of responses are influenced by context in systematic ways. This issue is discussed in greater detail in the next section.

THE LOCUS OF CONTEXT EFFECTS

Much research on judgment has been motivated by the psychophysical concern for the sensitivity of the human organism to environmental events. From that orientation some aspects of judgment that would intrigue many other psychologists tend to be dismissed by psychophysicists as "noise" that obscures data bearing on the sensitivity issue. Thus, Stevens (1958) dismissed as trivial context effects on judgment that could be traced to linguistic as opposed to perceptual factors. (In the terminology of the present chapter "perceptual", in Stevens' vocabulary, translates to "conclusion about an object" and "linguistic" translates to "response.") In psychophysical detection studies criteria have been offered for separating sensitivity effects from those due to response bias (Green & Swets, 1966; Swets, Tanner, & Birdsall, 1961). The response bias indicator reflects the operation of variables such as incentives, expectations, and the salience of correlated stimulus dimensions. These effects, which are anathema to the psychophysicist, are of considerable potential interest to social psychologists (see Upmeyer, 1981).

Criteria for Locating Context Effects in Non-scaling Tasks

In detection and recognition studies, the response dimension typically holds little intrinsic interest. The subject in the experiment is usually asked to indicate whether a stimulus event has occurred either by pushing an appropriate button or by uttering words such as "yes" or "no," "new," or "old." In identification the subject indicates which of a set of stimuli is judged to have occurred on a particular trial, and in discrimination the subject indicates in some straightforward way which of a pair of stimuli has more of a particular attribute. Again, the response by which identification and discrimination is conveyed is usually not of great interest. In all of these tasks it can usually be assumed that the judgmental conclusion has been directly and fully conveyed in the response, unless the subject has more-or-less deliberately biased the response for strategic reasons. Such reasons might include caution to prevent premature commitment, dissimulation, or other purposes that are in competition with the basic judgmental task. Methodologically, a context effect that operates on the response, as opposed to the judgmental conclusion that is conveyed by the response, is indicated by a systematic bias in the judgments (i.e., differences across experimental conditions in the level of the distribution of judgments). Effects upon the variability of responses might reflect influences upon judgmental conclusions and/or responses (Gravetter & Lockhead, 1973; Upshaw, 1969).

Scaling presents the same challenges as the other forms of judgment to the investigator who wishes to establish the locus of context effects. In addition, it poses some interesting problems in regard to the manner in which responses are made. Scaling responses are sometimes made as graphical or numerical ratings. Sometimes they are made in terms of units of physical measurement, such as inches and ounces. Indeed, it has been demonstrated repeatedly in cross-modal psychophysics that virtually any sensory dimension over which the subject has control can serve as a satisfactory response scale (Stevens, 1966, 1974).

Criteria for Locating Context Effects in Scaling Tasks

In scaling, the job of the judge is to map a domain comprising the subjective representations of a set of stimuli onto a range of responses. In the undimensional case this mapping requires that the judge establish a minimum of two equivalent points on the subjective quantity and response dimensions corresponding to the two parameters that define a linear relationship (Upshaw, 1969). In this formulation the subjective quantity consists of stimuli and their associated judgmental conclusions. Together, the stimuli and the conclusions concerning them may be viewed as subjective representations of objects which are similar to "true scores" in psychological test theories (Lord & Novick, 1968). As is often done in the theoretical analyses of tests, the response variable can be imagined to be regressed on the subjective quantity. Under the assumption of linearity, the regression constant can be interpreted as an indicator of the response scale origin and the regression coefficient as an indicator of the response scale unit (Torgerson, 1958; Upshaw, 1969; see also Johnson & Mullally, 1969).

In psychological testing it is not uncommon to develop multiple tests of the same trait. Distinctions have been made among several senses in which two tests may be said to be equivalent. One class of equivalent measures is what Jöreskog (1971) called "congeneric tests." Two tests are said to be congeneric if they differ only in the mean and standard deviation of scores. That is to say, the scores on two congeneric tests are both linear functions of the same true scores. By analogy, two response scales may be called congeneric if they differ only in terms of origin and unit.

The methodology developed by Jöreskog for analyzing congeneric tests can be applied in order to determine whether two judgment scales are congeneric. If they are, then any context effects that are found on one but not the other would reflect influences upon that particular response scale. Any effect upon the underlying subjective quantity logically must be manifested on all congeneric scales because it would be an effect upon the "true scores."

The logic of the congeneric-scale-criterion was employed in an attitude change study in order to determine the locus of influence by a persuasive source (Upshaw, 1978). Attitude was measured as a dependent variable for all subjects on two apparently congeneric scales. The persuasive message (an independent variable) varied in different experimental conditions according to which of the scales was targeted. Half of the subjects were exposed to variable levels of advocated years of imprisonment for a law-breaker, but with a constant level of leniency-sternness. The remaining subjects were exposed to variable levels of advocated leniency-sternness in regard to sentencing, but with a constant level of years of imprisonment corresponding to the advocated position. Effects were observed only on those dependent variable scales that corresponded to the particular target of influence that defined the independent variables. It was concluded that the social influence in the study occurred in the output phase of judgment because the effects were scale-specific. "True" attitude change would have affected both congeneric scales, according to the logic of the criterion that we have asserted.

The question of whether context affects judgmental conclusions or responses has divided theorists. Some theories such as Adaptation-Level (Helson, 1964) and Social Judgment-Involvement theory (C. Sherif, 1980; M. Sherif & Hovland, 1961) assume that context affects the subjective quantity, whereas other theories such as Range-Frequency (Parducci, 1965), Perspective (Upshaw, 1965, 1969; Volkmann, 1951), Accentuation (Eiser, 1971; Eiser & Stroebe, 1972), and a mathematical model offered by Gravetter and Lockhead (1973) assume that context effects are response phenomena. A number of experiments have been designed to resolve this theoretical issue (e.g., Dawes, Singer, & Lemons, 1972; Hicks & Campbell, 1965; Krantz & Campbell, 1961; Manis, 1967; see also Upmeyer, 1981), but the conclusions of these studies depend upon criteria for isolating the locus of the effects which are not universally accepted.

THE ANCHORING OF JUDGMENTAL SCALES

Most attempts to explain context effects in scaling invoke a poorly understood process of anchoring. The concept of anchoring originated in the psychophysical laboratory. There, it referred to part of the instructions given to subjects concerning how their judgments were to be made. Thus, a stimulus line of a given length might be shown to be a subject who is told that it is to be considered an example of a stimulus that should be judged in a particular way (depending upon the prescribed response language, "long," "eleven," or as equivalent to a squeeze of a hand dynamometer of a given force, and so forth). In that setting it is clear that anchoring serves to conjoin a stimulus and a response dimension by means of a prejudgment of a particular stimulus.

An experimental shift in the stimulus value that is associated with a particular response should and does produce a corresponding shift in the entire distribution of judgments. Systematic variation of the stimulus value that is associated with an invariant response is the paradigm for studying context in psychophysics (see Parducci, 1974). As the value of the anchor stimulus increases, the judged values of other stimuli in the set can be expected to decrease. As the anchor stimulus decreases, the judged value of other stimuli should increase. This negative correlation between anchor value and the typical judged value defines a widely observed phenomenon called "contrast."

The prediction of judgmental contrast as a consequence of variable anchoring is a straightforward implication of the anchor concept. However, it is not always observed. In fact, an opposite phenomenon was apparently demonstrated by M. Sherif, Taub, and Hovland (1958), which the investigators designated "assimilation." They found that the modal judgment of a set of stimulus weights shifted toward the anchor (assimilation) in one experimental condition whereas, in other conditions, the shift was away from the anchor (contrast).

Parducci and Marshall (1962) replicated the assimilation effect, and provided a plausible explanation of it. They noted that in the Sherif et al. (1958) study the anchor stimulus always preceded the variable stimulus. In that situation Adaptation-Level theory predicts a shift in the remembered value of the anchor toward the adaptation level (in the direction of the center of the stimulus distribution). Thus, an anchor of precisely the stimulus value of the most extreme variable stimulus (as was the case in the critical condition of the Sherif et al. [1958] study) is remembered as less extreme than it truly is. Consequently, some of the stimuli near the boundary of the series are judged more extreme than the anchor, and the entire distribution of judgments is shifted toward the anchor.

Assimilation effects have not often been reported in the psychophysical literature. The Parducci and Marshall study may explain the infrequency in that the effect required both that the anchor stimulus have the same value as the most extreme variable stimulus, and that the anchor be presented before the variable stimulus on every trial.

Traditional psychophysical research on anchoring has generally varied the stimulus value of anchors while maintaining a constant response repertoire. That was the design of the Sherif et al. (1958) study, as well as the study by Parducci and Marshall (1962). With a modification of the design to vary the response repertoire while holding the stimulus series constant, an effect resembling assimilation would be generally expected whereby the modal judgment shifts toward the value ascribed to the anchor stimulus. In an unpublished study by the present author, subjects estimated the weight of cylinders in the presence of an anchor that weighed 271 grams. In one condition subjects were told the true value of the anchor. In another condition subjects were told that the anchor value was 374 grams, and in a third condition, that it was 454 grams. Varying the announced stimulus value of the anchor resulted in a systematic shift in the judged value of all stimuli in the direction of the stated anchor value. A similar effect was observed in a social judgment study (Upshaw, 1978).

The anchor concept that appears straightforward in classical psychophysical research is far less so when applied to judgments in social settings. One difficulty in making the transition from the laboratory to social application results from the uncontrolled anchor stimuli that people bring to bear on social judgments. Thus, in judging a series of attitude positions that does not include the judge's favored position, a person might invoke his or her own position as an anchor stimulus (Upshaw, 1962). Furthermore, ambiguity often exists concerning the way in which a subject defines the judgmental task. Consider, for example, an attitude change study in which a relatively extreme position is advocated. Subjects are often free to define the advocated position as an anchor for the judgment of their own position or, alternatively, to define their own position as an anchor for judging the advocated position. Depending upon how subjects interpret this task, any change from the initial to final report of their attitude reflects either of two phenomena. It might indicate a response shift that results from reanchoring the scale. Alternatively, it could indicate a "true score" change resulting from reaction to an interpretation of the advocated position that was induced by differential anchoring by judges of varying attitudes. The social judgment-involvement theory as applied to attitude change appears to presuppose that the recipients of a message invoke their attitude as an anchor for judging a persuasive communication rather than employing the advocated position as an anchor to judge their own position. Evidence that judges in fact define their task in that way has generally not been reported (see, for example, C. Sherif, M. Sherif, & Nebergall, 1965).

Self-supplied anchors are not always at the extremes of the stimulus series. Marsh and Parducci (1978) presented evidence that judges often anchor the neutral point. According to the investigators, such anchoring is manifested by a failure of context manipulations to produce shifts of judgments across neutrality from painful to pleasurable, beautiful to ugly, and so forth. Speaking strictly, however, the evidence reported by Marsh and Parducci might best be interpreted to mean that different scales are employed for judging beauty versus ugliness, pain versus pleasure, and so forth. Because the concept of scale literally implies linear differences among anchor conditions (Upshaw, 1969), it is somewhat misleading to view nonlinear shifts of the sort that Marsh and Parducci reported as simple scale effects. (For a very readable discussion of the strict meaning of "scale" see Ellis, 1966).

The cognitive processes that are involved in anchoring have received little attention in the literature. It is generally agreed that an anchor functions as a standard with which stimuli are compared. How that comparison is accomplished, however, has not been analyzed precisely. It has been suggested that anchors serve to define category boundaries and that stimuli are compared, in turn, to those boundaries (Gravetter & Lockhead, 1973; Parducci, 1965). It has also been suggested that the anchors determine the origin and unit of a response scale. According to this model, stimuli are compared, in turn, with the origin and the resulting distance is described in terms of the unit (Upshaw, 1969). In addition, it has been suggested that individual stimuli are compared directly with the anchor (Ostrom & Upshaw, 1968), or an average stimulus (Helson, 1964).

Presumably in the comparison of stimuli with anchors, whether that comparison is direct or indirect, the judge evaluates the similarity of a focal stimulus and an anchor. If this presumption is true, then it may be the case that similarity judgments are basic to all anchor phenomena. This possibility implies the need for knowledge of the determinants of perceived similarity as well as for knowledge concerning how judged similarity results in anchor effects. Gregson (1975) presented a comprehensive review of the literature on similarity and its measurement. More recently, Tversky (1977), Tversky and Gati (1982), and Gati and Tversky (1982) have challenged the model that is generally implied in most psychometric research involving the similarity concept, and have compared it with another model that was described by Tversky (1977). The contested model views dissimilarity as an analogue to spatial separation between elements. Thus, similarity is assumed to be symmetric and determined entirely by attributes that are unique to the judgment objects. The alternative model, which has generally fared well in the research program, focuses on feature matching. Hence, the more common attributes, the greater the perceived similarity of stimuli.

Tversky's model allows for the possibility that context affects the salience of attributes that are brought to bear on the similarity judgment. On the other hand, it does not provide a detailed rationale for context effects. In a recent article, Krumhansl (1978) presented a model of similarity judgments that contains a mechanism to account for context effects. Specifically, discrimination among stimulus pairs in terms of similarity is said to be influenced by the density of stimuli in the perceptual region of those that are judged. The possibility of context effects on similarity judgments does not threaten an explanation of anchoring by reference to the perception of similarity. Insofar as context affects similarity judgments through discrimination rather than through anchoring, the explanation is complex, but not circular.

There has apparently been no systematic effort to relate any of the various conceptions of similarity perception to judgmental anchoring. The fact that anchoring can be achieved between virtually any stimulus dimension and any response dimension poses an intriguing challenge for research.

JUDGMENT AS A MEDIATOR

The act of judgment is a worthy topic of study in its own right. It is a delimitable segment of behavior that often has consequences for other people as well as for the judge. Another perspective on judgment as a psychological subject matter, however, is provided by considering it as a mediator of other behaviors on which research interest is focused. An important example of this function of judgment exists in the enormous literature on decision-making. Most approaches to decision research posit one or more acts of judgment in every choice or decision (c.f. Einhorn & Hogarth, 1981). The classical decision model, for example, assumes a utility judgment for every salient alternative. The utility judgment, in turn, is comprised of two prior judgments, the probability that some outcome state will occur, and the value of the outcome if, in fact, it is obtained.

In the recent literature on decision processes there has been increasing emphasis on the effect of judgmental variables on subsequent choices and decisions. Illustrative of this trend is the formulation by Kahneman and Tversky (1979) of the prospect theory of decisions under risk. A critical feature of the theory is the concept of gain or loss as measured from a subjective origin. The origin corresponds to the *status quo,* which, of course, defines context. This subjective origin is presumably equivalent to what Thibaut and Kelley (1959) called the *comparison level.* As such it might be expected to change as a function of variables such as perceived personal power, vicarious experiences of loss or gain by similar others, and the general salience of outcome values. It is conceptually similar to comparison level (Thibaut & Kelly, 1959), and like it, strongly influenced by judgmental context.

Illustrating another instance of judgment as mediator, Sherman, Ahlm, Berman, and Lynn (1978) demonstrated that experimentally induced contrast effects influence subsequent behavior if the affected judgment is made salient. In that study a context manipulation produced a contrast effect on the rating of the importance of recycling. Subjects in an experimental condition in which the rating was made salient subsequently volunteered differential support for a recycling project. Presumably, the judgment (rating) that was influenced by the immediate context was later retrieved from memory and interpreted in the new context. The demonstration appears to illustrate an important and subtle form of social influence.

A particularly interesting instance of judgment as a mediating variable is to be found in recent applications of cybernetics (Wiener, 1948) in psychology (Powers, 1973, 1978; Carver, 1979; Carver & Scheier, 1981a, 1981b). Fundamental to the cybernetic model of the way in which human beings control themselves is the concept of negative feedback which arises as a function of the discrepancy between behavior and a standard. In the model described by Miller, Galanter, and Pribram (1960), tests are made periodically to determine whether behavior is proceeding as planned. The result of the test is presumably a judgment concerning the magnitude of the discrepancy from the standard. A decision to operate or not upon the action in progress is then based upon the discrepancy judgment.

Powers (1973) advocates a somewhat different model in which judgment does not play an essential part. He argues that behavioral control is automatic, much like the way in which the temperature in a room is controlled by a thermostat. The thermostat does not act in response to anything analogous to a judgment. Indeed, it is acting when it turns the heat on, when it turns the heat off, or when it does nothing at all because the temperature is within the predetermined range. Pursuing the thermostat analogy, Powers believes that judgment cannot be part of the control process. Any judgment that is associated with control is presumably to be viewed as a side effect, and not as an integral part of the regulatory process. The implications of the postulated intervening judgment in the Miller et al. (1960) model have not been explored, nor has there been research confronting the differences between the Miller et al. model and that of Powers (1973).

CONCLUSION

The study of judgment includes too many topics to permit reasonable coverage in a single chapter. That this is so is a tribute to the vitality of research in cognitive psychology in recent years. The present chapter has accordingly focused only on a limited part of the literature of social judgment; that dealing with output processes. Developments in understanding these processes have not been as impressive in the past few years as they have been in other aspects of judgment. However, with our rapidly increasing understanding of memory, information integration, and reasoning—all part of judgment—we are probably at the threshold of creative new approaches to all of those processes with which this chapter has been concerned. If one can judge the future of judgment research, it looks good!

REFERENCES

Attneave, F. *Applications of information theory to psychology,* New York: Holt, 1959.
Attneave, F. Perception and related areas. In S. Koch (Ed.), *Psychology: A study of a science* (Vol. 4). New York: McGraw-Hill, 1962.
Birnbaum, M. H. Controversies in psychological measurement. In B. Wegener (Ed.), *Social attitudes and psychophysical measurement.* Hillsdale, N.J.: Lawrence Erlbaum Associates, 1982.
Bruner, J. S., Goodnow, J. J., & Austin, G. A. *A study of thinking.* New York: Wiley, 1956.
Bruner, J. S., & Tajfel, H. Cognitive risk and environmental change. *Journal of Abnormal and Social Psychology,* 1961, *62,* 231–241.
Burnstein, E., & Schul, Y. *Journal of Experimental Social Psychology,* 1982, *18,* 217–234.
Carver, C. S. A cybernetic model of self-attention processes. *Journal of Personality and Social Psychology,* 1979, *37,* 1251–1281.
Carver, C. S., & Scheier, M. F. A control-systems approach to behavioral self-regulation. In L. Wheeler (Ed.), *Review of personality and social psychology* (Vol. 2). Beverly Hills, CA: Sage, 1981. (a)
Carver, C. S., & Scheier, M. F. *Attention and self-regulation: A control-theory approach to human behavior.* New York: Springer-Verlag, 1981. (b)
Dawes, R. M., Singer, D., & Lemons, F. An experimental analysis of the contrast effect and its implications for intergroup communication and the indirect assessment of attitude. *Journal of Personality and Social Psychology,* 1972, *21,* 281–295.
Einhorn, H. J., & Hogarth, R. M. Behavioral decision theory: Processes of judgment and choice. In M. R. Rosenzweig & L. W. Porter (Eds.), *Annual Review of Psychology,* 1981, *32,* 53–88.
Eiser, J. R. Enhancement of contrast in the absolute judgment of attitude statements. *Journal of Personality and Social Psychology,* 1971, *17,* 1–10.
Eiser, J. R., & Stroebe, W. *Categorization and social judgment.* London: Academic Press, 1972.
Ekman, G. Is the power law a special case of Fechner's law? *Perceptual and Motor Skills,* 1964, *19,* 730.
Ellis, B. *Basic concepts of measurement.* Cambridge: Cambridge University Press, 1966.
Fechner, G. T. *Elemente der Psychophysik.* Leipzig: Breitkopf and Hartel, 1860.
Galanter, E. Contemporary psychophysics. In R. W. Brown, E. Galanter, E. H. Hess, & G. Mandler (Eds.), *New directions in psychology.* New York: Holt, 1962.
Gati, I., & Tversky, A. Representations of qualitative and quantitative dimensions. *Journal of Experimental Psychology: Human Perception and Performance,* 1982, *8,* 325–340.
Gravetter, F., & Lockhead, G. R. Criterial range as a frame of reference for stimulus judgment. *Psychological Review,* 1973, *80,* 203–216.
Green, D. M., & Swets, J. *Signal detection theory and psychophysics.* New York: Wiley, 1966.
Gregson, R. A. M. *Psychometrics of similarity.* New York: Academic Press, 1975.
Guttman, L. A new approach to factor analysis: The radex. In P. F. Lazarsfeld (Ed.), *Mathematical thinking in the social sciences.* New York: Free Press, 1954.

Helson, H. *Adaptation-level theory.* New York: Harper, 1964.

Hicks, J. M., & Campbell, D. T. Zero-Point scaling as affected by social object, scaling method, and context. *Journal of Personality and Social Psychology,* 1965, *2,* 793–808.

Johnson, D. M., and Mullally, C. R. Correlation-and-regression model for category judgments. *Psychological Review,* 1969, *76,* 205–215.

Jöreskog, K. G. Statistical analysis of sets of congeneric tests. *Psychometrika,* 1971, *36,* 109–133.

Juola, J. F., Fischler, I., Wood, C. T., & Atkinson, R. C. Recognition time for information stored in long-term memory. *Perception and Psychophysics,* 1971, *10,* 8–14.

Kahneman, D., & Tversky, A. Prospect theory: An analysis of decision under risk. *Econometrica,* 1979, *47,* 263–291.

Krantz, D. L., & Campbell, D. T. Separating perceptual and linguistic effects of context shifts upon absolute judgments. *Journal of Experimental Psychology,* 1961, *62,* 35–42.

Krumhansl, C. L. Concerning the applicability of geometric models to similarity data: The interrelationship between similarity and spatial density. *Psychological Review,* 1978, *85,* 445–463.

Lord, F. M., & Novick, M. R. *Statistical theories of mental test scores.* Reading, Mass.: Addison-Wesley, 1968.

Luce, R. D., & Green, D. M. Detection, discrimination, and recognition. In E. C. Carterette & M. P. Friedman (Eds.), *Handbook of perception* (Vol. 2). New York: Academic, 1974.

Mandler, G. Recognizing: the judgment of previous occurrence. *Psychological Review,* 1980, *87,* 252–271.

Manis, M. Context effects in communication. *Journal of Personality and Social Psychology,* 1967, *5,* 326–334.

Marsh, H. W., & Parducci, A. Natural anchoring at the neutral point of category rating scales. *Journal of Experimental Social Psychology,* 1978, *14,* 193–204.

Miller, G. A. What is information measurement? *American Psychologist,* 1953, *8,* 3–11.

Miller, G. A. The magical number seven, plus or minus two: Some limits on our capacity for processing information. *Psychological Review,* 1956, *63,* 81–97.

Miller, G. A., Galanter, E., & Pribram, K. H. *Plans and the structure of behavior.* New York: Holt, Rhinehart, and Winston, 1960.

Ostrom, T. M., & Upshaw, H. S. Psychological perspective and attitude change. In A. G. Greenwald, T. C. Brook, & T. M. Ostrom (Eds.), *Psychological foundations of attitudes.* New York: Academic Press, 1968.

Parducci, A. Range-frequency compromise in judgment. *Psychological Monographs,* 1963, *77,* (Whole no. 565).

Parducci, A. Category judgment: A range-frequency model. *Psychological Review,* 1965, *72,* 407–418.

Parducci, A. Contextual effects: A range-frequency analysis. In E. C. Carterette & M. P. Friedman (Eds.), *Handbook of perception* (Vol. 2). New York: Academic Press, 1974.

Parducci, A. Category ratings: Still more contextual effects! In B. Wegener (Ed.), *Social attitudes and psychophysical measurement.* Hillsdale, N.J.: Lawrence Erlbaum Associates, 1982.

Parducci, A., & Marshall, L. M. Assimilation vs. contrast in the anchoring of perceptual judgments of weight. *Journal of Experimental Psychology,* 1962, *63,* 426–437.

Pettigrew, T. F. The measurement and correlates of category width as a cognitive variable. *Journal of Personality,* 1958, *26,* 532–544.

Pettigrew, T. F. Cognitive style and social behavior: A review of category width. In L. Wheeler (Ed.), *Review of personality and social psychology* (Vol. 3). Beverly Hills, CA: Sage, 1982.

Powers, W. T. *Behavior: the control of perception.* Chicago: Aldine, 1973.

Powers, W. T. Quantitative analysis of purposive systems: Some spadework at the foundations of scientific psychology. *Psychological Review,* 1978, *85,* 417–435.

Rule, S. J., & Curtis, D. W. Levels of sensory and judgmental processing: Strategies for the evaluation of a model. In B. Wegener (Ed.), *Social attitudes and psychophysical measurement.* Hillsdale, N.J.: Lawrence Erlbaum Associates, 1982.

Schank, R. C., & Abelson, R. P. Scripts, plans, goals and understanding: An inquiry into human knowledge structures. Hillsdale, N.J.: Lawrence Erlbaum Associates, 1977.

Schiffman, S. S., Reynolds, M. L., & Young, F. W. *Introduction to multidimensional scaling.* New York: Academic Press, 1981.

Shannon, C. E., & Weaver, W. *The mathematical theory of communication.* Urbana: University of Illinois Press, 1949.

Shepard, R. N. The circumplex and related topological manifolds in the study of perception. In S. Shye (Ed.), *Theory construction and data analysis in the behavioral sciences.* San Francisco: Jossey-Bass, 1978.

Sherif, C. W. Social values, attitudes, and involvement of the self. *1979 Nebraska Symposium on Motivation,* 1980, *27,* 1–64.

Sherif, C. W., Sherif, M., & Nebergall, R. E. *Attitude and attitude change: the social judgment-involvement approach.* Philadelphia: Saunders, 1965.

Sherif, M., & Hovland, C. I. *Social judgment—Assimilation and contrast effects in communication and attitude change.* New Haven: Yale University Press, 1961.

Sherif, M., Taub, D., & Hovland, C. I. Assimilation and contrast effects of anchoring stimuli on judgments. *Journal of Experimental Psychology,* 1958, *55,* 150–155.

Sherman, S. J., Ahlm, K., Berman, L., & Lynn, S. Contrast effects and their relationship to subsequent behavior. *Journal of Experimental Social Psychology,* 1978, *14,* 340–350.

Stevens, S. S. Adaptation-level vs. the relativity of judgment. *American Journal of Psychology,* 1958, *71,* 633–646.

Stevens, S. S. On the operation known as judgment. *American Scientist,* 1966, *54,* 385–401.

Stevens, S. S. To honor Fechner and repeal his law. *Science,* 1970, *133,* 80–86.

Stevens, S. S. Perceptual magnitude and its measurement. In E. C. Carterette & M. P. Friedman (Eds.), *Handbook of perception* (Vol. 2). New York: Academic Press, 1974.

Swets, J., Tanner, W. P., & Birdsall, T. G. Decision processes in perception. *Psychological Review,* 1961, *68,* 301–340.

Tajfel, H. Value and the perceptual judgment of magnitude. *Psychological Review,* 1957, *64,* 192–204.

Tanner, W. P., & Swets, J. A. A decision making theory of visual detection. *Psychological Review,* 1954, *61,* 401–409.

Thibaut, J. W., & Kelley, H. H. *The social psychology of groups.* New York: Wiley, 1959.

Thurstone, L. L. A law of comparative judgment. *Psychological Review,* 1927, *34,* 273–286.

Torgerson, W. S. *Theory and methods of scaling.* New York: Wiley, 1958.

Tversky, A. Features of similarity. *Psychological Review,* 1977, *84,* 327–352.

Tversky, A., & Gati, I. Similarity, separability, and the triangle inequality. *Psychological Review,* 1982, *89,* 123–154.

Upmeyer, A. Perceptual and judgmental processes in social contexts. In L. Berkowitz (Ed.), *Advances in experimental social psychology* (Vol. 14). New York: Academic Press, 1981.

Upmeyer, A., & Layer, H. Accentuation and attitude in social judgment. *European Journal of Social Psychology,* 1974, *4,* 469–488.

Upshaw, H. S. Own attitude as an anchor in equal-appearing intervals. *Journal of Abnormal and Social Psychology,* 1962, *64,* 85–96.

Upshaw, H. S. The effects of variable perspectives on judgments of opinion statements for Thurstone scales. *Journal of Personality and Social Psychology,* 1965, *2,* 60–69.

Upshaw, H. S. The personal reference scale: an approach to social judgment. In L. Berkowitz (Ed.), *Advances in experimental social psychology* (Vol. 4). New York: Academic Press, 1969.

Upshaw, H. S. Social influence on attitudes and on anchoring of congeneric attitude scales. *Journal of Experimental Social Psychology,* 1978, *14,* 327–339.

Volkmann, J. Scales of judgment and their implications for social psychology. In J. R. Rohrer & M. Sherif (Eds.), *Social psychology at the crossroads*. New York: Harper, 1951.

Wiener, N. *Cybernetics: control and communication in the animal and the machine*. New York: Wiley, 1948.

Wolford, G. Function of distinct associations for paired-associate performance. *Psychological Review*, 1971, *78*, 303–313.

Wyer, R. S. The acquisition and use of social knowledge: Basic postulates and representative research. *Personality and Social Psychology Bulletin*, 1980, *6*, 558–573.

Wyer, R. S., & Srull, T. K. Category accessibility: Some theoretical and empirical issues concerning the processing of social stimulus information. In E. T. Higgins, C. P. Herman, & M. P. Zanna (Eds.), *Social cognition: The Ontario symposium on personality and social psychology*. Hillsdale, N.J.: Lawrence Erlbaum Associates, 1981.

Author Index

Subject Index

269

memory, relation to, II: 190–195
  and motivation, I: 267
  persistence of, I: 270–275
  and personality, I: 205
  and self, III: 155–156
  primitive or advanced, I: 246–254
  types of,
    availability, I: 193, 204, 209–218, 234–
      235, 248–251. II: 190–193
    representativeness, I: 193, 197–209, 226–
      228, 234–245, 249–251
    simulation, I: 193, 218–224, 229–230,
      249–251
Hierarchies, I: 98–102
Hypothesis testing, I: 213

I

Illusion of control, I: 226–227. III: 139
Illusory correlation, I: 217–218, 267
Imagery, I: 45, 58, 122, 124. II: 242, 246,
    249–251, 264
  vs. word concreteness, II: 264
  in Kosslyn model, II: 242, 246
  substitute for perception, II: 249–251
Implicational molecules, II: 85–94
  definition, II: 85–87
  implications for cognitive balance, II: 87–91
  role of,
    in attribution, II: 91–92
    in cognitive balance, II: 87–91
    in syllogistic belief organization, II: 92–
      94
Inconsistency of information,
  effect on recall, II: 98–101, 124–129, 169–
    172
  evaluative vs. descriptive, II: 128–129
Individuating information, I: 230–234
Inferences (see also Social inference), I: 74,
    80, 84, 86–87, 108–109
  from schemas, I: 148
  from event sequences, II: 109–110
Information, ease of generating, I: 215
Information integration theory, I: 191
Information processing,
  levels of, I: 43
  limitations on, I: 194–195. III: 1–2, 6–7,
    11–12, 29, 33, 35
  parallel vs. serial, I: 43
  psychology of, I: 129, 135
Innate perceptual biases, III: 17–18

Introspection, III: 142
Involvement, as determinant of conscious pro-
    cessing, III: 32–33, 35–37

J

Judgment (see also Inference)
  components of,
    discrimination, III: 241–242
    identification, III: 238–246
    recognition, III: 238–246
    recognition, III: 237, 243–247
    scaling, III: 238, 242–248
    stimulus detection, III: 238–246
  context effects in, III: 245–248
  contrast effects in, III: 248, 252
  input processes in, III: 239–242
  meaning of, III: 237
  mediating function of, III: 238, 251–252
  output processes in, III: 238–239, 242, 247,
    253
  theories of,
    range-frequency, III: 248
    signal detectability, III: 239–251

K

Knowledge, representation of (see also
    Schemas)
  acquisition of, I: 51–58
  analogues, II: 240–242
  as a mapping, II: 235, 247
  perceptual vs. conceptual, II: 246
  propositional, II: 240–242
  specificity of, II: 236
Korsakoff syndrome, III: 134, 168

L

Labeling
  context effects on, III: 106–107
  role in memory, III: 104–106
Law of small numbers, I: 199
Learning,
  as affected by prior knowledge, II: 185–186
  implicit, I: 56–57
  social, I: 51
Linear orderings,
  of event sequences, II: 106–108
  processing of, I: 58–60
Linear separability, I: 93–94